The State of Art Criticism

University College Cork
Coláiste na hOllscoile Corcaigh

Art criticism is spurned by universities, but widely produced and read. It is seldom theorized, and its history has hardly been investigated. *The State of Art Criticism* presents an international conversation among art historians and critics that considers the relation between criticism and art history, and poses the question of whether criticism may become a university subject. Participants include Dave Hickey, James Panero, Stephen Melville, Lynne Cook, Michael Newman, Whitney Davis, Irit Rogoff, Guy Brett, and Boris Groys.

James Elkins is E.C. Chadbourne Chair in the Department of Art History, Theory, and Criticism at the School of the Art Institute of Chicago. His many books include *Pictures and Tears*, *How to Use Your Eyes*, and *What Painting Is*, all published by Routledge.

Michael Newman teaches in the Department of Art History, Theory, and Criticism at the School of the Art Institute of Chicago, and is Professor of Art Writing at Goldsmiths College in the University of London. His publications include the books *Richard Prince: Untitled (couple)* and *Jeff Wall*, and he is co-editor with Jon Bird of *Rewriting Conceptual Art*.

The Art Seminar

VOLUME 1
ART HISTORY VERSUS AESTHETICS

VOLUME 2
PHOTOGRAPHY THEORY

VOLUME 3
IS ART HISTORY GLOBAL?

VOLUME 4
THE STATE OF ART CRITICISM

VOLUME 5
THE RENAISSANCE

VOLUME 6
LANDSCAPE THEORY

VOLUME 7
RE-ENCHANTMENT

Sponsored by the University College Cork, Ireland; the Burren College of Art, Ballyvaughan, Ireland; and the School of the Art Institute, Chicago.

The State of Art Criticism

EDITED BY

JAMES ELKINS AND MICHAEL NEWMAN

University College Cork
Coláiste na hOllscoile Corcaigh

Routledge
Taylor & Francis Group
NEW YORK AND LONDON

First published 2008
by Routledge
270 Madison Ave, New York NY 10016

Simultaneously published in the UK
by Routledge
2 Park Square, Milton Park, Abingdon, Oxon, OX14 4RN

Routledge is an imprint of the Taylor & Francis Group, an informa business

Transferred to Digital Printing 2010

Typeset in ACaslon-Regular by RefineCatch Limited, Bungay, Suffolk

Library of Congress Cataloging-in-Publication Data
The state of art criticism / edited by Michael Newman and James Elkins.—1st ed.
p. cm.—(The art seminar ; v. 4)
Includes bibliographical references and index.
ISBN 978-0-415-97787-6 (pbk.)—ISBN 978-0-415-97786-9 (hardback)
1. Art criticism—Congresses. 2. Art—Historiography—Congresses. I. Newman, Michael, 1954– II. Elkins, James, 1955–
N7475.S73 2007
701′.18—dc22
2007028043

ISBN10: 0-415-97786-X (hbk)
ISBN10: 0-415-97787-8 (pbk)
ISBN10: 0-203-47930-0 (ebk)

ISBN13: 978-0-415-97786-9 (hbk)
ISBN13: 978-0-415-97787-6 (pbk)
ISBN13: 978-0-203-47930-8 (ebk)

TABLE OF CONTENTS

Series Preface

James Elkins

It has been said and said that there is too much theorizing in the visual arts. Contemporary writing seems like a trackless thicket, tangled with with unanswered questions. Yet it is not a wilderness; in fact it is well-posted with signs and directions. Want to find Lacan? Read him through Macey, Silverman, Borch-Jakobsen, Žižek, Nancy, Leclaire, Derrida, Laplanche, Lecercle, or even Klossowski, but not—so it might be said—through Abraham, Miller, Pontalis, Rosaloto, Safouan, Roudinesco, Schneiderman, or Mounin, and of course never through Dalí.

People who would rather avoid problems of interpretation, at least in their more difficult forms, have sometimes hoped that "theory" would prove to be a passing fad. A simple test shows that is not the case. Figure 1 shows the number of art historical essays that have terms like "psychoanalysis" as keywords, according to the *Bibliography of the History of Art*. The increase is steep after 1980, and in three cases—the gaze, psychoanalysis, and feminism—the rise is exponential.

Figure 2 shows that citations of some of the more influential art historians of the mid-twentieth century, writers who came before the current proliferation of theories, are waning. In this second graph there is a slight rise in the number of references to Warburg and Riegl, reflecting the interest they have had for the current generation of art historians: but the graph's surprise is the precipitous decline in citations of Panofsky and Gombrich.

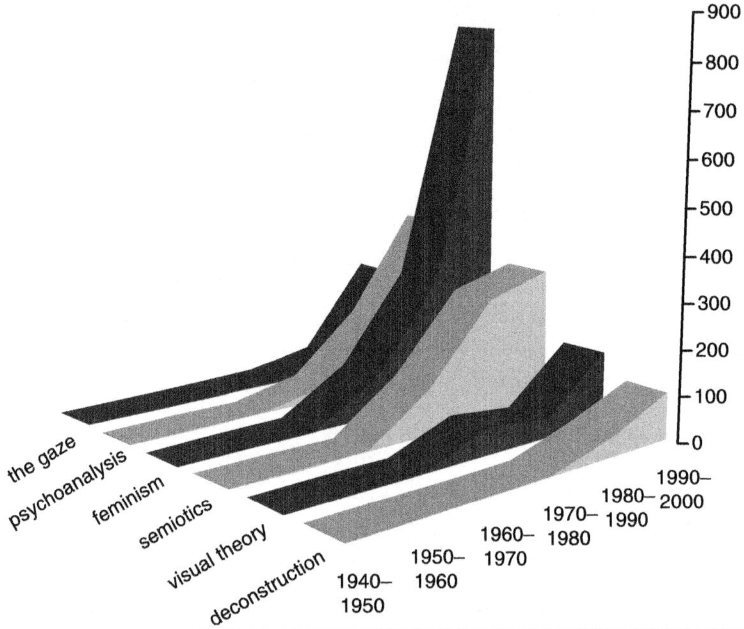

Figure 1 Theory in art history, 1940–2000.

Most of art history is not driven by named theories or individual historians, and these graphs are also limited by the terms that can be meaningfully searched in the *Bibliography of the History of Art*. Even so, the graphs suggest that the landscape of interpretive strategies is changing rapidly. Many subjects crucial to the interpretation of art are too new, ill-theorized, or unfocused to be addressed in monographs or textbooks. The purpose of *The Art Seminar* is to address some of the most challenging subjects in current writing on art: those that are not unencompassably large (such as the state of painting), or not yet adequately posed (such as the space between the aesthetic and the anti-aesthetic), or so well known that they can be written up in critical dictionaries (the theory of deconstruction). The subjects chosen for *The Art Seminar* are poised, ready to be articulated and argued.

Each volume in the series began as a roundtable conversation, held in front of an audience at one of the three sponsoring institutions—the University College Cork, the Burren College of Art

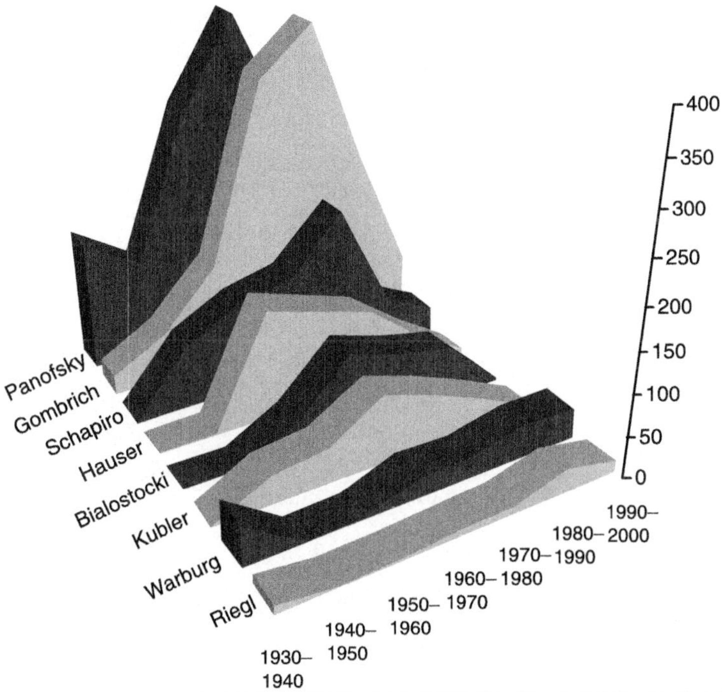

Figure 2 Rise and fall of an older art history, 1930–2000: Citations of selected writers.

(both in Ireland), and the School of the Art Institute of Chicago. The conversations were then transcribed, and edited by the participants. The idea was to edit in such a way as to minimize the correctable faults of grammar, repetitions, and lapses that mark any conversation, while preserving the momentary disagreements, confusions, and dead-ends that could be attributed to the articulation of the subject itself.

In each volume of *The Art Seminar*, the conversation itself is preceded by a general introduction to the subject and one or more "Starting Points," previously published essays that were distributed to participants before the roundtable. Together the Introductions and "Starting Points" are meant to provide the essential background for the conversation. A number of scholars who did not attend the events were then asked to write "Assessments"; their brief was to consider the conversation from a distance, noting its strengths and its blind spots. The "Assessments" vary widely in style and length: some are highly structured, and others are impressionistic; some are under a page, and others the length of a commissioned essay. Contributors were just asked to let their form fit their content, with no limitations. Each volume then concludes with one or more "Afterwords," longer critical essays written by scholars who had access to all the material including the "Assessments."

The Art Seminar attempts to cast as wide, as fine, and as strong a net as possible, to capture the limit of theorizing on each subject. Perhaps in the future the ideas discussed here will be colonized, and become part of the standard pedagogy of art: but by that time they may be on the downward slide, away from the centers of conversation and into the history of disciplines. At the moment they are unresolved, and their irresolution has much to tell us.

1
Introduction

THE RECOVERY OF CRITICISM

Michael Schreyach

> *Certainly, for us of the modern world, with its conflicting claims, its entangled interests, distracted by so many sorrows, with many preoccupations, so bewildering an experience, the problem of unity with ourselves . . . is far harder than it was [in the past]. Yet, not less than ever, the intellect demands completeness, centrality.* [1]

> *If art is again to play a more central part in our lives, it means that our lives will have to change, and that is a process which does not depend on artists and art critics alone; but there is no harm in making a small and very modest beginning.* [2]

When I chose the epigrams for this essay, I had the sense that I wanted to write about what I take to be a general skepticism towards the idea that art criticism can do little more than establish some context for the art under consideration, and offer a few remarks about that art's market value, popularity, its social significance (or lack thereof). I wanted to write against the idea that art criticism could—either now or in the future—offer nothing *substantive*, that is, nothing that would nourish and sustain a prevalent desire on the part of the public for a meaningful engagement with art. Although I was not sure how to proceed, I intuitively knew that amassing data and information about art criticism in the press—when and where it is read, how often, by whom, for what reason, what concrete impacts it makes on dealers and collectors, museums and auction houses, and so on—was not a viable option. The way of the epigram seemed most promising: it would allow me to avoid a pre-determined argument, to proceed as if by intuition or association. It is my initial choice of the two quotes that led me to consider the following, admittedly academic, episode as an important way to address my sense of the problem.

In "The Dead-End of Formalist Criticism," Paul de Man takes the literary critic I.A. Richards to task for operating under the once common, and perhaps commonsensical, belief that signifying form (such as a poem or a painting) can lead us to the experience that produced the form—and that the task of criticism is to facilitate this passage, to articulate an "exact correspondence between the author's [or artist's] originary experience and its communicated expression."[3] For Richards, a normative notion of communication was fundamental for a theory of criticism, and "the arts [were] the supreme form of the communicative activity."[4] De Man, Richards's critic, is skeptical of the presupposition "that language, poetic or otherwise, can *say* any experience, of whatever kind, even a simple perception."[5] De Man, like many since, thinks it cannot, and he cites the work of Richards's student, William Empson, to demonstrate that poetic metaphor compromises formalism's claims on a recovery of an originary experience. Why? Because metaphor produces an indefinite number of associations—a "limitless anteriority" that "deploys the initial experience into an infinity of associated [ones]."[6] This is a fundamental ambiguity of poetry; but, as de Man reads Empson, it proceeds not just from the ambiguity of all linguistic communication. Rather, it proceeds from a more serious problem: "the deep division of Being itself," the unbridgeable gap between the world of "spirit" and the world of "sentient substance."[7] The realization of this division leads to an unhappy consciousness, one that for the "new" Anglo-American criticism (de Man was writing in 1956) is "essentially divided, sorrowful, and tragic."[8] To their detriment, New Critics intuitively react with a "tendency to expect a reconciliation from poetry; to see in it a possibility of filling the gap."[9] This form of naïve criticism erroneously believes that art is capable of such reconciliation "because it provides an immediate contact with substance through its own sensible form."[10] For de Man, no such reconciliation is possible.

Surely, many would agree that the notion of an "immediate" contact with substance through form is one that was rightly jettisoned long ago, discarded as so much anachronistic, metaphysical nostalgia. De Man cautions his readers against any criticism claiming to overcome the incommensurability of sensory experience and its representation in art.[11] This division is crucial for de Man: "In a way, if it were not for the fact that substance is problematic and absent, there would not be art."[12] It is difficult to judge the extent to which this philosophical insight has affected the imagination of modern criticism. For while there continue to be refined efforts, like de Man's, to assess the incommensurability of language and being (an incommensurability nonetheless given depth and meaning by criticism), there is also a great volume of what James Elkins calls "ephemeral" criticism—that of newspapers, magazines, some journals—which intentionally confines itself to less philosophical speculations in order to provide more-or-less strategic and useful readings of artworks to a general readership.[13] Common to both, though, is a belief that art criticism supplies access to the context and meaning of art. In this sense, Richards's attempts to make criticism a more exact human science, one that could repay the application of principles to interpretation by the revelation of human meaning, value, and even truth, takes on a heuristic value for a society increasingly looking for answers, even as it stands in opposition to the spirit of de Man's position. Richard's scientific impulse, ironically, could be seen to be driven by the same positivist outlook that surreptitiously converts the richness of perception, "sensation, imagery, feeling, emotion, together with pleasure, unpleasure, and pain" into quantities that can be isolated and measured.[14] The pervasiveness of such an outlook, it seems, has only undermined criticism's initial attempts to "say" experience. The question remains: how best to proceed?

Between stultifying doubt and scientific certainty lies a pragmatic position that acknowledges the ultimate contingency of signification yet believes in the ability of art criticism to locate and develop human meaning in and through artworks. We undergo experiences, and we find value in modes of representing them—of handling them—that give those experiences depth.[15] The salient feature of good writing about art is its ability to resist, if only for the duration of reading, the conversion of every phenomenon into a dematerialized sign, and to restore to the object (or process) under investigation the palpability of lived experience. Some writers of criticism, that is, have the capacity to develop a mode of description that does more than just mirror its object. They instead produce an "equivalent" of it. Writing, for these critics, assumes the burden of reproducing the effects a first encounter with a new phenomenon might have produced in them (or someone else), but which now, at a physical distance or temporal remove, threaten to be lost to history—and perhaps to any consciousness. An assertion: a central aim of art criticism is conservative: it means to preserve, even to perpetuate, the latent or manifest possibilities of understanding that threaten to disappear from historical encounters. But not in any naïve way: an appeal to preserve "original" or "authentic" experience is bound to the perspective of the writer, whose inventive task it is to convert that experience into one with value for those with other perspectives, in the present. This is a performative task, the significance of which should be judged not only by how adequately the writer attends to his or her objects, or how well the piece of writing conforms to the conventions governing the production and publication of art criticism. It should also be judged by the manner in which the writer takes hold of her medium to give readers the sense of a meaningful encounter—and the degree to which she handles the vertiginous shifts in perspective (authorial, historical, social) afforded by the indeterminacies of writing.

To attend to the materiality of writing as a means of discovery is to attend to the heterogeneity of experience, because writing itself, whether a personal or professional activity, creates—more than it conforms to—the subjects it treats. Writing may be more or less conventional (rhetorical strategies can be learned and mastered), but the techniques through which writing is accomplished exert their own force over the writer, with the result that writing—even as it is carried out by the self-conscious, reflexive writer attending to his or her own production of meaning—is never entirely tractable, entirely mastered. This is axiomatic: the medium of representation reveals more about the materiality of the medium than it does about the object it represents. The materiality of writing causes interference;

but, at the same time, it is this interference which provides the conditions for the inventiveness of the writer.[16]

Framing

In 1963 the art historian (and sometimes critic) Edgar Wind lamented the "dehumanizing of artistic perception" by contemporary artists, who seemed to treat inventiveness not as a creative activity, a performative task, but as an end in itself, to be accomplished through rational analysis or strategic variation.[17] Artistic perception, for Wind, cultivates a mode of consciousness that is characterized by what Richard Shiff, in another context, has described as "a heightened critical awareness, an all-encompassing and perhaps disabling attentiveness to things, events, ways of life."[18] Artists busy themselves with activities that might not serve any purpose in a social framework concerned with production and progress. This mythology of artistic perception is associated with another that serves as its foundation: the myth of the modern artist, that she is an individual who is capable of resisting the pressure of means-end activities, notwithstanding the inevitable conversion of the products of her activity into commodities, which nonetheless assume for the culture at large the symbolic value of being relatively free from commodity forces.[19] According to Wind, focusing on mere "inventiveness" instead of cultivating creative, passionate attentiveness generates a situation in which art is increasingly "experimental" in a nearly scientific sense, and thus distant from a genuine connection to the world of human value. Wind traced some of the roots of the problem back to his own discipline, art history. Vienna school formalism, it seemed to Wind, detached art historians from passion, "reduc[ing] . . . artistic perception to an emotionally untainted sense of form" and thus presenting us with an art object "radical[ly] purge[d] of emotions."[20] Wind criticized Heinrich Wölfflin and Alois Riegl, along with later art critics Roger Fry and Clive Bell, for losing contact with art's "imaginative forces" in their methodical attempts to detach their studies of artistic form (which holds aesthetic interest) from their own personal prejudices and passions (governed by practical interest or desire).[21]

Nonetheless, the methods of formalism appeared to accomplish one of the central goals of the cultural sciences: to articulate the relationships that obtain between an objectively existent symbolic order (comprised of signs, either in the form of material objects, such as works of art, or of immaterial means, such as language) and a correlative subjective worldview (that particular horizon of shared social competencies and expectations in light of which those signs are manipulated and become meaningful to a group). In an effort to recover and interpret the past, various methodologies have tried to come to terms with the materiality of art (permanence) from the point of view of history (contingency).[22] Formalism was such a method. Because formalists assumed that the social dimension could be known to us historically only through the development of plastic structure, they tended to avoid narratives in which local forces, tensions, or contexts caused stylistic change.[23] The formalists aimed to provide the basis for an objective historical interpretation of artistic and cultural meaning—to yield a picture of history at the level of objectified general behavior read out of form. Whitney Davis notes: "The success of formalism as critical description [of individual works of art] suggests that it might also be successful in offering history . . . a fully historical, an anthropologically and psychologically exact, account of . . . others' perception[s] of the works [of art] they have made and viewed."[24] The benefit to formalism lies in its potential merging of horizons of understanding: from the subjective point of view of a writer to the recovery of an objective "historical grammar" (and, crucially, the subjective intentions that generated it), formalism provides a passage.[25]

But a drawback to the extremity of formalism's refinements, Wind continues, is the reaction it provoked: "In the place of an art of disengagement, which rejoiced in its separation from ordinary life, we are now to have an art which completely involves us in real life."[26] Wind was writing in the early 1960s, during a period when artists increasingly investigated their own performativity and their audience's participation as legitimate means for art.[27] From our present vantage point, Wind's point seems to have anticipated the dominance of the performative mode in art since the 1960s. Arguably, the phenomenological turn associated with Minimalism, radically extended by performance artists through the 1960s and experimental video artists in the 1970s, had been transformed, by the 1980s and early 1990s, to an all but total reliance on the audience's potential participation, through a call for action, for the social and political efficacy of the event or art "work" under consideration. The former notion of a modernist "beholder" or "spectator," surveying the field from a putatively objective viewpoint, was scrutinized and rejected. Within the political context of an accelerating disappearance of opportunities for dissident public discourse during the 1980s, this activation by artists of the alternative spaces and practices was nothing less than a renunciation of the ideology of aesthetic autonomy and a demonstration of a commitment to direct participation and intervention in politics. In such a situation, the boundaries traditionally maintained between aesthetic and actual participation eroded the artificial divisions between art criticism and criticism of society—divisions that seemed to have been installed as a consequence of the predominance of Greenberg's formalist criticism (not to be confused with the formalism of the Vienna school, of course) after the 1960s. The result was a re-unification of political and art criticism.[28] In actuality, the political dimension of art criticism was maintained in Greenberg's formalism, albeit in a latent form. What was new was the energy with which the manifest connection between art and political criticism was taken up by activist critics. Certainly, an important dimension of these moves was to reject the autonomy claims then being advanced by modernist formalism. Another was to encourage critics to reflect on the objects they investigated, but to question, while they were doing so, the legitimacy of their own viewpoints and practices in the hopes of making the evaluations based on their analyses politically efficacious. Such self-criticism was carried out through an attempt to specify, or make visible, the terms and assumptions of whatever discursive framework governed art making and art writing—not in order to lend to the work the appearance of ideological transparency (mere self-confession), but to accelerate the process of developing methods to continue the process of self-criticism.[29] The radical aspect of discerning the frameworks would ideally advance inquiry, not divert it from its aim of developing reliable knowledge.

The ubiquity of writing that claims to make objective, critical judgments—ironically—from the standpoint of the utmost personal and political engagement has been enabled by what Mark Bauerlein has in this volume called the "reflective turn," which entails the endless acknowledgement of positionality; that is, the writer's or critic's own "frame"—that structure of assumptions and presuppositions which mitigates the ideal of a disengaged subject surveying the world from a depersonalized vantage point.[30] The strategy marks a curious moment in art critical writing. It goes without saying that faith in the neutrality or objectivity of judgment has withered away under the pressures of self-reflexive critical practice over the past five decades. Still, one of the premier conditions of criticism—if it is to count as such—is an explicit acknowledgement on the part of the critic of his or her own frame. The idea is that once you divulge your assumptions, prejudices, predilections, tastes, interests, politics, investments, problems of subjective preference are solved, simply because you have acknowledged them. But admitting one's preferences and investments is self-exposure, not self-criticism. When such admissions serve primarily to neutralize anticipated counter-arguments based on some other set of assumptions (someone else's frame), they are strategic.[31] But in no sense can they claim to be complete, because anyone writing from a frame is bound to write within a frame that is at best partially conscious to the writer. Being able to acknowledge part of the frame does not mean that the frame is rendered unproblematic or that its influence over the subject at hand is reduced or obviated. Instead, the frame continues to operate, for better or ill, outside the conscious purview of most writers. As George Santayana wrote: "This subjective matrix and envelope of all my knowledge, though I may overlook it, underlies knowledge to the end."[32]

Crisis

Wind saw the studied inventiveness and performative engagement of the artistic generation of the 1960s compensating, or perhaps overcompensating, for the procedural methods of formalism—methods which had been developed in order to stabilize historical claims by adjusting the historian's subjective access to objectively existing instances of social communicability through form, albeit at the cost of losing some degree of investment in art's emotional value.[33] One result was, arguably, to diminish the idea that criticism was, as Northrop Frye contended in 1949, "a structure of thought and knowledge existing in its own right, with some measure of independence from the art it deals with."[34] The assumption that art criticism is an autonomous sphere of activity, the judgments of which should avoid extra-artistic frameworks and key themselves to a framework derived from an inductive survey of current practices of art, now appears hopelessly anachronistic.[35] Indeed, the critical pressure put upon the fundamental assumptions of disciplinary cohesion by poststructuralist critics since the 1960s has all but eroded the idea that art criticism can legitimately identify its own objects of inquiry or even demarcate its own boundaries. This condition reflects our current skepticism of systematic structures of knowledge—we can't make the assumption of total coherence for art criticism, as Frye might have, because "criticism" has become at best a generality without any organizing principle. The art critical text is thus now defined by its "heterogeneity, multiplicity, and dispersion."[36] We witness a proliferation of frameworks that complements what Wind noticed as the renunciation of "imaginative" synthesis in preference for the establishing an objective "historical grammar." Both circumstances contribute to the erosion of belief in the passionate recovery of historical meaning, the restoration and fusion of subjective perspectives.

Thus readers will find James Elkins, in an accessible and highly useful introduction to the state of art criticism published in 2003, stridently remarking that "art criticism is in a worldwide crisis."[37] Part of the reason this is the case, he says, is that while art criticism is produced in ever increasing amounts and bolstered by ever increasing opportunities for distribution (journals, magazines, gallery brochures, blogspots, and so on), no one really takes it seriously. Art criticism is "massively produced, and massively ignored"; it is in a state of "vigorous health and terminal illness."[38] Elkins would prefer a situation, it is fair to say, of reciprocity, in which art criticism is taken seriously by interested readers who are somewhat informed in the history of art criticism, art history, aesthetics, and art education and can participate in contemporary intellectual debates as they appear. But Elkins acknowledges that the sheer volume of art criticism is "outstripping its readers." He continues: "[T]here is more of it around than anyone can read . . . [we] can't read everything."[39] Yet Elkins concludes his short book by suggesting an impossible proscription: for a vital art critical dialogue, "all that is required is that everyone read everything. Each writer, no matter what their place and purpose, should have an endless bibliography, and know every pertinent issue and claim. We should all read until our eyes are bleary, and we should read both ambitiously . . . and also indiscriminately."[40] Whether or not this proscription would advance or hinder the development of art criticism is an open question.[41]

To inquire into the "state" of art criticism expresses an interest not only in defining what art criticism *is*, or in finding the limits or parameters of art critical practice; it also expresses an interest in making some kind of judgment about the condition such a practice—art criticism, if it is defined—generally finds itself in. However, a definition of criticism, and an evaluation of its state, might appear to mitigate the heterogeneity of art critical practices, making them appear similar and uniform. As some historians have argued, the birth of art criticism as a literary genre in mid-eighteenth-century France and its extension into a variety of forms of "Kunstliteratur" in the nineteenth (museum guides, exhibition reviews, travel accounts, monographs, historical studies, art correspondence) anticipated its modern heterogeneity and multiplicity.[42] Historically, then, art criticism is characterized exactly by its *lack* of codification: one does not have to prepare to be an art critic by engaging in any specific professional training; art criticism has no common rules; no common set of objects to which it applies; it does not share a standard mode of writing, presentational format, or rhetorical conventions; it is not located in a single place. By all accounts, criticism has no "internal coherence," as Michael Orwicz has pointed out.[43] Still, this heterogeneity is frequently taken a sign of health. In his Assessment, Julian Stallabrass takes art criticism's "fundamental lack of clarity" and the " 'undecidability' of its objects" to be its greatest virtue. So why worry about a "state"?

Perhaps because, as Lane Relyea indicates in this volume, "The terms that underwrote an older conception of criticism—notions of the public, of culture, of value—are in deep crisis, seemingly indistinguishable today from naming mere market functions in our transnational capitalist economy."[44] If the recent history of roundtables and publications on art criticism is any indication, there is a shared sense that criticism is in a crisis, unsure of its place and function within society.[45] Perhaps this is a problem with defining an audience: it is not clear who reads criticism, nor what is expected from it. Or perhaps this a problem with disciplinary boundaries: it is not clear what criticism *is*, what it should address itself to, and what (if any) standards it should hold itself to (and who would define those standards in the first place?). Reading over the roundtable discussions and responses to them, what becomes evident is the uncertainty many individuals have over whether it is worthwhile—were it even possible—to reform criticism. Of course, the parameters of this reform are an open question, but there does seem to be a common desire, articulated by Katy Siegel in another context, to see art critics "try to *understand* the social and historical conditions that they experience as the crisis of art criticism."[46] Doing so might imbue criticism with a relevance greater than it enjoys at present.

What are the conditions under which such understanding and writing can occur? Does it require the anticipation of a readership, or a secure understanding of the constituency of the audience that is being addressed? Some respondents certainly think so: "Art audiences and art writing constantly intersect," says Robert Enright in his Assessment, "and one of the prerequisites of good criticism is figuring out who you are writing for and in what way." According to Elkins, the audience for art criticism is unable to keep up with its production. So his call for everyone to read everything might be a way to increase the opportunities for art criticism of quality to emerge. Increasing the amount readers interested in art read is one way to solve the problem of art critics, a problem Elkins identifies in naming the title of the first chapter of his book *What Happened to Art Criticism* (partly reprinted here as a Starting Point essay) "Writing without Readers." If understood from the point of view of a critic who wants to make a connection with an audience, who writes for a possible or imagined readership, writing without readers is an unfortunate situation. It is especially problematic for the market, which relies on criticism to provide marks of distinction to artists in an overcrowded system, to advance their careers, and to turn a profit. But why should the audience matter? It is only convention that stresses the importance of one's writing for a communicative exchange with another person. If understood from the point of view of an individual writing for *no* audience, then the situation might provide a salutary effect. In isolating one's practice of writing from the external forces which shape its reception, and its meaning—to the extent such isolation is possible, if one decides it is desirable—one writes within a space that is relatively free of those constraints explicitly or implicitly imposed by audience that would limit what could be written. Of course, this freedom is never absolute—one always writes for readers, even if just one. The circuits of identification and projection which propel writing demand as much. And of course, the rebuttal argument would be that such hermetic writing no longer counts as criticism.

Ethics

Assertions can function as a stimulus for discussion. Art criticism aims to understand, through the description and evaluation of artworks, broader aspects of experience than those usually associated with art as a semi-autonomous sphere of activity generated by and responsive to its own demarcated historicity. Simply put, art criticism can reveal through its handling of artworks a spectrum of concerns confronted by individuals or groups at different times and in different contexts: from attitudes towards concrete historical situations or dynamics, to more abstruse categories such as embodiment.[47] The veracity of the first part of this claim is based on the assumption that a connection exists between society and human forms of expression; that of the second, on the idea that all conditions of viewing are physiologically or psychologically grounded. In regard to the first, it is perhaps unnecessary to reiterate that a fundamental hypothesis in the development of the idea of culture is that the art of a period reflects the general worldview of that period.[48] The idea that the art of an era and the society which produced it are integrally bound together is one of the defining characteristics of our current scholarship within the discipline of art history, and is arguably the premier methodological—and ideological—configuration of modern historical inquiry. An important implication of this connection for art criticism is that aesthetic judgments are inseparable from social and ethical judgments. Michael Orwicz has found this to be definitive: "Criticism is generally differentiated from the fields of aesthetics and art history by virtue of the values (explicit or not) that art-critical judgment seeks to mobilize, and the defined position from which the critic speaks. It is precisely its mobilization of judgments of value concerning works of art that constitutes the specificity of the art-critical text."[49] The question emerges: is contemporary art criticism characterized by its capacity to articulate this correspondence, and to imbue its pronouncements with a moral authority? Does art criticism, as it is practiced in its various "publication vehicles" (as Dario Gamboni has called the network of texts that feature and distribute criticism) regularly attain the insights into society (and concomitant insights into the ethical character of that society) characteristic of the best criticism?[50]

A first example. John Ruskin was a key figure in the establishment of a mode of criticism that understands—and judges—society through interpreting its cultural artifacts, its forms of expression. What makes him a compelling figure to return to in any discussion of contemporary criticism is that his personal commitments enabled him to think that contemporary, as much as historical, forms of expression and the way we interpret them were not just consequences of unchangeable historical conditions, but were rather instances, and instruments, of a transformative cultural program. Ruskin, looking back from the vantage point of a society undergoing rapid change to a time he perceived as more holistic (the Middle Ages), attempted to save or revitalize an organic mode of living, thinking, and feeling he thought was being eradicated by technologies of industrial mechanization. This mode of being might be characterized as one of fullness or directness, perhaps as one of honesty and truthfulness. Ruskin did not advocate a return to the middle ages; he neither wanted the life nor the decorations of the thirteenth century back again. But he was nonetheless cognizant of a loss he hoped could be recuperated by criticism. Progress entails an erasure of former modes of thinking as well as of behaving. Recognizing what was being lost from the past was most important to Ruskin, and it is this sensitivity that informs much of his thought about art. His writings are best read as an attempt to preserve or reinstate modes of consciousness that were imagined to be more fulfilling and genuine than the alternative—the increased atomization or quantification of all aspects of life, drained of any qualitative moral or spiritual significance and ultimately devoid of human meaning.[51]

A second example. Walter Pater, writing about Winckelmann's legacy as the figure who transmitted to Goethe the "true essence" of Greek art, noticed that the features Winckelmann discerned in Hellenic culture, namely "breadth, centrality, with blindness and repose," were more evident to us now than they perhaps were even at the time. "The local, accidental colouring of its own age has passed from it," Pater wrote, "and the greatness that is dead looks greater when the link with what is slight and vulgar has been severed."[52] If Winckelmann restored to Goethe not just a plausible but an authentic and viable understanding of Hellenic culture, Pater's criticism of Winckelmann concentrates and intensifies that understanding. In so doing, Pater reveals Winckelmann to be exemplary of his own eighteenth-century moment; simultaneously, Pater's own work may become for the sensitive critic not only a passage to what is true about Winckelmann (or the Greeks for that matter), but also an exemplification of the historical truth of Pater's Victorianism. In both moves, from Pater to Winckelmann, and from our critic to Pater, writing restores to the reader a sense of historical veracity, refracted, as it always must be, through a lens of subjectivism. But this subjectivism can, in critical practice, convert into what Whitney Davis has called a "plausible historical psychology," in which the critic approximates, identifies, or articulates a fully historical account of how people other than ourselves understood the world.[53]

Whether or not it is desirable to accept these models of ethical criticism from our postmodern standpoint, characterized by skepticism and disbelief more than by conviction and faith, their relevance for contemporary debates lies in their self-reflexivness—in Ruskin's or Pater's attempt to grasp simultaneously their own (present) situational context and a (past) horizon of meaning. Interpreting the past, these critics substantially record their own attitudes and judgments.[54] But readers sense that this historical refraction is more substantial than the form of cultural critique often characteristic of ephemeral art criticism, with all its recognition of its own institutional, ideological, and discursive frameworks. Focusing on positionality, or framing, can be beneficial under conditions that are sensed to prevent, or to inhibit, inquiry and evaluation of a cultural situation. We might expect such a condition to be present when the amount of material or information under consideration reaches a point of maximum availability. Facing an overabundance of evidence, critics are neither able to discern, nor to present, a synthetic picture—

a meaningful representation—of the most important features of a given cultural moment. Unmanageability becomes a symptom of a defunct critical procedure. It may be compensated for by self-reflexivness, distinct from strategies of reflective positioning, which replaces external constraints on writing (for instance, pressures to adhere to conventions of presenting historical evidence in an argument) with internal ones (for instance, the regulation of writing by a keen sense of personal desire).

Equivalence

A conventional assumption about art criticism is that it mediates between the critic (a professional who produces specialized knowledge about artists and artworks) and a public that seeks to be educated or enlightened about a market of artistic or intellectual products.[55] It serves an intermediary role, shuttling back and forth between two poles, illustrating aspects of art and arbitrating its economic and cultural value. Art criticism presents its objects to an audience, and in so doing is thought to be culturally relevant, to have a purpose and to fulfill a function. But what about criticism that is not written to explain, nor to demonstrate, nor to evaluate, but instead to collapse the distance between the two poles? This criticism would be characterized by its ability to create for readers an experience that possesses qualities of the critic's original confrontation with the object, text, or process that serves as the occasion for writing. This would be a criticism that performs what it putatively describes; the kind of writing, as Richard Shiff argues, produced by Walter Benjamin to represent the "shock" of the modern world as registered in nineteenth-century photography and poetry. "Benjamin's writing," Shiff explains, "figures modernity in a language of analogy that *acts* upon the reader in lieu of explaining."[56] To preserve in writing the force of a physical or emotional encounter with an object (or process, or event) would be to register the resistance of that object to immediate assimilation, to habitual understanding. It would be a figured writing that imposes upon readers the character of experience.[57] Adjusted to the form of its object, this subjective writing could serve as its equivalent, as Darby English argues.[58]

An example might help to elucidate this point. It is a commonplace of interpretation that modern artists, in breaking finally with the principle of imitation, were concerned with making objects that not only simulated perceptual processes (primarily those of vision) for a viewer, but which could also adequately stand as a surrogate for the experiential world, equal in its intensity and depth.[59] By the mid 1940s, this view was widely held by artists of the Abstract Expressionist generation. For instance, responding to Hans Hofmann's admonition that he should paint from nature, Jackson Pollock supposedly retorted, "I *am* nature."[60] Pollock was driven to make such an assertion because he wanted Hofmann to understand that the model for his painting was not in the visual aspect of nature "out there," but rather was identified with the processes of the natural world (such as change, continuity, constancy, and disruption). Because these rhythms were common to both nature and human beings, Pollock believed he was capable of producing paintings that not only pictured the natural world, but also stood as equivalent to it. In a handwritten note found among the artist's papers after his death, Pollock expressed his desire for his art to exhibit "states of order—organic intensity—energy and motion made visible." Pollock went on to indicate that he wanted his work to manifest nature or experience "in terms of painting—not an illustration—(but the equivalent)."[61] In other words, the artist thought his paintings might not only depict a natural world, but might exemplify it.[62] In a classic discussion of depiction and exemplification as complementary modes of representation, Nelson Goodman argued that depictive realism (naturalism) in art was complemented by a less arbitrary mode of representation: when a painting *refers* to something while at the same time *possessing* some properties of the thing it refers to, it exemplifies. Goodman put it succinctly: "exemplification is possession plus reference."[63] Following Goodman's lead, we might think of *Autumn Rhythm* as being more than a depiction of an autumn landscape. It is also its sample: it conveys some of autumn's colors, cadences, moods, atmosphere. Like many of Pollock's large-scale drip paintings, *Autumn Rhythm* manifests a physical sense of the environment: the work generates effects analogous to those we experience when we are in an environment.

Is it desirable to expect from art critical writing such a motivated connection to its object? It would be, if what a reader expected from art criticism was more than a contextualization of the art under consideration within a general history of art, a comparative analysis of the art with other contemporary practices, and an evaluation of its success or failure. Ambitious criticism strives for equivalence, because it allows the reader to share the subjective position of the writer, whose technique ideally facilitates the passage from representation to experience.[64]

Recovery

If art criticism is in disarray—a view it would be difficult to resist, given the diversity of opinions represented in the roundtables and commentaries—the question becomes, is it necessary or advantageous to regularize it as a practice, or indeed, to even agree on its functions? Twenty years ago, addressing these questions—questions of disciplinary responsibility and specialization—seemed relevant, even desirable. For instance, Richard Wollheim, always pragmatic and incisive in his clarification of central problems, straightforwardly asks, "What then is the end of criticism?"[65] And the answer he gives is likewise straightforward: art criticism aims to understand, to grasp the meaning of, artworks. The theoretical problem, of which Wollheim was well aware, is that there are numerous interpretations of "meaning." Two views predominate. On the one hand, meaning can be thought of as something adhering to the work of art, some quality to be discovered by the critic through discovering the original conditions of its creative manufacture. On the other hand, meaning is constructed by the critic and subsequently imposed on the work of art. The difference is between meaning that originates in the creative process, and that which derives from the critical process. While it may be difficult to distinguish exactly when a critic operates according to one or the other mode, Wollheim distinguishes the approaches by calling the first "criticism as retrieval" and the second "criticism as revision."[66]

Between these alternate poles are an indefinite number of critical positions, more or less representative of one technique or the other. It is not necessary to choose one over the other, because they are not mutually contradictory: they are tendencies, and each critic will emphasize, according to his or her needs, the one that suits the purposes of the moment. Arguably, it will be the critic who is able to exchange positions with ease who will be most adept at communicating meaning for the art he or she encounters. For such flexibility enhances two simultaneous operations, both crucial for convincing criticism: an openness to the circuits of projection and identification that allow different horizons (historical, personal, cultural) to merge, or to be adjusted to one another (however much we are accustomed to disavow the authenticity of this process); and a resistance to accepting the non-contingent truthfulness of those projections and identifications outside the subjective positioning that makes them possible. This is arguably constitutive of a critical approach to the recovery of human meaning.

Notes

1. I would like to acknowledge Michael Golec for his helpful reading of a draft of this essay. Walter Pater, "Winckelmann" [1867], *The Renaissance* [1893] (Berkeley CA: University of California Press, 1980): 182.
2. Edgar Wind, *Art and Anarchy* [1963] (Evanston IL: Northwestern University Press, 1985): 21.
3. Paul de Man, "The Dead-End of Formalist Criticism" [1956], *Blindness and Insight* (Minneapolis MN: University of Minnesota Press, 1971): 231.
4. I.A. Richards, *Principles of Literary Criticism* [1925] (New York and London: Harcourt Brace Jovanovich, n.d.): 26. If this were not the case, art would be unable to fulfill those functions Richards believed were of paramount importance: "The arts are our storehouse of recorded values . . . Both in the genesis of a work of art, in the creative moment, and in its aspect as a vehicle for communication, reasons can be found for giving to the arts a very important place in the theory of Value. They record the most important judgments we possess as to the values of experience" (32).
5. de Man, 232.
6. de Man, 235. For Empson, the transformation of unity into multiplicity leads to an ambiguity that nonetheless can be constrained or limited by intelligent exegesis.
7. de Man, 237. De Man elucidates what he takes to be Empson's chief insight over the work of Richards: "[T]rue poetic ambiguity proceeds from the deep division of Being itself, and poetry does no more than state and repeat this division. . . . The ambiguity poetry speaks of is the fundamental one that prevails between the world of the spirit and the world of sentient substance: to ground itself, the spirit must turn itself into sentient substance, but the latter is knowable only in its dissolution into non-being. The spirit cannot coincide with its object and this separation is infinitely sorrowful" (237).
8. de Man, 241.
9. de Man, 245.
10. de Man, 244.

11. On this point, see Richard Shiff, "Homeopathic Criticism," *Common Knowledge* 7 (Winter 1998): 4.
12. de Man, 244.
13. A related distinction between "journalistic" and "academic" art criticism is taken up in earnest by contributors to this volume. See especially the responses by Peter Plagens, Margaret Hawkins, Robert Enright, Sheila Farr, Blake Gopnik, and Saul Ostrow.
14. Richards, 92. Although his method of criticism was principled, Richards did not believe that science could provide all the answers to questions of artistic value: "If we knew enough it might be possible that all necessary attitudes could be obtained through scientific references alone. Since we do not know very much yet, we can leave this very remote possibility, once recognized, alone" (267).
15. My sense of criticism "handling" it objects derives from Richard Shiff. See "On Criticism Handling History," *Art Criticism* 3:1 (1990).
16. See Shiff, "Self-Interference,"
17. Wind, 21.
18. Shiff, "Performing an Appearance: On the Surface of Abstract Expressionism," in *Abstract Expressionism: The Critical Developments* edited by M. Auping (New York: Harry N. Abrams, 1987): 94.
19. See Shiff, 94–95.
20. Wind, 23.
21. Later formalist critics, especially Clement Greenberg, to some extent reiterated this Kantian distinction between aesthetic and practical interest, but nonetheless positively valued artistic perception as a meeting point of sense and reason [See Bernard Bosanquet, *A History of Aesthetic* [1892] (Cleveland OH and New York: World Publishing, 1961): 265.] The unity between feeling and sense on the one hand, and reason and intelligence on the other, found an expression in Greenberg's writings, who recognized that "[t]ruth of feeling in art is in great measure an effect of detachment," but who also knew that in order to be aesthetically convincing, artists had to "have the nerve to impose [their own] truth on art." See Clement Greenberg, "Feeling is All" [1952], in *Clement Greenberg: The Collected Essays and Criticism*, edited by Joan O'Brian, 4 vols. (Chicago IL: University of Chicago Press, 1993), vol. 3, 102–103.
22. See Whitney Davis, "Formalism in Art History," in *Encyclopedia of Aesthetics*, edited by Michael Kelly, 4 vols. (Oxford: Oxford University Press, 1998), vol. 2, 223.
23. Meyer Schapiro criticized formalism's tendency to "lose sight of the structure of the historical object, namely, the particular human society, and deal with absolute general categories that seem to produce history by their own internal logic." See Schapiro, "The New Viennese School" [1936], in *The Vienna School Reader*, edited by Christopher Wood (New York: Zone Books, 2000): 453–85.
24. Davis, 222–23. Sentence order reversed.
25. Wind, 23.
26. Wind, 24. For Wind, both the formal approach and an approach of "*art engagé*" have their problems: "Both try to escape, in opposite directions, from the plain and fundamental fact that art is an exercise of the

imagination, engaging and detaching us at the same time: it makes us participate in what it presents, and yet presents it as an aesthetic fiction. From that twofold root—participation and fiction—art draws its power to enlarge our vision by carrying us beyond the actual, and to deepen our experience . . ." (24). Wind's view is consistent with certain aspects of Roger Fry, whom he criticizes. Fry famously articulated the theory of aesthetic disinterest on the grounds that the "clarified sense perception which we discover in the imaginative life" allows us to ignore the need for "responsive action" and to focus on and develop instead the emotions of imaginative life. See Roger Fry, "An Essay in Aesthetics" [1909], reprinted in C. Harrison and Wood, editors, *Art in Theory 1900–2000* (London: Blackwell Publishing, 2003): 78.

27. Wind's *Art and Anarchy* is the published version of the Reith Lectures of 1960, which he delivered at St Catherine's College, Oxford.
28. The consolidation of Greenberg's formalism as authoritative is often associated with the publication in 1961 of *Art and Culture*, (Boston MA: Bedcon, 1961), an anthology of his essays. But it would be a mistake to understand Greenberg's formalism as apolitical.
29. I owe this point to my reading of Mark Bauerlein's response. Bauerlein notes: "Once it has made inquirers aware of potential bias, [the reflective turn] has done all the work it can. At that point, we need methods to handle the problem, not reiterations of the problem." Bauerlein calls for criticism to advance reliable knowledge by developing standards through communal conversation, contestation, and consensus.
30. On this point, see Shiff, "Flexible Time: The Subject In/Of Art History," *Art Bulletin* 76:4 (December, 1994): 584.
31. Another strategy of current critical writing is to criticize the arguments and claims made prior to one's own. An evaluation of the failings of other writers usually precedes the claim that a new study will rectify previous errors, methodological or otherwise. Negative criticism takes the place of a collective discussion, a back-and-forth conversation about the significant aspects of some practice or object.
32. George Santayana, *Scepticism and Animal Faith* (New York: Charles Scribner's Sons, 1923): 240.
33. Davis, 224.
34. Northrop Frye, "Polemical Introduction," a revised version of "The Function of Criticism at the Present Time" [1949], *Anatomy of Criticism* (Princeton NJ: Princeton University Press, 1957): 5.
35. Fry calls these "extra-literary schematism[s]," *Anatomy of Criticism*, 7.
36. Michael Orwicz, "Art Criticism," 465.
37. James Elkins, *What Happened to Art Criticism?* (Chicago IL: Prickly Paradigm Press, 2003): 2. Raphael Rubinstein prefers the word "mess" to indicate what he perceives as a "hopelessly confused" situation of art criticism which has developed naturally, "mostly through inaction." See *Critical Mess: Art Critics on the State of their Practice*, edited by Raphael Rubenstein (Lenox MA: Hard Press Editions, 2006): i. Elkins's essay is reprinted in excerpted form in Rubenstein's book.
38. Elkins, 4 and 6.
39. Elkins, 4.

40. Elkins, 85.
41. Olu Oguibe essentially agrees with Elkins when he advocates a return of art critics to modes of learning and understanding characteristic of "an earlier age when to be enlightened meant to read—and explore—widely . . . [and] to pay no mind to disciplin[ary boundaries]" (xx). Issues of economic, institutional, or vocational privilege that would support such engagement are relevant here. For a related discussion of "insiders" and "outsiders," see Katy Siegel, "Everyone's a Critic," in *Critical Mess*, edited by Raphael Rubenstein, 43–47.
42. The term is Julius von Schlosser's, and refers to any number of discourses related to art. See *Die Kunstliteratur. Ein Handbuch zur Quellenkunde der neueren Kunstgeschichte* (Vienna: Scholl, 1924): 1–2. The different examples of "Kunstliteratur" I include here are those common to the lists compiled by Michael Orwicz and Dario Gamboni in two very well-informed articles on art criticism. See Orwicz, "Art Criticism," 463; and Gamboni, "The Relative Autonomy of Art Criticism," in *Art Criticism and its Institutions in Nineteenth-Century France* edited by M. Orwicz (Manchester and New York: Manchester University Press, 1994): 182. Additionally, Orwicz includes dictionary entries, caricatures, essays, poetry, biography, and fiction as examples of Kunstliteratur; Gamboni also lists press articles, art chronicles, polemical texts, manifestos, and collections of aphorisms.
43. Orwicz, "Art Criticism," xx.
44. For a compelling assessment of art criticism from the point of view of the transition from modernism to postmodernism, see Relyea's "All Over At Once," in R. Rubenstein, 49–59 [originally published in *X-TRA* (Fall 2003)].
45. See for instance, *The Crisis of Criticism* edited by Maurice Berger (New York: The New Press, 1998); "Round Table: The Present Conditions of Art Criticism." *October* (Spring, 2002); James Elkins, *What Happened to Art Criticism?* (Chicago IL: Prickly Paradigm Press, 2003); and *Critical Mess: Art Critics on the State of their Practice* edited by Raphael Rubenstein (Lennox MA: Hard Press Editions, 2006).
46. Katy Siegel, "Everyone's a Critic," in R. Rubinstein, 45. Emphasis added.
47. Michael Fried's work is exemplary in its combination of historical argumentation and philosophical interpretation. See *Menzel's Realism: Art and Embodiment in Nineteenth-Century Berlin* (New Haven CT and London: Yale University Press, 2002).
48. Raymond Williams, *Culture and Society: 1780–1950* (New York: Columbia University Press, 1958): xvi–xviii. Williams takes the awareness of connection between art and society to be most prominent in the nineteenth century, and quotes Kenneth Clark on the point that "[t]he idea of style as something organically connected with society, something which springs inevitable from a way of life, does not occur, as far as I know, in the 18th century" (130).
49. Orwicz, "Art Criticism," 463.
50. Dario Gamboni, "The Relative Autonomy of Art Criticism," in M. Orwicz, 184.
51. Ruskin's passages on the effects of industrialization on individual self-

realization are justifiably famous. Ruskin wrote: "We have much studied . . . the great civilized invention of the division of labour; only we give it a false name. It is not, truly speaking, the labour that is divided, but the men—Divided into mere segments of men—broken into small fragments and crumbs of life . . ." See Ruskin, "The Nature of Gothic," in *The Stones of Venice* [1853]; reprinted in abridged form in *The Art Criticism of John Ruskin* edited by R. Herbert (New York: Da Capo Press, 1964): 97–98.

52. Pater, *The Renaissance*, 181.
53. Davis, "Formalism in Art History," 221–25.
54. On this point, see Richard Shiff, "Flexible Time: The Subject In/Of Art History," 583.
55. Orwicz, "Art Criticism," 465.
56. Richard Shiff, "Handling Shocks: On the Representation of Experience in Walter Benjamin's Analogies," *Oxford Art Journal* 15:2 (1992): 91 (emphasis added). It should be mentioned that Shiff's own practice of writing aims to achieve analogous effects: it is Shiff's writing that restores—or rather, equips the reader to attend to—the shock of Benjamin's analogies, just as Benjamin's writing had restored shock to his subjects.
57. Shiff argues that both Charles S. Peirce and Theodore Adorno understand experience as "whatever we cannot immediately either assimilate or repulse, whatever imposes itself as a foreign substance, forcing alteration or adjustment of existing psychic and somatic mechanisms" (90).
58. English seems to call for such a mode in his Assessment, when he calls for criticism that would secure "greater resemblance to that which it would clarify." He continues: "If criticism . . . record[s] . . . an artwork's provocations to thought, then perhaps it is at its best when it articulates such provocations in a way that *retains rather than assimilates* [those] element of surprise. . . . What would it mean for a critical practice to be 'continuous' with aesthetic practices . . .?" Such inquiries are not unilaterally shared, of course. Maja Naef points out the "impossibility of recouping the experience of the artwork in writing . . . it is precisely this irretrievable residuum that motivates [art criticism]."
59. For an insightful theoretical and historical overview of this point, see Tzvetan Todorov, *Theories of the Symbol* (Ithaca NY: Cornell University Press, 1982): 147–222.
60. This part of Lee Krasner's account of the meeting between Hofmann and Pollock is well known, and quoted repeatedly in the scholarly literature. Krasner related in an interview: "I brought Hofmann up to meet Pollock for the first time and Hofmann said, after looking at his work, 'You do not work from Nature.' Pollock's answer was, 'I am nature.' " Lee Krasner, "Interview with Bruce Glaser" [1967], in *Jackson Pollock: Interviews, Articles, and Reviews* K. Varnedoe and Karmel, editors (New York: Museum of Modern Art, 1999): 28.
61. Jackson Pollock, "Handwritten statement" [c. late 1950s], in Karmel, et al., *Jackson Pollock: Interviews, Articles, and Reviews*, 24.
62. For an investigation of the Abstract Expressionist interest in equivalents through the lens of cognitive psychology, see Claude Cernuschi, *"Not an Illustration but the Equivalent": A Cognitive Approach to Abstract Expressionism* (London: Associated University Presses, 1997).

63. Nelson Goodman, *Languages of Art: An Approach to a Theory of Symbols* (Indianapolis IN: Hackett Publishing, 1976): 52–54.
64. Nancy Princenthal's notion of "surplus" in art criticism might be relevant in this regard. See "Art Criticism, Bound to Fail," in R. Rubenstein, 83–90.
65. Richard Wollheim, "Art, Interpretation, and the Creative Process," *New Literary History* 15:2 (Winter, 1984): 241–53.
66. Wollheim, 243.

2
Starting Points

The Specificity of Criticism and Its Need for Philosophy[1]

Michael Newman

If there is a crisis in art criticism, it would seem tempting to turn to philosophy for a solution. I will argue that philosophy is not in a position to provide a solution to the problems faced by art criticism, since it is implicated in them. While both art criticism and theory are inadequate alone, each calls for supplementation by the other.[2] This mutual need cannot—for reasons I will go on to explore—be fulfilled in a synthesis, but when subjected to a genealogy, might indicate the nature of the problem. In the first section of this paper, I will consider the determinations of the problem faced by art criticism today. In the second, I will attempt to defend the specificity of art criticism as a practice against "sublation" (*Aufhebung*) into philosophy. This defense will hinge on a radical notion of judgment which may be retrieved from Kant's third *Critique*.[3]

In the third section this emphasis will be reversed: I will consider why, after—and indeed within—Kant, the "art of judgment" could not be sustained. It is in the art theory, and theory of criticism, of the German Idealists and Romantics that the reconciliation of the British tradition of "taste" and the German tradition of "aesthetic" which Kant attempted bifurcates again, but in a new form which presages the modern avant-garde.[4] It is at this point that the universality of philosophical critique becomes the destiny of the particular work of art, to be attained via the act of reflection, at the cost, arguably, of the dissolution of singularity in the transcendentalism of irony. This provokes the question of the extent to which certain approaches to art practice and theory repeat the structure of Romantic irony.

I

One merely has to peruse most of the art journals and magazines to see that the quality and rigor of art criticism has declined dramatically since the mid-1980s, if not before. Why has this occurred?

To say that the decline of criticism has resulted from the decline in quality of its object, works of art, is too simple, as this presumes what needs to be called into question: first, that criticism is merely an extrinsic, descriptive supplement to its object; and, second, that the nature of its object is not itself reflective and critical. It could be argued that one of the reasons for the problem of criticism today is its redundancy when changes in art practice, notably Conceptual art, displaced criticism from its role in relation to the avant-garde by incorporating critique—including the critique of a descriptive, objectifying epistemology—into the practice itself: art theory replaces art criticism as the appropriate way of mediating the practice, and is often carried out by the artists themselves.[5] In this context, the role left to the critic is either to become himself a writer or artist, or the meta-critique of this move, of the turn to theory.[6] Insofar as taste and judgment are subject to critique whether explicitly or implicitly by the works—or the practice—themselves, the return to judgmental as opposed to theoretical criticism during the 1980s tended to be understood as indicative of a neo-conservative revival of elitist taste or the bad faith of adopting an independent posture while serving the market.

These developments since the late 1960s need to be understood in relation to the historical transformation of relations between modernism, the avant-garde and mass culture. Conceptual art took up the project of the twentieth-century avant-garde of the critique of the institution of art. What needs to be accounted for is not simply the way in which the avant-garde provides a reflective critique of the institution of art,[7] but the repeated failure of this move—the (re)unification of art and life—to have its intended extra-aesthetic consequences, which is not necessarily to imply that the reasons for the failure are each time the same.

The criterion of success assumed in the very question "Why has the avant-garde repeatedly failed?" presupposes an enlightenment project for art. To be more precise, art takes over when enlightenment reason has been perceived to have failed to deliver what it promised: art becomes the sphere in which *la promesse de bonheur*, the promise of happiness, continues to be figured.[8] The function of criticism would be as an elucidation and mediation of the emancipating and fulfilling potential of art practice. A problem arises, however, with the structural involvement of both art and criticism in the conditions which prevent such emancipation and fulfillment taking place.

According to the Frankfurt School analysis, those conditions include above all the actualization of the categorial implications of commodification (instrumentalization and exchangeability) within the "culture industry." Where "life" itself is governed by the commodity-form, the avant-garde project of the dissolution of art into life is bound to fail in its revolutionary aim—or perhaps succeed all too well, but in the wrong way insofar as "life" has become aestheticized as phantasmagoria or simulation.

For Adorno, under such conditions the avant-garde project would merely instrumentalize the artwork. Whereas the twentieth-century avant-garde came to include a critique of modernism as aesthetic autonomy, Adorno provides a modernist critique of the avant-garde as a project of the *premature* dissolution of the autonomy of art.[9] A condition for Adorno's critique is the perception of the failure of left social movements with which a progressive avant-garde must ally itself: in the phase of post-liberal organized capitalism, the proletariat had been absorbed as consumers.

Clement Greenberg's response to this situation was to press the philosophy of history which served to validate the avant-garde into service as a legitimating account of modernism, which thus becomes the culmination of the history of art as a process of art's purely internal progressive self-criticism and self-limitation. This was sustained by an undialectical opposition of the theoretical object, the Greenbergian artwork constituted by the elision of the different categories of "modernism" and "avant-garde," with "kitsch" mass culture,[10] the basis for the discrimination of which ultimately lay in the taste of the critic, as a time when the Kantian claim for the universality of judgments of taste implied the hegemony of an particular ideology rather than the potential emancipation of universal mankind.

While it would be wrong to say that Adorno, like Greenberg, "opposes" modernism to the culture industry, since, rather, he conceives them as dialectically interrelated moments of a historical totality,[11] the existence of modernist *works* provides for Adorno the basis in actuality for critique, insofar as they show that the "culture industry" itself does not saturate the totality. Only through the autonomous artwork could the contradictory, rather than flatly homogenous, nature of the totality be upheld. Nonetheless, Adorno offers no comfort: there is nothing in principle to prevent the complete homogenization of the totality.

Moreover, as Adorno himself demonstrates, the work of art becomes the "absolute commodity" in its perfect substitution of exchange for use value—it is exchange-value which is consumed:

> The appearance of immediacy takes possession of the mediated, exchange value itself. If the commodity in general combines exchange-value and use-value, then the pure use value, whose illusion the cultural goods must preserve in completely capitalist society, must be replaced by pure exchange-value, which precisely in its capacity as exchange-value takes over the function of use-value. . . .
>
> . . . The more inexorably the principle of exchange-value destroys use-values for human beings, the more deeply does exchange-value disguise itself as the object of enjoyment.[12]

In other words, according to this somewhat hyperbolic argument, with the commodification of art, the *promesse de bonheur* of the particular work becomes the servant of exchange value: indeed, happiness becomes exchange-value and exchange-value becomes happiness. If this is the case, then it may be only the critical text, as theoretical text, that can remain truly "critical" by disclosing the dialectical mediations at work in the art object and in its relation to the "culture industry" and capitalism. However, there are at least two problems with this move.

The first, acknowledged by Adorno, is that as "theory" disconnected from social movements the critical text cannot accomplish its critique on a practical level. The institutionalization of modernism itself by the late 1960s affected both Adorno's reception in Germany by the new left,[13] and the critique of Greenberg in the USA by artists and critics associated with Conceptual art. Hence the phase which succeeds Adorno, from 1968 to 1974 (the year of the publication of Bürger's *Theory of the Avant-Garde*), is that of the attempt to renew the avant-garde project, this time separated from modernism (predominantly in its interpretation according to Clement Greenberg) and including modernist autonomy as the object of its critique on both practical (happenings, performance, inter-media, and so on) and theoretical (Conceptual art) levels. It should be noted that both procedures are unable in the end to break out of the institution of art, insofar as the latter provides the only possible condition for their cultural visibility. The incorporation of structuralism in post-Conceptual art theory of the 1970s resulted in the dissolution of the particularity of the autonomous artwork (aided by the use of strategies of reproduction and language as media), which was henceforth to be understood as text within an inter-text or language. A consequence of this was the occlusion of judgment as a question even to be raised.

If the critical text is to become what the modernist work of art ought to have been, this means that the critical text must itself suffer the fate of the art work, namely commodification, which brings us to the second problem. Criticism, even if it involves critique, contributes in its role as mediation with the public to the extension of the culture industry, which comes to include modernism, the avant-garde, and the institution of criticism itself. Furthermore, the indication of criticality itself becomes essential to the appearance of distinction of the artwork from mass culture upon which, for a time, its successful commodification depends: the "critical" critic finds him/herself in a contradictory position, since the attribution of criticality may serve to legitimate the work in the market (this also undermines the Conceptual art approach).

Once this was acknowledged, it became apparent that it is only from within the culture industry itself that critique may be carried out. This defines the parameters of the "post-Conceptual" phase of radical art from the late 1970s to the mid-1980s, during which period the strategy becomes that of internal subversion drawing on the philosophical mode of deconstruction. This represented a last chance—or desperate wager—on the possibility of sustaining the criticality of practice and theory. It is the failure of this strategy (for both "internal" and "external" reasons) which is one of the immediate causes of the "crisis" of art criticism today (that is, from the mid-1980s to the 1990s).

To suggest, then, that a turn to philosophy is somehow going to resolve this crisis is to forget the latter's history, which has taken the form of repeated turns to theory or to philosophy as a way of attempting to redeem art from reification. This is why I want to go on to argue, in the next section, for the specificity of art criticism as distinct from art theory as at least figuring—preserving and anticipating—a certain possibility inherent in the call to and practice of judgment. But we must also consider why this possibility has *not* been realized. The most obvious way of doing so is to re-examine the first time when, after this possibility became explicitly available, it could not be fulfilled. The aesthetic theory of early, post-Kantian German Idealism and Romanticism marks the first turn from judgment to philosophy as the destiny of the particular work of art. Insofar as these tendencies represent the first avant-garde, the seeds of all the subsequent strategies of the avant-garde, and their failure, are already present. It is necessary to reconsider this history if the call to philosophy for salvation from reification is not to be merely an unreflective repetition.

II

It is largely Greenberg's use of the notion of taste which accounts for its repudiation as a valid basis for the evaluation of artworks since the 1960s, and with it the occlusion of the question of judgment. The recourse to subjective taste in Greenberg substitutes, as a form of legitimation, for the absence of an explicit account of the connection between the autonomous history of art and the socio-historical totality. As an at least symptomatic example of the rejection of taste as a criterion, one has only to think of the critic and Minimalist artist Donald Judd's substitution of "A work needs only to be interesting"[14] for Greenberg's criterion of "quality." The Minimalist approach to the object provides no solution, though, insofar as it remains based on a positivist epistemology and purely phenomenological conception of experience.[15] Nonetheless, Minimalism did provide a performative demonstration of the role of the gallery as an experiential frame for the encounter with the "specific object," indicating the necessity for this to be broadened to the institutional critique carried out by Conceptual art, which included a theoretical critique of taste, consolidating its repudiation. That the rejection of "taste" also involves a suppression of judgment becomes apparent when, in the 1970s, the discourse of art comes to be dominated by "theory" drawing on structuralist thinkers. However, certain re-assessments of Kant in philosophy allow the question of judgment, in its aesthetic and political implications, to be raised anew.

An exemplary study in this regard is Howard Caygill's book *Art of Judgment*.[16] What it allows us to do is to construct a genealogy of the contemporary crisis of criticism, of the problematic relation of judgment to theory, and to appreciate more clearly, perhaps even in a new way, what is at stake. Behind the call for a "philosophical criticism" lies an aporia which became apparent when Kant attempted to orient his thinking on judgment in relation to the two traditions of "taste" and "aesthetic."

The British philosophers of the eighteenth century (Cumberland, Shaftsbury, Hutcheson, Kames, Hume, Burke) used "taste" as the basis for the moral justification of "civil society" from within. Their problem was to reconcile individual interest with the general good or end (48). The legality of the state is subordinated to the morality of civil society (47), which is immediately felt by sentiment rather than rationally known. The pleasure of taste becomes the sense of beauty and virtue as the immediate experience of providence:

> Individuals behave affectively, according to sentiment, but providence ensures that the sum of their actions realizes the common good. In this way the freedom and autonomy of the individual at the level of sense is reconciled with the lawlike characteristics of universality and necessity at the level of idea. The price of this solution was the disembodiment of taste; it became an intangible medium of exchange between the rational will of providence and the irrational individual sentiment. (43)

Thus, according to Caygill, since the activity of taste is interpreted as the work of providence, British theorists "devolve the responsibility for self-legislation—the ordering of civil society—upon providence, and violently exclude its productive moment." The exclusion of productive self-formation and self-legislation is the ideological correlate of the exclusion of the laboring classes from civil society as an alliance of aristocracy and commerce. Adam Smith, at the end of this tradition, recognizes the role of productive activity, thus initiating the transition from the theory of taste and civil society to political economy (44), but he separates the moments of invention and judgment, dematerializing and occluding the latter as the famous "invisible hand" of providence.

Thus, within the British tradition lawlike properties are attributed to the discriminations of sense, resulting in what Kant criticized as the "amphiboly" of sensualizing the concepts of the understanding and rationalizing, in an immediate way, the discriminations of sensibility (98). The role of "providence" was to exclude the need for the state to legislate the common good, thereby freeing commerce to pursue its own interests untrammeled. However, this resulted in a contradiction, since the productive moment in the conformity of individual and universal, of sensibility and intellect, of law and discrimination, could not be acknowledged.

> In the realm of circulation the moral sense is king; but its writ does not run to production—here rules compulsion and the threat of slavery. Yet the goods on which the virtuous circulation of civil society depend cost effort to produce, and were the source of conflict, but this conflict is relegated from civil society. The producers are not recognized as part of civil society, their productive activity does not fall within the orbit of wealth and virtue. And yet the whole of the harmonious circulation of civil society depends on the *je ne sais quoi* of their effort. (101)

While the theory of taste emerged in Britain as a way of legitimating civil society—the pursuit of individual interests as leading, via providence, to the common good—the theory of aesthetic in the German-speaking countries, above all Prussia, developed from the attempt to accommodate pleasure in the systematic philosophy which provided the theory and ideological legitimation for the bureaucratically administered *Polizei* state.[17] Whereas the British theoreticians began with a sense and then had to justify its validity with respect to the common good, the philosophers of *Polizei* began with the equation of rational perfection with the common welfare. For Wolff, perfection was legislated from above, by the "higher faculty," while the "lower faculty" of sense does not participate in judgment at all. However, this subsumptive model cannot accommodate the experience of beauty. The problem arose of how the higher and lower faculties were to be related as the question of how beauty and pleasure were to be mediated. Wolff's critics, the Swiss Bodmer and Breitinger, influenced by British theories of taste, argued that taste involves recognition and not ascription, and gave an active role to the imagination which they consider

> to work according to its own rules which only become apparent in works of art. The task of criticism is to draw out the rules of imagination as they manifest themselves in the work, and not to discriminate between works according to a body of rules already established by reason. (146)

Baumgarten then attempted to extend the Wolffian system in order to accommodate the experience of art.

The aesthetic, Caygill points out "was awkwardly placed within and without [Baumgarten's] system, being both a discrete part of it—the philosophical treatment of art—and, as the science of sensibility, its foundation" (148). Thus the attempt to incorporate the experience of art—aesthetic pleasure—ended up undermining the system as a whole when the productive role attributed by Baumgarten to the lower faculty but restricted by him to theory, is extended by Herder to practical philosophy, resulting in a philosophy of history of dynamic human self-formation. Modeled on the tactile activity of sculpting rather than the visual perception of the image or reflection, this reinstated the etymological relation of taste to *tasten*, to discriminate by touch in an active and productive way, rather than *Geschmack* as the German equivalent of the French *goût*, the *je ne sais quoi* (183).

The theories of taste and aesthetic have an antinomial relation to each other, the one attempting to work from the bottom up, the other from the top down. Without the incorporation of the productive moment, taste cannot justify its validity except by recourse to an unknowable providence. Similarly, without an account of how the principle of discrimination is formed, aesthetic cannot show how the pleasure in beauty might be related to perfection and the common good. The pleasure in beauty had a crucial role in provoking the crisis of both the theory of taste and the systematic philosophy of aesthetic. As Caygill writes,

> In the theory of taste, the law of discrimination is given by providence, while production becomes a *je ne sais quoi*. In aesthetic, the law is administered upon its subjects and objects, denying them any autonomy. In both cases the proportionality produced by judgment can only be recognized through pleasure in beauty. Beauty holds the promise of a freedom which legislates and produces for itself, and becomes not only the necessary supplement of the theories of civil society and the police-state, but also their point of crisis and disruption. (184)

In his first *Critique*, concerned with the conditions of possibility for knowledge and the critique of metaphysics, Kant attempted to resolve the problem of the relation between sensibility and the universal by making the transcendental distinction between intuition and understanding, which involved the restriction of both: neither by itself could provide knowledge, which could only be *produced* through an *act* of synthesis by the subject. However, while introducing the moment of production lacking in both the theories of taste and aesthetic, Kant's model of judgment in the first *Critique* remained subsumptive, violently subordinating the sensibility, and thus dividing the subject into transcendental and empirical. However, the experience of pleasure in beauty lodges a claim for sensibility which appears to be prior to its rational subsumption, yet nonetheless universal, and throws into question the adequacy of the account of synthesis in the second edition version of the "Transcendental Deduction of the Pure Concepts of Understanding" and the "Schematism." In order for the manifold of intuition and the concepts of the understanding to be conformed in a synthesis without the violent subsumption of the former, where understanding and sensibility are divided into active and passive modes, there must be a prior proportionality or harmony—prior to and exceeding judgment and intimated in pleasure—which would ultimately amount to the unity of nature with freedom in "life." Hence, in considering judgments of beauty in the third *Critique*, Kant develops another model of judgment which is "reflective" rather than determinative or subsumptive.

Rather than, as in cognitive judgments according to the first *Critique*, beginning with the universal and subsuming the particular under it, the reflective judgment of beauty is obliged to ascend from the particular to the universal.[18] If such judgments are not merely statements of contingent liking, but make a universal claim, the universality of the reflective judgment must be, for Kant, contained not in the categories of the understanding, but by reference to a proportion which underlies the employment of sensibility and understanding. Caygill summarizes:

> The fundamental proportion inspires the mutual vivication of the knowledge powers, a vivication which occurs in every experience but which is only recognized in the case of beautiful objects. It can only be determined in terms of feeling, since it founds and exceeds cognition, but this feeling is not one of the sensibility, but is the *sensus communis*. (336)

The accord or proportionality of the knowledge powers in the *sensus communis* is made into a normative idea from which the necessity of the aesthetic judgment of taste is to be established. The source of the necessity of the *sensus communis* itself is established by Kant through a consideration of genius and tradition. What we are allowed to glimpse is the possibility that the productive imagination might be "*free and of itself conformable to law*,"[19] which amounts to a claim for invention surpassing the governance of the understanding yet required for the latter's operation and therefore not arbitrary. In order to justify the intrinsic lawfulness of invention, of the productive imagination, Kant needs a notion of finality, but does not allow himself the appeal to providence which we have encountered in the British theory of taste. Hence, for Kant, the finality itself must be humanly constituted, and this is analogically perceived in reflective judgment which "can dispose itself finally without presupposing an end (*Zweckmässigkeit ohne Zweck*) because it is the disposition that constitutes ends" (369). This purposiveness, which Kant conceives as purely formal, is the law which the reflective judgment gives to itself as the transcendental principle of its universality. The fundamental accord thus apprehended and justified overcomes the problem of the self-alienation of the understanding in a purported objectivity: from the "top-down" perspective the understanding "inscribes finality on nature, and then subjects itself to its own laws as if they were objective; in other words, it disowns responsibility for inscription, allowing its spirit to become letter" (371). Rather, the agreement or disagreement of finalities, felt in pleasure and unpleasure, is foundational: "It founds the possibility of inscription, but cannot itself be inscribed. In Kant's terms, the agreement of concept and intuition cannot be explained in terms of concept and intuition" (372). Nature—Creation—is to be justified "by a being which has been ordained to legislate its own freedom. The self-cultivation of such a being is shown to be the cultivation of the entire creation" (380). Hence Kant's contribution to the overcoming of the aporias of taste and aesthetic, of civil society and state, of reason and sensibility, and of freedom and law, is the thought of dynamic, productive self-legislation which we find in his discussions of the reflective judgment of beauty and the creativity of genius.

However, the "conformity of free activity and law," and the "notion of a beautiful relation between humans and between them and nature," are threatened in the sublime, where might and dominion are in disproportion, and reason is again divided in its superiority from sensibility and imagination, which may be not unrelated to Kant's views on the Terror which succeeded the popular revolutionary assertion of freedom and self-legislation in France. A violent subsumption of individuals under law is reinstituted: "the discourse of proportion and realization, which exceeds the transcendental distinction, is reduced to its terms. An unconfigured and internally destructive manifold is opposed by a centralized unity," and

> The proportioned ethical life is presented in terms of civil society and the police-state . . .: a civil society which no inherent principle is ordered by a police-state which possesses reason . . ., the language of the beautiful—*Ubereinstimmung* [agreement]—is surrendered to that of the sublime—*Entgegensetzung* [setting against]. (391)

Nonetheless, Kant had evoked the possibility of "a transcendental proportionality inaccessible to categorial thought" (394) through the consideration of the validity of judgments based on the experience of pleasure in beauty.

A claim for judgment—and with it for art criticism—as a specific practice irreducible to theory, may be based on Caygill's discussion of Kant in relation to the traditions of taste and aesthetic. However, I will now go on to suggest that art criticism cannot do without the philosophy of art. This is not a purely philosophical claim, but rather an historical one. We need to confront the barriers to the actualization of the harmonious proportionality implicit in the pleasure of beauty and reflective judgment as the ethical life of the community. The overcoming of these barriers came to be the project of the avant-garde.

III

At stake in the two traditions of taste and aesthetic is the relation of civil society to the state, with taste implying a providential unity towards the common good of particular interests, aesthetic a conceptual unity, in the "police" or welfare state. Kant attempts a reconciliation by finding in the productive practice of reflective judgment as formative of tradition the requirement for a hypothetical ("as if") telos towards the *summum bonum*, the highest good of the moral "kingdom of ends." Self-production is legitimate insofar as it is also self-legislation. However, in the end for Kant the telos can only be upheld at the cost—as a response to the Terror in France and also as a result of the anthropocentrism at the root of both traditions—of a violent subsumption which conceals the claim of beauty of a harmonious proportion prior to judgment. Law, self-production and the harmonious proportion of mankind and nature, which are figured as bound together in the pleasure of beauty and anticipate ethical community, break apart.

However, what Caygill seeks to retrieve from Kant's working through of the aporia of taste and aesthetic is the notion of an art of judgment, constitutive of tradition, responsive to the claim of a harmonious proportion prior to judgment, and exceeding therefore not conceivable within the terms of the transcendental distinction (that is, between intuition and understanding, exemplified in the antinomy of the traditions of "taste" and "aesthetic," both of which suppress the productive moment).

The implication of this for our problem is the claim for the possibility of an art criticism as a form of judgment which, on one hand, is not reducible to merely contingent judgments of taste, and on the other, not subsumable by theory. From Kant's thinking on the art of judgment we may be able to derive a model for the political as neither the centrally planned (*Polizei*) state, nor liberalism (which still remains dependent on an irrational idea of providence). In the notion of the *sensus communis* as the basis for the universality of judgments of taste, is figured a reciprocal communicative *praxis* (in the Aristotelian sense, as retrieved, through an Aristotelian reading of the third *Critique*, by Arendt[20] among others).

If this claim could be justified, it would have at least the limited consequence of redeeming art criticism as a specific practice from the attempt to absorb or abolish it by the turn to "theory" which followed in the wake of Conceptual art in the 1970s. It would also save art criticism from the kind of sociological critique which seeks to reduce judgments of taste to markers of social status, an approach which depends on the reduction of Kantian "reflective judgment" to "taste" as understood by British eighteenth-century thinkers; which is not, however, without a certain truth, as this is what judgment historically reverted to under the pressure of commodification.[21] However, such an approach misses the philosophical implications of Kant's text, where the very status of judgment is transformed, such that subsumptive judgment is dependent on a prior reflective judgment, the condition for which is a fundamental proportionality.

The problem for the thinkers who followed Kant was precisely the immanent and actual realization in a form of life of critique as reflective (rather than subsumptive) judgment, with its underlying proportionality as the basis for non-repressive and non-dominating self-legislation in aesthetico-ethical community. This project is sketched in the "Earliest System-Programme of German Idealism" (1796?).[22] The increasing hegemony of commerce and instrumental reason made the barrier against such actualization seem all but insurmountable. Although it is not possible here to enter with the detail the topic deserves into the complexity of the distinction between speculative Idealism and early or "first" Romanticism,[23] the response of post-Kantian thinkers could in general be said to involve a renewed bifurcation of the empirical and the transcendental. On the empirical level, they attempted to establish an esoteric form of life, thus abandoning the enlightenment attempt to establish a bourgeois public sphere, but insofar as they did seek to re-establish, on new terms, the connection between art and life, constituting the first avant-garde according to Jochen Schulte-Sasse.[24]

Post-Kantian (and perhaps more accurately post-Fichtean) thought sought to develop the possibility of a transcendental vantage point within art as a way of answering the requirement for an inherent purposiveness opposed to the endless chain of instrumentality in a society increasingly dominated by commerce. Indeed, it is at precisely this historical moment that the critique of the aesthetic—which Kant had attempted to constitute and maintain as a unified project after the collapse of criticism based on normative rules for the individual arts (which is related to the transition from stratified to functionally differentiated but economically unified societies)—bifurcates into art criticism and aesthetic theory, as becomes clear in Friedrich Schlegel. Jochen Schulte-Sasse describes the distinction as follows:

> Whereas aesthetic philosophy reflects on the *status* of the particular and of the individual within modernity in general terms, criticism reflects on the particular as it is portrayed in individual works. Criticism's treatment of the particular, though, always remains related to the reflection carried on in aesthetic theory, without being able to use aesthetic theory's conclusions to systematize its critical praxis. As an individual representation of the particular, art is not amenable to systematic forms of criticism. (131)

This amounts to a re-division of the transcendental and the empirical—of universal and particular—which comes to be reflected in the ontological structure of the artwork itself (that is, Romantic irony) and the relation of particular work to art in general implied by it.

Once the transcendental vantage point is separated from the actuality of society, how is it to be justified? More precisely, once the transcendental vantage point, after Kant and Fichte, is understood to be the outcome of a process of self-production or self-formation (*Bildung*), the formation of form, as Lacoue-Labarthe and Nancy put it, the question arises of its authority as more than a merely relativized perspective, that is, of what justifies such a standpoint as critical. The solution attempted is to equate the standpoint of critique with the Absolute: for the Idealists the Absolute as posited (Fichte), as primal ground (Schelling), or as determinate dialectical result (Hegel); for the Romantics as infinite self-reflection towards the Work yet to be achieved. The turn to the philosophy of history (Hegel) and the history of art (Romantics) may be understand as an attempt to solve the problem of the authority or legitimation of the critical standpoint which arises once reason itself is taken as posited or subjectively self-generated after Descartes' destruction of tradition and Kant's critique of the substantialism of the Cartesian self-conscious subject.[25] The Romantic philosophy of history projected the critical standpoint of reflective reason into a future which became transcendent with respect to the actuality of the present dominated by commerce and instrumental reason, thus transforming the enlightenment schema of progress into a static opposition:[26] giving rise to "transcendence of surpassing instead of progress or advancement,"[27] or else a cyclical and organic conception of history replaced one which was rational and could be planned.

If, as I have suggested, the Romantics needed a philosophy of history insofar as the valorization of individuality against the abstraction of exchange raised a problem of justification or validity, on the aesthetic plane the question which arose was: how could the justification of the particular, objectified work be achieved without subsuming individuality under a general idea of perfection? Art history would sublate the contradiction of the individual and the general in the ideal of art, by taking art as the basis for a higher form of history where universality and individuality would be reconciled.[28] In essence, an individuality-yet-to-be-achieved, which would overcome the antinomy of particular and universal, was projected into the future. In the Romantic attempt to reconcile individuality and progress, aesthetic theory (or "Art" in the singular, which became current as a term at that time, as opposed to the individual arts) becomes the destiny of particular works, to be achieved through critical construction, and providing the validity which they cannot provide for themselves by uniting the particular with the whole: "Criticism here is the constitutive instrument for a form of art, not yet realized, that is no longer viewed in terms of works but rather as aesthetic reflection through the medium of individual works," writes Schulte-Sasse (138). All particular works were regarded by the Romantics as incomplete, the task of criticism being to project their completion through dissolution and construction, anticipating the Absolute, the Idea, but not as abstract, rather as the absolute individual which would sublate the diremption of universal and particular. The problem is that the task of attaining such an absolute Work becomes an infinite one, so the Work becomes the aesthetic equivalent to Kant's postulates of pure practical reason as the infinite deferral of the ethical substance of the moral law. With regard to the Romantic avant-garde, the implication is that the self-productive freedom of infinite reflection is ultimately only equivalent to the abstract, formal freedom of liberal society.

For the Romantics, as Lacoue-Labarthe and Nancy point out, criticism is situated "simultaneously in the space of the 'auto-illumination' of the beautiful work and in the space, in every work, of the absence of the Work."[29] Kantian reflective judgment is pushed beyond its reflective or analogical limits by identifying judgment with the very production of form, completing that which in the work is limited by its contingent objectification. On the side of Idealism (with the exception of Hegel), the procedure is to raise judgment to the level of idea by positing the aesthetic idea which in Kant is not posited but rather reflected. This Idealist act of positing is the subject's reflection of the primordial Identity present in each form. Thus reflective judgment reverts to a metaphysical (but imaginative rather than rational) intellectual intuition of the Identity prior to analysis and the division of subject/object and transcendental/empirical. A route is thus opened to philosophies of the origin and the pre-original. Philosophy, for Schelling, is not only the destiny of the work of art, since only philosophy can reveal the truth of the work with respect to the whole, but even displaces art in its productivity:

> Only philosophy can reopen the primal sources of art for reflection, sources that for the most part no longer nourish production.[30]

While in many ways Schelling anticipates Adorno, there is also an important difference between them. For Adorno, theory of art discloses the unrealized possibility contained in the work of a unity arising from the elements of the work themselves, and not violently imposed from without. The philosophy of "negative dialectics," which remains conceptual, cannot take over the role of producing that unity, but rather must establish why it cannot be produced non-violently under the conditions of the totality. By contrast, the role given by Schelling to philosophy as the affirmative "science" of art leads, in the perceived absence of the conditions for achieving ethical life, to the annulment of the particular as the precondition for the translation of critical reflection into the intuition of primordial Identity. Similarly, if in a different direction, for the Romantics the aesthetic provides the model for an as yet to be achieved justification of history projected into a future separated by an unbridgeable (in practical terms) gulf from a totalized instrumental contemporaneity. For both Schelling and the Romantics, the problem of the historical contingency of the subject leads to the philosophy of origins and originary mimesis; for Hegel and Adorno it leads to the question of beginning, a beginning which must take place in and out of a socially riven "unrealized" present and must bear the burden of its contingency.

The cost of the Romantic aesthetic utopianism is that the transcendental division reappears within aesthetic discourse itself, which, as I have suggested, breaks up into transcendental and empirical, aesthetic theory and art criticism, insofar as—at least from an Adornoian point of view with which I only partially concur—the reconciliation of particular and universal remains unrealized in actuality. While having to avoid subsumption under the universal, which would void its claim to express particularity, art criticism is continually threatened by the lapse into "taste" according to the British tradition which, in the context of the domination of the bourgeois public sphere by the economic, means an instrumental role in the formation of fashion to promote the circulation of commodities. Hence, while approaching the problem from opposite directions, both Idealist philosophy of art and Romantic criticism answer the need to redeem the work from its objectivity by fulfilling its blocked potential for subjective self-reflection in the former and subjective self-formation in the latter. The occlusion of the question of judgment begins here, insofar as the judgment of beauty comes to be associated with political economy and reification and with the passive, heteronomous determination of the subject by the objectivity of the particular work. In Romantic practice, objective presentation takes the form of fragments as a stimulus for active integration and self-development of the subject as an anticipation of the *Roman* (novel), the fusion of poetry and prose, universal and particular, in the *Bildungsroman* of the universal individual yet to come.

"Reflection" and "judgment," which Kant tried to hold together in his conception of "reflective judgment", broke apart in the philosophy of Idealists such as Fichte and Schelling and the criticism of the early Romantics. For the latter, *any* pre-existent unified objectivity was held to be alienating under conditions of increasing commodification, not least, to their immediate concern, of the book trade. In addition, art comes to be functionalized as a compensatory realm,[31] which tends to defuse any radical criticism contained in individual works. If the productive moment revealed by Kant is not suppressed, it is displaced into the realm of pure transcendental self-reflection and self-production.

The particular work (especially when fragmented in form) becomes the medium or occasion for the act of free constitution of an infinitely reflecting subjectivity—that is, for constitution *against* and beyond socialization and dialogue in civil society (that is, the Kantian model of critique). Emancipation from instrumental reason—"petrifying and petrified" according to Novalis—becomes the condition of possibility for authentic subjectivity. The infinite inexhaustibility of reflection, as productive of the free, self-producing and self-exceeding subject, is supposed to free art from reification. But this necessarily leaves the *particular* work in its objectivity behind, insofar as the work's destiny thus becomes the infinite productive reflection of the self-transgressing subject—the reflecting self is to transcend its objectified ego, and the reified, commodifiable particular work as well. Critical construction and philosophical reflection seek to translate the particularity of the work, through the elaboration of its form, into an ethical substance yet to be achieved, in which particular and universal will no longer be at odds.

The problem arose of how to transform this projected self-formation based on transcendental reflection back into social critique without submitting to reification. While Hegel criticizes Romantic irony as a continuation of Fichtean self-positing,[32] it can also be argued that insofar as the effect of irony is dependent upon recognition by the other—it is only possible to be ironic "for another"—irony has a necessarily social dimension.[33] Irony is thus the mode in which subjectivities freed from dependency on an instrumentalized totality interact which one another,[34] and therefore may be seen as social and communicative rather than monadic, and hence the way in which the Romantic (self-) productive imagination is intended to become *social* critique. If the Romantics turned Kantian "understanding" (*Verstand*) into a social category, the same is true in their transformation of reason (*Vernunft*) into irony. The reason this transformation has to take place is that it was no longer considered possible to transform society by means of rational regulative ideals, since rationality itself has been degraded into instrumental reason (such transformation would therefore be "more of the same," that is, a quantitative not qualitative one). Therefore the reflective capacity is transferred from reason/judgment to the productive imagination (hence the importance of "incomprehensibility" for Schlegel), which is to free reason from quantitative thinking and thus dissolve the ossifications of social reality and of language itself. The assumption behind this is that the imagination (as the ecstatic movement towards the infinite absolute) is independent of the social process (that is constitutes its own origin). Along with this "freeing" of the imagination from society goes its separation from sensibility, from the "aesthetic" in the older meaning of the term, preserved in Kant, as the science of sensibility. Once pleasure and beauty are left behind by the now transcendental imagination, the aporia of judgment can no longer be thought, and with it the connection of this aporia to historically embedded socio-political life. When the social is understood governed by identity logic, "otherness" is to be sought elsewhere—in poetry, a poetry which does not yet exist, as the medium of the "appropriate state of dialogue" (Novalis).[35] This practice of reciprocal reflection is not to be normative and competitive (the contestation of judgments in pursuit of the "correct" meaning), which would reduce it to the function of the market, but rather an infinite *Symphilosophie* and *Sympoesie*, the performance of philosophizing and poeticizing together.

Insofar as what we might call the "community of irony" is constituted as a socially ineffective esoteric elite, bolstered by a compensatory philosophy of history of their ultimate triumph, Hegel's critique of irony may remain applicable: the community of irony may be the manifestation in actuality of a collective Fichtean self-positing subjectivity, the universality of which is projected into a utopian and unrealizable future. The contradiction of subjectivity and objectivity, inner freedom and objective unfreedom, comes to be suspended in the paradoxes of irony as the corollary of a subjectivity striving infinitely towards the absolute which it cannot attain without the destruction of its own actuality.

Thus the early Idealists and Romantics began with the intention of what was to become known as the avant-garde, of realizing in life as a whole the ideal of art. With increasing commodification, the objectification of the particular work of art becomes problematic. Hence, a philosophy modeled on what art *ought* to be becomes the destiny of the particular work, in order to salvage its critical and reflective possibilities from reification and instrumentalization.

If the ideals of art cannot be actualized in the life of society, they can at least form the basis of the community of philosopher-poets, whose mutual recognition takes place in the performative medium of irony. This moment is also that of the retreat of the Idealist-Romantic avant-garde to the university (as institutionalized universality) whereby, in effect, the production of ideas becomes separated from social production and sensibility, corresponding to the separation of imagination from sensibility and the former's assignment to the task of infinite, autonomous self-reflective self-forming. This historical development prefigures that of the transition from the avant-garde to modernism.

Modernist aesthetic autonomy is therefore, from the start, an outcome of the failure of the (post-Kantian) avant-garde, the avant-garde of the "Earliest system-program . . . ."[36] In the distinction between the "sublations" of the work of art carried out by Idealism and Romanticism, criticism and philosophy each remain in need of supplementation by the other, but cannot achieve a synthesis (a distinction which Hegel attempted to overcome, at the cost of the sacrifice of beauty). This indicates a displacement to the difficulty of the relation of theory and criticism of the irresolution of the contradiction between subjective and objective, or formal and substantive aspects of the artwork itself, where under prevailing conditions beauty cannot be achieved without violence in production (the unification of the elements into a "work" by force) and recuperation in the sphere of circulation.

If the philosophy and theory on which the art-theoretical discourse of the 1980s drew (Barthes, Lacan, Derrida, de Man, Lyotard, and so on) shares a problematic with that of the German Romantics and Idealists,[37] this is no coincidence, nor merely a question of the a priori unsurpassability of metaphysics. The currency of this philosophy, and indeed its success for a time in the academic and cultural market in the 1980s and 1990s, needs in part at least to be understood in the context of the failure of the avant-garde movements of the 1960s. In the sense that I have outlined above, it is *modernist* philosophy. We are therefore confronted with the paradox that supposedly "postmodernist" tendencies in art and art theory, which appear to oppose aesthetic modernism drew for their self-understanding from a modernist philosophy. Moreover, as I have suggested, the notion that the criticality of the work of art might be saved by its sublation into philosophy is already manifested in the first transition from the avant-garde to philosophico-poetic modernism (a transition which is repeated in the formation of what is more generally considered to be modernism in the visual arts after 1848). And, if I am correct that the crisis of criticism in the 1980s—a crisis that continues—has been provoked at least in part by the commodification of theory, recourse to the early Idealist and Romantic solution—which was precisely to escape reification by taking the philosophy of art or critical (re)construction as the destiny of the particular work—must be acknowledged to be untenable.

The effects and significance of this move can be gauged in relation to Kant's conception of the proportionality revealed by and underlying reflective judgment, as retrieved in Caygill's study. If reflective judgment bifurcates into critical-ironic theorizing reflection, and art criticism which serves the market, does this indicate a break-up of the transcendental and empirical after the failure to achieve the form of life intimated in the experience of beauty? Both sides bear the marks of the struggle to overcome this fate. Philosophy from Nietzsche through Heidegger to Derrida involves a problematization of the transcendental[38] and the attempt to give itself linguistic materiality; while art criticism attempts to raise itself from the mire of commodification by recourse to theory. A focus of the problem, which I cannot elaborate in any detail here, is the question of exemplarity.

Briefly, what exemplarity (of the work of genius) reveals for Kant is the self-formative telos of the culture of mankind towards a destiny of freedom and self-legislation: "free and of itself conformable to law." That telos, I have suggested, became blocked in actuality, resulting in diremption (*Entzweiung*). The return to Kant in philosophy during the 1980s, and the return of the question of judgment, is, I suspect, connected with the attempt to reconceive the public sphere of civil society. If exemplarity is taken to mean the subsumption of singularity, or if the destiny of the particular—paradigmatically the particular work of art insofar as the experience of beauty raises the possibility of a non-violent relation to the other—is taken to be its sublation into philosophy as categorial theory, this would indeed be analogous to the political domination of identity. On the other hand, if the singular is not to be thinkable rationally, not to be available to critique, to conceptual mediation with respect to the totality, then one might fear the regression to a providential legitimation of liberalism, for how else are the plurality of "language games" not to become mutually destructive or subject to domination by one or another of them?

The aporia of judgment in modernity—in modernity as a historical fate—is, rather, that we must judge, but "we" cannot.[39] The impossibility or aporia of judgment does not have to be transposed to the register of the quasi-metaphysical. And this "we" does not have to be understood as the reduction of plurality into a homogeneous consensus, if it is otherwise thought as the not-yet achieved self-*legislation* attuned to the non-subsumptive proportion, thus making possible a distinction between a not-yet achieved democracy, and a dehistoricized, mystified and providential liberalism. For this the subject of political speech and action—the subject of a community neither transparent to itself nor utterly opaque, neither a homogenous totality nor a mere aggregate of particular interests—would need to be reconceived rather than abolished. Therefore it is vital to maintain, rather than dissolve prematurely, the tension between criticism and philosophy where, in the aporetic space thus opened, the work of art figures the place of a promise repeatedly broken.

IV

Thomas Crow tells us that the Paris Salon, which began to be held in 1737, "brought together a broad mix of classes and social types, many of whom were unused to sharing the same leisure-time diversions,"[40] and he asks: "could the crowd in the Louvre be described as anything more than a temporary collection of hopelessly heterogenous individuals?" (3). Crow cites a contemporary description:

> Here the Savoyard odd-job man rubs shoulders with the great noble in his *cordon bleu*; the fishwife trades her perfumes with those of a lady of quality, making the latter resort to holding her nose to combat the strong odor of cheap brandy drifting her way; the rough artisan, guided only by natural feeling, comes out with a just observation, at which an inept wit nearby bursts out laughing only because of the comical accent in which it was expressed; while an artist hiding in the crowd unravels the meaning of it all and turns it to his profit.[41]

Clearly that "crowd" contained not just heterogeneous individuals but members of groups in conflictual and antagonistic relations with each other. Crow goes on to consider the question of what transforms this concrete, "empirical" audience into a public, and specifically, how does the art exhibition become a "public space"—the space for a purportedly unified public, a "public sphere" with a normative dimension. While Crow's approach is to consider struggles in discourse over different kinds of painting, I want to emphasize the role of the rhetoric of art criticism in calling forth a public that did not yet exist.

The critic "represents" the public in two ways. First of all, critics represent the public by taking the point of view of a public visitor to the exhibition, somebody who is neither an artist, nor an official of the exhibiting institution or the state. These people do not write as artists, whereas previously the discourse on art was either by artists or for them, in the form of poetics or instruction. The critics, however, write as members of the public visiting exhibitions and they dramatized their visit, describing works that struck them, and encounters with other visitors. The critic also "represents" the public in another sense: by creating, in and through the writing, a representation of something called the public. That process is therefore circular. The critic represents the public "he" helps to constitute. The critic "stands for" a member of the public but on the basis of a representation of the public that he creates through his writing. The descriptive dimension of criticism serves to legitimate its hidden performative dimension: that in addressing a unified public it seeks to bring it into being.[42] This is more obvious in the early period, before the public could be taken for granted, and the criticism of the time is at times overtly theatrical, placing itself within the space of the Salon and among the visitors. In his Salons, Diderot incorporates an interlocutor, sometimes named as his editor Melchior Grimm, into dialogues, creating a mode of address that is at once intimate yet capable of inviting the identification with the addressee of a future public, thus combining particularity and universality. A good, compressed example is his piece on a painting by Jacques-François Amand:

> As for *Joseph and His Brothers,* that I saw. Choose, my friend: do you want a description of this picture, or would you prefer a story?—But the composition doesn't strike me as being all that bad.—I agree.—This big chunk of rock on which the child's price is being counted out works well in the center of the canvas.—Certainly.

And the review concludes:

> —Ah! Let's not speak of the color and the drawing, I close my eyes to those. What I feel here is a mortal chill overtaking me, and this in front of the most affecting of subjects. What gave you the idea it was permissible to show me a scene like this without breaking my heart in two? Let's speak no more about the picture, I beg you; the mere thought of it pains me.[43]

In this theatrical act of self-blinding, the reader far away in space and time, who cannot see the picture (it would not have been illustrated) is fused with the direct addressee in front of the painting—non-experience becomes experience mediated through writing which constitutes the (absent) reader as the member of a public. Elsewhere in Diderot's descriptions of paintings, the performative constitution of the public is grounded in the idea of the transparent representation of nature, the nature that all human beings share, to the extent that the reader might be invited to enter the landscape as is the case in his descriptions of the paintings of Claude-Joseph Vernet in "The Salon of 1767."[44]

In relation to the emergence of what came to be called "the bourgeois public sphere," the art criticism that developed in the eighteenth century in France around the Salon, and the philosophy of the aesthetic that developed later in Germany, shared a common project, yet had distinct roles and different relations to actually existing politics—the French Revolution and the Terror divided them historically, as well as the very different political institutions in France and the German states. With the idea of the *sensus communis* through which freedom and nature might be reconciled for finite human beings, Kant posits a possible basis—in a "sense" that was not strictly speaking one of bodily sensibility—for the universality of reflective aesthetic judgments. Art criticism in its very performance provides a bridge between the intimate, subjective response of the individual critic and the "general" public that such criticism interpolates and supposedly represents.

Aesthetic judgment is more than a private interest; rather, it involves a new configuration of private and public. Jürgen Habermas in *The Structural Transformation of the Public Sphere* (1962) has described the emergence of the "bourgeois public sphere" in which private individuals come together to engage in rational critical debate in spaces outside those controlled by the state—such spaces include both the coffee house and the literary journal. Criticism has been leveled at Habermas for focusing insufficiently on the exclusions from the public sphere: exclusions both on the basis of gender and class, and of the empirical bodily being of the individual. The argument is that, in the name of a reason according to which the force of the better argument alone will prevail, Habermas idealizes the public sphere, occluding the constitutive role of exclusion, conflict and antagonism. In relation to this, we can witness the art criticism of the Salon performatively generating the idea of a unified public, and "disinterested" aesthetic judgment contributing the "disincorporation" necessary to sustain the normative status of the public sphere.[45]

What one might, despite these criticisms, still call the "bourgeois public sphere" that emerged in the eighteenth century dissolves in the nineteenth, according to Habermas, when private commercial interests take over its institutions (for example, when newspapers and periodicals become primarily profit-making businesses based on circulation and advertising): instead of the private as public, this is the public as a collection of private interests. At the same time, politics partially reverts to the publicness associated with feudal monarchy in which something invisible is supposed to be made visible through the body and attributes of the ruler:

> The aura of personally represented authority returns as an aspect of publicity; to this extent modern publicity indeed has affinity with feudal publicity. Public relations do not genuinely concern public opinion but opinion in the sense of reputation. The public sphere becomes the court *before* whose public prestige can be displayed—rather than *in* which public critical debate is carried on.[46]

This transformation of the sense of publicity from the transparent publicness necessary for rational debate to the publicity of display coincides with the emergence of a consumer culture based in commodity and spectacle. While all the arts are affected, the visual arts are particularly susceptible insofar as, with the exception of certain forms of public art and until the emergence of avant-garde strategies of resistance, since the renaissance they have generally taken the form of portable, commodifiable objects. The bifurcation of practical art criticism and theory—as well as the turn to philosophy as a court of appeal—needs to be understood in relation to this context.

During the first decade of the twenty-first century the situation is changing once again. The art world is more dominated by the market than ever before, and this influence extends into museums and other institutions. Simultaneously, globalization has affected publicity, distribution and production in a number of ways. Globalization has coincided with fragmentation. Technological innovations, above all the Internet, have transformed not only the dissemination of and access to information, but also the generation of critical writing: through a blog, anyone with access to the Internet can become a critic. Furthermore, it no longer makes sense to speak of a single public or a single public sphere—rather, there are now multiple publics and potential publics, distributed in various ways, sometimes geographically, sometimes within the same national or urban space;

and an individual might participate in more than one public. At the same time, the relation to artists' works and projects has become at once more local—an audience might be constituted in a particular place for a short time—and more mediated, since information tends to be distributed more quickly and widely than ever before. These changes pose particular challenges to criticism. If the task of unifying a confictual multiplicity into a single public required that the role of the performative dimension of criticism, after an initial florescence, conceal itself, the existence of multiple publics exposes the fact that critical writing has an address, and involves exclusions and forms of repression, some of which are constitutive of the practice, and some contingent. And given the very different kinds of art that are being produced concurrently—not only paintings, sculpture, photographs, films, installations but also forms of direct social intervention and collaboration with various participants who may not be artists and possibly with no lasting outcome—the role of critical judgment, and indeed whether art criticism continues to involve judgment at all, is thrown into question again, as it was in the 1960s and 1970s. But have not reflective aesthetic judgments always had to discover their criteria, which are never given in advance?

Notes

1. This essay was originally completed in November 1990, and published in a French translation as "La spécificité de la critique et la nécessité de la philosophie" in *La place du goût dans la production philosophique des concepts et leur destin critique*, Rennes, Archives de la critique d'art, 1992. The essay was written at a time when art criticism was under attack by theory, as reliant on taste and entangled with the market, which had at the point become very powerful. It also coincided with a period for me of research in philosophy at the University of Essex, after having worked as a freelance art critic and lecturer. The engagement with philosophy brought home to me the extent to which the then-current "theory," while drawing on philosophical authors and having sources in German Idealism and Romanticism, had a different project to philosophy, including that in the Continental tradition. The essay, then, was intended both as a defence of the irreducibility of art criticism to either theory or philosophy, and as a historical genealogy of these different approaches and their mutual entwinement. For this English publication I have changed it only very slightly to make it readable in the present, including cutting the word "postmodernism"—which I now feel is too vague and compromised a term—and adding a few notes, although I have not attempted to update the references to include subsequent publications in the field. I have also

added a short section on the performative constitution of the "public" in art criticism.

2. As will become clear below, I use "art criticism" to refer to the practice of judgment of particular works, and "theory" to refer to the philosophical theory of art (rather than a body of rules) which was developed somewhat differently by the Idealists and the Romantics.
3. It is worth remembering that the words "criticism" and "critique" (French *critique*, German *Kritik*) derive from the Greek *krinein*, to judge, as does the Greek *krisis*, discrimination and dispute, but also decision in the sense of judgment or appraisal, which is the etymological source for "crisis". For a discussion of these etymologies, and the significance of criticism in the eighteenth century, see Reinhart Koselleck, *Critique and Crisis: Enlightenment and the Pathogenesis of Modern Society* (Cambridge MA: MIT Press, 1988) 102ff.
4. Philippe Lacoue-Labarthe and Jean-Luc Nancy write of the group around the Atheneum, "C'est en fait, il n'est pas du tout exagéré de le dire, le premier groupe d' 'avant-garde' de l'histoire." *L'absolu littéraire: Théorie de la littérature du romantisme allemand* (Paris; Seuil, 1978) 17.
5. For example, Daniel Buren, Robert Smithson, Joseph Kossuth, Dan Graham, Jeff Wall, Art & Language, Victor Burgin, Mary Kelly among others. All of these exigencies of contemporary criticism are prefigured in German Romanticism.
6. See my "Revising Modernism, Representing Postmodernism" (1985), reprinted in *Postmodernism*, ICA Documents (London: Free Association Books, 1989) 95–154.
7. For the most influential account of the avant garde as involving the critique of the institution of art, see Peter Bürger, *Theory of the Avant-Garde* (Minneapolis MN: University of Minnesota Press, 1984) which was first published in German in 1974.
8. Baudelaire cites the phrase from Stendhal in "The Painter of Modern Life", *The Painter of Modern Life and Other Essays*, translated by Jonathan Mayne (New York: Da Capo, 1964) 3. According to Theodor Adorno, "Art is the ever broken promise of happiness", in *Aesthetic Theory*, translated by Robert Hullot-Kentor (London: The Athlone Press, 1997 [first German edition 1970]) 136.
9. Theodor Adorno, "Art is . . . happiness".
10. See Clement Greenberg, "Avant-Garde and Kitsch" (1939), in *Art and Culture* (London: Thames and Hudson, 1973) 3–21.
11. On March 18, 1936 Adorno wrote to Benjamin: "the dialectic of the lowest has the same value as the dialectic of the highest, rather than the latter simply decaying. Both bear the stigmata of cazpitalism, both contain elements of change. . . . Both are torn halves of an integral freedom, to which however they do not add up. It would be romantic to sacrifice one to the other, either as the bourgeois romanticism of the conservation of personality and all that stuff, or as the anarchistic romanticism of blind confidence in the spontaneous power of the proletariat in the historical process—a proletariat which is itself a product of bourgeois society." (*Aesthetics and Politics* [London: Verso, 1980] 123). For a discussion of this issue, see Peter Osborne, "Torn

Halves and Great Divides: the Dialectics of a Cultural Dichotomy", *News from Nowhere*, No. 7, Winter 1989, 49–63, and "Aesthetic Autonomy and the Crisis of Theory: Greenberg, Adorno and the Problem of Postmodernism in the Visual Arts", *New Formations*, No. 9, Winter 1989, 31–50.

12. "On the Fetish Character of Music and the Regression of Listening" (1938), in *The Essential Frankfurt School Reader*, edited by Andrew Arato et al. (New York: Urizen Books, 1978) 279.
13. See Peter Uwe Hohendahl, *The Institution of Criticism* (Ithaca NY: Cornell University Press, 1982) 32.
14. "Specific Objects" (1965) reprinted in Donald Judd, *Complete Writings 1959–1975* (Halifax: The Press of the Nova Scotia College of Art and Design and New York: New York University Press, 1975) 184. There is a parallel to this in the Romantic's conception of the goal of modern art as the "*interessant*" rather than the "beautiful": see Kathleen Wheeler, "Introduction", *German Aesthetic and Literary Criticism: The Romantic Ironists and Goethe* (Cambridge: CUP, 1984) 6. If my argument is correct, both follow from the collapse of a paradigm of the judgment of taste.
15. For explicit criticism of Donald Judd and Minimalism, see Karl Beveridge and Ian Burn, "Don Judd." *The Fox*, no.2 (1975) 129–42, and for an implicit indication of the absent reference to social experience outside art, Dan Graham, "Homes for America," *Arts*, XLI, 3 (December–January 1966–67).
16. Howard Caygill, *Art of Judgment* (Oxford: Blackwell, 1989), to which page numbers in this section refer.
17. The "*Polizei*" state regulates welfare, security, morality, and so on in a "top-down" manner within its boundaries.
18. Kant, *Critique of Judgment*, second introduction, sect. IV.
19. Kant, *Critique of Judgment*, sect. 22.
20. See Hannah Arendt, *Lectures on Kant's Political Philosophy*, edited and introduced by Ronald Beiner (Chicago IL, The University of Chicago Press, 1982).
21. See Pierre Bourdieu, *Distinction: A Social Critique of the Judgment of Taste* (London: Routledge, 1984).
22. For an English translation of the "Earliest System-Programme of German Idealism", see Appendix 3 of H.S. Harris, *Hegel's Development: Toward the Sunlight, 1770–1801* (Oxford: Oxford University Press, 1972) and the discussion on pp. 249–57; for a French translation and discussion of "Le plus ancien programme systématique de l'idéalisme allemand", see Lacoue-Labarthe and Nancy, *L'absolue littéraire*. There has been considerable debate concerning who among Schelling, Hölderlin and Hegel is/are its author/s. See Jacques Rivelaygue, *Leçons de métaphysique allemande: Tome I* (Paris: Grasset, 1990) 211–55.
23. This is the topic of the two outstanding treatments of early Romanticism: Walter Benjamin, "The Concept of Criticism in German Romanticism" in *Selected Writings Volume 1 1913–1926*, editors Marcus Bullock and Michael W. Jennings, (Cambridge MA: and London: MIT Press, 1996) 149–78, where the distinction between Fichtean subjective self-positing and the "medium-of-reflection" of F. Schlegel and Novalis is discussed; and

Lacoue-Labarthe and Nancy, *L'absolue littéraire*, who consider, following Blanchot, Romanticism to be the "interruption" of Idealism.

24. Jochen Schulte-Sasse, "The Concept of Literary Criticism, in German Romanticism", *A History of German Literary Criticism, 1730–1980*, edited by Peter Uwe Hohendanl (Lincoln NE: University of Nebraska Press 1988) 140, to which I am indebted for parts of the following account.
25. Cf. Lacoue-Labarthe and Nancy, "C'est en fait" 39–52.
26. Cf. Schulte-Sasse, "The Concept of Literary Criticism" 133–40; also Koselleck, *Critique and Crisis*.
27. Gisela Dischner, *Bettina von Arnim: Eine weibliche Sozialbiographie aus dem 19. Jahrhundert* (Berlin: Wagenbach, 1977) 133, quoted in Schulte-Sasse, "The Concept of Literary Criticism", 136.
28. See Johann Joachim Winckelmann, *Reflections on the Imitation of Greek Works in Painting and Sculpture* (La Salle IL: Open Court, 1987), and *The History of Ancient Art* (Boston MA: J. R. Osgood, 1880).
29. Lacoue-Labarthe and Nancy, "C'est en fait," 105.
30. F.W.J. Schelling, *The Philosophy of Art* (Minneapolis MN: University of Minnesota Press, 1989) 11.
31. Cf. Herbert Marcuse, "The Affirmative Character of Culture" (1937), in *Negations* (London: Free Association Books, 1988) 88–133.
32. See G.W.F. Hegel, *Aesthetics: Lectures on Fine Art*, translation by T.M. Knox (Oxford: Oxford University Press, 1975, Vol.I) 169–71. Hegel's central point is that irony is mere formal freedom, detached from all obectivity which it dissolves: in other words, subjective freedom without objective freedom, and ultimately self-destructive since it must destroy its own objectivity as well.
33. For a discussion of this aspect of irony, see Gary J. Handwerk, *Irony and Ethics in Narrative: From Schlegel to Lacan* (New Haven CT: Yale University Press, 1985). The most important Romantic discussion of irony is Friedrich Schlegel, "On Incomprehensibility [*Uber die Unverständlichkeit*]" (1800), reprinted in English in *German Aesthetic and Literary Criticism: The Romantic Ironists and Goethe*, edited by Kathleen Wheeler (Cambridge: Cambridge University Press, 1984) 32–40.
34. Cf. Schulte-Sasse, "The Concept of Literary Criticism", 154–5.
35. Quoted, Schulte-Sasse, "The Concept of Literary Criticism", 161.
36. Cf. Novalis in "Monologue" (date uncertain), translated into English in *German Aesthetic and Literary Criticism: The Romantic Ironists and Goethe*, edited by Kathleen Wheeler (Cambridge: Cambridge University Press, 1984) 92–93: "It is amazing, the absurd error people make of imagining that they are speaking for the sake of things; no one knows the essential thing about language, that it is only concerned with itself."
37. Blanchot, Heidegger and Derrida provide the horizon for Lacoue-Labarthe and Nancy's discussion of Idealism and Romanticism in *The Literary Absolute: The Theory of Literature in German Romanticism*, translated by Richard Barnard and Cheryl Lester (Albany NY: State University of New York Press, 1988). For the following, by contrast, discussion of the Romatics and Idealists provide a basis for the critique of contemporary philosophy: Manfred Frank, *What is Neostructuralism?* (Minneapolis MN: University of Minnesota Press, 1989); Peter Dews, *Logics of Disintegration:*

Post-Structuralist Thought and the Claims of Critical Theory (London: Verso, 1987); Andrew Bowie, *Aesthetics and Subjectivity: From Kant to Nietzsche* (Manchester: Manchester University Press, 1990).

38. See Rudolphe Gaché, *The Tain of the Mirror: Derrida and the Philosophy of Reflection* (Cambridge MA: Harvard University Press, 1986).
39. Cf. Jean-François Lyotard and Jean-Loup Thébaud, *Au juste* (Paris: Christian Bourgeois, 1979).
40. Thomas E. Crow, *Painters and Public Life in Eighteenth-Century Paris* (New Haven CT: Yale University Press, 1985) 1.
41. "Lettres sur l'Académie Royale de Sculpture et de Peinture et sur le Salon de 1977", reprinted in *Revue Universelle des Arts*, XIX, 1864, 185–6, cited in Crow, *Painters and Public Life*, 4.
42. A "performative" utterance is one that does something (such as one vested with the authority to perform marriages declaring a couple married) by contrast with a "constative" utterance that purports to describe a state of affairs in the world. The distinction was made by the philosopher J.L. Austin in *How to Do Things with Words* (1962) (Oxford: Clarendon Press, 1975).
43. Denis Diderot, *Diderot on Art Volume 1*, edited by John Goodman (New Haven CT and London, Yale University Press, 1995) 139. This form of address, at once to an individual and through that individual to a wider public, must be connected with the peculiar conditions of publication, secret at the time of their writing, yet addressed to a future "universal" public. Diderot's writings on art produced between 1759 and 1781 were not publicly available during his lifetime, being circulated as part of a manuscript newsletter, the *Correspondance littéraire*, edited by Melchior Grimm, and sent to a secret subscription list that according to Thomas Crow never numbered more than fifteen. See Thomas Crow, "Diderot's Salons: Public Art and the Mind of the Private Critic" in Denis Diderot, *Diderot on Art Volume 1*, x–xii.
44. Denis Diderot, *Diderot on Art Volume II*, translation by John Goodman (New Haven CT and London, Yale University Press, 1995) 86–128.
45. See Michael Warner, "The Mass Public and the Mass Subject" in *The Phantom Public* edited by Bruce Robbins *Sphere* (Minneapolis MN: University of Minnesota Press, 1993) 234–56; Nancy Fraser, "Rethinking the Public Sphere: A Contribution to the Critique of Actually Existing Democracy" in Robbins edited by, *op.cit.*, 1–32; and M. Jonathan Hess, *Reconstituting the Body Politic: Enlightenment Public Culture and the Invention of Aesthetic Autonomy* (Detroit MI: Wayne State University Press, 1999).
46. Jürgen Habermas, *The Structural Transformation of the Public Sphere: An Inquiry Into a Category of Bourgeois Society* (Cambridge MA: MIT Press, 1991) 200–201.

Critical Reflections

Boris Groys

For a long time now, the art critic has seemed a legitimate representative of the art world.[1] Like the artist, curator, gallery owner, and collector, when an art critic shows up at an opening or some other art-world event, nobody wonders, What's he doing here? That something should be written about art is taken as self-evident. When works of art aren't provided with a text—in an accompanying pamphlet, catalogue, art magazine, or elsewhere—they seem to have been delivered into the world unprotected, lost and unclad. Images without text are embarrassing, like a naked person in a public space. At the very least they need a textual bikini in the form of an inscription with the name of the artist and the title (in the worst case this can read "untitled"). Only the domestic intimacy of a private collection allows for the full nakedness of a work of art.

The function of the art critic—perhaps art commentator would be a better way of putting it—consists, it is thought, in preparing such protective text-clothes for works of art. These are, from the start, texts not necessarily written to be read. The art commentator's role is entirely misconstrued if one expects him to be clear and comprehensible. In fact, the more hermetic and opaque a text, the better: texts that are too see-through let works of art come across naked. Of course, there are those whose transparency is so absolute that the effect is especially opaque. Such texts provide the best protection, a trick well-known to every fashion designer. In any case, it would be naïve for anyone to try to read art commentary. Luckily, few in the art world have hit upon this idea.

Thus, art commentary finds itself today in a confusing position, at once indispensable and superfluous. Other than its sheer material presence, one doesn't really know what to expect of it or desire from it. This confusion is rooted in the genealogy of contemporary criticism: the positioning of the critic within the art world is anything but self-evident. As is generally known, the figure of the art critic emerges at the end of the eighteenth and beginning of the nineteenth century, alongside the gradual rise of a broad, democratic public. At that time, he was certainly not regarded as a representative of the art world but strictly as an outside observer whose function was to judge and criticize works of art in the name of the public exactly as would any other well-educated observer with the time and literary facility: good taste was seen as the expression of an aesthetic "common sense." The art critic's judgment should be incorruptible, that is, bear no obligation to the artist. For a critic to give up his distance meant being corrupted by the art world and neglecting his professional responsibilities: this demand for disinterested art criticism in the name of the public sphere is the assertion of Kant's third critique, the first truly important aesthetic treatise of modernity.

The judicial ideal, however, was betrayed by the art criticism of the historical avant-garde. The art of the avant-garde consciously withdrew itself from the judgment of the public. It did not address the public as it was but instead spoke to a new humanity as it should—or at least could—be. The art of the avant-garde presupposed a different, new humanity for its reception—one that would be able to grasp the hidden meaning of pure color and form (Kandinsky), to subject its imagination and even its daily life to the strict laws of geometry (Malevich, Mondrian, the Constructivists, Bauhaus), to recognize a urinal as a work of art (Duchamp). The avant-garde thus introduced a rupture in society not reducible to any previously existing social differences.

The new, artificial difference is the true artwork of the avant-garde. Now it is not the observer who judges the artwork, but the artwork that judges—and often condemns—its public. This strategy has often been called elitist, but it suggests an elite equally open to anyone insofar as it excludes everyone to the same degree. To be chosen doesn't automatically mean dominance, even mastery. Every individual is free to place himself, against the rest of the public, on the side of the artwork—to number himself among those constituting the new humanity. Several art critics of the historical avant-garde did just that. In place of the critic in the name of society arose social critique in the name of art: the artwork doesn't form the object of judgment but is instead taken as the point of departure for a critique aimed at society and the world. The art critic of today inherited the older public office along with the avant-garde betrayal of this office. The paradoxical task of judging art in the name of the public while criticizing society in the name of art opens a deep rift within the discourse of contemporary criticism. And one can read today's critical discourse as an attempt to bridge, or at least conceal, this divide. For example, there is the critic's demand that art thematize existing social differences and position itself against the illusion of cultural homogeneity. That certainly sounds very avant-garde, but what one forgets is that the avant-garde didn't thematize already-existing differences but introduced previously nonexistent ones. The public was equally bewildered in the face of Malevich's Suprematism or that of Duchamp's Dadaism, and it is this generalized nonunderstanding—bewilderment regardless of class, race, or gender—that is actually the democratic moment of the various avant-garde projects. These projects were not in a position to suspend existing social differences and thereby create cultural unity, but they were able to introduce distinctions so radical and new that they could over-determine differences as they stood. There's nothing wrong with the demand that art give up its Modernist "autonomy" and become medium of social critique, but what goes unmentioned is that the critical stance is blunted, banalized, and finally made impossible by this requirement. When art relinquishes its autonomous ability to artificially produce its own differences, it also loses the ability to subject society, as it is, to a radical critique. All that remains for art is to illustrate a critique that society has already leveled at or manufactured for itself. To demand that art be practiced in the name of existing social differences actually means affirmation of existing structure of society in form of social critique.

In our time art is generally understood as a form of social

communication; it is taken as self-evident that all people want to communicate and strive for communicative recognition. Even if the contemporary discourse of art criticism understands the famous "other" not in the sense of particular cultural identities, but as desire, power, libido, the unconscious, the real, and so on, art is still interpreted as an attempt to communicate this other, to give it voice and shape. Even if communication is not achieved, the desire for it suffices to secure acceptance. Also the work of the classical avant-garde is accepted when it is understood as subordinated to the earnest intention of bringing the unconscious and the otherness into expression: the incomprehensibility to the average observer of the resulting art is excused by virtue of the impossibility of any communicative mediation of the "radical other." But this "other" that desires unconditionally to convey itself, that wants to be communicative, is, of course, not other enough. What made the classical avant-garde interesting and radical was precisely that it consciously shunned conventional social communication: it excommunicated itself. The "incomprehensibility" of the avant-garde was not just the effect of a communication breakdown. Language, including visual language, can be used not only as a means of communication, but also as a means of strategic dis-communication or even self-excommunication: that is, a voluntary departure from the community of the communicating. And this strategy of self-excommunication is absolutely legitimate. One can also wish to erect a linguistic barrier between oneself and the other in order to gain a critical distance from society. And the autonomy of art is nothing other than this movement of self-excommunication. It is a question of attaining power over differences, a question of strategy—instead of overcoming or communicating old differences, new ones are produced. The departure from social communication repeatedly practiced by modern art has often been described, ironically, as escapism. But every escapism is always followed by a return: thus the Rousseauian hero first leaves Paris and wanders through forest and meadow only to return to Paris, set up a guillotine in the center of the city, and subject his former superiors and colleagues to a radical critique, that is, to cut off their heads. Every revolution worth its salt attempts to replace society as it is with a new, artificial society. The artistic impulse always plays here a decisive role. That so many attempts to produce a new humanity have so far met with disappointment explains many critics' trepidation that they will put too much hope in the avant-garde. Instead, they want to drive the avant-garde back to the stable ground of facts, fence it in, and tether it to the real, to existent differences.

Still the question remains: What are these real existing differences? Most are artificial through and through. Technology and fashion generate the important differences of our day. And where they are consciously, strategically produced—whether in high art, design, cinema, pop music, or new media—the tradition of the avant-garde lives on (the recent enthusiasm for the Internet, reminiscent of the time of the classical avant-garde, is a case in point). Social art critics don't go in for such technical or fashionable differences, even though they have the success of such artificial differences to thank for the fact that their brand of discourse is in style (or at least was until fairly recently). So many years after the rise of the avant-garde, the discourse of contemporary art theory continues to suffer because artificial, consciously produced differences still remain unprivileged. Just as in the era of the historical avant-garde, those artists introducing artificial, aesthetic differences are reproached for being motivated exclusively by commercial and strategic interests. To react to the fashionable with enthusiasm and hope, to see in it a chance for a new and interesting social difference, is considered "improper" in "serious" theory. The unwillingness of the critic to identify himself with specific artistic positions is chalked up theoretically to the opinion that we have reached the end of art history. Arthur Danto, for example, argues in *After the End of Art*[2] that those programs of the avant-garde intended to define the essence and function of art have finally become untenable. It is thus no longer possible to privilege a particular kind of art theoretically as those critics who think in an avant-garde mode—in the American context the paradigm remains Clement Greenberg—have again and again tried to do. The development of art in this century has ended in a pluralism that relativizes everything, makes everything possible at all times, and no longer allows for critically grounded judgment. This analysis certainly seems plausible. But today's pluralism is itself artificial through and through—a product of the avant-garde. A single modern work of art is a huge contemporary differentiation machine.

If the critics had not, as Greenberg did, taken specific works of art as the occasion for drawing new lines of demarcation in the field of theory and art politics, we would have no pluralism today, because this artistic pluralism certainly cannot be reduced to an already existing social pluralism. Even the social art critics can only make their distinctions between the "natural" and the "socially coded" relevant for art criticism because they place these (artificial) distinctions like readymades in the context of modernist differentiation. And Danto makes the same move as Greenberg when he attempts to draw all the consequences from Warhol's *Brillo Box* and to think this artwork as the beginning of an absolutely new era. Today's pluralism definitely means that no single position can be unequivocally privileged over another. But not all differences between two positions are of equal value; some differences are more interesting than others. It pays to concern oneself with such interesting differences—regardless of which position one advocates. It pays even more to create new, interesting differences that further drive the condition of pluralism. And since these differences are purely artificial, a natural, historical end cannot be attributed to this process of differentiation.

Perhaps the real reason today's art critic no longer passionately champions a particular attitude in art and its relevance for theory and cultural politics is more psychological than theoretical. First, in so doing, the critic feels he is left in the lurch by the artist. One might easily have supposed that after the critic has crossed over to the side of the artist he would have won the artist's gratitude and become his friend. But it doesn't work this way. The critic's text—so most artists believe—seems less to protect the work from detractors than to isolate it from its potential admirers. Rigorous theoretical definition is bad for business. Thus, many artists protect themselves against theoretical commentary in the hopes that a naked work of art will be more seductive than one dressed in a text.

Actually, artists prefer formulations that are as vague as possible: the work is "charged with tension," "critical" (without any indications of how or why), the artist "deconstructs social codes," "puts our habitual way of seeing into question," "practices an elaboration" of something or another, and so on Or artists prefer to speak themselves, to tell their personal histories and demonstrate how everything, even quite trivial objects that fall under their gaze, takes on a deep, personal meaning for them (at many exhibitions, the observer has the feeling of being put in the place of a social worker or psychotherapist without receiving any corresponding financial compensation, an effect often parodied in the installations of Ilya Kabakov and, in a different way, in the video work of Tony Oursler).

On the other hand, the critic's attempts to turn back to the public and offer himself as the defender of its legitimate claims lead to nothing: the old betrayal hasn't been forgiven. The public still regards the critic as an insider, a PR agent for the art industry. Ironically, the critic wields the least power of anyone in that industry. When a critic writes for a catalogue, it's arranged and paid for by the same people who are exhibiting the artist he's reviewing. When he writes for a journal or newspaper, he is covering an exhibition the reader already assumes is worthy of mention. The critic thus has no real chance to write about an artist if the artist isn't already established; someone else in the art world has already decided that the artist is deserving of a show. One could object that a critic can at least give a negative review. That is certainly true—but it makes no difference. Through these decades of artistic revolutions, movements and countermovements, the public in this century has finally come around to a position that a negative review is no different from a positive one. What matters in a review is which artists are mentioned, where, and how long they are discussed. Everything else is everything else.

As a reaction to this situation, a bitter, disappointed, nihilistic tone pervades the art criticism of today, which clearly ruins its style. This is a shame, because the art system is still not such a bad place for a writer. It's true that most of these texts don't get read—but for this very reason one can, in principle, write whatever one wants. Under the pretext of opening up the different contexts of a work of art, the most diverse theories, intellectual takes, rhetorical strategies, stylistic props, scholarly knowledge, personal stories, and examples from all walks of life can be combined in the same text at will—in a way not possible in the two other areas open to writers in our culture, the academy and the mass media. Almost nowhere else does the pure textuality of the text show itself so clearly as in art criticism. The art system protects the writer as much from the demand that he convey some kind of "knowledge" to the masses of students as it does from the competition for readers among those covering the O.J. Simpson trial. The public within the art world is relatively small: the pressure of a broad public forum is missing. Therefore, the text need not necessarily meet with the concurrence of this public. Of course, fashion does emerge as a consideration—sometimes one should sense authenticity in an artwork, at other times perceive that there is no authenticity, sometimes emphasize political relevance, at other times slip into private obsessions—but not a strict one. There are always those who don't like the prevailing fashion because they liked an earlier one, or because they're hoping for the next, or both. But above all, the art critic cannot err. Of course, the critic comes under repeated accusation of having misjudged or misinterpreted a particular art form. But this reproach is unfounded. A biologist can err, for instance, if he describes an alligator as being other than an alligator, because alligators don't read critical texts and therefore their behavior is not influenced by them. The artist, in contrast, can adapt his work to the judgment and theoretical approach of the critic. When a gap arises between the work of the artist and the judgment of the critic, one cannot necessarily say that the critic misjudged the artist. Maybe the artist misread the critic? But that's not so bad, either: the next artist might read him better. It would be false to think somehow that Baudelaire overrated Constantin Guys, or Greenberg Jules Olitski, because the theoretical excess the two produced has its own value and can stimulate other artists.

It's also not that important which artworks the art critic uses to illustrate his theoretically generated differences. The difference itself is important—and it doesn't appear in the works but in their use, including their interpretation—even if various images seem suited to the purposes of the critic. There is no dearth of useful illustrations, because we're observing a tremendous overproduction of images today. (Artists have increasingly recognized this—and begun to write themselves. The production of images serves them more as a cover than as an actual goal.) The relationship between image and text has changed. Before, it seemed important to provide a good commentary for a work. Today, it seems important to provide a good illustration for a text, which demonstrates that the image with commentary no longer interests us as much as the illustrated text. The art critic's betrayal of the criteria of public taste turned him into an artist. In the process, any claim to a metalevel of judgment was lost. Yet art criticism has long since become an art in its own right; with language as its medium and the broad base of images available, it moves as autocratically as has become the custom in art, cinema, or design. Thus a gradual erasure of the line between artist and art critic completes itself, while the traditional distinction between artist and curator, and critic and curator, tends toward disappearance. Only the new, artificial dividing lines in cultural politics are important, those that are drawn in each individual case, with intention and strategy.

Notes

1. This essay first appeared in *Artforum*, 1997.
2. *After the End of Art: Contemporary Art and the Pale of History* (Princeton NJ: Princeton University Press, 1997).

On the Absence of Judgment in Art Criticism

James Elkins

This is excerpted from a pamphlet published in 2004.[1] *It was divided into four parts. The first part proposed that no one reads art criticism (a notion that has since been both criticized as unfactual and taken as a virtue), and that art criticism is in crisis if only because it has largely given up judging artworks in favor of describing them. The second part, which was the bulk of the pamphlet, distinguished seven kinds of criticism, from philosophic essays (such as the Introduction to this book) to journalistic criticism (represented here by Ariella Budick, among others). I am not reprinting that section here, except its opening pages, because the two roundtables were themselves an attempt to embody something of the diversity of art criticism. The pamphlet continued with a list of attempts to "cure" the malaise of criticism, which is reprinted here, and an envoi with several proposals, which are omitted.*

Art criticism: writing without readers

Art criticism is in worldwide crisis. Its voice has become very weak, and it is dissolving into the background clutter of ephemeral cultural criticism. But its decay is not the ordinary last faint push of a practice that has run its course, because at the very same time, art criticism is also healthier than ever. Its business is booming: it attracts an enormous number of writers, and often benefits from high-quality color printing and worldwide distribution. In that sense art criticism is flourishing, but invisibly, out of sight of contemporary intellectual debates. So it's dying, but it's everywhere. It's ignored, and yet it has the market behind it.

There is no way to measure the sheer quantity of contemporary writing on visual art. Art galleries almost always try to produce at least a card for each exhibition, and if they can print a four-page brochure (typically made from one sheet of heavy card stock, folded down the middle) it will normally include a brief essay on the artist. Anything more expensive will certainly include an essay, sometimes several. Galleries also keep spiral-bound files on hand with clippings and photocopies from local newspapers and glossy art magazines, and gallery owners will gladly copy those pages for anyone who asks. An afternoon walk in the gallery district of a city in Europe, North or South America, or southeast Asia can quickly yield a bulky armful of exhibition brochures, each one beautifully printed, and each opening with at least a hundred-word essay. There is also a large and increasing number of glossy art magazines, despite the fact that the market is very risky from an entrepreneur's point of view. Large magazine displays in booksellers such as Eason's and Borders carry dozens of art magazines, and glossy art magazines can also be found in newsstands near museums and in college bookstores. No one knows how many glossy art magazines there are because most are considered ephemeral by libraries and art databases, and therefore not collected or indexed. There are so many that no one I know even attempts to keep track. As a rule, academic art historians do not read any of them. At a rough guess, I would say there are perhaps two hundred nationally and internationally distributed art magazines in Europe and the United States, and in the order of five hundred or a thousand smaller magazines, fliers, and journals. No one knows how many exhibition brochures are produced each year, mainly because no one knows how many galleries there are in the world. Large cities such as New York, Paris, and Berlin have annual gallery guides, but they are not complete and there is no definitive listing. As far as I know no library in the world collects what galleries produce, with exceptions at the high end of the market. Daily newspapers are collected by local and national libraries, but newspaper art criticism is not a subject term in any database I know, so art criticism published in newspapers quickly becomes difficult to access.

In a sense, then, art criticism is very healthy indeed. So healthy that it is outstripping its readers—there is more of it around than anyone can read. Even in mid-size cities, art historians can't read everything that appears in newspapers or is printed by museums or galleries. Yet at the same time art criticism is very nearly dead, if health is measured by the number of people who take it seriously, or by its interaction with neighboring kinds of writing such as art history, art education, or aesthetics. Art criticism is massively produced, and massively ignored.

Scholars in my own field of art history tend to notice only the kinds of criticism that are heavily historically informed and come out of academic settings: principally writing on contemporary art that is published in art historical journals and by university presses. Art historians who specialize in modern and contemporary art also read *Artforum, ArtNews, Art in America*, and some other journals—the number and names are variable—but they tend not to cite essays from those sources. (A few historians write for those journals, but even then it's rare to find them citing art magazines.) Among the peripheral journals is Donald Kuspit's *Art Criticism*, which has only a small circulation even though it should in principle be of interest to any art critic. The others are a blur—*Art Papers, Parkett, Modern Painters, Tema Celeste, Frieze, Art Monthly, Art Issues, Flash Art, Documents sur l'art*—and the list melts away into the glossy magazines that are just not read much inside the academy—*Revue de l'art, Univers des arts, Glass, American Artist, Southwest Art* . . . Art historians generally do not get very far along that list. The same can be said of art historians' awareness of newspaper art criticism: it's there as a guide, but never as a source to be cited unless the historian's subject is the history of an artist's reception in the popular press. If an anthropologist from Mars were to study the contemporary art scene by reading books instead of frequenting galleries, it might well seem that catalog essays and newspaper art criticism do not even exist.

Do art criticism and catalog essays function, then, primarily to get people into galleries and to induce them to buy? Probably, but in the case of catalog essays the economic effect does not seem to depend on the writing actually being read—often it is enough to have a well-produced brochure or catalogue on hand to convince a customer to buy. It is not entirely clear that criticism affects the art market except in prominent cases, when the buzz surrounding an artist's show can certainly drive up attendance and prices. In my experience, even art critics who work at prominent newspapers receive only a modicum of letters except in unusual cases. The same phenomenon occurs on the Internet, with regard to e-zines and groups: weeks and months can pass with no sign that the texts are being read, and those deserts are punctuated by flurries of e-mails on controversial issues.

So in brief, this is the situation of art criticism: it is practiced more widely than ever before, and almost completely ignored. Its readership is unknown, unmeasured, and disturbingly ephemeral. If I pick up a brochure in a gallery, I may glance at the essay long enough to see some keyword—perhaps the work is said to be "important," "serious," or "Lacanian"—and that may be the end of my interest. If I have a few minutes before my train, I may pause at the newsstand and leaf through a glossy art magazine. If I am facing a long flight, I may buy a couple of magazines, intending to read them and leave them on the plane. When I am visiting an unfamiliar city, I read the art criticism in the local newspaper. But it is unlikely (unless I am doing research for a book like this one) that I will study any of those texts with care or interest: I won't mark the passages I agree with or dispute, and I will not save them for further reference. There just isn't enough meat in them to make a meal: some are fluffy, others conventional, or clotted with polysyllabic praise, or confused, or just very, very familiar. Art criticism is diaphanous: it's like a veil, floating in the breeze of cultural conversations and never quite settling anywhere.

The combination of vigorous health and terminal illness, of ubiquity and invisibility, is growing increasingly strident with each generation. The number of galleries at the end of the twentieth century was many times what it was at the beginning, and the same can be said of the production of glossy art magazines and exhibition catalogues. Newspaper art criticism is harder to measure, although it seems likely there is actually less of it, relative to the population size, than there was a hundred years ago. According to Neil McWilliam, in 1824 Paris had twenty daily newspapers that ran columns by art critics, and another twenty revues and pamphlets that also covered the Salon. None of those writers was employed *as* art critics, but some were virtually full-time just as they are now. Today, even counting the Internet, there is nowhere near the same number of practicing critics. So it is possible that newspaper art criticism has gone into a steep decline, and that would be in line with the absence of art criticism from contemporary cultural programming on television and in radio. Some of the early nineteenth-century art critics were taken seriously by contemporaneous philosophers and writers, and others—the founders of Western art criticism—were themselves important poets and philosophers. The eighteenth-century philosopher Denis Diderot is effectively the foundation of art criticism, and he was also a polymath and one of the century's most important philosophers. By comparison Clement Greenberg, arguably modernism's most prominent art critic, bungled his philosophy because he was uninterested in getting Kant any more right than he needed to make his points. A good case can be made that Charles Baudelaire enabled mid-nineteenth century French art criticism in a way that no other writer did, and he was of course also an indispensable poet for much of that century and the twentieth. Greenberg wrote extremely well, with a ferocious clarity, but in the hackneyed phrase he was no Baudelaire. These comparisons are perhaps not as unjust as they may seem, because they are symptomatic of the slow slipping of art criticism off the face of the cultural world. Who, after all, *are* the important contemporary art critics? It is not difficult to name critics who have prominent venues: Roberta Smith and Michael Kimmelman at the *New York Times*; Peter Schjeldahl at the *New Yorker*. But among those who aren't fortunate enough to work for publications with million-plus circulation, who counts as a truly important voice in current criticism? My own list of most-interesting authors includes Joseph Masheck, Thomas McEvilley, Richard Shiff, Kermit Champa, Rosalind Krauss, and Douglas Crimp, but I doubt they are a canon in anyone else's eyes, and the cloud of names behind them threatens to become infinite: Dave Hickey, Eric Troncy, Peter Plagens, Susan Suleiman, Francesco Bonami, Kim Levin, Helen Molesworth, Donald Kuspit, Buzz Spector, Mira Schor, Hans-Ulrich Obrist, Miwon Kwon, Germano Celant, Giorgio Verzotti—there are hundreds more. The International Association of Critics of Art (called AICA after the French version of their name) has over four thousand members and branches, so they claim, in seventy countries.

Early twenty-first-century art critics may or may not be university trained: in a way it does not matter, because virtually none is trained *as* an art critic. Departments of art history almost never offer courses in art criticism, except as a historical subject in courses such as "The History of Art Criticism from Baudelaire to Symbolism." Art criticism is not considered as part of the brief of art history: it is not a historical discipline, but something akin to creative writing. Contemporary art critics come from many different backgrounds, but they share this one crucial absence: they were not trained as art critics in the way that people are trained as art historians, philosophers, curators, film historians, or literary theorists. There is a limit, I think, to how little this might matter. Just because a field has no academic platform does not mean that it is less rigorous, or less attached to the values and interests of adjacent fields that do have the imprimatur of formal training. But the lack of an academic practice of art criticism—with a few interesting exceptions, such as the program at Stony Brook—means that art criticism is unmoored. Its freedom is exhilarating, occasionally, but for a steady reader it is stultifying. Among the various reasons for art criticism's vertiginous freedom, its swoops and feints in and out of a dozen disciplines, is its lack of a disciplinary home. I do not mean that criticism would be better off if it were constrained by a conservative or fixed pedagogy: but if it were disciplinary in *any* sense, it would have a center of some kind against which to push. At the moment art critics feel very little resistance. A critic who writes exhibition brochures and catalogues will be constrained a little by the expectation that the piece will not be unfavorable, and a critic who writes for a large-circulation newspaper will be constrained because the public is unused to new art, or accustomed to moderate opinions. But those and other sources of constraint are minor in comparison with the lack of restraint that is granted to art critics by the absence of an academic home. An academic discipline, as fractious and contradictory as it may be, puts two kinds of pressure on a practitioner: it compels an awareness of colleagues, and it instills a sense of the history of previous efforts.

Both are absent, with spectacular and fantastical effect, from current art criticism.

This is the picture of art criticism as I would paint it: it is produced by thousands of people worldwide, but it has no common ground. Art criticism involves a fair amount of money by academic standards, because even modest exhibition brochures are printed in large numbers, on coated stock, with high-quality plates that are rare in academic publishing. Even so, art critics very rarely earn their living from writing criticism. More than half of those with jobs at the top American newspapers earn less than $25,000 per year, but successful freelance critics may write twenty or thirty essays per year, at a base fee of $1,000 per essay or $1 to $2 per word, or $35 to $50 for a brief newspaper review. (My own experience is probably about average; I have charged between $500 and $4,000 for essays between one and twenty pages long.) Critics who are actively writing will also be asked to lecture at art schools and travel to exhibitions, with all expenses paid and fees between $1,000 and $4,000. Articles in glossy art magazines pay between $300 and $3,000, and those essays can be used both to augment the critic's income and generate further invitations. By comparison an academic art historian or philosopher may easily spend a long and productive career without ever being paid for any publication. Criticism is ubiquitous, then, and sometimes even profitable: but it pays for its apparent popularity by having ghosts for readers. Critics seldom know who reads their work beyond the gallerists who commission it and the artists about whom they write: and often that reading public is ghostly precisely because it does not exist. A ghostly profession, catering for ghosts, but in a grand style.

As recently as the first half of the twentieth century, art criticism was very different. Art critics were more likely to be concerned with the history of art, including the history of their own practice. It was more common then for critics to think on large scales, comparing their judgments on different occasions, or considering the differences between their positions and those of other critics. Bloomsbury critics like Roger Fry and Clive Bell felt they could stand back and assess large regions of history. Bell's manifesto *Art* demotes everything between the twelfth century and Cézanne: he calls the Renaissance "that strange, new disease," and says that Rembrandt was a genius, but also "a typical ruin of his age." Judgment itself was presented more ambitiously in Bell's generation, as a matter of broader comparisons. Contemporary critics tend not to think outside the box of the exhibition or particular work at hand, or rather they write as if they weren't thinking outside the box. At glossy art magazines, that's sometimes the implicit charge: do not pontificate or wander: stick to the theme.

Early and mid-twentieth century American art critics were also fiercely opinionated and even polemical. At the turn of the century Royal Cortissoz, the stubbornly conservative critic for the *New York Tribune*, fought everything modern except Matisse, and a generation later John Canaday, the backward-looking critic for the *New York Times*, battled Abstract Expressionism with a sarcastic violence that seems outlandish today. Cortissoz, known as a "square shooter," found most European art of the first two decades of the century "crude, crotchety, tasteless," and "arrogant." In a column written in 1960, Canaday critiqued a "dried and caked puddle of blue poster paint" that he found on a wall, pretending it was painting called *Blue Element* by a painter named Ninguno Denada. He wrote a full-length review of the spill, declaring it "deeply impressive, a profound interpretation of our century of crisis," comparing Denada to the real-life painters Modest Cuixart, Antoni Tàpies, and Joan Miró, and then refusing to distinguish between his "satire" and the "brainwashing that goes on in universities and museums." It is hard to imagine a *New York Times* critic these days being that sarcastic. (And the comparison to Cuixart, Tàpies, and Miró are entirely unfair. Even Cuixart's most uncontrolled paintings have carefully drawn elements superimposed. The real target, of course, was Pollock.)

It is not necessarily the case that critics have become less opinionated: there are many reasons for the changes I am describing, and I will be more specific later on. But I do mean that critics have become less ambitious—if by ambition is meant the desire to try to see the landscape of some art practice and not just the one thing in apparent isolation. There are few living art critics who have gone on the record with what they think of the twentieth century's major movements. Local judgments are preferred to wider ones, and recently judgments themselves have even come to seem inappropriate. In their place critics proffer informal opinions or transitory thoughts, and they shy from strong commitments. In the last three or four decades, critics have begun to avoid judgments altogether, preferring to describe or evoke the art rather than say what they think of it. In 2002, a survey conducted by the Columbia University National Arts Journalism Program found that judging art is the least popular goal among American art critics, and simply describing art is the most popular: it is an amazing reversal, as astonishing as if physicists had declared they would no longer try to understand the universe, but just appreciate it.

These differences, which I am going to try to flesh out, are enormous. During the same decades that art criticism proliferated around the world, it also receded from the firing lines of cultural critique into the safer and more protected domains of localized description and careful evocation. I do not at all mean that criticism's intellectual purview has shrunk to fit the pluralism, jargon, and epistemological evasiveness that are so often associated with the academic left. I wouldn't argue that we need to regain the hairy-chested health of the impetuous critics of high modernism. It is true that the contemporary critics who are most ambitious in the sense I am using that word are also arch-conservatives, but I do not consider conservatism a promising or even relevant ideological direction for criticism. Writers like Hilton Kramer are deeply detached from what is most interesting in the art world, and it is in part their ambition that prevents them from being able to engage current questions in a promising manner. Yet I want to continue using the word "ambition" because it strikes me as a fascinating mystery that art criticism has turned so abruptly from the engaged, passionate, historically informed practice it was before the later twentieth century, into the huge, massively funded but invisible and voiceless practice it has effectively become.

I have just two questions in mind. First: does it make sense to talk about art criticism as a single practice, or is it a number of different activities with different goals? Second: does it make sense to try to reform criticism? [*Here, I reprint the opening to the first, and the whole of the second.*]

How unified is art criticism?

If I were to draw a picture of current art criticism I'd make it a hydra, fitted with the traditional seven heads. The first head stands for the *catalog essay*, the kind commissioned for commercial galleries. (It has been said that catalog essays are not art criticism, because they are expected to be laudatory. But that begs the question: If they aren't art criticism, what are they?) The second head is the *academic treatise*, which exhibits a range of obscure philosophic and cultural references, from Bakhtin to Buber and Benjamin to Bourdieu. It is the common target of conservative attacks. Third is *cultural criticism*, in which fine art and popular images have blended, making art criticism just one flavor in a rich stew. Fourth is the *conservative harangue*, in which the author declaims about how art ought to be. Fifth is the *philosopher's essay*, where the author demonstrates the art's allegiance to or deviation from selected philosophic concepts. Sixth is *descriptive art criticism*, the most popular according to the Columbia University survey: its aim is to be enthusiastic but not judgmental, and to bring readers along, in imagination, to artworks that they may not visit. And seventh is *poetic art criticism*, in which the writing itself is what counts. This is the third-most popular goal of art criticism according to the Columbia University survey, but I suspect it is also one of the most widely-shared goals across the board.

I don't mean that these are the hydra's only heads, or that the heads couldn't be renumbered for other purposes. The critic Peter Plagens has suggested a schema with three parts, and for many writers the only important division is between academia and everything outside of it. The seven heads swerve and blur together, and sometimes it seems there are many more, or else just one conglomerate Babel. Yet often enough the combined practice of art criticism can be imagined as seven—or so—separate practices. At least it seems useful to me to picture it that way. . . .

Seven unworkable cures

It is tempting to try to escape the fog of current art criticism and run out into the clear air of certainty. Of course, everyone has their own idea about where that clear air might be found. The people on the

October roundtable on art criticism—one of the texts that is central to the roundtables in this book—wanted more attention to rigor, theoretical sophistication, and "levels of complexity in discourse." Others would prefer it if art critics had rules, norms, theories, or at least some concerns in common. There have been laments that the twenty-first century has no guiding voice—even one that might guide us through the decaying labyrinth of pluralism. Newspaper calls for the reform of art criticism usually attack jargon, and promote simple ideas. Conservative commentators want to boost art's moral purpose. Kramer wants to bring in a bit of old-fashioned discipline, "discrimination," and firm standards. Newspaper critics themselves sometimes want to reform criticism by removing its connection to the market.

I think things are more difficult. The very idea of finding something wrong with the current state of criticism is itself historically determined. Why should *October* have a roundtable discussion on criticism, a kind of writing it has largely refrained from publishing, in the fall of 2001? Why does a text with the title "What Happened to Art Criticism?" appear in spring 2003? It is important to understand why a problem comes to the surface at a given point in time, because we all ride currents of historical thinking of which we're only intermittently aware. Thinking about the reasons for various calls for the reform of criticism helps reveal that the proposed solutions tend to be born from nostalgia for specific moments in the past. Let me try to demonstrate that with seven examples of increasing length and difficulty. (These do not correspond to the seven hydra heads, but once you start thinking in sevens it is hard to stop.)

1. *Criticism should be reformed by returning it to a golden age of apolitical formalist rigor.* In *A Roger Fry Reader*, the art historian Christopher Reed proposes Fry can be interpreted as a "postmodern" critic on account of his complexity, his "iconoclastic relation to authority," and his "social mission." Hilton Kramer wrote his usual impatient review, claiming Reed's perspective is unworkable and false: a typical product, Kramer thinks, of postmodern "historical nullification." In place of Reed's version, Kramer wants a thoughtful but conservative Fry, one who was never an "avant-garde incendiary." Kramer's dislike of politically-inflected art criticism prompts him to

stress Fry's interest in finding laws of art in "a realm apart from life"—a phrase Reed uses to remind readers that is not *all* that Fry did. There's nothing to stop Fry from being reborn for each new generation: that is the nature of historical reception. Yet Kramer's Fry is Kramer *avant la lettre:* a brilliant formalist, who knows and respects the older history of art, and is unafraid of proposing "a realm apart from life." Clearly, Kramer's polemic is driven by nostalgia. He wants things the way he imagines they once were, and that is not a plausible model for contemporary criticism.

2. *Criticism lacks a strong voice.* In 1973 the artist and art historian Quentin Bell lamented the decline of authoritative art critics using the same observation with which I began: "while the literature of art is, in publishers' terms, booming, it has in one respect suffered a loss." What Bell misses is a critic who can be a "censor" and "apologist for the contemporary scene, a Diderot, a Baudelaire, a Ruskin or a Roger Fry." Why is there no such "grand pundit" on the art scene? Perhaps, Bell thinks, it is the "character of modern art," which is difficult to discuss, or maybe it's the spread of high-quality illustrations, which obviate the need for description. Unfortunately for Bell's argument the history of criticism shows that many, perhaps most, decades since Vasari have lacked a strong critical voice. Criticism was weak and dispersed before Winckelmann, as Thomas DaCosta Kaufmann has shown. It was weak after Diderot, as Michael Fried has argued. After Baudelaire there were many interesting critics, among them Theophile Thoré, Ernest Chesneau, Jules Castagnary, Edmond Duranty, Félix Fénéon or Albert Aurier, but none have been as important for modernism as Baudelaire. Criticism was arguably weak again before Bloomsbury, and again before Greenberg. It doesn't reflect poorly on us that we have no prophet at the moment. Bell's complaint is another instance of a nostalgia for something past: in this case, mainly a Bloomsbury past.

3. *Criticism needs systematic concepts and rules.* To some observers criticism just seems like a mess. In the 1940s the aesthetician Helmut Hungerford wanted to arrange paintings in "classes," and to work out standards such as organization, integration, and skill, that are relevant for each class. Behind his dogged rationalism I read an anxiety about

the fate of formal analysis. Hungerford's criteria crumbled around him, even while he tried to shore them up by proposing additional criteria of "coherence" within classes and standards. These days, as far as I can see, he is entirely forgotten. Perhaps art criticism cannot be reformed in a logical sense because it was never well-formed in the first place. Art criticism has long been a mongrel among academic pursuits, borrowing whatever it needed from other fields (the sublime and the beautiful, of judgment and imitation, of the gaze and the spectacle). It has never been a matter of the consistent application of philosophic concepts, and there is little sense in hoping that it ever will be.

4. *Criticism must become more theoretical.* Perhaps, then—lowering the bar a bit here—art criticism might make use of shared theoretical interests, no matter where they're cribbed from. The film critic Annette Michelson argues that in a brilliant essay on Pauline Kael. She compares Kael to Umberto Eco (who wrote an essay on *Casablanca*): the "very obvious difference," Michelson says, is that Eco is convinced that "the infusion and support of an evolving body of theoretical effort will work to the advantage of communication." Michelson thinks that Kael's "intransigent resistance to the theorization of the subject of her life's work inhibited her ability to account for film's impact in terms other than taste and distaste." As the years went on, Kael "ceased to renew her intellectual capital, to acknowledge and profit by the achievements of a huge collective effort." This is an admirable way of putting the point: it is crucial to be part of the same reservoir of concepts and theoretical tools as the rest of the generation, even if they only enter into the work in the form of unused capital. I would find it difficult to argue against this: it is not dogmatic, and it isn't propped up by nostalgia for some earlier state of perfect passion and eloquence. I'll have more to say about it at the end.

5. *Criticism needs to be serious, complex, and rigorous.* This call is more or less the consensus recommendation in the 2001 *October* roundtable, and it has a particular lineage: it can be traced to the critics associated with *Artforum* from its founding in 1962 to around 1967. Critics including Carter Ratcliff, Rosalind Krauss, John

Coplans, Max Kozloff, Barbara Rose, Peter Plagens, Walter Darby Bannard, Phil Leider, Annette Michelson, and others were part of a loose and ultimately divisive group that nevertheless shared a sense of criticism's newly serious purpose. Amy Newman's book of interviews, *Challenging Art: Artforum 1962–1974* is a good source for the group's elusive sense of community. In *Challenging Art*, John Coplans suggests that the wave of commitment to analytic criticism came indirectly from expatriate German scholars, preeminently Erwin Panofsky, despite the fact that several of the art critics began their careers by repudiating work by art historians such as Sydney Freedberg. Coplans points out that the only prior American model for serious criticism was *The Magazine of Art*, especially when Robert Goldwater became editor in 1947. The *Magazine of Art*, he says, was "absolutely against the French method," which was perceived as a tradition of poets. Several of the critics and historians Newman interviews make analogous claims: the poet and critic Carter Ratcliff recalls how some poet-critics remained interested in "a private history, a personal history," while others, the *Artforum* group especially, "tried to establish some *defensible* scheme, a schematic of history," into which they placed new art. "And in that way," he concludes, "they could keep track of history *right as it happened*." In the same book, Rosalind Krauss distinguishes between the *Artforum* kind of criticism and a preeminently French "*belle lettristic*" kind of writing, where "poets would compose emotive catalogue prefaces for artists." The criticism published in *Artforum* was indebted, she says, to Anglo-American New Criticism, which "involved a textual analysis in which the project was to make statements about the text in front of you that had to be verifiable. You couldn't introduce things about the artist's biography or about history. It was really limited to what was on the page so that any reader who was at all competent could *check* what you were saying about the work." Aside from Greenberg, Krauss says, she had been "very frustrated by the vagueness and unverifiability of *opinion*" in English-language art critics such as Sidney Janis, Thomas Hess, Dore Ashton, and Harold Rosenberg. Nothing they wrote struck her as "*hard*, verifiable." Fried, similarly, mentions "all that fustian writing—Hess and the others." (*Fustian*, a very sharp-edged word for a woolly fabric, meaning not only bombastic and inflated, but also, as a consequence, worthless.)

Coplans says the only criticism that seemed interesting in London in the early 1960s was "Lawrence Alloway fighting it out with Sir Herbert Read" over the importance of surrealism. Robert Rosenblum sums up the situation at *Artforum* by recalling an article by Max Kozloff called "Venetian Art and Florentine Criticism" (December 1967). "I loved the title," Rosenblum recalls, because "it put its finger on one of the problems of *Artforum* classic writing, namely it was Florentine, it was intellectual and bone-dry, and never really could correspond to the sensuous pleasures of looking at art." Rosenblum's special viewpoint aside (his writing is famously full-blooded, in these terms), the metaphor of Florence and Venice is accurate: *Artforum*, and later *October*, stood for rigor as against fustian writing of all sorts.

All that is the foundation of what "serious criticism" continues to mean. Since 1976, it has also been exemplified by *October*, and by essays written by Thomas Crow, Thomas McEvilley, and a score of others in different venues. Calls for a return to criticism that is serious, complex, and rigorous are indebted to the model provided by *Artforum* and its descendents. That means, in turn, that it is important to ask whether it makes sense to revive those particular senses of commitment, verifiability, and intellectualism. It seems to me the only defensible answer is that such values are no longer a good fit for art at the beginning of the twenty-first century. Metaphors of intellectual *labor*, of difficulty, of challenge recur in *Artforum* discussions, beginning with Greenberg: when it is good the work is dry, hard, obdurate and irrefragable . . . it is not easy to imagine how those values can be transposed to the present, and even if they were, it is not easy to picture how useful they would be.

6. *Criticism should become a reflection on judgments, not the parading of judgments.* This is essentially what Rosalind Krauss argued in 1971 and again in 1985, and it is put into practice in reception histories and institutional critiques, mainly in academic writing. If you conceive of the art world as a matrix of institutional and power relations, then there is no immediate sense to words like "quality" or "value": they are determined by divisions of labor within the art world, and produced for different purposes including academic power and market value. If you are interested in reception history, then the hard-fought battles in the art world become objects of historical

interest. You will want to know the historical contexts that produced interest in words like "quality" or "value," and your interest will be purely historical or even philological—you won't have any more investment in the outcome than an entomologist has watching one tribe of ants battle against another. Even the explanation offered by institutional critique will become susceptible to reception history: the idea of institutional critique began in the 1980s, and has its own historical trajectory. Within that course, its explanations for words like "quality" or "value" will have weight, but before, after, or outside it they will not.

The problem that faces both institutional critique and reception history is the present. We live in it, we make judgments in it. When we judge contemporary art, we engage concepts that we believe in—there is no other way to judge. For a person who practices reception history, that poses a truly difficult problem. Such a writer will be acutely aware that no concepts are born in the present. Concepts that are used to judge art must have their own histories, and once those histories become apparent, it will not be possible to believe in the concepts with the whole-hearted commitment that they once commanded. If a figure like Greenberg has already receded far enough into the past to that his discourse is an object of historical analysis, that means concepts at play in contemporary art are entirely unrelated to his. If they aren't—if Greenberg's senses of words like "flatness," "abstraction," "kitsch," and "avant-garde" are still echoing in the present—then the evaluation of contemporary art becomes extremely problematic. How, after all, is it possible to judge a work using criteria that are no longer believable, that belong to another time? When concepts all belong to past writers, criticism becomes chronicle, and judgment becomes meditation on past judgment. The present is immersed in history, and finally drowns in it.

These are difficult points, and I have put them as clearly as I can. As far as I can see, critics such as Buchloh who practice institutional critique and reception history do not take the confluence of everyday judgment and considered neutrality about judgment to be problematic: like everyone, Buchloh judges new work as he encounters it, and he understands older works as the products of the conversations of their time. As a prescription for art criticism, the turn to reflection on judgment is still ill-resolved, especially when its aim is to replace art criticism.

7. *At least a critic should occasionally take a stand or have a position.* This seems sensible, an even inevitable: it is a minimal demand. It is, however, exactly what is most in contention in contemporary criticism. Met me pose it as a contrast between two writers I take to be pretty much diametrically opposed. The first is Jerry Saltz, currently art critic at the *Village Voice;* the second Michael Fried, once the leading figure in *Artforum*. I know both of them, and I can hardly think of two more opposite people. Michael Fried, as everyone who has met him can testify, is absolutely and unswervingly faithful to certain theoretical commitments he developed in the 1960s: the project of modernism as he has delineated it; the indispensability of a fully informed sense of art history; the central critical and historical importance of art that compels, for a given time and audience, conviction. Jerry Saltz is a kind of inversion of those values: it's not that he isn't argumentative—he is as sharp and funny and talkative as they come—but in my experience at least his arguments are ad hoc, and he wants them that way. This is just as relevant to Saltz's art criticism as Fried's ferocious commitment is to his, because Saltz's writing is effervescent and colloquial, as if he were continuously surprised by himself. Saltz has a collection of forty thousand slides—the collection is so large that MoMA has asked for it when he retires—and when he lectures, he shows pictures of all sorts of things: his taxi ride in from the airport, the look of the streets in the city he's in, and the outside of the galleries he visits. It is not just a distraction, it's a warm-up for the swerving observations that will follow.

When I asked Saltz what essay of his best addresses the conundrum of the contemporary critic's position, he sent me to a piece called "Learning on the Job," which he wrote in the fall of 2002. In it he reports being buttonholed by Barbara Kruger, who reacted to his apparent lack of critical method by saying, "We really need to talk, buddy boy!" Part of the essay is Saltz's position statement, or rather lack-of-position statement. He is against theory, by which he means Procrustean formulas that shape experience before the fact. "My only position," he writes,

> is to let the reader in on my feelings; try to write in straightforward, jargon-free language; not oversimplify or dumb down my responses; aim to have an idea, a judgment, or a description in every sentence; not take too much for granted; explain how artists might be original or derivative and how they use techniques and materials; observe whether they're developing or standing still; provide context; and make judgments that hopefully amount to something more than just my opinion. To do this requires more than a position or a theory. It requires something else. This something else is what art, and criticism, are all about.

There are nine parts to that long sentence, separated by semicolons. The first, second, and third are matters of tone and audience, and are not directly relevant at the moment. The fourth—to "aim to have an idea, a judgment, or a description in every sentence"—is a position against illogic, although it is also not a position in favor of a continuously developed logical argument. (I think it is actually impossible to write a grammatical sentence that doesn't express an idea, a judgment, or a description.) The fifth part, that he does not want to "take too much for granted," says again that he does not want to have a "theory" that guides experience. The sixth, seventh, and eighth clauses (beginning "explain how artists might be original or derivative" and including explaining to artists "how they might be original or derivative" and providing "context") are one hundred percent art history, not art criticism, and they contain a hint of a theory because they imply that innovation is better than repetition—that the avant-garde, or some multiplied pluralist form of it, remains an indispensable guide to criticism.

The ninth and final clause, promising to "make judgments that hopefully amount to something more than just my opinion," is to my mind the lynchpin of the paradox of positionless, or theoryless, art criticism. It is also the only clause of the nine that is about critical judgments, as opposed to art historical information, style, logic, or audience. It is likely, given human nature, that the judgments Saltz makes in *The Village Voice* will be shared by other people. Logically speaking, if everything he said were shared by only a few of his readers, his criticism would be extremely unpopular, and if everything he said were shared by none of his readers, it would be perceived as nonsense. But the clause "make judgments that hopefully amount to something more than just my opinion" means more than that, because what is at stake is not popularity or sense, it is historical connection. Saltz's judgments amount to more than just his own opinion, and they do so by sharing common ground with judgments that can be assigned to streams of modernist and postmodernist thinking. This is where the paradox enters, because in my reading Saltz is saying both "I do not want to be fettered by theory," and "My criticism needs to connect to previous theories." He needs to connect, but not know too much about that connection: not to worry it, not to get too serious or systematic about it. To keep the edge, stay nimble, and be able to make acute judgments, it is necessary not to think about other people's theories, but when the job is done—in the ninth clause—it is also important that the common ground is evident for those who choose to look.

It is not common practice to read newspaper criticism quite as slowly as I have here, or to read quite as much into it as I have. I don't doubt I have gotten this wrong from Saltz's viewpoint, but I also know this is what the sentence says. And just to be clear: Saltz's positionless position has granted him any number of wonderful insights. Consistency is the hobgoblin of little minds, he might say, and for the purposes of his writing and his encounters with objects consistency certainly has limited appeal—in fact it tends to appear as "theory." I do not object to any of that: spontaneity may be a fiction, and pure openness to an object may be impossible, but that is wholly irrelevant when it comes to the effects those putative states actually have on Saltz's writing. The difficulty begins when the sum total of his criticism is weighed against other people's criticism—not that Saltz has ever said he thought such a project would be worth anything. But from my point of view, historical meaning cannot be kept back: once it begins to leak into a text, as it does in several of the nine clauses, the text will soon be soaked. Once a single judgment is made whose sense depends, no matter how obliquely, on judgments made in the previous history of art, then sooner or later every judgment will want to take its significance from history. And that means, according to the logic of floods, that no wall can keep historical meaning at bay: in the end it is not only possible but necessary to ask how the sum total of Saltz's writing compares with other critics' writing. This is the crucial point that is so often missing from arguments in favor of pluralism: if individual judgments, the building blocks of the text, are significant on account of their connection to art history, then the entire corpus has to be weighed in an historical balance. Not every day, luckily, and not while you are encountering the art or arguing with Barbara Kruger—but eventually, if *anything* is to make sense.

This same point is made with characteristic concision in Greenberg's "Complaints of an Art Critic," just after he has proclaimed that aesthetic judgments are "given and contained in the immediate experience of art," and wholly "involuntary." Even so, he writes, "qualitative principles or norms are there somewhere, in subliminal operation," because "otherwise aesthetic judgments would be purely subjective, and that they are not is shown by the fact that the verdicts of those who care most about art and pay it the most attention converge over the course of time to form a consensus." Greenberg did not suppose that the uncovering of such a consensus was any of his business, and I do not think it is part of the brief of every piece of art criticism: but it becomes necessary whenever the question pertains to the sense and significance of a critic's *entire* position, or sum of positions. That is where Saltz's ninth clause becomes evasive. To "make judgments that hopefully amount to something more than just my opinion": they will inevitably amount to something more than his opinion, so the question is why only hope? Why not be the one who watches and keeps count?

What is *not* opposed to this in Fried's art criticism? The strength of his beliefs, and the way they are tempered with reasoned explanations, are especially clear in an exchange that took place at Brandeis University in 1966, during a panel discussion on criticism that also included Barbara Rose, Max Kozloff, and Sidney Tillim. Rose recalled that Greenberg once quoted Matthew Arnold to the effect that the task of the critic was to define the mainstream. But, she said, "at any given moment the mainstream is only part of the total activity, and in our time it may even be the least part. Thus to concentrate on the mainstream is to narrow one's range to the point where even tributaries to the mainstream, such as Dada, Surrealism, and Pop art, are not worthy of consideration." Fried replied:

> I feel tempted to say, if someone likes *that* stuff—putting aside the question of what, in a given instance, that stuff *is*—I simply can't believe his claim that he is *also* moved or convinced or flattened by the work of Noland, say, or Olitski or Caro. I mean that. It's not that I *refuse* to believe it, I really *can't*. I have no way of understanding what I am asked to believe. The most I can do is assume that whoever makes this claim admires Noland's or Olitski's paintings or Caro's sculptures, not for the wrong *reasons* exactly, but, as it were, in the grip of the wrong experience—an experience of mistaken identity.

This is different but analogous to Greenberg's claim that he did not always agree with his own judgments, but that he was forced to make them. Fried implies he is in the grip of a position that is both reasoned—as the cogently imagined reconstruction of an opposing position testifies—and also passionate to the point of being irrevocable. Greenberg's most forceful articulation of his position on his own powerlessness in the face of his own judgment was made in the same essay "Complaints of an Art Critic," which was a contribution to an *Artforum* series of essays on the state of criticism. The most compressed statement of his position against the idea that a critic should have a position is this:

> You cannot legitimately want or hope for anything from art except quality. And you cannot lay down conditions for quality. However and wherever it turns up, you have to accept it. You have your prejudices, your leanings and inclinations, but you are under the obligation to recognize them as that and keep them from interfering.

Both Fried's and Greenberg's positions on the matter of conviction are outlandishly strong, and I do not know any critic or historian who has taken them as seriously as they want to be taken. Some art historians, including Thierry De Duve, have thought about what they imply, but that is as it were from the outside, as historical observers of other people's theories. No one, I think, has taken them to heart, by which I mean considered the possibility or the desirability of having such convictions, entirely apart from the kinds of art that Greenberg or Fried championed. (As Fried said, "putting aside the question of what, in a given instance, that stuff *is*.") The usual attitude is to conflate Fried's or Greenberg's positions on conviction with the art they defended, making it possible to discard the former on account of the latter. That misunderstanding is what allows people to write off Fried after they have decided they don't like Olitski as much as he does, or to stop reading Greenberg once they've discovered he did not like Pop art. Things are more difficult than that.

Fried's *position* in the early essays is a matter of allegiance to modernist painting and sculpture, but it is not a position that can be *taken* in the sense in which a person says, "He took that position." It is a position that Fried held then and still does hold, but not one he chose out of a selection of other positions. If it were that kind of position, readers would be able to read his texts in such a way as to disclose the prior position that enabled him to "take up" the modernist, anti-literalist position. It would be possible to follow the antecedent positions, be persuaded by them, and take them up. The Greenberg of "Complaints of a Critic" would say that Fried's position is not a position that he needs to have *agreed with:* it is simply one he "accepted," because it compelled conviction and therefore drove the writing forward.

Saltz's *theory*—his theory abut how art critics should not have theories—is more akin to the kind of position that a person can *choose to take*, because Saltz thinks of theory as a thing that springs from some irrelevant prior experience. If you decide your Theory of Everything over coffee before you go to the gallery opening, your review is apt to be atrocious. That kind of theory, or position, ruins the possibility of open-minded encounters with objects. In the course of his essays, Saltz does take up less permanent positions, but they are short-lived, sensitive to the changing art, the time of day, and his mood at the moment. Those kinds of unstable positions are probably better called *stances*. The word is common in contemporary art criticism, because it helps suggest that full-blown positions are too unwieldy in the current pluralist climate. *Stance* also suggests something that Fried and Greenberg would find wholly unacceptable: that the critic is an agent who stands back from the writing, picking and choosing positions to suit different occasions. That is the rhetorical force of the phrase, "My stance on that is . . ." as opposed to "My stand on that is . . ." The question that "stance" begs is the source of the authority that invests the critic-as-agent with the ability to pick and choose stances. What stand, what position, could permit and orchestrate the lightning-fast changes of stances that comprise contemporary art criticism? Saltz is like a weather vane, spinning around to match the breeze at any given moment, and Fried is like a thermostat, either on or off, with no intermediate setting. Between the two there is a curious and unexplored territory. Clearly, if art criticism is to be reformed be requiring critics to take definite positions, they cannot be the kinds of positions Fried exemplifies because those can't be taken: and if criticism is to go on without positions, it cannot go the way Saltz goes without running into the problem of not having positions.

Perhaps it is best not to worry the problem of positions at all, but to reform criticism by making it more honest, immediate, and engaging. Saltz writes energetically on all sorts of things without worrying about how he's doing in the absence of "theories," and Fried's pronouncements on criticism are rare in comparison to the essays that propose judgments about art. Still, positions can never entirely disappear. Robert Hughes is a curious example. He has weighed in on virtually the whole of Western painting after the Renaissance—his writing is significantly more comprehensive than all but just a few art historians—and in all that writing he has almost never pondered his positions. In a brilliant essay on Francesco Clemente, he sighs over the "elusive," "curiously polymorphous" art, which "always looks hasty," and is "usually banal." He quips: when Clemente "is light, he is very, very light." And he complains: most of the time, Clemente "draws like a duffer." Then he settles in to look at just one image, an enigmatic beach scene with five red wheels. Could they be from a child's cart? An allusion to Ezekiel's wheels of fire? Symbols for the rank of angels called Thrones?

> By the simplest means, one is shifted sideways into a parallel world of improbabilities. At its best . . . Clemente's work lives a tremulous, only partly decipherable life at the juncture of eros and cultural memory. It is rarefied, intelligent and decadent, although its intelligence is more literary than plastic and its decadence never fails to make collectors want to cuddle it.

This is wonderful writing: judicious, measured, improvisational. The final "cuddle" is a typical hit: Hughes made much of his reputation by deflating reputations. Reading Hughes, I have often had the feeling that if he were to say what he was looking for, or what he found himself responding to—if, in other words, he would present observations as if they were theories—then I wouldn't be interested. He has said he values clarity, poise, technical skill, solidity (de Kooning's early drawings are "all nuance and doubt on top" and "iron below"), senses of space, a redeeming "cultural synthesis" (Pollock), an "unmistakable grandeur of symbolic vision" (Kiefer), concreteness over abstract ideas, and art with its own scale and density" as opposed to mass media. These ideals are insubstantial and tend to evaporate in the face of the works. They are also, as he would acknowledge, mainly late romantic and early modernist concepts. (Most can be found in Cortissoz's criticism at the turn of the century.) Hughes is broadly popular in America and England, but in my experience he is not regarded with any special interest in academia. Aside from all the usual reasons including academic élitism, the neglect is caused by the lightness of the ideas that serve as his positive criteria. Readers like him, I think, because they like his impatience with sham, and they enjoy the rawness of the reasons he gives. Those attractions may keep their minds off the uninteresting reasons why art succeeds.

It really does matter that Hughes can write great salt-and-pepper prose, and that he comes out with brilliant images, like the one of Greenberg's disciples "rocking and muttering over the last grain of pigment" in Morris Louis's canvases, "like students of the Talmud disputing a text, before issuing their communiqués about the Inevitable Course of Art History to the readers of *Artforum*"—or, my own favorite, the notion that Max Beckmann is poised "between the sleep walk and the goose step." But when the subject comes around to twentieth-century art criticism as a whole, in its relation to art history and to wider intellectual debates, then it does matter when debunking takes precedence over thinking about the shape of history, and it matters that Hughes's positions, insofar as they can be gleaned between the lines, are not put to the test by comparing them with previous judgments. Hughes doesn't care much about what other people have written, so he focuses on debunking received ideas and on finding the right words for his own responses.

Positionless art critics, including those like Hughes who are just not interested in positions, can still be compelling. Yet there is a difference between a critic such as David Sylvester, who was scrupulous about his own reactions even though he often had no idea how they might fit in with other people's, and a critic like David Banks, who recently praised installation art by the Bristol artists Sonya Hanney and Adam Dade by admitting that "in the grand tradition of art criticism, I don't know a lot about it, but I know what I like." Often what Sylvester has to say springs directly from his own visceral reactions: "art affects one in different parts of one's body," he told the critic Martin Gayford in an interview in 2001. "For example, sometimes in the solar plexus or the pit of one's stomach, sometimes in the shoulder blades . . . Or one may get a feeling of levitation—an experience I particularly associate with Matisse." Sylvester's narrow focus is justified because phenomenology frames his critical approach; Banks's opinions can't be defended in the same way, and neither can Hughes's.

There is a lot of treacherous ground between the kind of unwanted convictions that possessed Greenberg, and the positionless position—the theory of theorylessness—espoused by Saltz. In between are the intense convictions, both possessed and possessing, that drive Fried's art criticism, and the fugitive criteria that sometimes appear in Hughes's writing, and then vanish just as quickly. Art critics who do not seem to have positions can end up having them anyway, when the sum total of many judgments seem to point in one direction, the way a swarm of gnats slowly rises or falls even though the individuals are moving in all different directions. A position can materialize out of the most concerted efforts to avoid being consistent. All that is par for the course: it's the way writing works. Positionlessness finds its limit, however, when the writing itself implies there should be a position. A critic who recoils from theories may fall prey to an autoimmune reaction when his own criticism implies that he does in fact have a position. On the other hand, a ferociously strong position or Theory of Everything limits discourse with other critics and historians, and in Greenberg's case it even seems to have limited his articulation of the genesis of his own preferences. Clearly, it is dubious at best to reform art criticism by requiring art critics to have positions: it leads back along an uneven path toward a kind of commitment so ferocious even the person who held it, Greenberg, described it as a force outside himself. It's not that the opposite is best—it's that positions are not things to which a person can return.

This ends my list of seven proposals for reforming criticism. My moral is simple: no reform comes without the very severe penalties of anachronism and historical naïveté.

Note

1. *What Happened to Art Criticism?* (Chicago IL: Prickly Paradigm Press, distributed by the University of Chicago Press, 2003).

What is a Theorist?[1]

Irit Rogoff

Undone

A theorist is one who has been undone by theory.

Rather than the accumulation of theoretical tools and materials, models of analysis, perspectives and positions, the work of theory is to unravel the very ground on which it stands. To introduce questions and uncertainties in those places where formerly there was some seeming consensus about what one did and how one went about it. In the context of a question regarding what an artist might be, I would want to raise the question of what a theorist might be, to signal how inextricably linked these existences and practices might be. The old boundaries between making and theorizing, historicizing and displaying, criticizing and affirming have long been eroded. Artistic practice is being acknowledged as the production of knowledge and theoretical and curatorial endeavors have taken on a far more experimental and inventive dimension, both existing in the realm of potentiality and possibility rather than that of exclusively material production. The former pragmatic links in which one area "serviced" another have given way to an understanding that we face cultural issues in common and produce cultural insights in common.

Instead of "criticism" being an act of judgment addressed to a clear-cut object of criticism, we now recognize not just our own imbrication in the object or the cultural moment, but also the performative nature of any action or stance we might be taking in relation to it. Now we think of all of these practices as linked in a complex process of knowledge production instead of the earlier separation into to creativity and criticism, production and application. If one shares this set of perspectives, then one cannot ask the question "what is an artist?" without asking "what is a theorist?"

The narrative of theoretical unraveling, of being undone, is a journey of phases in which the thought we are immersed in is invalidated. Those moments of silent epiphany in which we have realized that things might not necessarily be so, that there might be a whole other way to think them, moments in which the paradigms we inhabit cease to be self-legitimating and in a flash are revealed to be nothing more than what they are: paradigms. In my own particular case this was a journey from a discipline called art history, via great roads of critical, theoretical study to some other and less disciplined place, which for the moment and very provisionally we might call *visual culture*.

Furthermore, I come to the formations of visual culture from a slightly different perspective of cultural difference, and it is one of the privileges of the culturally displaced that their view is always awkward and askance, never frontally positioned, and often exists in an uneasy relation to dominant paradigms. Initially from a long, conventional and very anti-intellectual training in art history, which left me at its end at a complete loss on how to navigate the interstices between who I was, what I did and the world that I inhabited.

In my own particular case the distance between these three was such that fairly acceptable exercises in stretching and expanding a professional practice to make it accommodate one's concerns seem, in retrospect, to have not been able to bridge the gaps. Therefore in the first instance my attention was caught by what possibilities there might be for formulating a project not out of a set of given materials or existent categories, but out of what seemed at each historical moment a set of urgent concerns. Roughly speaking these emerged for me as:

- in the 1980s a concern with gender and sexual difference, which resulted in an exploration of feminist epistemologies

- in the 1990s a concern with race and cultural difference, which resulted in trying to take on the authority of "geography" as a body of knowledge with political implications
- and currently a concern with questions of democracy and of what modes; parliamentarian and performative, might be open to us to take part in it, which I am currently thinking about as an exploration of participation and of what does it mean to take part in visual culture beyond the roles it allots us as viewers or listeners.

Obviously I am speaking of a long journey of some eighteen years now, which has included encounters with, on the one hand, the ways in which global politics constantly reformulate and reformat themselves, and on the other, tremendously exciting encounters with critical theory that asserted that things aren't necessarily what they seem and gave me the tools to see through them.

But have no fear, I am not about to rehearse upon you the long march from Structuralism to Deleuze with detours through feminism, psychoanalysis and colonialism. Instead, I am concerned with the dynamics of loss, of giving up and of moving away and of being without. These dynamics are for me a necessary part of my understanding of visual culture, for whatever it may be it is *not* an accumulative, an additive project in which bits of newly discovered perspectives are pasted on to an existing structure, seemingly augmenting and enriching it, seemingly making it acceptable to the pressures of the times. In my own thinking it is not possible to divorce the notion of *criticality*, which I see as foundational for visual culture from the processes of exiting bodies of knowledge and leaving behind theoretical models of analysis and doing without certain allegiances. Criticality, as I perceive it, is precisely in the operations of recognizing the limitations of one's thought, for one does not learn something new until one unlearns something old, otherwise one is simply adding information rather than rethinking a structure. It seems to me that within the space of a relatively short period we have been able to move from criticism to critique to criticality—from finding fault, to examining the underlying assumptions that might allow something to appear as a convincing logic, to operating from an uncertain ground which, while building on critique, wants nevertheless to inhabit culture in a relation other than one of critical analysis;

other than one of illuminating flaws, locating elisions, allocating blames. One is, after all, always at fault; this is a permanent and ongoing condition, since every year we become aware of a new and hitherto unrealized perspective which illuminates further internal cultural injustices. Criticality is therefore connected, in my mind, with risk, with a cultural inhabitation that acknowledges what it is risking without yet fully being able to articulate it.

Without

I have called this section "Without" because for some time now I have been very interested in this condition as a starting point for embarking on new thought and new research projects. It seems to me to indicate a state in which we acknowledge that we had some navigational principles and some models of critical analysis to hand, but that they no longer quite serve us in relation to a new and emergent conjunction of problems. And more than simply acknowledge them, we pay them the respect due by recognizing what strong supports these models of analysis had been to us, of how aware we are of their lack. The events of 9/11 are for me a very actual example for the state I am trying to articulate. In the context of critical thought, these events, dreadful and tragic, came in the wake of a slowly growing realization that the twin models of post-colonial theory on the one hand and discourses of globalization on the other, were no longer equal to the task of trying to think through intercultural relations on a global scale. Suddenly we were faced with what I have called elsewhere "geography in real time." Real time is the moment in which some nebulous half-acknowledged entity, previously no more than a vague unease or a partially avowed recognition, crashes into our own reality by becoming a reality itself. The events of 9/11 were an instance of suddenly being forced to live in real time. But with hindsight, many of us will confess to having been uneasy for over a year then; G8 summit meetings in Seattle, Gothenburg, and Genoa disrupted by increasingly violent protests, the Intifada in Palestine and Israeli response spiraling out of control, evermore exasperated spokespersons for international aid agencies trying to warn of impending disaster, cities in which NGOs are the only infrastructure still in place, open discussion of the consequences of slavery and racial violence across the globe taking place in Durban. Therefore intellectuals who have been thinking about geopolitical power relations through their cultural manifestations found themselves for a moment in a state of being "without." The old ordering of the world between colonizers and colonized was not sufficient to come to terms and analyze these events, nor was the more recent ordering viewed through the logics of multinational corporations and free trade agreements and Internet blurrings of national, cultural boundaries. Had we not been through those models of analysis, post-colonialism, and globalization, we would not have understood our state of simultaneously knowing and being unable to know, which characterizes the condition of being "without." I will come back to the moment crystallized by these events at the end of this paper, but I would like to return to a more detailed characterization of my understanding of visual culture as a state of being without.

What is it that has been given up in the shift from the investigative and the analytical to the performative and the participatory? Most people would say that it is the absence of a solid sense of history that anchors and legitimates everything that is the source of greatest insecurity. I myself do not feel that, since I have always seen it as an amalgam of tropes and narrative structures. Historical research often contains fascinating materials but rarely actually explains anything at the level at which I want it explained, as dissonances and disruptions and trivial performances that say as much about us as they do about the outside world. The answer lies, to my mind at least, in substituting the historical specificity of that being studied with the historical specificity of he/she/they doing the studying. In order to effect such a shift without falling prey to endless anecdotal and autobiographical ruminating which stipulate experience as a basis for knowledge, we attempt to read each culture through other, often hostile and competitive, cultural narratives. This process of continuous translation and negotiation is often exhausting in its denial of a fixed and firm position, but it does allow us to shift the burden of specificity from the material to the reader or viewer and prevents us from the dangers of complete dislocation. Perhaps it might even help us to understand that at the very moment in which historical specificity can provide liberation and political strength to some of the dispossessed, it also imprisons others within an old binary structure that no longer reflects the conditions and realities of their current existence. The Delueze-inspired replacement of working with a model of a culture of *singularity* (singular to a logic of its own organization) rather than one of *specificity* (specific to one particular location) has been of great importance to this discussion.

Certainly the security of a discipline and with it all the comforts of a coherent identity, of having clear sources for funding applications, of knowing which subject panel your work should be sent to for assessment. Even the simple question of knowing what to answer when you are asked at a party "And what do you do?", which always elicits panic-stricken silences and particularly lame answers. Now I am bolder and more confident and look them straight in the eye and say "Visual culture" and wait for *them* to look away in embarrassment, when they clearly have not a clue what I am talking about. In the recent *Manifesta* exhibition in Ljubljana there was a piece by Lithuanian artist Arturo Raila called "The Girl is Innocent," which simply tracked on video a group of professors at the Vilnius Art Academy doing end of the year critics of the students' work and assigning final grades.[2] In the simplest form this piece rehearsed the ways in which aesthetics and ideologies are linked at moments of crisis and demise to a point that none of the participants, who had made their name in a previous era, had any principles by which to navigate the current moment. They spoke of their loss, insecurity, confusion—one bearded, middle-aged professor said in a sorrow-choked voice: "and now we can't even speak of beauty." The piece did not assign progressive or retrograde positions to the protagonists, did not rehearse all the obvious political arguments around communism vs. democracy, but simply staged the confusion inherent around teaching, judging and locating art within dramatically redefined paradigms.

What else has been given up? More problematic to give up has been the very notion of a methodology, of the certainty of an approach, of a problematic, of a set of analytical frames which we can use to tackle whatever issue of problematic we are preoccupied with. It was relatively easy to give up notions of history or notions of disciplines because we had inherited them and had to either accept or agitate to make changes within them, but methodology was something we struggled for and invested in its operations all of our hopes for producing an intellectually broader, a politically more inclusive, and a subjectively more imaginative field of activity. I have for some time been interested in space and spatialization and have been very excited about what is commonly called "the discourse on space," and particularly in those discussions which seemed able to unravel some less familiar manifestations of both sexual and cultural difference. However, recently and to my surprise, I understood that it is not space as such that interests me but rather what it has allowed me to perceive about the dynamics and performances of ambivalence and of disavowal in public-sphere culture.

Which leads me to understand that perhaps the thorniest of the forsaken elements has been the notion of the subject of the work one is doing. Increasingly I have become wary of occupying areas which have an agreed-upon and sanctioned subject for their activities. In the wake of all the posts we have read and internalized, I understand that both the consensus around a subject (for example, that we all understand each other perfectly when we say "I am working on the representation of female subjectivity in domestic interior paintings at the turn of the century," or the ways in which everyone hummed reassuringly when someone said they were working on the "The Body") and the assumptions, systems and boundaries sustain its very existence in the world as a subject. Instead I think we are in that phase when all of the work goes into the constitution of a subject for the work. We have a set of concerns, of issues, and we have a set of nagging doubts about what lies behind the manifest, and we have a certain investigative freedom, and we set those to work and wait to see what comes up. So many of our PhD supervisions now dance around the inconvenience of what the dissertation is about, of what its subject is, of what we might name it when it finally comes into the full exploration of its concerns. Increasingly we seem to interview potential research students for the motivation that underlies their project and not for what they want to do. The less they seem certain of what precisely their project is, the more we seem to like them, but the less likely they are to receive AHRB [since 2005, the AHRC] funding unless we can rally to repackage all of that uncertainty into a set of plausible questions, methods, and assertions, and perhaps the work is really in this translation between the twin poles of doubt and certainty.

So what then, where is the work located? Perhaps that is the wrong question, perhaps a "where" intimates a fixed and known location where we might conceivably go and look for and actually find the work. Perhaps even better is the notion of how does the work function and what does it produce, of what effects it has in the world rather than of what existing meanings it uncovers.

Again and again in recent years I have found myself dealing with a particular question, critically analyzing the contexts and conditions of its emergence, the assumptions on which it might rest, and the languages in which its is articulated. But having gone through all of these analytical steps, I would find myself at a loss to imagine the next step: the one that would go beyond critical analysis into the possible imagining of an alternative formulation, an actual signification of that "disrupted-through-analysis" cultural phenomenon. On occasion, certain encounters with Conceptual artworks which are taking up the same issues I am preoccupied with, would provide a bridge to the next step for thought: an actual cultural making, not an analysis, of a condition I perceived of theoretically. They address how culture is perceived when it is viewed from the back door or from an oblique angle, through miscomprehension and mistranslation, and what it means to be in a position of culturally longing for that which is historically and politically forbidden to you.

My current theoretical articulations locate the artists' work within a set of cultural debates in which the visual arts rarely find representation. It assumes the form of a practice, of a "writing with" an artist's work rather than writing about it, a dehierarchization of the question of whether the artist, the critic, or the historian, the advertising copy-writer or the commercial sponsor, the studio or the director, has the final word in determining the meaning of a work in visual culture.

Unfitting

When we began to theorize visual culture as an entity in the mid-1990s, it was very much geared towards an amalgam of all of the "withouts" that I have just tried to elaborate here. In a sense, what prompted that enterprise—and I am speaking in the context of the United States, where I was working at the time—was a recognition shared by many of us that it was simply no longer productive to continue a battle with the strictures of art history as a discipline and with all the efforts to force it to expand its boundaries. Boundaries, small or large, limited or expanded, are in the end just that, setting the limits of the possible. What was required instead would be an open and fluid space in which numerous forms of experimental conjunctions between ideas, politics, images, and effects might take place. Furthermore, in this space neither materials nor methodologies would dominate, and the endless taxonomy of constitutive components that characterizes so-called interdisciplinarity could be suspended with. Depending on the problematic one was investigating or thinking through, one would bring into the discussion anything that seemed important or illuminating without having to align it with the histories of the disciplines it might have been culled from. Here we return to the argument of singularity vs. specificity I mentioned earlier, and to the Deleuzian view of matter as being self-organizing rather than filling up previously structured organizing principles.

Since then a certain amount of institutionalization has inevitably taken place in the field; departments and programs, readers and monographs, journals and teaching curriculums are proliferating. Fair enough, and since I am at the heart of all this and know full well that no one actually knows what visual culture is in that simple form of definition, what we were experiencing was perhaps a slightly more organized form of that same hoped-for fluidity. However, more recently I have been hearing about a certain kind of policing of what visual culture is—apparently it is this not that, can be defined in this manner not that one, can be spoken by these but not by those. In short, the processes of territorialization have begun, and in their wake will probably trail the entire gamut of subject fixing and method valorizing, of inclusions and exclusions which we had tried to escape from a few years ago in the aim of fixing our attention on what needs to be thought rather than on arguing with what had already been thought. I would have wanted to reiterate my belief that the work of *unfitting* ourselves is as complex, as rigorous, and as important as the work that goes into fitting within a disciplinary paradigm or that of expanding it in order to accommodate our concerns. That it shares much with Derridean deconstruction though its is perhaps less preoccupied with shifting consciousness and is more focused on enactments and cultural effects.

Most recently we have all, in our different countries and

institutions and practices, had to think about the institutionalization of what we do. About the newly emergent names and titles and so called "fields" which we inhabit and of how they might interface both with each other as well as with funding structures and job descriptions, as witnessed by my friend, the artist ShuLea Chang, who has now begun to call herself a "conceptualizer" to the great envy of all of us.

These thoughts are for me an unwelcome diversion, though obviously a necessary one in the circumstances, for what I had really wanted to think about here was—seven years on from writing texts that had tried to characterize the study of visual culture—what it was like to actually be in visual culture, working in it and living it out, rather than to talk about its coming into being. To me the most surprising thing that has happened recently has been a shift in the direction I am facing. At the beginnings I had described earlier I was firmly facing the academy and intellectual work; they were the frames of references through which I arrived at artworks and they were the arenas in which the work circulated, albeit with many hiccups, and with which it was in dialogue. Suddenly I find myself facing the art world, by which I mean not simply that this is where the work is gaining response but is spurring something in response. The process is still much the same, a lot of eclectic reading, going to talks and exhibitions, and finally writing. The effects, however, are very different. I have not had enough time fully to understand or to think about the implications of this shift, but it does seem to me to have something to do with the shift to a performative phase of cultural work in which meaning *takes place*, takes place in the present rather than is excavated for. Where its operations are not through signifying processes or through entering a symbolic order, which I suppose are the hallmarks of academic intellectual work, but through forms of enactment. Through languages and modes of writing that focus on address rather than on what Barthes called the filial operations of texts. As Peggy Phelan says, "I am also interested in the ways in which the performative *inspires* new terms; I think that's one of the *performances* the term performativity enacts." Perhaps what I am trying to say is that it is my understanding of a response that has changed. Perhaps it has moved from response as affirmation of what you have said, which is what happens when someone quotes your work, to response perceived as the spur to make something as yet nonexistent.

Entangled

In closing I wish to go back to that process of recognition of the limitations of post-colonial and of globalization discourses I mentioned in relation to the moment of 9/11. Earlier in my thinking I had been interested in the possibilities that visual culture might offer as a field constituted out of sexual or cultural difference, out of performativity or out of multiplicities, rather than these becoming the subject of the work or that they be applied as critical models of analysis to various materials. That these would produce questions rather than characterize conditions, and that those questions could be taken anywhere at all, far from their seemingly appropriate materials.

More recently I have been wondering about the possibilities inherent in notions of creolization to provide more complex and more appropriate modes of cultural engagement. Wondering whether within notions of creolization we might enable to get away from binaries of colonizers and colonized as well as from later notions of hybridity in which this and that came together into something else, some newer and more contemporary cultural formation. In particular, I have been trying to think of what the creolized museum might seem like as a form of encounter between the structure of the museum and issues of cultural difference.

At the Documenta platform of Creolite and Creolization, which took place in St. Lucia in January 2002, a model began to emerge that does seem to have potential as an alternative to some of the post-colonial, post-feudal paradigms. In this understanding, as articulated by Stuart Hall, Gerardo Mosqueras, Derek Walcott, and many other participants, creolization is a process of cultural mixings, an entanglement of cultures in the result of slavery, colonialism and plantation culture. Its components are highly slippery signifiers, since the originals Creoles are Whites who, through long exposure, have lost their originary identity. White settlers who have become indiginized, facing black slaves, Africans born in the location of their enslavement. Creolite is the construction of a project out of these entangled mixings.

The existence of a culture as a form of entanglements which have lost their origins and exist as mutual interlocutions rather than as, for example, hybridized outcomes seems very intriguing. While thinking of it I was also watching hours of video work by Kutlug Ataman, trying to write the catalogue for his exhibition in at the BAWAG Foundation in Vienna. In one of the works, "Women Who Wear Wigs,"[3] which was shown at the Venice Biennale and in London at the Lux Gallery in 2000, we meet four Turkish women who wear wigs for various reasons. One is a political activist who has been on the run for thirty years and who uses wigs as part of her disguises. One is a sophisticated journalist who has breast cancer and has lost her hair through chemotherapy; she wears a wig to reproduce the luxuriant hair she has lost and of which she was so proud. One is a devout Muslim student who is not allowed to cover her head with a scarf at the secular university, so she experiments with a wig as some form of covering protection. The fourth is Demet Demir, transsexual, prostitute, political activist for left-wing youth associations, human rights, the environment, feminism, experimenter with Lesbian relationships, ironic raconteur of personal melodramas, teller of hair-raising tales of police brutality which included repeated harassment, beatings and the shaving of her head.

Demet Demir became a student in 1982 immediately following the military coup in Turkey by joining a night school where she organized a meeting to mark the 1st of May, and was ultimately expelled from the left-wing youth Association for Homosexuality. She was the first transvestite to become a member of the Human Rights association, had an early sex change operation, educated herself to become, she says, a feminist and an environmentalist, has fought long legal battles with the police. All this side by side with ruminations about clients who are disappointed to find out that she doesn't have both a penis and a vagina, for these days, she says, one needs both. All of these are not contradictions, they are entanglements and mixings that produce a rich field of possibilities. In this work Ataman has produced a new subject in the world, a creolized subject in which something called WWWW unframes all the tedious narratives about women and Islam, women and the Muslim state told in the West about the East, and produces instead a heady mix of women and sexuality and Islam and patriarchy and the state and vanity and desire and rebellion and melodramatic sentiment—all connected through wigs and exceeding the boundaries of anything that might actually circulate under the aegis of the proper name of woman.

In a sense that is what I wish for us in visual culture, that we become a field of complex and growing entanglements that can never be translated back to originary or constitutive components. That we never be able to hold on to the divisions that have separated artist from theorist, since like the White settlers and the Black slaves of Caribbean culture in the eighteenth century, we endlessly mimic one another. That we produce new subjects in the world out of that entanglement and that we have the wisdom and courage to argue for their legitimacy while avoiding the temptation to translate them, or apply them, or separate them.

Notes

1. This essay originally appeared in German as "*Was Ist ein Kunstler?*" edited by Katharyna Sykord et al. (Munich: Wilhelm Fink, 2004).
2. Arturas Raila, "The Girl is Innocent" in *Borderline Syndrome—Energies of Defence*, catalogue of Manifesta—European Biennial of Contemporary Art, Lubljana, Slovenia 2000.
3. www.kutluataman.com, Women Who Wear Wigs, 1999.

Is This Anything? or, Criticism in the University

Stephen Melville

I

I've borrowed my title from a recurrent segment on David Letterman's *Late Show*. The curtain rises and there, flanked by what one may take as the ornament or the distraction of Grinder Girl and Hula Hoop Girl (who each at one time featured in this segment) will be someone doing some form of vaudeville-like performance. After about 30 seconds the curtain comes back down, and Dave and his band leader Paul Shaefer decide whether or not that was something. In the event that they agree that it was something, the judgment is direct and devoid of nuance: that was something. Where the act fails to be something, there's room for considerable qualification; my favorite among the standard forms of qualification is one I think usually comes from Paul: "Well, that could have been something, but it wasn't." Disagreement between them is rare and sometimes kind of interesting: the other night they had a man riding a little tiny bicycle around in circles with a woman on his shoulders sort of waving her arms around. Ruthie and I, always willing to weigh in, knew this was nothing, and Paul seemed distinctly unexcited, but Dave was clearly quite taken with it and dwelt particularly forcefully on how very small the bicycle was—evidently entirely deaf to Ruthie's riposte that it was still only riding a bicycle and the woman added nothing to that. In the end Paul gave in. A night to two later, it was a guy in a serape and sombrero doing a goofy dance to Mexican music, and Dave, Paul, Ruthie, and I were once again all tracking together: "Oh Thank God!" Paul said as the curtain came down, and Dave said, "Well, that was certainly nothing." After a commercial break, Dave said he just been informed that the contestant worked regularly at a theater in New York, and that it cost fifteen bucks to get in.

Well, that's it—criticism—in a nutshell, isn't it? Judgment amidst distraction and in the face of a possibly senseless market. A part of the pleasure in watching "Is This Anything?" has—I think this isn't just me—to do with its absolute clarity: you see the thing, you say what it is—something or nothing—and you're done. No reasoning your way from some first grasp to some justified conclusion and not a lot of room for discussion—it's hard to know where Dave's insistence on the smallness of the bicycle could have gone had Paul not folded. That one can in fact say something like "that could have been something, but it was nothing" is certainly worth a pause.

In the 1950s and 1960s in the United States, art criticism—the best of it anyway—may have looked a little like this; in our current unkind retrospects it's come to look a lot like this, just as most current criticism looks nothing like it. It's not in fact clear that most current criticism looks like anything at all. I spent a day this fall at a symposium on American art (now organized by Darby English), most of which was not very surprisingly devoted to remarks about the global and the local and the collapse of the national. It seemed to me interesting that we got through some six hours of papers by a distinguished group of curators and art historians without the words "critic" or "criticism" coming up once, and when I asked about this, the entire panel was agreed that criticism was nothing, not part of what it mattered to talk about. One might expect this of the curators, who seemed quite happy to say that they now did the job critics used to do, and perhaps also from a group of art historians strongly given to what has for some time now been called "theory" (I understand from the *New York Times Magazine*'s year-end summary of New Ideas that theory has now been declared dead by *Critical Inquiry*, a matter I will touch on again, albeit obliquely), but it was at least a little surprising that Arthur Danto, also on the panel and pretty widely considered our leading critic, should also have been of this view. Not a huge surprise of course: his theory of art doesn't seem to leave a lot of room for criticism, and his talk that day—not quite in line with the globalizers on the rest of the panel—had mostly focused on the art school as not so much a place for learning, or failing to learn, something in need of teaching but as a simpler site for "the pursuit of happiness" where admission alone amounted to a ratification of one's declaration of one's self as an artist and graduation—or for that matter, failure to be graduated—was no better than a sort of afterthought. So much not only for criticism, but presumably also the hallowed institution of "the crit."

II

It's not an entirely bad description of the critic to say that what he or she does is "get about" and "say what's what." The getting about is presumably important, and it means, among other things, that the critic tends to have a grasp of "what's going on." Sometimes this will even seem the critic's defining feature; certainly much current writing seems little more than the display of such knowledge and so can remind one that if this is all you've got, you're finally only dealing with a gossip column—or, as we say in the university, sociology—and not criticism. The "what's what" part is important and not reducible to, possibly not even particularly dependent on, knowing what's going on.

In any case, the contemporary critic does not in fact do very well by the getting about part of the job. The people who really manage to get about, now, are collectors and curators. In a small city like Columbus, the world of collectors has a certain transparency. At the top of the heap, or one of the heaps anyway, is Les Wexner, founder of The Limited retail chain, major arts patron, donor of Ohio State's architecturally notable Wexner Center, and collector, primarily, of classic European modernist work. Just below him would be the developer Ron Pizutti, who focuses on somewhat more recent, mostly American work—from, say, the 1960s on. Both of these men have formed major collections of the kinds museums keep a close eye on, heavily advised and, at least in Wexner's case, possessed of their own in-house curators. Below this level, there's a group of collectors of distinctly contemporary art; their motives tend to be rather various, so the collections—not necessarily terribly large—sometimes reflect something like taste or principle and sometimes appear comprehensible only as speculative instruments or records of relatively raw, if highly mediated, social fact. And these people do get about, both at their own initiative and through various collector's tours and the like, often bound up with the local institutions they actively support and on whose acquisition committees they often serve. They go to Venice and to Kassel and to Basel and to Sundance; they are friends—in an artworldy kind of way—with New York and LA and maybe even some European gallerists, and so on. In Miami, it's a group of collectors of more or less this kind who are the driving force behind the emergence of Art Basel Miami, the development of the Design District, and a host of thick relations between museums, artists, and various urban schemes. Typically such collectors see a vastly larger amount of contemporary art than a presumed academic specialist in the field, myself for example, can ever dream of seeing. They probably see a great deal more than even a working critic in an established center like New York or LA typically sees.

And certainly curators get themselves very much about. The past decade in particular has seen the emergence of the international curatorial star, who may have no actual home base or have only the loosest of ties to such a base (to the point that in hiring a curator of contemporary art it is an active question whether or not a candidate is actually willing to stay home and work). There's now a very real community—a sort of airport-and-kunsthalle community—of curators in more or less continuous conversation with one another as they circulate from Rio to Venice to Johannesburg to wherever the next newly invented Biennial is being held, and these conversations effectively amount to both what is going on and the knowledge of what is going on. The critic mostly does not travel in these circles, does not get about in these ways, and is now more often than not a distinctly belated arrival in front of work that has already been received, swathed in discourse, located and described, and, often enough, already sold. To a considerable degree there appears to be no job to be done beyond ratifying that situation, and the language of contemporary criticism has, accordingly, has become a curiously reduced version of languages once central to criticism's way of embedding judgment in description—of saying what's what: it now seems enough to note that a given work "references" another or refers to itself or to art to imagine that one has somehow made contact with the whole complex of issues that were once carried by the term "self-criticism."

These are facts not simply about the institutional world through which we might imagine art to travel, conditions to which it simply submits willy-nilly. They are intimately related to a range of new shapes art is proposing for itself, or at least that artists and curators and, indeed, critics are proposing for their selves. It's a matter of, I suppose, a sort of tipping of balance at first: it's not unusual for an artist to act, as it were temporarily, as a curator—as, for example, Mona Hatoun is currently doing at the Museum of Modern Art—but something tips a bit when artists curate their own work and present that act of curation as itself part of the work, as Chris Williams and Albert Oehlen did a couple of years ago at the Wexner Center; similarly, we are used to the idea that an artistic work might take the form of a curatorial intervention, as in Fred Wilson's work, but something will seem to have tipped a bit when the artist's work seems to consist in nothing but the formation and exhibition of a collection, as in much of the work of Annette Messager, among many others. And finally, the absolutely familiar business of a curator putting together a show around a theme or argument will seem to be tipping into something else when the curating itself is reviewed as if it were the work—as seems increasingly the case of the large, international exhibit (and as Diarmuid Costello has recently argued may be the case of Tate Modern overall). The cumulative effect of all these little shifts in balance is an increasing uncertainty about what counts as work and what as an exhibition of it, and the past couple of years have seen this uncertainty increasingly jell into a new vocabulary of "platforms" and "stations" that presumably means to make it possible to speak of art activity—a phrase to be preferred, I think, in this context to the more familiar "artistic activity"—without having to speak separately of works, their exhibition, and the relations between them.

But of course now the question of who gets about and how has turned up a new wrinkle in the shape of that other question about what's what.

Before leaving this turn around the critic's way of going about his or her business, it's maybe worth dwelling about on how or where the critic mostly got about. One might say that typically the critic got about on foot—that is, participated in a certain urban situation and history, sharing features with such other urban inhabitants as the flaneur and the dandy, and typically the places the critic got to were studios and galleries and museums and their social extension into various bars and cafes, assorted openings and parties, and so on—very much the same ground on which collectors and curators now move with their new or at least greater visibility and the considerable aid of the airlines. A place the critic typically did not go was the university. Critics often came from the university, in the sense that they were educated there, although often not in the field—art or art history—central to their activity as critics. And in a slightly different sense they often continue to come from the university—they may teach or be studying in it—but are quite clear about leaving it behind insofar as they engage in criticism. It may be that the university-based critic brings a notable art historical sensitivity to her criticism, but for the most part she is entirely clear that she is setting aside most of the protocols that guide and define her as an art historian in moving out into this rather distinctly other world. Typically, too, the critic has not been taught to be—not been actively formed as—a critic (and we often, I think, feel that one of the things that a critic somehow has to discover is what it is for him or herself to be a critic: the thing we call "voice" counts a lot here and is found only in a certain kind of sustained trying of it). This means, mostly, that one cannot major in "criticism"—it's just not on offer. There are, increasingly, exceptions to this, and they are perhaps interesting: art schools seem to be taking an interest in what are often called "writing courses," sometimes explicitly oriented to "criticism" but also, I think, conceived as giving art students a presentational skill they are taken to need, and criticism appears as an explicit field in at least some art education programs, where it comes complete with textbooks with titles like How to Criticize a Photograph—sorting this out can't really be separated from a larger question about what kind of thing art education is or is becoming. Apart from these two developments, Bard College has recently supplemented its rather interesting graduate program for curators of contemporary art with a separate track in criticism.

The university has historically not been a place friendly to criticism; it is, after all, basically organized around shapes of knowledge and it's not clear that criticism has that shape or even that it has an object in the sense that we assume for knowledge. The contrast is perhaps particularly pronounced in art history. I think it works pretty much the same way in literary study, but it's certainly true that literary academics will easily refer to themselves as literary critics even if they don't so easily call what they do criticism, and it's also true that they don't, simply as a matter of names, have the same inescapable attachment to "literary history" that art historians do to art history. And of course criticism is itself a literary genre and so more or less teachable within a literary curriculum at least as a history—courses in the history of criticism are pretty much standard fare in English departments and, to the best of my knowledge, almost non-existent in art history programs.

More to the point, literary study's institutional invention is substantially less explicit than art history's. The art history we have now is the product of, among other things, a very active project of foundation—which has itself been the object of deeply interesting re-examination in recent years—that includes strong, if also sometimes deftly subterranean, arguments for, for example, historical distance of a very particular kind as a precondition for any art historical knowledge, thus cutting the contemporary and the critical out of the field from the outset. The contemporary has, of course, crept back but its curricular presence remains fragile, the place most frequently filled by someone suspected of not being a real art historian or of not teaching at the heart of the thing. The heart of the thing is, of course, still the Renaissance, and it is so because it is now deeply established within the discipline as the mirror in which the art historian repeatedly discovers and recognizes himself.

The critical too has found its way back into the disciplinary margins of academic art history, and these margins are perhaps particularly interesting because they are inhabited by a number of the most intellectually powerful figures in the field—such figures as (my little list is merely exemplary) Michael Baxandall, Michael Fried, Tim Clark, Rosalind Krauss, Leo Steinberg, and Joseph Koerner. That's at least enough of a list to allow one to see that this is not simply a matter of working in contemporary or modern art, although a certain tropism is clear enough and certainly not accidental; it's also, I think, not a list that depends on an underlying commitment to "theory" in its current sense, although once again there is an orientation of sorts that shouldn't be simply ignored. When I say that the critical finds its way back into art history in the work of people like these I mean, quite simply, that they all, with varying degrees of explicitness, understand their art historical activity as essentially critical, thus understand the discipline not in some sharp distinction from criticism but as a particular modality of it. Baxandall is in a number of ways the most interesting figure on this list—the most explicit about referring art history always to criticism and the one whose work is most fully at home in the very place—the Renaissance—in which art history had seemed to secure its distance and distinctness from criticism.

But before turning more directly toward his work, it's perhaps worth offering a few remarks on Fried and Krauss. Both not only belong importantly to the history of recent criticism, but also come quite directly out of the notably sustained and self-conscious exploration of criticism that *Artforum* was in its glory days. There's some tendency to think of Fried as having turned from criticism to art history with his departure from *Artforum*—Fried has himself, I suspect, entertained this view at times—but I'd argue that his most recent book,[1] on Adolph Menzel and including what amounts to a renewal of the conversations with Stanley Cavell that so informed his writing of the 1960s, makes that view untenable. Krauss, on the other hand, seems to have considerable success in maintaining a continuing critical contact with contemporary art over a long period in a time arguably distinguished by real difficulty in maintaining such contact, in sustaining a career in criticism; at the same time, her way of continuing *Artforum*'s impulse clearly moves the whole enterprise much closer to the university—*October* is, admittedly somewhat uneasily, an academic journal in a way *Artforum* was not and did not aspire to be. One might, of course, feel that whatever *Artforum*'s conscious aspirations, *October* does show something about its inherent trajectory, and one might feel also that what shows in that trajectory is criticism losing touch with its actual situation and audience, becoming academic and in the process ruining the particular clarity and openness that has always been the hallmark of great critical writing. Maybe. I prefer to think of this as showing something about the possible scope of criticism and so also the actual standards of "theory."

Viewed as a kind of experiment in criticism, *Artforum* was open to a fairly wide mix of writers, and in that mix Fried and Krauss are particularly distinguished by their indebtedness to Clement Greenberg's criticism. It's important that Geenberg shows up here, and it's important not only—maybe not at all—because he's a figure it's altogether too easy to see emerging through the comedy of "Is This Anything?," but because whatever the fate of Greenberg's particular art historical claims—they've certainly come in for all sorts of attack and criticism, by Fried and Krauss among many others—Greenberg has exerted a strong, if not entirely clear, claim on art history itself. We've been, you might say, unable to relegate him, for better or for worse, to his moment within the history of art or the history of criticism but instead find him repeatedly showing up as if offering something that bears on the possible shape and self-understanding of the discipline, as if offering at least hints toward how it might re-imagine itself on the grounds of its attachment to the contemporary rather than its distance or detachment from the past. In trying to think about this situation, one may find oneself also having to think about the angle of incidence with which "theory" strikes or might strike a discipline that has its construal as criticism as a distinct problem and possibility. This doesn't seem to me as true of literary study in its moment of being struck by "theory," and so it's been a bit of a problem for art history, running behind as it tends to do, that so much of the "theory" by which it was eventually struck was reflected off of literary study.

Thus, however oddly, to Baxandall.

III

Baxandall's favored rhetorical mode is irony, leavened, particularly in *Patterns of Intention*, with a strand of pun-driven allegory, so that even his most explicit moments remain systematically understated. I like passages like the following:

> The specific interest of the visual arts is visual, and one of the art historian's specific faculties is to find words to indicate the

> character of shapes, colors, and organizations of them. But these words are not so much descriptive as demonstrative: I am not sure how firmly we have grasped the implications of this.[2]

Of course what he means is that we mostly have no clue what we are doing when we set about saying the various things we say faced with a particular work—not just no clue about how our words attach or fail to attach to their presumed object, but why we are saying them at all, particularly in an age of mechanical and other reproduction that would seem, on the face of it, to spare us whatever need we might once have had (say, in the Renaissance) to produce words just because we could not produce the thing, and no clue perhaps most of all about how clarity about the words we produce in such circumstances might amount to a radical clarification of art history altogether. Take it this way: Baxandall's suggestion is that art historians demonstrate their objects in something like the way one might be said to demonstrate those toys called Transformers: one can describe one of these things pretty easily—"It's a truck that turns into a robot"—but demonstrating it is a different matter, a matter of making explicit how it turns and how it doesn't turn, the degrees and sites of freedom and constraint that make it be just that and nothing else. It's possible that some things intended as Transformers might turn out to be indemonstrable: you fold and unfold and flip and flop and suddenly you've got a senseless shape you can't get out of. It meant to be a Transformer, and there may even have been a truck-shape and a robot-shape within the sequence of permissible transformations, but the thing was falsified, undone, by a particular kind of failure. I suspect Transformers can't actually fail this way, but it seems to me not a bad analogy for at least one way in which putative works of art fail.

Baxandall's ostensive demonstration of works amounts to a kind of proof of them, very much, I think, along the lines Hegel standardly proposes for his kind of argument: "Philosophy has to consider an object in its necessity . . .; it has to unfold and prove the object, according to the necessity of its own inner nature. It is only this unfolding which constitutes the scientific element in the treatment of a subject" (*Aes*, Intro). Hegel, of course, eventually harnesses this somewhat peculiar sense of "prove" to a more familiar and logical construal of it, but the formulation itself seems one in which the critic catches a glimpse of his or her own activity. If Baxandall's verbal pointing can carry this kind of resonance it is at least in part because Baxandall and Hegel share an understanding of art's work as essentially thought; as Baxandall puts it, in his favored not quite theoretical idiom: "One can work the ostensiveness of one's language hard, so as to draw the hearer sufficiently into his own active act of perception for his attention to shift away from one's own. One can also shun expository sequences that look like representations of perceiving, for example descriptions, in favor of ones that assimilate themselves to thinking."

Thoughts like this are important to me as an art historian: if art history is a mode of criticism, then its objects—and its object in the larger, disciplinary sense—remains in need of proving, its or their thought not yet exhausted. By the same token, where art history cannot grasp itself as criticism, as having always this task of proof in front of it, it has, I would suggest, no object, or at least does not have the object—art—it seems to claim. It is, whether it admits or not, simply the study of visual culture (in this sense, much of the current fuss around this term has relatively little to do with the particularities of French thought of the 1960s and 1970s and everything to do with the path Panofsky laid out for art history in the United States).

Taken directly as thoughts about criticism, this view does something to move criticism out of what might otherwise seems its pure belonging to some continuously moving present in which it finds no support outside either that present's sheerest social facts or the always empty or badly formed promise of a future that will administer "the test of time." "My question," Stanley Cavell writes, pointedly bringing out the complicity of empty promise and social fact, "is: *What* will time tell? That certain departures in art-like pursuits have become established (among certain audiences, in textbooks, on walls, in college courses); that *someone* is treating them with the respect due, we feel, to art; that one no longer has the right to question their status?"

Recognizing that art history is a modality of its criticism is recognizing also that the arena of art's presence, its unfolding and proof, is always also the past, not because the past stands as its guarantee—"what counts," Cavell also writes, "as the genuine article is not *given*, but itself requires critical determination"—but because art has no other objectivity than this. This is why Baxandall calls criticism "an heroically exposed use of language" and it's also what underlies Jean-Luc Nancy's formulation, which I like very much, that "art is each time radically another art . . . but is at the same time each time all that it is." Criticism is the continuing proof of what is never given other than in time, "infinitely finished" Nancy writes.

Nancy and Cavell and Baxandall are all in agreement about what this means: that what is called for—what it takes to say what's what—is reading, an activity whose relation to both description and interpretation is, at best oblique (*Patterns of Intention* is, among other things, a sustained quarrel with Panofsky, conducted on terms only intermittently recognizable to him). It's likewise an activity uninterested in and unsecurable by any methodological guarantee, thus not in that sense an exercise of theory: here the cunning ordinariness of what Baxandall calls "plain reading" and the high post-Hegelian idiom of Derrida and Nancy go, maybe not so simply, hand in hand. That American academics may have thought Derrida and others had something other than that to offer may be reason to underline one of Baxandall's closing thoughts: "Newly professionalized and academicized activities like art criticism tend to don special authority rather fast . . ." Baxandall is inclined—it's near the heart of the motives to his systematic virtuoso irony—to think that this is reason also to refuse idioms like Nancy's, or at least to bury his awareness of them in, for example, the calculated choice to let the Renaissance Italian *commensurazione* guide him through his discussion of Piero rather than be drawn into Foucault and Lyotard and Davidson et al. on "incommensurablity," but it seems to me that the justice of this will depend in no small part on what it is you have before you. My worries start at the moment you allow yourself to think that you don't have to worry about what's before you because you have a method.

Baxandall's "plain reading" is, in any case, hardly simple and gives rise to its own, complex demands, most of which center on the ways in which we—Baxandall's readers, followers of his book—are asked to find or assume our present both as a condition for our work and a consequence of it. What remains simple about reading—even in its high theoretical modes—is that it finally claims no support apart from an experience that is, in principle, yours as well as—sometimes even over and against—say, Baxandall's. This does of course mean that you may find your experience corrigible by his—that seems to me one of the most serious things we expect criticism to do. "Publication" emerges as an interestingly key term in *Patterns*'s closing pages: it is what is entailed by the work's essential exposure, what Fried poses as the deep convention that artworks exist to be beheld. Unlike research, criticism writes not to notate its results but because writing is the actual shape of the proofs it offers. As Baxandall means the word, the accent falls on the "public" bit—on, say, how one makes out what's what by being willing to make out one's experience, testing its and your capacity for articulation and so for conversation—that's perhaps a clue to the deep relation between the critic's interest in getting about and in saying what's what.

Baxandall calls this "democratic," and I think that's right too. Of course he doesn't mean that any of this is a matter of opinion or resolvable by voting, but that democracy—presumably in general—is the willingness to demand sense of one's opinions, thus risking the discovery of their senselessness. It sounds like a good idea.

IV

I used to joke that the History of Art department at Ohio State only hired me—given my utter lack of art historical training—because they needed someone who could explain the Wexner Center, Peter Eisenman's newly built and presumably radically deconstructive or deconstructivist campus arts center. That was, of course, before I started struggling with trying to write about the thing—trying, more particularly, to say something about how it might be seriously taken as a sort of curricular intervention. There are a number of reasons why I'm doing this, but certainly mixed up in the middle of the more straightforward intellectual motivations there are a lingering bundle of real questions about what, after some dozen years, I am in fact doing at Ohio State, in the History of Art department, looking out my window at the Wexner Center.

The museum, the art school, and the university, say more particularly the department of art history, form a fairly familiar triangle. We might think of these three things as facing one another really quite directly, people regularly passing out the door of one building and entering another as they go about their business nodding in recognition to those they pass headed some other way. It doesn't, I guess, always work out exactly like that; I remember, a bit late at one party, a colleague who normally doesn't have much to say to me coming over to announce that the problem was that since Courbet the artists really haven't listened to us art historians, so there are perhaps some bits of grit in the system. But it is or has been largely a sensible and workable piece of landscaping, and it has likewise made sense that these three institutions might sit comfortably together on a university campus—knowledge and object of knowledge, practice and standards, theory and practice, all more or less smoothly opening into one another.

The Wexner Center—not only an architectural form that is certainly odd-looking and perhaps actually radical or critical, but also a *kunsthalle* rather than a museum—is in fact a disturbing presence. For one thing, you're very likely to be stopped on your way to lunch by someone trying to find the door. This is one of the many minor ways in which the terms of its conception—a game played on the different grids of campus and city—mean that it literally does not face the university it sits within. As a *kunsthalle*, it likewise seems to face more fully toward the art world in which the objects it shows for a time largely circulate than it does toward the university and its shapes of study; certainly it cannot do the job most art historians want of a campus museum, which is to be a site for real engagement with the objective givens, the given objects, of the field.

The disturbance runs both ways: it's clear that those who have to look out the Wexner's windows (this often means having to get down on one's knees, but never mind) are often puzzled by what's out there, uncertain what it wants from them or what they might have to do with it. If the Wexner is not to be the art historian's other home, is there some other intellectual or disciplinary stake it can find for itself in the university? Should it have, for example, a curatorial kind of appointment somehow aimed at intellectual or academic programming? A critic-in-residence, more or less in parallel with the artists it regularly invites in? (And what would that be, given the critic's deep desire to get about?) And what might the Wexner be to the studio program beyond a sort of animated art magazine? Or perhaps a chance for its faculty to show their work (most places of the Wexner's size and prominence don't have to worry about this one, but the building that became the Wexner was initially proposed as merely a better gallery for the art department and nothing of the difference $48 million dollars and Eisenman's involvement made was actually sorted out until the building was pretty well up and running, so there's a peculiar history still at play around these matters).

Mostly Ohio State hasn't much cared about these things—like too many other colleges and universities, it is these days overwhelmingly interested in excellence, rebranding, budget restructuring, and so on—bits of business that tend to get slowed down if you insist on worrying about curriculum, program, and things of that sort. Art education, the leading edge, in our particular stretch of terrain, of the social sciences that now order the university, is the only relevant part of the university that has had no trouble swallowing the Wexner in its capacious maw. You can't get indigestion if nothing calls for digesting.

The Wexner, I've come to feel and would like to find my way to argue, sits on the campus essentially as an unanswered demand for criticism, and its architectural overlaying of two grids awkwardly angled across and through one another might thus be read as a concrete allegory of how thought—the proving of objects—and knowledge might be put to work within and against one another, a model for an interdisciplinarity that doesn't consist in slicing the pie of the given ever finer but of asking after the relation between the object and its giving—its invention or discovery or continuity. When I say "might be read," I am pointing on the one hand to something someone like me might write and publish and so on—except that so far I don't know how to write it without its turning out to be willful and merely mine—and on the other hand to something that would have its proper and compelling publication as a curriculum, a rearticulation of the university around the Wexner's complication of its axes. Among the prominent features of such curriculum would, I think, be an insistence on the real continuity of acts of material making with the apparently more abstract business of thinking as well as a determination to renew, or at least strongly test, the still, it seems to me, unreceived promise of theory as criticism (and so also as exposed to essentially critical conditions of objectivity, of conversational and demonstrative sense).

These remarks yield no particularly strong or pointed conclusion. I suppose I've simply been trying to think a bit about critical positions—positions in criticism, positions on criticism, about the ways in which the critic is perhaps asked now to get about a bit differently and about how such critical movement might affect the practices and institutions it would then find itself variously traversing or engaging. We are now and have for some time been at a funny moment—unsure about the justification and availability of our objects, not sure what in our institutions and the larger world calls for diagnosis and what demands embrace, what's what and what's a symptom of what. My hope is that I've given a plausible picture of the terrain and of what a position for criticism might be in it.

Notes

1. Michael Fried, *Menzel's Realism: Art and Embodiment in Nineteenth-Century Berlin* (New Haven CT: Yale University Press, 2002).
2. Michael Blaxandall, *Patterns of Intention: On the Historical Explanation of Pictures* (New Haven CT: Yale University Press, 1985).

3
The Art Seminars

First Roundtable

Ballyvaughan, Co. Clare, Ireland

This conversation was held June 17, 2005, at the Burren College of Art in Ireland. The participants were: Guy Brett (London), Whitney Davis (University of California, Berkeley), James Elkins (University College Cork/School of the Art Institute of Chicago), Jean Fisher (Royal College of Art/Middlesex University), Boris Groys (ZKM, Karlsruhe), Timothy Emlyn Jones (Burren College of Art), Irit Rogoff (Goldsmith's, London), Abigail Solomon-Godeau (University of California at Santa Barbara), and Gemma Tipton (Dublin).

James Elkins: I propose we concentrate on four subjects: the forms of criticism that already exist in art history, the ways art criticism is or isn't taught, the role of judgment, and the sum of practices we might want to call "art criticism." That way our conversation can be a clear jumping-off place for the next roundtable, the one in Chicago.

I

JE: Let's begin by considering how art history, as a discipline, may also be said to be critical. There are four of us here—Abigail, Boris, Whitney, and myself—who might not mind being called art historians, and one of us—Abigail—who has had an influential critical practice and also reads in the history of criticism (especially nineteenth-century French Salons). In doing so she reads texts that were intended to be critical and have become sources for art history.

So we're invested, to varying degrees, with the possibility that art history includes criticism, and perhaps *is* critical. I'll open with an anecdote. In 1994, I was asked to write the entry for "Art Criticism" in the thirty-four-volume Grove *Dictionary of Art*.[1] (The *Dictionary* is a massive compendium of art historical facts, with entries by some 7,500 scholars.[2]) In the essay, I reviewed theories of criticism that claim all statements amount to judgments, and I remarked in passing that such a position would imply that the entire thirty-four volumes of the *Dictionary* are actually art criticism. When I got the copy-edited manuscript back for review, I noticed that sentence had been deleted. So I sent the editor a letter, saying, "There are reasons to say that, and I think it would be a good idea to keep it in." I got a nice letter back, and I put the sentence back in; but when the *Dictionary* was published, the sentence had vanished.

Now I don't mean to say this is a fair indication of the state of thinking about art criticism within art history, but it is symptomatic. This is a problem within art history—a limit of how it conceptualizes itself—and it matters for any sense of art criticism that takes account of its relation to history.

Abigail Solomon-Godeau: I would begin by saying that the existence of a *canon* in art history attests to the fact that criticism has made its way into what is ostensibly an objective, scientific discourse. Insofar as one accepts the idea that the canon is a kind of natural, organic element of art production, one obscures the fact that criticism, in the sense of making determinations of value, has already been at work. That is why it seems extremely odd to me that the sentence you wrote should have been unacceptable to the people at the Grove *Dictionary*.

Whitney Davis: I would distinguish two senses of art criticism in this regard. In art history there is a deep interest in the critical standards applied by people in the past (evaluative, descriptive, prescriptive, or phenomenological criteria that were brought by historical or traditional cultures, often very remote from us in time or place) to the assessment of works of painting, sculpture, architecture, and so on, produced in those situations. Art history must have a deep interest in such acts of criticism conducted in the past. Of course it's an open question how we would recognize the critical activities of cultural groups whose indigenous aesthetics, if you want to use that kind of terminology, would be remote from our own. (They were not affected, for example, by the Kantian analysis of the structure of judgment.) There has also been a debate over whether we can take our own critical practices and expect to find anything even remotely like them in the past. But as a working hypothesis, it has been of interest to some art historians to attempt to assess, for example, the degree to which an ancient Egyptian sculptor was making critical evaluations of one kind or another—evaluations of well-formedness, of appropriateness, and so forth. Art history must be interested in that problem, whether or not we can solve it.

There is also the nineteenth-century philological sense of criticism, of which Biblical criticism is the prime example: the clarification of evidence, sources, and contexts, which make it is possible to determine the object of study. I think it is relatively straightforward in the case of contemporary art to know what the object is—to identify the subject of critical description and evaluation. But in art historical contexts it is often unclear what the object of critical or historical analysis itself *is*. There needs to be a kind of critical clarification of that problem. Such an inquiry might use very conventional methods—iconographic, philological—but it may also require the most advanced phenomenological, hermeneutic critical activities on our part, simply to clarify what that Bronze Age site up the hill consists of, for the purposes of any further description or evaluation. That, to me, is the essential critical activity in art history.

Boris Groys: Art history is of course merely a history, and history means *story*. So art historical writing itself can always be interpreted as a fiction, as a novel—as a kind of practice.

I would like to draw our attention to what happens to art history in museums today. We think about art history as being represented in our museums by permanent collections. But the weight and value of permanent collections continuously decreases, and the value of temporary exhibitions increases, including temporary exhibitions of traditional art. Every curatorial project rewrites the interpretation of history, finds new contexts, and discovers things that were overlooked. That means that contemporary exhibition practice operates by permanent re-evaluation of the critical judgments that were formulated in the past and of the inclusions and exclusions based on these judgments. Contemporary curators also function as art critics by redefining the canon, by confirming or reversing traditional critical judgments, and by modifying the museum's strategy of display. Contemporary art historians can't help but let themselves be affected by this new fluidity of curatorial practice, rewriting the traditional art history time and again.

JE: And can't we extend this to art historical writing in general, aside from exhibition catalogs? Any book picks and chooses its subject, and in doing that it alters the available art historical narratives. The sheer bulk of writing on Michelangelo, for example, constitutes a critical act (and a curatorial act, in your sense), regardless of the content of the writing.

Perhaps this fact of merely choosing, whether it happens in museums or in art historical texts, would be a third critical function of art history, in addition to the two Whitney named.

WD: It may also be the same as Abigail's fundamental and well-taken point about canon formation in art history. The sheer directing of our attention to this work of art rather than that is ipso facto going to create a critical valuation skewed in that direction, whether or not a canon emerges in the strict sense.

JE: For me the fundamental question in regard to this third sense of criticism in art history is whether it needs to be regarded as *passive*, as an effect of the activity of art history, or whether—

WD: Well, now we're told by the so-called new art history, or postmodern poststructuralist art history, that in fact the activity of hermeneutic interpretation and judgment in art history as a critical possibility needs to be actively and self-reflectively recognized and theorized.

JE: We're *told* that, but—

WD: I'm sympathetic to that, although it is not clear to me that you can *prescribe* how to be sensitive, observant, and contextually aware, in all cultural situations. I'm not sure there's a golden rule—

JE: Exactly. One of the reasons I wanted to begin with this theme, which may seem marginal to a roundtable on art criticism, is because as art historians, we're all taught this first thing: we're instructed, as students, that we're not writing objective texts, and that neutrality is an incoherent proposition. But it seems no one knows what to *do* with that information. How might it influence what you say, or how you say it?

Guy Brett: Boris, that's a fascinating observation about temporary exhibitions, and I had never thought of it before. At the same time, the permanent collections are always being reordered in accord with the curator's point of view. Things are brought out of the storeroom, and put back on show . . .

BG: The display of art-historical canons and art historically relevant works is changing rapidly. Today almost every important work travels from one exhibition to another. Walter Benjamin wrote about this; we're constantly taking artworks out of their contexts and putting them in new ones—putting historically significant works alongside contemporary ones, for example. I think there is a precise analogy between art critical, art historical, and curatorial practices, because to rewrite history is merely to change context. Such changes alter the conditions of comparison, the conditions of time and space under which the viewer experiences the art, and finally also the historical narratives.

There is an enormous difference between traditional curatorial practices—of gradual canon formation—and the new curatorial practices, involving high-speed changes of context.

Jean Fisher: Boris, I'd like to extend that to writing. When I first thought of putting together a collection of my essays on contemporary art, I approached an editor who was assembling a series of books, but my essays were rejected because they weren't "art history," but I had thought I was doing something similar to what you mentioned in the curatorial field: that I was at an initiating point of art history, by virtue of the kinds of debates I was engaging with and the new artists I was putting into the pool of mainstream discourses. I was, I thought, reconfiguring the narrative.

Not to mention the work we were doing at *Third Text*, which, among other things, was a critique of the choices and judgments made in the "mainstream" art historical, critical and curatorial fields vis-à-vis the work of artists of non-European origins who were not recognized as making any legitimate contribution to Western art historical canons—and this despite ample evidence that modernism was a two-way street encounter between the "West and the Rest" and not the sole property of the former.

Art history should be capable of functioning as a living and transformable archive, always rich in new possibilities of interpretation, and in which the story never forms a reductive closure.

JE: It is interesting to me that curatorial practices have easy access to an awareness of this issue—it seems unproblematic to think of every new curatorial initiative as a move in the game of art history, and equally plausible to see any art critical work as an "initiating point" of some art history. In art history, I'd say we're both aware of this issue and paralyzed in relation to it: we see it, but we don't know how to act.

I will add an example at the intersection of art history and curation: Victoria Newhouse's new book, *Art and the Power of Placement*, is a study of how the placement of artworks affects their meaning. Newhouse does some fairly thorough art historical research, showing, for example, the various settings of the *Nike of Samothrace* and the *Laocöon*. But she is mainly a formalist—actually, she's a kind of interior decorator—she loves thinking about how private collectors arrange their own Picasso paintings and Giacometti sculptures. Those decisions have little to do with historical meanings—but I would never say they have *nothing* to do with historical meanings. Even shifting your Picasso painting a little closer to your Giacometti will create a tiny shift in *historical* meaning. Very tiny, and often private, but sometimes measurable.[3]

Gemma Tipton: I don't think you can dismiss Newhouse's contribution to the debate as simply "interior decoration." One of the things I thought interesting about her book was the way in which she returns consideration of some artists who are normally now only seen and understood in an institutional (museum) context, to a domestic setting, albeit in the homes of millionaires. It's a reminder of the influence of private, rather than institutional, taste in shaping collections and therefore canons.

Irit Rogoff: If you bring the curatorial to the art historical, you immediately throw things into relief. You show that art history is a theory of knowledge that is grounded in a notion of immanence. Curators have come to understand how contingent knowledge formations are. For example, if you assemble the same group of images under different titles, they will invoke very different perceptions.

That's something that a scholarly formation of knowledge can't do, and that's why talking about something like art criticism within art history becomes very difficult. All you're going to get is a sense of expanded boundaries: you'll include a bit more of this or that, become a bit more aware of this or that. But that kind of basic immanence does not shift.

WD: I agree that a doctrine of immanence or emergence, if you like, is fundamental to art history's conceptualization of art's having a history. But it's also the fact that acknowledging the very immanence of, say, cultural significance, or ethical value, or aesthetic innovativeness, as opposed to acknowledging fully emerged and positive qualities, itself requires a critical act. There is going to be no empirical, straightforward evidence coming from history to tell us that such-and-such a work in the past may or may not have had such-and-such effects, valences, possibilities, transgressions, or legitimations. The immanence of those historical phenomena requires *our* speculative, theoretical, and critical reconstruction, as an extra-positivistic act. In that function of art history, we would become theoretical in your sense, Irit: we would become theorists of the image—critics of the immanent possibilities of the past.

IR: One can juxtapose a much more contemporary notion, which is that of actualization. There's all that *stuff* in there, in history, and our task is not to trace its lineages, to link it to a kind of immanent trajectory, but to actualize it: to make it do something in the world today. What happens behind the screen is not yet known.

GT: In terms of that idea of creating contemporary links, of making works "work" in the world today, we have come up against a new issue: the increasing prevalence of temporary exhibitions that have adopted media strategies in curation, and their espousal of advertising and marketing's love of the new. Their love of the alliterative title, of the antithetical title. Often what's created as links between works don't bear a huge amount of scrutiny from art criticism or art history. Glib curatorial practices provide *seemingly* new meanings for work, or heavy-handedly impose meanings that exclude other subtler readings. Perhaps it's a new responsibility, or function, of art criticism and art history to draw back from that a bit, and say, "Just because the names of the artists in the show rhyme doesn't mean there's a connection."

BG: Or take a drastic example, Nazi art: there has still been no major exhibition in Germany that shows the art produced in the time of National Socialism in the same space as any *other* art of the twentieth century—of course including the so-called "degenerate" art—and there are also still difficulties involved in showing the official art of the GDR and West Germany from the period of the

Cold War. So-called totalitarian art is systematically excluded for political and moral reasons. The same applies to Stalinist art. I have written a book comparing Russian avant-garde art to Stalinist art production; it was shocking for many people.[4] A curatorial or critical contextualization is not simply a neutral delineation of immanent, pre-existing connections, but is rather a matter of making political, aesthetic, and moral choices.

Timothy Emlyn Jones: The difference between traditional and current curatorial practices, of which Boris spoke a few minutes ago, is very interesting from my point of view as an artist. Many of my contemporaries and those I teach want to have a place in the art historical canon, whether they get there through its gradual formation or sudden context change, and one of the ways they get there is through the art critics and curators. Therefore, it would be inappropriate just to see this as an intellectual issue—art critics and curators can be in a position of power, or at least influence. No wonder so many artists adopt a curatorial stance in their work; they want the power of self-historification. It's ironic then that so many curators seek to assert their practice as creative, sometimes in a Romantic manner that would seem odd if asserted by an artist. Each wants to be the other. Nevertheless, there is a sense in which art critics are midwives of art history, even if not the parents that some might wish to be.

GB: I was involved in a project that was simultaneously an act of curating, art history, and art criticism. (Although I'm not an art historian.)

JE: Nice to hear you deny that. And, so the audience knows, I suspect that we'll all be denying we're art critics!

GB: The exhibition was called *Force Fields*.[5] On the one hand, it was a revisiting of the kinetic art phenomenon in the 1960s; on the other hand, it disturbed the configurations in place at the time by putting together two movements that were apparently in total opposition to one another: *l'art informel* and *l'art concret*. The two had conventionally attacked one another, but I felt there was a thread connecting them despite their stylistic differences. That project was, I'd say, a combination of all three activities.

WD: Is it the case that an artist can simply entirely circumvent the mediating, publicizing, historicizing functions of the critic, and simply do it by him- or herself?

JE: That is *required* at the graduate level, but risky at the professional level.

GT: It also suggests that the critic is superfluous, perhaps even a parasite, and forgets the important level of separation from the work that a critic brings. While you can't be absolutely objective (in the sense that you are always going to have some form of a position), you do have a sort of "subjective objectivity," for want of a better way of putting it. This provides an antidote to all the material that is now written about an exhibition, by the artists, curators and publicity staff of galleries and museums. I frequently come across incredible amounts of, often densely written, cogent argumentation wrapped around an exhibition or event.

That makes it difficult to review the exhibition, because all the alibis are in place, with the result that some potential readings, perspectives and extrapolations are lost. Also some conceptual art begs such a large amount of text from the artist, that I sometimes wonder whether they should just have written a book instead. What the practice does do, however, is demonstrate the importance of words, the acknowledged influence of critical writing—even if it is from the subjects themselves.

GB: An artist might write articulately about his work, so that it seems he knows how he wishes the work to be received, but at the same time he may be longing for new insights.

BG: An artist can't immunize himself from criticism, but it is possible for him to protect himself somewhat by writing. Mondrian and Malevich are good examples. That robs the critic of the freedom to write as he pleases.

JE: On the other hand, some books, like Julian Schnabel's silly *C.V.J.*, are like pouring gasoline on the fire of criticism—they leave the artist more vulnerable than ever.[6]

AS-G: There has never been two pages of serious criticism about Julian Schnabel. That has not affected his entry into the textbooks of contemporary art. With respect to the art of the last twenty years, the absence or presence of serious criticism has not materially determined who gets into the books and who doesn't. Let's not have any illusions about the importance of art criticism in contemporary art. It's less important than the activities of galleries, corporate collections, publicists, auction houses, and so forth.

JE: There is exactly *one* page of serious criticism on Schnabel, in *Art Since 1900*. The authors force themselves, more with reluctance than with rage, to say how appalling Schnabel is, and how he takes the easy bits of modernism and presents them as postmodernism.[7]

I want to introduce one of the stranger attempts to define what counts as art criticism within art history—or rather, in this case, what counts as the boundary between art history and art criticism—and that is Michael Fried's account in the introduction to *Art and Objecthood*.[8] He has said that he recognizes art history in part by the fact that it doesn't matter how things come out: it would be acceptable if he were surprised by some discovery about a nineteenth-century artist, for example. He is, in his art history, "resolutely nonjudgmental."[9] He recognizes art criticism in part by the experience that what happens *matters*. He works both as a critic and an historian, and the place where the two practices meet is sometime in the early 1960s: when he writes about art before then, it appears as art history, and when he writes about more recent art, it's art criticism. There is an "unbridgeable gulf" between the two, and at that moment, "somewhere around 1960," the structure of time undergoes what he calls a "twist."[10] He doesn't theorize the twist—it's apparent it is grounded in personal experience, and there is no way he can proceed at that point.

Now that is an astonishingly clear analysis, but also astonishingly hard to take on board. (Not that it's meant to be taken on board—Fried only gives it to explain his own practices.) Yet it seems impossible on several counts. Can it really be a matter of indifference to you, as an historian, if an artist you're studying turns out to have done something radically at odds with the thesis you've been meaning to propose? Is there no possibility of writing criticism of recent art that works to accept unexpected changes in art? Can such a boundary between history and criticism always, or even often, be located? Can it be located often, or always, in the historian's own experience?

I offer this is as an example of how rarely, and even then how unconvincingly, the relation of criticism to historical writing has been theorized in art history, beyond the ubiquitous allowances that criticism exists always already everywhere in history.

AS-G: Fried's comment is particularly ingenuous because when he approaches his historical material he has already got the ending scripted. What he does with Courbet, Manet, or Greuze when he is wearing his art historical hat is by no means different from the story he casts for art in the period after the 1960s. In fact, it's exactly the same story. So it seems a a bit deceptive to suggest that that he's neutral about where Manet comes out in the art historical lottery but avowedly partisan when it comes to Anthony Caro.

WD: In some respects when art historians are writing about contemporary artists, and especially artists they know personally, in some strange way that we haven't put our fingers on, the interpersonal relation between the artist and critical theorist—the dialogue, collaboration—has elements that do not seem to exist in the same way that they do, for example, in the relation between an art historian and an Egyptian sculptor in the third millennium BCE.

We haven't much talked about that relation, but Fried is presumably quite sensitive to it because he worked closely and personally over a number of years with a small number of artists whose project he is trying to defend according to the historical teleology of modernism he himself has laid out in his own work as an art historian, and conversely his teleology as an art historian flows from his experience supporting those very American painters whose work interested him in the early 1960s.

IR: Fried isn't someone who is very central on my horizon. It's that old Barthes idea of lineage (so-and-so is the son of so-and-so, who begat so-and-so). The person who studies them absorbs their knowledge as if by osmosis, and comes to embody their project.

I have a different image in mind: we're all standing together in a line and looking out toward the same thing. *That's* what creates the connection. I have very little interest in the personalities of the people I work with; most of the time I may dislike them profoundly. What we share is a common set of concerns, which we're addressing very differently: but we don't embody those concerns, or become the living heritage of those concerns. That creates a mutuality, a collaboration, but not in the sense of making things together.

JE: What do you think the historical limitations of that picture might be? Could you "collaborate" with Raphael?

IR: It's an interesting possibility, but it's not something I've thought out—and I don't want to just start speaking nonsense for the sake of speaking.

JE: Oh, too bad.

BG: That idea, of "collaborating" with Raphael, was a typical practice for many art critics and historians in the nineteenth century. Collaborating with the dead by imagining what the historical figure might say or do in the contemporary situation. It can be done with incredible obsession: I have met some people in Russia who did that in the 1950s and 1960s.

JE: Ilya Kabakov, one of your friends, has been "collaborating" with an artist he invented.[11]

BG: Yes, and many people have said I'm obsessed by Kabakov! That's collaboration with the living, or with the fictional. But there are people obsessed by the dead, with whom they identify themselves. I agree with Irit: we're not in that period of thinking and feeling. At the same time, I would not exclude it as a possibility: it can come again.

JE: I like this idea of thinking about collaborations, and even "collaborations" with dead artists (and even "collaborations" with "dead" artists like Kabakov's invented artist Rosenthal) as a way of getting at what counts as criticism in art history, but I'm not convinced there's a difference. A living artist can contradict you more quickly than a Raphael can, but there may not be a deeper difference.

GT: A living artist can also respond to your critique with a shift in direction, an alteration in practice, or perhaps a more trenchant implementation of their existing project. That is not to say that the primary purpose of criticism should be to influence future works of art, but it is a possibility, every time you write something.

WD: I agree with Irit that one kind of critical practice might embody an interpersonal relation with living artists that does not tend toward identification, embodiment, or even friendship. But there are many counter-examples, right? There are many instances of art criticism and art history that flow from deep identification with the artist: there are historical and present-day examples of that. I wouldn't dismiss the validity of those kinds of equations when they emerge. They are *difficult* equations for art historians to find themselves in. We are told as art historians that building an identification with the "object" of our historical and critical analysis contaminates the possibility of arriving at certain kinds of assessments, of achieving certain historical understandings. Now I don't know if I agree with that, but there certainly seems to be a theoretical threshold over which we are not supposed to pass as art historians. Art critics might be allowed to take a step over that line if they choose to do so.

JE: I think that's well put: it's a kind of official limit to theorizing. The nineteenth century and the Renaissance, for example, were periods whose self-understanding depended on intense engagements with what they understood as their pasts, which the artists were actively trying to recapture, reimagine, or reconstruct. That means, however, that art history is *itself* a discipline that is out of its time, particularly when art historians develop that kind of embodied, "collaborative," critical relation.

WD: The imaginative project of art history today has largely shifted from the reconstruction of the immanent identities, trajectories, and teleologies of individual artists to a complementary reconstructive engagement with so-called cultural contexts or cultural systems differently construed.

JE: Yet psychologically or narratively, that can result in analogous sorts of engagements.

Well, I notice we have begun to drift from our initial subject of criticism in art history. We have sketched three models of criticism in art history but we have also begun to lose our theme. (In the first model, critics shaped the canon, as Abigail said; in the second, as Whitney observed, people in the past operated as critics; in the third, also Whitney's, there is a critical question concerning what art historians study; in the fourth, Boris's, art history is already fictional; and in the fifth, which I am assigning to Michael Fried, history is what happens when you don't care how it comes out.) But we have drifted. I want to say our inability to remain on topic is not just the ordinary drift of conversation—real philosophy, as Diderot would say—but it has something to do with what Whitney called the "theoretical threshold" that is built into art historical self-understanding. But that's for another day—and perhaps for the second roundtable.

II

JE: Our second topic is entirely different: the place of art criticism in pedagogic institutions. I don't think it's often noted that art criticism is not taught in universities: it's one of the few subjects in the humanities that can still be said to be anathema. Any medium-sized art history department will be likely to offer classes in the history of criticism—you can learn about Baudelaire, Diderot, and other moments in the history of criticism—but art criticism does not appear in those contexts as a field that leads to a practice. (Those classes are principally to train art historians.)

The absence of art criticism in universities is partly, but not wholly, explained by the perception that criticism is perceived not to possess a hierarchy of knowledge: it's thought that you can't teach a student to become a critic by taking her from one level to the next, as in all other fields recognized as such in the university.

At the same time art criticism is routinely taught in art schools (including here, at the Burren College of Art), but again not as a systematic, hierarchized subject. Instead it is taught unsystematically and idiosyncratically, according to the particular interests of the critic who is teaching the individual class.

I thought we might spend a few minutes talking about this,

because art criticism is frequently said to be "institutionalized" or "academicized," but it isn't, at least not as those expressions are usually meant. Its exclusion from humanities programs is tremendously interesting, because exclusion of any kind is unusual in this period of interdisciplinarity and continuously reconfigured fields of study.

WD: I wonder if there aren't counter-examples: degree-granting programs that produce art critics.

JE: There are: in Frankfurt there's Daniel Birnbaum's program at the Städelschule, and at the Art Institute in Chicago we're trying to teach criticism in a systematic way—we offer a sequence of graduate-level classes in History of Art Criticism, Theory of Art Criticism, and Practices of Art Criticism.[12] But those are art schools. Examples in universities are rare.

AS-G. There's Stony Brook.[13]

JE: Yes, although that's an eccentric example, because it has an art-school orientation even though it's nominally a university. There are other counter-examples; New York University does elements of criticism as well, and you could enlist Visual Studies curricula at places like Rochester and Irvine.

JF: Middlesex University has thought about creating an MA in Art Criticism, but then the university has some responsibility in considering what job opportunities are open to such graduates. Aside from journalism, art writing is an independent and freelance practice, for obvious reasons, and unlike art history or curating doesn't find salaried positions. I want to emphasize that writing is a practice; and in *Third Text* we started a review section precisely as a space for younger writers to practice. Rather than academic courses in criticism I might prefer to see residencies and bursaries for writers like those for artists that would enable them to do more thorough independent research.

But I'd like to ask: what kind of knowledge does art criticism actually involve and produce?

GB: Why can't we have a discipline that's not taught? A discipline that's self-taught?

JE: That's an incendiary opinion from a university standpoint!

GT: I agree with Guy, that we shouldn't necessarily worry about the absence of criticism in universities. One of the exciting things about criticism is the plethora of forms and modes it takes: it's not hammered down; you can travel and respond to new things, and it's not academicized. By that I mean it isn't fixed within the value-systems and hierarchies of academia.

TJ: Within the growing research culture of art schools, and the positioning of art research within the wider university context, criticism is taking on a new position within students' learning. Increasingly, students are expected to become self-theorizing, working with a new paradigm of intelligent, inquiring practice in which theory and practice are fused or unified. Art students have always been expected to be self-critical, but now they are expected to methodologically reflective too. This is a huge step away from the atelier approach. When faculty are no longer regarded primarily as instructors but as researchers—the senior researcher in a kind of supervisory partnership with the junior researcher who is the student—the idea of education as the transmission of knowledge and skill goes out the window. It is a different power relationship and a more facilitating one. There is a sense in which students are encouraged to become self-taught. That's the case if the pedagogical model is one of inquiry.[14]

WD: I'm still not sure of the nature of the question. Is it asking why, in universities, where it's possible to get degrees in chemistry or biology, you can't also get a degree in art criticism? Supposedly that doesn't happen, and we wonder why. So you're not asking about the emergence of art criticism as a practice that may be more or less professionalized and taught within art schools?

JE: In my experience in art schools, art criticism is always taught in some form, but the *way* that it is taught doesn't seem to be exportable into university settings as a field, or a free-standing program. It often does occur as a single class, taught by a visiting critic or a studio instructor with an interest in the subject. But it does not exist as a structured field. I don't necessarily want to get art criticism into universities. I'd like to know why it doesn't exist as a discipline or a field, because I suspect the answer to that question might illuminate how art criticism *is* taught in art schools, and ultimately why it appears to us as a series of disparate practices (that's our fourth and last subject today).

BG: In Germany and Austria, I have been involved in long discussions on this subject. The answer was generally that we don't have a canon of contemporary art, so we don't know what we have to study. And we also don't have a canon of contemporary art criticism. Both canons have to be established before the study of art criticism can be institutionalized.

My argument in those discussions (which was, I'll admit, ineffective) was that the *mechanisms* of contemporary art, rather than the results, could be a field of academic knowledge. How would a contemporary artist or art writer situate themselves in the context of the contemporary art world? What roles do critics, curators, and others play in the establishment of artists? Instead of studying works and canons, we would study processes and strategies.

GB: When I said "self-taught," of course, I did not mean people should teach themselves: I meant it's more an experiential process. You're taught, but not held in an academic system. You can navigate your way through a learning process, by talking to artists, reading, going to shows.

JE: There is an example of art criticism being taught in a systematic way, and that is the field Tim and I are interested in—the PhDs in studio art. There, the PhD dissertation is meant to be comparable in its rigor, its level, and its accomplishments, to dissertations in other fields. But the PhD in studio art is an emergent, quickly changing practice, and the standards for PhD-level art critical writing (in this case, writing the student-artist produces about her own work) has not yet been theorized. The people who supervise the students' PhD dissertations are typically their studio instructors, who have no special knowledge of art criticism as a field—because, I'd say, knowledge of that sort does not exist. There are no major texts, no brilliant essays on the subject that the supervisors can consult.

In academia, there are any number of writings about what constitutes non-fiction writing, and what might be regarded as "literature" or "philosophy," and all of that could be apposite.[15] But it hasn't yet been brought to bear.

JF: I'd like to point out that in the British colleges I am familiar with, supervision of PhDs in studio practice is not conducted by studio instructors alone (many of whom in any case now have doctorates), but in collaboration with an appropriately informed art historian or theorist in the academic group. Artists use art history, or more properly, artworks of the past, as a resource as well as philosophy, literature or pop culture, and much else besides, but not necessarily in any systematic way.

So it is, indeed, a very open and uncertain field that may gain more clarity as our experience of it deepens. So for the moment I try to instill a critical attitude toward whatever it is the students are researching and an ability to discuss their work in terms of the discourses that seem appropriate. However, being critically aware about one's practice is not the same as functioning as a practicing art critic; which is not to say that artists can't be effective writers about art—the reputation of *Artforum* was founded on artists' analytic writings.

TJ: There is a great deal of ground to be won, finding methodology appropriate to fine art, and methodology that is not borrowed from some other field and used in a distorted form. As you say, there aren't precedents. But that's a great opportunity. I supervised a dissertation that involved a great deal of research, but the student eventually opted to show the work with a shorter supporting text; she drilled through the dissertation and attached nuts and bolts so I could not open it. It is lodged in the library, not to be read. I happen to know the content, and it's a very powerful document.

JE: I've also had that experience. My student welded an iron frame around a book he had been working on, so I could not open it.

GT: But what you're talking about is something different from the academization of art criticism; you're talking about artists being trained to write about their own work, of finding ways of framing possible responses to their work. And as we discussed earlier, it's a strategy that's useful to learn, but not always successful, particularly when it's overdone. These artists may go on to practice critical writing about other artists' work: that is a different issue. It's also interesting that artists who seal their texts in the way your student did (or drill holes in their volumes, or paint over the words, or render them illegible in other ways) are demonstrating an ambivalence to the influence of words on the processes as well as products of art making.

TJ: The student I'm referring to decided to distance herself from her writing so that the work she presented for the PhD should appear as an exhibition might. But the pattern of formation of her work was innovative—the critical dimension is within the formation of the work: it is intrinsically intelligent practice, which is *such* a shift from just a few decades ago, when many an artist would just grunt and shuffle and try to look profound. Gemma is right, that this is different from the academicization of art criticism, but in my view this hybridization of artist and critic has the potential to change how we understand art criticism, and in what way it might be academicized.

WD: I don't have a fully worked-out answer to your question, but two thoughts.

First, a philosopher goes to graduate school and gets a PhD in philosophy not in order to be employed as a philosopher in the public square, spouting philosophy to whomever will listen. People get PhDs to teach other people. It's a self-sustaining, self-fulfilling academic operation. Why would somebody who had an interest in art criticism—that is, engaging in art being made in the public arena, engaging with artists, working in national or international contexts—why would they want to study art criticism in order to teach people in the academy, who would teach other people in the academy, about the possibility that one of them might go out into the public to become an art critic?

Second, critical theory exists in the academy as a massively legitimated operation. We may or may not want to make a distinction between art criticism and critical theory, but certainly critical theory exists as a field: there are many interdisciplinary programs in which a series of well-known, almost canonically legitimated texts, running from Nietzsche, Adorno, and Benjamin forward to their poststructuralist iterations, is consumed by hundreds of students annually, from undergraduate courses all the way to PhD courses. It's an enormous operation. It may well be that the functions of art criticism, theater criticism, restaurant criticism, have somehow been intellectually absorbed by the claims of that sort of operation. If you've read Adorno, you're ready to be an art critic.

JE: To the second point, I'd say that is one of the reasons why it is so interesting that art criticism has not developed in this way. The material is all there to be used, and it's the major opportunity and temptation for the PhDs in studio art.

I guess what I'd say about the first point is that the analogy isn't exact. Philosophers, to take the "average" case, do normally intend to teach other philosophers. But then there's the moment when they assemble their ideas, and try to put together their big book, their original contribution. That would be the analogue to the purposes of critics.

IR: Whitney, I think that's a uniquely North American model of education, that we're educating people at the level of postgraduate research, so that they become academics. The possibilities of employment for those people are gone, and they will probably never return. My experience at Goldsmith's is that the people who come for the PhD are practicing artists, who want to take a break and re-assess their practice. At Goldsmith's we have a large number of such students, and I'd say ninety percent are people who have come back from the art world after having been professionally active, because they need the space, and because the model of being an artist as a person who works alone in his studio and then exposes work in the public sphere has been largely abandoned. The model that is emerging is collaborative. Most are not training to be anything: they are trained. They are shifting gears.

BG: I am absolutely for the academization of art criticism in the university. But a advocatus diaboli argument is that it's unfair to ongoing art critical practices, because every new academization involves creating privileged positions. Academization makes every field less free. The new PhDs in studio art will result in artists who are trained in criticism and those who aren't, and we will have produced a new kind of inequality. I'm not against it, in fact. But if we do it, if we introduce this new inequality, we will be faced with some new critical choices, which is exactly what academics don't want to do. Not being willing to do that, to take responsibility, academics exclude art criticism.

WD: Boris is drawing attention to a contradictory situation: the responsibilities that come to an art critic raise precisely the evaluative responsibilities that a certain official ideology of the academy says the academy must withdraw from, if not abdicate.

JE: Yes, that's very well said. The whole issue of the PhD in studio art that Tim and I are interested in is very challenging, because it raises these fundamental issues of the academy's sense of itself. Art criticism as a field, as a teachable subject, is a virus: first it infects the "academization" of criticism, then it spreads to graduate instruction, and to the PhD, and finally it elicits an antibody reaction from the university.

I want to mention one last reason why art criticism is not taught in universities. This one is a bit ruder: it has to do with what happens when you sit in a seminar with postgraduate students and try to pay serious attention to a text of journalistic art criticism. A strange thing happens: you read and read, and you get nothing. I've had this experience in Chicago, where I teach, for example, Paul Goldberger—an architectural critic who gets wide play, and is more or less a popular spokesman for architectural criticism. He is not only a newspaper journalist; he also writes for the *New Yorker*. I've had the experience of reading his texts, taking say an hour for a two-page text—not an unusual speed, in general terms, for a close reading—and being almost at a loss to extract any proposition at all from the text.

There are also critics like Dave Hickey, who has a huge following among art students: if you try to read his texts in that way, he would be the first one to say you won't get anything out of them. They work differently: they have a rhetorical or enabling, permission-granting function that is not legible to close reading. (That is one reason he gets ill-treated in the *October* roundtable on art criticism, which we'll be talking about later.) A close reading succeeds only in extracting an enormous list of the number of times he's contradicted himself in the space of a few pages.

GT: The architectural criticism example is probably unfair; I have yet to read any really good contemporary architectural criticism. It's still grounded in description and formalism, and is only just beginning to develop strategies that respond to architecture in more affective ways.

WD: Where is the pressure coming from for the establishment of university programs in art criticism?

IR: I'll give you an example. In the extremely impoverished British educational system, we're always looking for outside funding sources. A well-known gallerist in London suggested to me that he put together a consortium of galleries, and give us a scholarship for a PhD in art criticism. I went back to my colleagues and proposed this, and they said, no way! It goes against the grain of the way we're thinking, and that is that there has to be a critical perspective on culture, and that the people coming out of our programs are critically well-educated to face culture. Its academization too, something that responds only to art goes against the grain. But we thought, it's idiotic to give up this money! And we sat there for three weeks, trying to think of a devious way to accept the offer, but we couldn't and in the end we said, no thank you.

JE: Whitney, I don't think there's any student or administrative pressure in or on universities for the creation or adoption of programs in art criticism. Sometimes there's pressure to have a critic in the university—that's been "solved" recently at the University of Chicago and Northwestern University, with the hires of Matthew Jackson and Lane Relyea, respectively—but not to implement a new field of study. To me, that's an opportunity to reflect on art criticism as a subject: from the university point of view, to ask what counts as a subject in the humanities; and from the art-school point of view, to put pressure on the very idiosyncratic, unaccountable ways art criticism is in fact taught.

GT: When I think of universities, part of me thinks of wonderful places where you can pursue your interests, work with your academic heroes, be inspired. But another part of me thinks of the Masons and Opus Dei; of sequestered places that draw you into their webs of patronage. Your student goes to Cambridge, yours to Berkeley, yours to Yale, and you all appoint one another and go to one another's conferences. Then there is the example of the academization of curatorial practice, which is now leading to the exclusion of many young, self-taught curators from our institutions. The idea that art critics would disappear into that system is deeply disturbing to me.

III

JE: Let's move on to the third topic for today, which is also arguably the most important undecided issue in art criticism: the place of judgment. I would like to try to structure our conversation by bringing in three pieces of evidence in turn. The first is a brief text—a bar chart, actually—from a book called *The Visual Art Critic*, which records the results of a poll of the top two hundred art critics of the United States, chosen according to the circulation of their newsmagazines, alternative weekly papers, or daily newspapers.[16] To the question "How much emphasis do you place on the following aspects of criticism?" the respondents ranked what matters in their practice according to five criteria. The top answer, rated most important by sixty-two percent of the respondents, was "providing an accurate, descriptive account of the artwork or exhibition": in other words, evoking or describing, rather than judging. The second most popular answer was "providing historical and other background information," which is, to some approximation, what art history does. The third answer was "creating a piece of writing with literary value," in other words, writing well. (I think that is an unobjectionable goal, but it doesn't help define art criticism.)

That leaves the two least-popular categories: number four, "theorizing about the meaning, associations and implications of the work" (in rough terms, art theory), and, at the bottom of the list, rated highly by only twenty-seven percent of respondents, is "rendering a personal judgment or opinion about the work." That last and least popular purpose to art criticism is, in fact, what criticism *was* for much of its history. So it seems statistically unimpeachable that most popular art critics, in the United States at least, conceive their purpose as something other than judging art.

AS-G: I think there is an immediate problem when we scramble together the categories of arts journalism and art criticism, because I do not think they are the same thing. So being asked to respond to the statistical breakdown in this particular report means being asked to ignore what can be considered a crucial distinction between two very different kinds of art writing. Is arts journalism really the same as art criticism?

JF: I agree. You're talking here about a range of genres I am not involved with, and can't comment on, although I have done the occasional press release—but that was publicity, not analysis. Is reportage criticism when the writer is not trained in looking at art, especially when the art concerns cultural difference? There has been an assumption that in art, as in politics, everyone is an "expert" and entitled to opinions; but opinions aren't "truths," or even informed judgments, because what are the criteria of judgment—one might even say here prejudices—being applied? Nowhere is this more starkly foregrounded than in the recent history of criticism in relation to cultural difference. One of the criteria in thinking about genres is to ask who is being addressed, and what their expectations may be.

At *Third Text* we were well aware that our primary readership were those folks who already had a vested interest in raising issues of racism and postcoloniality in art and culture, which, when *Third Text* began in 1987, were marginal, if not actually antagonistic to mainstream critical and curatorial concerns. I am ever mindful of the fact that black British artists emerging in the early 1980s had to be their own curators and writers because, unlike various artists' groups in the history of Western modernism, there was no informed or interested peer group of historians, collectors, curators, or critics to provide their work with a discourse.

This is one area in which art history has to confront itself as an unfinished and poorly conceptualized project.

BG: For a long time, art criticism was about judgment: it was understood as the ability of some specialist in art, a *connoisseur*, to make a judgment about art based on something like enlightened common sense and educated taste. That was a very Kantian attitude, and so I'd call it *Kantian criticism*. Today, Thierry de Duve even says that the distinction between art and not-art requires a judgment in this Kantian sense.[17]

But I think we are increasingly confronted with a different kind of attitude, which I will call *phenomenological criticism*. It has its roots in Hegel, Husserl, and Heidegger, and also Derrida and many other French philosophers of approximately the same generation influenced by phenomenology. It is about drawing attention to the artwork, exposing the artwork to the spectator by the means of a discourse, using the discourse to make the artworks visible in a certain light—in the same way that an artist, using for example a ready-made, brings certain things to visibility, exposes certain things to the spectator. Actually the curator does the same. Artist, curator, and critic collaborate in making things visible, bringing them into the focus, making them open to an experience that is not simply a pragmatic and instrumental.

Let me propose that there are two codes in reacting to artwork. The first is a traditional, nineteenth-century schema. One judges the work is either positive or negative, yes or no—the critical judgment functions here as an electrical discharge between plus and minus. But in our time we operate by a different, digital code, in which the option is either one or zero. One, we expose the artwork by a discourse; zero, we don't. The zero option is a decision—a political, aesthetic, and ethical decision—to overlook an artwork, to let it remain in obscurity, in concealment. That is where *real* decisions take place. To mention something, to bring it to exposure, or to withhold it from attention. For me that is an important change in the politics of art criticism, and I experience it every day in my own practice.

GB: There obviously is a distinction between art criticism in art journals, and newspaper art criticism. I've written in both: but I think I write in the same way whether I write in a newspaper or in a scholarly journal. I assume an average, curious viewer and reader. I try to do all the things that appear in that list, Jim: I try to link the work with other forms of experience, I try to write well, I try to describe it adequately . . .

JE: And you theorize.

GB: Sorry?

JE: That's the fourth one, theorizing.

GB: Well, I'll pass over that one. I don't know if what I write deserves the name theory. And the fifth purpose, judgment: I don't say I condemn this work, or approve of that one, but I accept there's a judgment implicit in all writing. And I've tried on the role of newspaper critic, the one who explicitly judges. I abandoned that because I came to think that the amount of space devoted to an artist is more important than what is actually said about the artist in the review. I decided not to write about artists who were already famous, whether I was for them or against them. I tried instead to bring overlooked work to people's attention.

JE: In that respect you moved, in Boris's terms, from an implicit form of "electrical" Kantian judgment to an explicit form of "digital" phenomenological judgment.

I would like to add, because it's part of our problematic, that the kind of writing documented in *The Visual Art Critic* does leach into more "serious" venues. *Artforum* is full of descriptive, neutral, evocative, nonjudgmental writing, in its brief reviews and in many of its essays, and so is *Kunstforum*, and any number of the hundred-odd national magazines of art around the world. I don't think there's a line to be drawn.

GT: I am really surprised that judgment is even an issue. I can't understand how one can believe themselves to be writing about something without judgment being implicated. It's there fundamentally in your choices of words, of emphases, of going to a particular exhibition, and then of electing to write about it at all. And if you don't acknowledge that, and pretend you're neutral, you are in a sense cheating the reader. If you allow people to follow how you came to your judgments, they can accept or reject them:

but it's not doing your job to pretend you have no position, or to refuse to come to a conclusion about what you're seeing.

WD: It is striking that only twenty-seven percent of these critics place a strong emphasis on rendering judgment. I agree with Abigail that clearly there is a distinction between what is happening in this journalistic context and art criticism in a broader, deeper sense, but nevertheless we would have to count these newspaper art writers at some level as performing one of the traditional functions of art criticism, and therefore it is in itself striking that even in the place where you would expect to find quick, categorical, relatively untheorized or decontextualized aesthetic or other kinds of judgments being made, that even there, in that arena, people are backing off and putting the making of judgments as the lowest possible priority.

I don't have a good explanation of that, but one might imagine that there is a crisis of judgment more broadly, right? It's not only in the arts that pressure mounts against the rendering of judgments, whether those judgments are categorical, political, moral, social, or aesthetic. It becomes increasingly difficult in an ideologically polarized society to argue for, or stand up for, certain kinds of things, and so it's not surprising that people find it increasingly challenging. Only some people will have, as it were, the kind of intellectual, political, or ethical fortitude to try to accomplish that given the current climates of opinion.

As Boris says, the nature of judgment has also shifted. There is classical aesthetic judgment in Thierry de Duve's sense, which asks, "Is this a good aesthetic experience?" Whether an experience is an experience of a work of art or not now calls for an ontological judgment about art as such: "Is this a work of art?" Those are two different kinds of judgments, and it may be that people are backing away from the classical aesthetic judgment and drawing nearer to the ontological judgment. I don't know, because the survey does not differentiate judgments in de Duve's sense.

AS-G: In saying that critics—so-called critics, art journalists, whatever we call them—are backing off from determinations of quality, of judgments of art as good or bad, we might also consider the institutionalization of the notion of pluralism as determining the field of contemporary art. The received wisdom is that there is no longer any dominant style, anything goes, let a thousand flowers bloom . . . that kind of not very interesting thinking about contemporary art *is* the doxa in the United States.

JE: I think the reasons for the shift away from judgments, in this group of critics, is a complicated issue. I have seven possible explanations in the pamphlet.[18] Briefly, I think there are academic and non-academic reasons. The academic reason, as both of you say, has to do with pluralism, coupled with a certain relativism.

The non-academic answer, the one that comes from the journalists polled in the survey, is that their readers are so unfamiliar with modern and contemporary art that they *need* to simply describe the work, in order to generate the enthusiasm that would help create a public.

We would then have a choice. We could accept the testimony of the people working in newspapers—we judge our public, and therefore we decide not to judge—or else we could say that what I called the academic explanation (the combination of institutions and philosophic positions that creates a damping pluralism) is itself responsible for what happens in newspapers, that the journalists are influenced, at several removes perhaps, by thinking that goes on mainly in universities.

BG: Today, if I write an article with negative judgments on a certain artistic work, I bring that work into focus, and that neutralizes the effect of the negative judgment. In today's media, a negative text is the best compliment to the artist. The artist then becomes an important, misunderstood, and rejected figure in a well-known tradition of *artiste maudit*, and therefore even more interesting. Kantian criticism is therefore simply ineffective nowadays.

It is much better simply not to mention art you don't like, and which you don't want other people to like. Just overlook the artist in a strategic way. Art criticism has always been an agonistic practice, and you have to have your strategy; phenomenological criticism is just more effective as a strategy.

AS-G: The range of writing about contemporary art, from the level of daily journalism through exhibition catalog texts and art magazines, provides few examples of *critical* critical writing. Everything ends up being implicitly about advocacy, even, to take your example, the occasional bad review of an artist. When you write a catalog essay, you're obviously not going to write something critical, let alone negative. For one reason or another, what was originally understood as a critical task *precludes* the possibility of critique: it just doesn't exist anymore.

BG: Abigail, you can also make critical judgments in the way I propose by putting works in certain contexts. For example, you can connect them with certain ethical or political positions, thus directing the reader's gaze toward the aspects of an artwork that make this work problematic, controversial, or naïve.

GT: My problem with your strategy, Boris, is that you're never going to be able to cover everything you endorse, and therefore those works will automatically be categorized with things you don't like, things you're giving the zero to by not mentioning. Your position isn't valuative enough.

BG: Of course not. But you know, our life is finite. We can't endorse everything we'd like to: if we could, we would be divine, and our life would be infinite. That's why art criticism is a kind of politics. It is also part of the realm of injustice.

JE: I love the idea that life is too short to be silent about everyone you don't like. Boris, your idea is compatible with Guy's notion that fame is directly proportional to the column-inches per week that mention an artist. Its inverse, your phenomenological zero, means an equal number of nonexistent columns need to be allocated for everyone whom you wish not to privilege.

IR: The notion of judgment is deeply alien to the way I think. I'm pondering the possibility of adopting Boris's strategy by ignoring it! I was thinking, though, that one might shift sideways into a sense of actualization. I remember what Kenneth Tynan wrote in that famous review of John Osborne's *Look Back in Anger*; he said, "I refuse to be friends with anyone who has not been deeply affected by this play." A German art critic friend of mine said of Denys Arcand's *The Decline of the American Empire*, "I won't be friends with anyone who doesn't value this."

I was thinking that this is actually a wonderful way of being a critic in the world. It isn't the Olympian notion of judgment—this is good, or bad, or ineffective, or whatever—it's a way of saying, "This is *so* important that it becomes a kind of tool for navigating, for differentiating between things in the world." It's always more interesting to try to say what a thing makes possible, than to try to say what it is.

JE: But one of the critics polled in *The Visual Art Critic* might say to you, "But my review—even my judgment—*does* make things possible. That's *how* things become possible." In other words, judgment is never just saying what the thing is anyway.

JF: For me, making judgments about artworks is not viable if by this is meant value judgments that primarily serve market interests. There are more interesting questions one can ask *of* art. What is art's relation, now, to the social sphere? How does this work enlarge my perception of reality? We all live with socio-political questions, shared questions, but perhaps art asks the questions that we haven't yet thought to ask! In which case what art does as engendering a process of thought is more interesting to write about than what it is as an "art object" as such. The "object" is art insofar as it functions as the trace of thought linking experience to world.

WD: There seems to be an assumption in the survey that judgment is a matter of taste. "I like this," "This gives me pleasure," and so forth. That would be a very primitive judgment to apply to art, and Kant himself did not say that. It would be a starting-point, or one of the moments of aesthetic or political judgment, which would pass through the judgment of taste toward winning the assent of others. It would be a misconstrual of the judgment of art that it could be stated *as* a judgment of taste.

It may be a sign of the maturity of art criticism that it can escape pure judgments of taste, and work its way through the phenomenology, the ethical and political effectiveness, and the contextuality of the work. Insofar as judgment retreats to a judgment of taste, it has abdicated its own philosophic possibility.

JE: I agree; I think some questions in *The Visual Art Critic* are posed as judgments of that restricted sort. But I wonder how far we can escape from the problems posed by the reticence to judge by saying we are more concerned with, say, shared questions about art's work in society. Those are also judgments, and not just phenomenological markers of interest.

JF: Of course as a writer I make choices about which pathways to follow when thinking about a certain art practice, but these are dictated more by the nature of the practice and my horizon of knowledge than by any prescribed mode of aesthetic judgment. On the other hand, I willfully make judgments about the *context* of art as a site of cultural politics, which was central to my engagement with American Indian–US relations. My critical and curatorial collaborations with Jimmie Durham in the mid-1980s were deliberate strategies toward to making visible contemporary native art practices, *not* because of their exclusion from the art world, but to get the sociopolitical conditions of American Indians on to an international cultural agenda where the American Indian Movement had failed in real politics. We may not have had much success in this respect, but Durham has emerged as an inspirational model for a younger generation of native artists and writers, who see in his position the possibility for indigenous voices to enter into an international dialogue. So something was achieved.

What art makes possible is the potential for a new configuration of reality, or an expansion of thought. I see the writer's task as drawing on this configuration and making connections with complementary strands of thought. Art is a practice closer to philosophy than to art history insofar as it enquires about the relation between human and world; and it speaks to its time, which compels the writer to address its context.

GB: I think judgment is important to me, because the word *judge* is linked to the word *justice*. The artworld is full of huge injustices. My sense of judgment might be directed at combating hype and inflated reputations.

GT: I'm still dismayed by the idea that opinion and criticality can't be linked, and that you can consider yourself a critic but not feel compelled for form a judgment. Not in the basic terms of the judgment of taste, Whitney, but in the wider sense of the terms the artwork presents, and how it creates new possibilities for understanding.

AS-G: I guess what disturbs me about the idea that once a critic is involved in valuation, it comes down to a question of taste, is that this precludes a certain form of polemical criticism which need not be concerned with particular artwork or particular artists. I speak in this instance as a feminist: a critical piece of writing is necessarily an intervention, and the world being what it is, it is more often than not in the denunciatory mode. That includes what you were calling "injustices," Guy. It's not just an issue of individually inflated reputations, but of systematic occlusions and marginalizations—all the apparatus of business-as-usual in the artworld, including intellectual and discursive structures themselves, which require the interventionary, the denunciatory, the polemical. Those issues should not be equated with judgments of taste.

BG: I think if you want to be political, and I think we all want to be—

AS-G: Do we? All of us?

BG: Hmm, I think yes, more or less. Because to be involved in art criticism is to be engaged in a certain kind of politics. If we're not art historians, and we intervene in the contemporary scene, it must be dictated by some political interest. It's a question of temperament.

So we have also to look at journalism, and at how the public is influenced. A while ago there was an enormous show of Julian Schnabel's work in Germany, and afterward there was a huge TV program on him. It was wholly negative, very critical. But all my acquaintances who were not art insiders said, "He must be the most important artist working today, because he had such a critique on television." If you experience that, you cannot be blind to it.

AS-G: I am not talking about critiques of individual artists, but institutional critique, structures of sexism and racism, and homophobia. The kind of activist, interventionist criticism that is being obscured in our discussion is not about denouncing a particular artist.

BG: Almost every artist I know wants to be critical. So what should an art critic do if the art itself is critical? In this situation, the sense of criticism is entirely different. It is not the artist any more who is the object of a critical evaluation, of a critical judgment. Instead, we *join* the artist, we support his or her critical attitude toward the society. In this sense criticism has a completely different direction: It is directed not toward art in the name of society but toward the society in the name of art. Actually, I completely support this kind of criticism.

IR: Because you share the same conditions as the artist: you're both citizens in the same culture. There were, for example, some tremendously interesting developments in Documenta X and Documenta XI, some tremendous paradigm shifts in the understanding of what is possible, and I do not think criticism has yet caught up with them.[19]

AS-G: I see no problem with critical collaboration, especially if one defines oneself as an oppositional voice, a critical voice. There is then no reason not to enter into these relations of partisanship or collaboration. Fine, no problem. But for all the very interesting and gratifying aspects of Documenta X and Documenta XI, women artists were, of course, marginalized. In Documenta X there were seventeen percent women artists, and in Documenta XI it was worse. (I always count the names of women artists. It's very old-fashioned, but I still do it.) So you can say a paradigm shift might have occurred, but women are still marginalized, in the Documentas as in the Museum of Modern Art. It's too easy to say, "We don't have to deal with these kinds of things because there have been paradigm shifts, and everything has changed." I think that argument needs defending.[20]

IR: I would not argue with you. Women were marginalized. But the question is: what is the relation between what doesn't take place, and what does take place?

AS-G: Was that the paradigm shift?

IR: I don't want to give a lecture about the two Documentas. I believe they were paradigm shifts, and they did include certain marginalizations. But you can't stay with the same demands and terms all the time. They have to be tinkered with continuously. *That*, to me, is critical activity. You have to rethink the political efficacy of your beliefs. The critical debate does not say, "these criteria override everything." It says, "these are emergent paradigm shifts that are taking place: what kinds of new relations can we write among them?"

WD: I think I'm very skeptical of the notion that something one might call a paradigm shift occurs in a couple of international art exhibitions, where many of the central geopolitical and socio-economic structures, intellectual and institutional, racial, ethnic, sexual structures, remain essentially the same. Like Abigail, I'm very concerned with the seeming absence of the possibility of an activist, necessarily judgmental criticism. Perhaps it's been replaced by what you're calling *criticality*, Irit—that is, a kind of horizon of openness to these kinds of possibilities, but seemingly without the evaluative moment. I can't speak about this from the point of view of a feminist criticism, which has worked for twenty years to find new possibilities, but I will state it from a queer-theoretical perspective. It concerns me very much. In the name of a certain kind of pluralism, which is sustained by a certain critical theory, certain possibilities of critique—the Kantian sense of self-critique, ideological critique, and activist critique in Abigail's sense—have been eroded, if not foreclosed. I am not saying this is due to the emergence of a critical theory that is in line with neo-liberal pluralism, but it's a suspicion that I have. Progressive ideological critique has been undermined by the alignment of neo-liberal pluralistic politics and critical theory that has tailored itself to the social reality of the academy, the art world, progressive politics in some general sense. I'm not sure of this, but I'm worried about it.

IR: I think there are activist politics everywhere you look. What they are *not* is identity politics. Several generations of identity politics have brought us to a place where we understand that identity is constituted from so many places that it cannot be reassembled under singular identities. Activism has widened.

WD: I am the last to suggest that political activism reduces to identitarianism. I have never argued that, I've never written that, I am not claiming that. I agree that there has been a tradition of identification between identitarian politics and certain traditions of criticism in the last twenty years or so. Perhaps that landscape has indeed changed.

JE: All our deflections in this conversation are interesting. In this case I'm intrigued by our seamless transition from the apparent lack of judgment in journalistic criticism to an apparent lack of judgment in the most sophisticated, contemporary collaborative criticality. But I would like to leave it at that for the moment.

Let me interpolate the second of the three texts pertaining to judgment. It is from your essay, Irit.[21] The passage proposes a simple, three-part schema, and it introduces an historical dimension into our discussion, which I think we need. Here's the passage: "It seems to me that within the space of a relatively short period we have been able to move from criticism to critique to criticality—from finding fault, to examining the underlying assumptions that might allow something to appear as a convincing logic, to operating from an uncertain ground which while building on critique wants nevertheless to inhabit culture in a relation other than critical analysis . . ."

I propose we consider this as an historical schema. In that case, *criticism* could be identified with the straightforward giving of judgment—let's say judgment in any of the forms Whitney enumerated—and in particular criticism could be identified with modernism. *Criticism*, in this sense, is the identification of the critical enterprise with judgment.

Critique would be the moment when the critic understands her purpose as the interrogation of her own assumptions regarding judgment—the assumptions that would make judgments plausible. That corresponds extremely well with something Rosalind Krauss wrote in 1981 and then repeated a number of times: it's a moment identified with postmodernism.[22] The claim was that criticism, as it had been understood, no longer had interest, and that a critic's purpose was to try to understand what led her to the moment when she felt that her response to a work could be written as a judgment. That has always been a very problematic position, and I don't think it has ever received a thorough critique. I also think it *and* the modernist project are still operative.

Irit, you give *criticality* as your third option. Would you mind expanding on that a little?

IR: What fascinated me was that within the twenty years I've been working, we have moved very rapidly from one of these to the next. And I agree, they all happen together: they aren't an historical sequence in the sense that one replaces another.

What my colleagues and I are trying to do is think of criticality as a situation in which one is fully theoretically armed—we have this vast structuralist, poststructuralist, feminist, postcolonial critical armature with which we can see through things and understand the assumptions on which they are based. On the other hand, we are fully implicated in the lived conditions of which we're a part. Hanna Arendt said it very beautifully: we're fellow sufferers. Criticality describes this double condition: you both acknowledge the condition in which you are embedded, and you see through it in a critical and theoretical way. Criticality is also in the present, and it's active.

JE: It's performative.

IR: It allows us to introduce the performative as an important way to understand contemporaneity. This notion that culture is not necessarily archivable, and may not be subject to historicizing impulses.

(By the way, criticality isn't a particularly good term, and we're looking around for other terms. It's easily misunderstood.)

JE: The reason I brought in your text, Irit, is to consider how we might extend our conversation into a history of criticism. Since Michael Newman couldn't make it to our roundtable, we have not explored this as much as we might, but I want to open this subject for the second roundtable. I would say that the three initially historical moments of your schema are also all living practices, each for a different reason.

In terms of your first moment, criticism: Greenberg is long

gone, but the opposites of his judgments are very much alive in the art world: they drive enormous quantities of art production in art schools and art academies. And yet it is rare to find people who acknowledge that they are following variously construed opposites of Greenberg's judgments—putative opposites of flatness, painting, modernism, and especially criticism. Even the last few minutes of our conversation, concerning Documenta, can be read as an aftereffect of the desire to *not* do Greenberg. So there is an incomplete understanding of the inverted heritage of modernism.

In regard to the second moment, critique: it is very well set out in those texts by Krauss and others, but I don't think the effects of the practice are understood. A practice like that (the reformulation of criticism as the interrogation of one's prospective judgments, and the conditions of judgment), if it were followed verbatim, would result in a self-interrogation that would not leave a reader free to extract *any* judgments of value, because the practice would be purely Kantian. But of course the body of literature that has been produced around that position has had anything *other* than a neutral, self-reflective effect. It's had all kinds of other effects.

And then in regard to the third moment, criticality—partly in relation to your essay, Irit, but also to other initiatives: I am still unclear about how it is conceptualized. It is necessarily non- or even anti-conceptual at a certain point, because it has to do with reaching a certain aporia based on a kind of self-interrogation, which is in fact the second of the two models, but *using* that model to reach a point where there is a gap in understanding, which allows the writer to move toward an encounter with, and a reciprocal relation with, an artwork, and then from there back into theoretical understanding. I can't see how this is a third model, or rather I can't see it *as* a model. I see it as a series of hopes and particular examples.

So I think there is inadequate conceptualization of all three moments, and I think they combine to produce some—not all!—of the current conceptual disarray of criticism.

IR: We need a different vocabulary. One of my colleagues, Simon O'Sullivan, speaks of the of critical affirmation: that which makes things possible, rather than sitting in judgment. Affirmation is the instance of actualization, of potentiality.

JE: And that is different from Boris's phenomenological affirmation-by-exposure.

IR: This is much more Deleuzian. Most every curator I speak to names two exhibitions as the most important ones of all: Harald Szeeman's *When Attitude Becomes Form*, and Jean-François Lyotard's *Les Immatériaux*.[23] They refer to those not as models for making exhibitions, but as moments when people realized something was possible. They opened a huge set of inventive possibilities for people, and that's what I'm calling a paradigm shift.

BG: Irit, that's a good distinction between your position and mine. Deleuze is talking about total fluidity, bodies without organs, and the unlimited expansion of desire. They are beautiful things, of course, but I think I'm too old for that.

JE: Too old for a body without organs?

BG: I never saw anybody without organs! I have a body with some dysfunctional organs, but that's not the same. I feel that I don't have unlimited desire, and my horizon of possibilities is pretty close. So I have a strong feeling that Deleuzian discourse does not adequately describe my personal situation.

I love recent French philosophical writing. It is very inspiring. But I have a feeling that it speaks about things that have no relationship to me whatsoever because it speaks permanently about infinite things—infinite work of difference, infinite play of signifiers, infinite flow of desire, democracy beyond democracy. But I am finite, my space is finite, my time is finite. Only if we take that seriously do we come to real choices. As long as we're talking about infinity, we still believe that we can deal with infinite visual fields or with infinite possibilities of the interpretation of every individual image. But if we organize an exhibition, we have to betray the original openness of the visual field—we have to select, to exclude, to limit the number of exhibited images, objects, or documents. And if we write a critical text we have to betray the infinity of interpretations—again we have to select, to close, to exclude.

To be finite is a very unpleasant thing. One has to be unjust and unfair. One has to be become political. But to be finite seems an unavoidable condition for art practice—at least, in our time.

WD: If we're considering the conditions of thought as a paradigm shift, then I think we have to look back to the eighteenth century. I find it hard to believe that we are looking at paradigm shifts when we're considering the current conditions of the art world in 2005. As Jim said, even in the second of the putative three phases or interlocking possibilities, there is a missing link: carrying out the project of critique verbatim would require a project that has not yet itself been realized, even by those who have set out to carry it out most systematically qua art criticism or art history. And as Abigail said, the project of critique in the second sense rarely occurs within art history, even though the question of it has been on the table since Panofsky's hermeneutics, if not before.

IR: The pressures are different now, and so are the paradigm shifts. The great paradigm shift of the Enlightenment age are not the same as the shifts that have come out of the geopolitical pressures that are currently being put on thought.

WD: Regarding the paradigm shift the art world and art criticism are putatively experiencing now, which is taken as a function of cultural, sexual, racial, ethnic, national, regional possibilities: if the content of that paradigm shift is the reconstruction of a notion of the horizons of thought, the conditions of possibility of thought—if that is the substantive claim for the content of this paradigm shift, then I can't understand it as a paradigm shift.

JE: That is related to another difficulty I have with new critical practices. They depend on the notion that one reaches a point where the critique—the Kantian critique—fails to find its "cleared ground" and continues to dig. One then reaches a point of maximal complexity, or maximal mutual contradictions of operative concepts, or maximal aconceptuality, and *that* is the momentarily desired state, the place where a gap opens that allows new practices to become visible. The problem is it's very hard to theorize that place. I remember there's a text by Rosalind Krauss in which she tries to find such a point by employing Freud's "A Child is Being Beaten" and Lyotard's "matrix": she is looking for a zero-level of sense, which however can't be simply or only a zero-level because if it were it would be a null rather than a productive, unpredictable, vacillating state.[24] It just isn't possible to theorize such a thing within rationality, and that is appropriate, because no one I know is interested in pure irrationality: what's wanted is a certain state of uncertainty. It's really an aesthetic interest despite all the reasons why one might say it isn't, because describing it, living within it, gives pleasure.

I also wonder about the idea that performance art and other ephemeral forms, because they are time-based and not susceptible to conventional forms of documentation, call for new forms of writing. It's not that I disbelieve that, it's that I don't see how it's possible to justify the connection between temporality, video capture, and so on, and specific decisions about narrative.[25]

All that—and I'm including Whitney's observation—is why I think the third term, criticality, is really a version of the second, and perhaps even a version of one of the opposites of the first. It's Latour's phrase, "we have never been modern," but in a different sense.

BG: It's a common assumption that a visit to an exhibition will encounter art. I don't think that's any longer the case. We are increasingly confronted with documentations of art practices, and they are not art in themselves, because the art is supposed here as being something that has taken place elsewhere, at some other time.

What we encounter on coming into an exhibition is a certain absence—namely, an absence of art—and that itself can call for a new kind of reaction, new kind of writing. As a critic I cannot aesthetically or otherwise appreciate and evaluate a work of art if I see only documentation of it. Rather, if I write something on a certain art project, my writing is simply added to an already existing documentation of this project. The opposition between spectator and artist has become blurred, and so has the distinction between critic and artist. By adding my writing to an exhibited documentation of an art project, I am actually collaborating with this project, participating in this project.

IR: Today there is a real revision in the notion of collaboration. The notion of two people cocooned inside a project, which then results in a work, has been superseded by an emergent notion of people working together in such a way that new possibilities are opened. What's happened with *Opensource*, for example, is a way of letting people in, of allowing new configurations and proliferations.[26] It's not right to demonize art history, because it's just a formation of humanities scholarship; but it always involves questions of boundaries and exclusivities. I think what is happening now, with the concept of collaboration, is an attempt to deal not with the individuals and their individual works, but with the boundaries and exclusivities.

JE: You're very interested in interesting configurations of things. I'm also interested in dull things, which continue to happen in a lot of the world.

WD: Irit, I would love to believe you. But I find it difficult to square your position with the dominance of well-entrenched economic structures of display, distribution, publication, dissemination, remuneration, in which a whole tier of artists, academicians, gallerists, public relations people, are all co-participants, co-exploiters, co-exploiteds. I would love to hear you say more about how these more mutual, relational practices are sustainable given the overall geopolitics of the art market, in which only a very small percentage of people will ever participate.

IR: I can't deny the very grave truth of capitalist realities, and I don't practice a romantic utopianism. I think one has the responsibility of a bit of resistance. I live in London, as several of us here do, and large on our horizon looms the Tate Modern. It's like a giant vacuum cleaner: it hoovers everything into itself, flattens it, makes it into dust. There's a real need to look away from it, to leave some mental space to see something else, and to allow a panorama that is subject to other indices, other comparisons. So it's not that I'm unaware of the well-oiled machines of the gallery system: but we can allow our attention to fragment. We can look at little things, like three people sitting in a basement somewhere: those three are then networked to three thousand people somewhere else—and it begins, from very little, to be something. Institutions like Tate Modern and MoMA do not have those kinds of global relations, even though they pretend to . . . But James, can you say more about your interest in dullness?

JE: By "dullness" I mean average art: mediocre art, normal art production, ordinary art-student production throughout the world. What concerns me here is the relation between an avant-guardist practice, such as yours, and a normative one. As a person with a special interest in dullness, I'd like to know if the new configurations you are interested in are conceptually dependent on some older practices that are, as Whitney said, still very much in place. Yours is a particular kind of contemporaneity that has very quickly come to take its points of reference from places other than what I'd like to call its pertinent pasts.

Anyway, it's time to introduce the third and last of the texts we can use to consider judgment. This one takes a few minutes to read out. It occurs in the roundtable on art criticism published in *October*.[27] The people in that conversation went back and forth on the question of judgment, as we have done. Several people there said what they would like judgment to do in art criticism, and one of the participants, Hal Foster, listened and collected the options. Late in the dialogue, he enumerates "the archaeological function, the exploratory function, the paradigm-marking function, and [the] mnemonic function." It's not perfectly clear to me which is which, but I'll mention a few points in the dialogue that correspond to the functions he names.

First, David Joselit says criticism "is about making a judgment and not simply an interpretation"—a clearer formulation than any we've had today.[28] A few minutes later, Helen Molesworth—she'll be in our second roundtable, so she can correct this if I've got it wrong—asks what he meant. Is it simply "whether the art is good or bad . . . or is it judgment something like Donald Judd's criterion of 'interest'?" (That's a word we have not used today, not in that direct fashion.) Hal Foster then asks, in an impeccably detached manner, "What terms does judgment call up for you when uncoupled from quality?" He notes that his generation of critics worked against the identification of criticism with judgment. So far, so good. But then Joselit gives two answers. First he says, "I would say one can judge what constitutes an object." And when Benjamin Buchloh asks, "An aesthetic object?" He says, "Yes, or an object of history." Those, it seems to me, are two entirely different possibilities. Foster then tries to sum up: "What David proposes, if I hear him right, is that one task of the critic now is disciplinarian, or, if you prefer, antidisciplinarian: to decide whether boundaries between categories of art and categories of visual culture should be drawn or crossed. It sounds like an academic task, but for you it is a critical one."[29] That, I'm guessing, is what Foster later calls the "archaeological function" of criticism.

I'll name the other three (that's exploratory, paradigm-marking, mnemonic) more briefly. The "exploratory function" comes up a moment later, when George Baker—he will also be at the Chicago roundtable—says, "one of my models for what I do as a critic is something like an explorer." In the absence of criteria, which "refer to judgments of quality" and are therefore inoperative, he says he's interested in "locating silences, articulating repressions, providing a space for certain types of work and certain artistic aspirations to continue and to evolve."[30]

Foster's third function for criticism, the "paradigm-marking function," comes up perhaps when Rosalind Krauss says she had always assumed a critic's job was "scanning the horizon for some new blip appearing on it"; and when Joselit notes that she didn't just report on "a preexisting phenomenon" but actually helped "produce a definition of postmodernism," she says, "It's true. A good critic produces as well as reports."[31]

Foster's fourth function of criticism, the "mnemonic model," is also Baker's. Baker says contemporary criticism might "resist precisely the changes in . . . what can be said within certain art magazines . . . the critical voice has to, in some sense, keep certain projects alive." Foster calls that the mnemonic model.

Okay, so that's four. What I would like to know is: Why are the people in that conversation content to let such a diversity of purposes coexist? Why is the very purpose of criticism allowed to float in and out of the conversation? Why does Foster play the role of historiographer or collector of the purposes of criticism? (What position is *that?*)

GT: It's such a jump from *The Visual Art Critic*. The terms of discussion have entirely changed, from two hundred newspaper critics who were writing "go see" or "don't go see," to an entirely different group of people who have their own project, their own implicit readership. I think you have to mark that the conversation has changed absolutely and fundamentally.

BG: I find this *October* material very dogmatic, and very artificial. I almost don't have the desire to discuss it, because it's just an exercise in a taxonomy. It's just not sexy. [*Laughter.*]

JE: Anyone else want to comment on *October?*

AS-G: As a group they seem extremely judgmental, and yet they appear relucant to acknowledge that judgment is any significant part of their critical tradition. That should do it. I'll say that for the record.

JE: I suppose I should say why I thought it was a good idea to read out that material, and then I'll introduce our fourth and last topic for the day. I have taught any number of texts from *October* and the writers associated with it, but I have to say that among my students in Chicago, that roundtable is something of a laughing stock. They laugh at the panelists—that moment Benjamin Buchloh asks who the YBAs are—

WD: Surely, however, that was ironic.

JE: Perhaps. I'm not so sure.[32] Anyway there are several points in the conversation that make my students laugh, and some—like the disparagements of Dave Hickey—that they find annoying and off the point. They just can't take it seriously as a representation of art criticism.

Now we've just dismissed it almost as quickly as some of my students have, but I suspect our reticence to discuss it has a very different origin. There's the weight of *October* in the critical scene, of course, and the overdetermined nature of the dialogue for those of us who have known the speakers (in some cases, for years) . . . there are lots of reasons to want not to engage.

And yet (and this is why I've brought that text into our conversation) I think it's a significant conversation, one of the best-informed on the subject in recent years. So it's odd that they let themselves float so easily among different models of criticism and understandings of judgment, *especially* because several of the speakers were architects of a kind of postmodern criticism that we have called critique. Several of them practiced an especially strong and problematic kind of criticism, and yet there they are, speaking informally about a whole zoology of options. I wonder how dangerous it is for us *not* to take that conversation more seriously, or to fail to see ourselves in it.[33]

JF: I find this discussion profoundly depressing insofar as it seems to pull us continually back to the standpoint of the (Western) reflective or intentional subject. As with art, I am more preoccupied with what criticism *does* as a responsible practice in the world than with categorizing it, and insofar as the *October* roundtable discusses possible critical functions it has value. However, it is a long time since I've found either journalism or *October* inspirational, and my reluctance to engage lies in the suspicion that *October* is now a vanity press, promoting the views of a small cadre of writers and acolytes. So what or whose reality are we being asked to address here? One seemingly unconcerned with what the rest of the world is thinking and therefore at once imperialistic and parochial.

To confront a relatively alien reality is to come face to face with the limits of one's own language or horizon of knowledge. To acknowledge these limits is also to accept that the reality of the other, especially the cultural other, is not—contrary to Western assumptions—transparent to the Western gaze. One is thus faced with the *ethical* decision whether or not to engage in a conversation (that is, listening as well as speaking), and hence one is also confronted with the problem of translation. In fact, it is indeed Joselit's comment that needs unpacking, because it begs the question: Can one justify a critical judgment without first understanding the aesthetic, social and historical context from which a work arises, or at least without a willingness to engage dialogically with the unknown territory it presents?

I am inclined to say that criticism is not simply about making a judgment according to quasi-objective criteria, but also about applying a range of interpretive tools capable of addressing a work's referential efficacy in the wider world. In other words, I am suggesting that the discussion might attend to the limits of critical language and bring into play some of the issues of hermeneutics as advanced by Gadamer and Ricoeur—not, alas, something I am competent to do!

IV

JE: So, on to the final topic. I don't think we'll make any headway with this one either, but I wanted to be sure to mention it so the next roundtable will have it as a subject.

The question here is what we want to count as art criticism. As Gemma said, there's an enormous gap between journalistic writing and stuff like the *October* roundtable. I think that gap—really it's more like an abyss—is significant for three reasons. First, journalistic criticism is what is actually read, if you just count heads: *Time* and *Newsweek* have circulations around 4,000,000, and *The New York Times* sells a little over 1,000,000 copies. Second, if things like newspaper criticism and essays in exhibition brochures aren't called art criticism, then you have a kind of problem with terminology. What would we call those texts? "Writing for hire?" "Commercial exhibition brochures?" It is more sensible, I think, to begin by calling them art criticism. Third, and most important, it is an interesting intellectual challenge to try to think of these kinds of writing together. This abyss is larger than abysses in other fields: it's deeper and broader than an internecine disagreement or factional dispute of the kind many disciplines have.

So let's spend the last few minutes trying to figure out what we want to call "art criticism."

GT: One fundamental thing to get straight is that it's not necessarily a difference in audience. The mode of writing is different, because the purpose differs, but the audience may be shared.

AS-G: What are the stakes for you in this question? You keep saying, "It's important, we have to consider it," but I want to ask why.

JE: I don't see firm lines between the kinds of writing. I have students who go out with art history MAs and then write for newspapers, without having undergone weird conversion experiences.

AS-G: But then what is the question?

JE: Can we talk about these kinds of writing at the same table, in the same conversation? Or is *October* correct at least in its exclusionary stance, if not in its other choices?

GB: I wonder if there is a popularization of art that's equivalent to the popularization of science. When I was at Harvard, I roamed around in the astrophysics library, and I was faced with things of such complexity I couldn't hope to understand them. There is popular science, but I don't think there is such a thing in the arts, because newspaper art criticism is not a popularization of other discourses on art. Unless perhaps we consider those incredibly irritating placards written by the education departments of museums and put up on walls to tell visitors how to see the work. Those are betrayals of the artistic experience, not popularizations of what any of us do.

JE: I think you might be assuming that there is no such thing in popular science as *vulgarized* science.

GB: I think there is.

JE: In that case you could say that newspaper art criticism is popular art criticism, instead of just a vulgarization or something wholly different.

GT: Newspaper art criticism absolutely has to be considered together with more academic writing. It's part of people's encounters with art; it's in the back of your mind when you enter an exhibition, and it forms part of the apparatus of apprehending and seeing, and therefore can't be discounted. I would put it in a continuum of writing, which together creates a textual environment in which it is made, shown and seen. Additionally, ideas from academic and theoretical art criticism enter the more popular discourse over time, and so the two areas are linked in that way as well.

WD: I guess I wasn't completely convinced by your answer to Abigail, and I'd ask her question again. There would seem to be an interest on your part in there possibly being a common ground between Michael Kimmelman writing for the *New York Times* or Peter Plagens writing for *Newsweek*, and Hal Foster working as an art critic and operating as a "theorist" in *October*, or Meyer Schapiro working as an art historian but proceeding at times as a critic. You seem to be interested in finding whether there might be some unifying activities that we could put our fingers on . . . again, like Abigail, I am interested in finding the stakes of the question.

JE: When you put it that way, then yes, there are disparate activities, and not much would be gained by lumping them together. The way you described them gives them different functions. But I would like to know the structure of the connections, like the ones Gemma mentioned, and if there are denials of such connections, then I would like to know their ideology. Our refusal to engage with the *October* roundtable, for instance, has reasons behind it, and if we were pressed, we could explain them. But our assertions that we're different in kind from newspaper art critics (especially because at least two of us are, or have been, newspaper critics!) might be harder to explain.

AS-G: You don't think there's a difference between what you're calling a "refusal" and a reasonable attempt to put things in a different space?

JE: I would have felt odd if I had been in that *October* roundtable and not mentioned some of those commercial and journalistic practices.

AS-G: That's the question, whether those journalistic practices are in fact continuous with ours.

JE: They are continuous with what we do, and we may even be responsible for their intellectual genealogies. Just as my students laugh at *October*, there may be people in the roundtable following ours who will laugh at us. The idea is not to exclude without knowing the reasons why.

AS-G: But particularly those of us who do not write in newspapers, we are for better or worse, professionally, structurally, and even politically, are more closely aligned with people who write in reviews such as *October* or *Parkett*, than we are with the art critic at the *Des Moines Register*. Those of us at this table are concerned with the *problem* of criticism.

GT: Yet I write for both *The Irish Times* and *Circa*, to take two Irish examples. And I am as concerned with the problem of criticism in one as in the other. Criticism underpins my writing about museum and gallery architecture, art exhibitions, and institutional structures, as well as my questioning of the role of my relationship to the art and artists I write about. My concerns are the same, it is just the manner of discourse, the analogies, allusions and citations I can employ are different. That is not to say I think I "dumb down" for the newspaper, just that I present things differently.

WD: I might step back from your question and make the historical observation that in no other culture has there been such a disparate array of discursive situations within which responses to the modern art of the culture have happened. Ancient Roman art writing is a singular genre, not widely shared; Egyptian responses to art are again a singular kind of phenomenon. Here, it's an interesting phenomenon that we have responses to art ranging through virtually all kinds of publication outlets that are possible in modern society. That's a strange phenomenon in itself.

JE: Thanks for that, and I think I'm finished flogging my dead horse.

Sabine Kriebel [*Question from the audience*]: Hi, I am an art historian; I work at the University College Cork. I wonder which direction do the various participants of the panel think criticism should take? That is, which sets of questions, judgments, ideological or political issues would you like to see future art criticism address so that it arrives at the critical standards that seem to have gone missing?

JF: There is no doubt that globalization and particularly its commodification of culture—and of thought itself—present a situation in which art history, art, and critical practices risk stagnating and becoming irrelevant to the wider sociopolitical issues that affect us globally. That is especially so when art, history, and criticism restrict themselves to debates about Western internal institutional concerns. We all need to maintain vigilance to the lived conditions in which we function, which means being informed about the way ideology and political expediency subtly inscribe and direct practice (which is all too familiar for those of us working in academia). For a society to remain vital and open it needs to keep in circulation alternative and critical voices that act as counter-discourses to the ever-increasing instrumentalization of everyday life. While this should not be the exclusive responsibility of art and criticism, these practices are among the few spheres of life whose relative autonomy is capable of enabling some degree of in depth social and political critique. This is not to advocate art as protest, but to understand how art may open onto a new thought of the political, globally conceived.

GT: One issue I would like to see addressed is that of exclusivity. By this I mean the acceptance of dense, allusive and referential discourse as a viable mode of art criticism. While I appreciate the necessity for professional language, and for a certain level of technical and theoretical references, there is also a need for lucidity. With artists being influenced, as Irit said, by such a diversity of sources, there is much to be gained by a refusal to make art criticism opaque to sociologists, scientists, philosophers, poets, and political scientists, as well as those with backgrounds that depend more on experience than theoretic acumen.

I would like to see more critical thinking from the perspective of the making of art—the view from the studio. I don't mean just what artists might have to say in a way that intrinsically excludes others—anyway, some artists have been notoriously unreliable in their accounts of what they do—but how it is that works of art come into the world. For me this would mean better and fuller theorization of art considered as a process of inquiry and eventually the development of a new paradigm for what I would call art research. I can't open that topic here, but I would say that the views of critics, philosophers, historians, psychologists, and others would be important to such a new kind of discourse. So much of aesthetics has been concerned with looking at works of art—at style. I would like to see an aesthetics of method, of the pattern of formation of art.

SECOND ROUNDTABLE

Chicago, Illinois, USA

*This conversation was held October 11, 2005, in the Art Institute of Chicago. The participants were: Dave Hickey (freelance art critic), Lynne Cooke (Dia Art Foundation), James Panero (*The New Criterion*), Ariella Budick (*Newsday*), James Elkins, Gaylen Gerber (School of the Art Institute of Chicago), Stephen Melville (Ohio State University), and Michael Newman (School of the Art Institute of Chicago).*

Later on it becomes relevant that the panelists seated themselves in that order, with Dave Hickey on one end and Michael Newman at the other. Gaylen Gerber is an artist, and he produced a backdrop painting for the symposium. It was an architecturally-scaled gray monochromatic painted canvas that was the exact size of the rear wall of the auditorium; it was installed behind the panel and, in combination with the discussion, was meant to constitute an artwork.

James Elkins: Hello, everyone, and welcome. Well, I don't think this panel will make Jean Fisher any happier: we're still all White, and we're all from North America or Western Europe, and I imagine the people who write Assessments for the book will want to address that. However, there is arguably an even greater diversity of opinions, politics, and methodologies at this table than there was at the Irish roundtable.

I propose that we address four topics this afternoon. First I want to pursue a link that did not quite materialize between the first roundtable and the *October* roundtable.

Then I'd like to address issue of judgment, which took up so much time on the first roundtable and resulted, I think, in so little progress. Third, let's take up where the first roundtable ended, and ask what is the sum total of practices we might want to call art criticism.

Fourth and last, let's talk about the relation of art criticism to its past. In the first roundtable, when questions of art criticism's histories came up, they died away, and no one seemed to notice or care. History has been somewhat ghostlike in our own conversations as well, and so this afternoon I want to save an encounter with those ghosts until the end.

I

JE: Let's begin with the problem of the *October* roundtable, by which I mean the fact that it elicited relatively little interest in the first roundtable.[34] Is that, I wonder, a tenable reaction?

Let me get things started by proposing an *uninteresting* reason why the panel wanted to ignore the *October* text; then I'll suggest a possibly more interesting reason. The uninteresting reason is that most of us know people in the *October* roundtable, and so we didn't want to say anything. But I don't like that as an explanation, because in some people didn't especially want to bite their tongues about what they felt, and in other cases there was no love lost anyway.

A more interesting reason may be that some of the panelists in the Irish event felt *independent* of whatever was happening in *October*. There was Boris Groys's sharp and funny comment about

October not being sexy, and Jean Fisher's observation that *October* is not relevant to her. Can it be that there are critical discourses that are so independent of *October's* terms and interests?

I thought this might be a good place to begin because we have at least one panelist—Dave Hickey—who really doesn't have much to do with *October*, and at least one other—Steve Melville—who really does.

James Panero: *October* is sexy in a kind of unsexy way, if that's possible. And I disagree with the panelists in the first roundtable. What *October* did, and what it still does, directly impacts the way we write about art criticism, if only as something to refute.

Dave Hickey: I agree. The *October* discourse is certainly part of my universe. Annette Michelson was my first friend in the New York art world, and we write about the same things. There are large points upon which we disagree, of course; *October* is more optimistic about the revolution than I am and much more trusting of Freud. They're not interested in the public vogue of art, which is my principle interest, but I think it's nice that they have some ideological fervor. It's kind of corny, but it's serious. I don't have any problem with them.

JP: I'll agree, it's kind of cute. But what I want to know, Dave, is why you factor into their commentary to such a degree. Buchloh calls you a "critical placebo," and elsewhere Hal Foster says you've developed a kind of "pop-libertarian aesthetic."[35] That seems like a—

DH: —sign that I bother them more than they bother me. It's understandable. They are concerned with the reform and redefinition of criticism. I am a non-conforming critic, so I bother them. I am interested in discouraging bad art, and they are not artists, so they don't bother me. Also, I am an independent contractor. They work for the Man. They are creatures of institutional virtue and instruments of its power. I am a creature of the marketplace. Our jobs do overlap, however. Yve-Alain Bois and I write about many of the same artists. Rosalind Krauss is brilliant and exquisitely teachable, if deluded in recent years.

So we differ? So what? So they talk trash? I've said worse about others, and, in truth, I'm always happy to dine my enemies. It's fun

I'm not intellectually insecure, and the discourse surrounding art is not that that personal. Also, I'm sure these people don't really dislike me, personally. They are distrustful of libertines and people who are glib. They're suspicious of rhetoric. They think people are being seduced into wrong thinking by the cosmetic glamour of my writing, and this is so delusional about the nature of rhetoric that it's not even flattering.

Stephen Melville: Talk about *October* tends to get all over the place fairly quickly. One thing perhaps worth saying about it is that it has always seemed to me in part an attempt to inherit the very broad permissions that *Artforum* gave to criticism in the 1960s, so that it was born with a worry about art criticism as a part of what it is. For me it continues to be an interesting place for thinking about criticism and theory.

Michael Newman: I'd like to try out something, at least, around this *October* moment. To a certain extent, the development from *Artforum* to *October* has to do with breaking away from Clement Greenberg's shadow, in the particular sense of continuing to do criticism, but doing it in a different way. (Although in retrospect *October* criticism may not have been quite as different from Greenberg as they may have hoped.) Greenberg's approach combined aesthetic judgment with a certain kind of theory of history of art, leading towards a goal, which then turned out to legitimate the judgments that he made. So the critics writing in *October* wanted to go on writing criticism, therefore necessarily involving a certain kind of judgment, but not the same kind of judgment as Greenberg was using.

To be schematic, I'd say that *October's* sense of judgment in criticism differed from Greenberg's in two ways. One difference is Rosalind Krauss's move from judgment to meta-judgment, which came up in the first roundtable: you make judgments, but at the same time you're writing about the conditions for making judgments. The other difference—the other side of the *October* move—had to do with trying to ground judgments, and in a sense to dissolve judgments into their ground.

Broadly, that second difference or move happened in two ways. Krauss's way was to ground judgment in a theory of subjectivity, ultimately using psychoanalysis. Benjamin Buchloh's way was to ground judgment in a theory of society, using Frankfurt School theory. So judgments were made, but the claim was that what legitimated judgment was the relation of art either to some aspect of subjectivity, or to some aspect of social critique.

Ultimately, that is problematic. I would tend to go along with Jean-François Lyotard when he says that aesthetic judgment is judgment *without* grounds. The point of a judgment is a kind of exposure of the groundlessness of the judgment itself.

SM: I don't think I want to accept Michael's distinction of judgment and meta-judgment, and I'm also inclined to distinguish Buchloh and Krauss much more sharply: Buchloh really does have a theory that produces standards capable of determining judgments. I'm not at all sure that's true of Krauss; it seems to me she uses theory largely descriptively—to show what something is and what it addresses—and not as a ground for her judgments. Like Lyotard, she seems to me in that broad sense "Kantian."

Whether the point of a Kantian judgment in this sense is "a kind of exposure of the groundlessness of the judgment itself" is, I suppose, another question. Taking the formulation at face value, it's hard to see why such judgments should matter to anyone, so Lyotard must mean more or other than just that.

MN: That brings me to another question I'd like to raise, and also pose to the other members of the panel. The attendance for these events is quite flabbergasting.[36] That suggests there is a resurgence of interest in art criticism. I started writing art criticism in 1977—I had a bout of it then—and that was before I started studying art history. I studied art history because I had been writing criticism; that is how I got into it. I then stopped for a couple of years, and started again at the end of the 1970s. At that time, in England, the feeling was: theory would replace judgment in criticism. You would no longer base criticism on judgment; judgment was utterly disreputable because it was associated with an implicit, hierarchical, Western, phallogocentric position. So you replaced judgment with theory, which made criticism something completely different: you give a theoretical account of the work, rather than, as it were, an aesthetic account. The thought at that time was, "Art criticism is at its last gasp, and will continue as a kind of market legitimation." Criticism was to be replaced by theory.

That moment seems to be over. It doesn't mean theory is not relevant, but its role is different from the role it had before. *October* was an attempt to reconcile theory and criticism, in a certain way. I wonder what that moment, in the 1970s, has to say about the moment we are living through now, and the context for the renewed interest in art criticism.

Lynne Cooke: It seems to me that if there had been a roundtable in the late 1960s, say, on art criticism, then some of the key people on the panel would have been artists. If you look at the Summer 1967 issue of *Artforum*, the one that is often called the "sculpture issue," the contributors included Sol LeWitt (his manifesto on conceptualism), Robert Smithson, and Robert Morris, as well as Michael Fried ("Art and Objecthood").[37] If you look at the 2002 *October* roundtable, one of the most glaring things is that almost no artists participated.

JE: Except Andrea Fraser and—

LC: Yes. But proportionately it's very different.

JE: There's an interesting text I've just been shown by someone here: *Conference on Art Criticism and Art Education*, held in May 1970. The participants in that were already mainly historians and critics: Lawrence Alloway, Barbara Rose, Hilton Kramer, Robert Rosenblum, Robert Pincus-Witten, Horst Janson, Irving Sandler—and Brian O'Doherty, who says he's responding not as an artist but as an "ex art-critic" who is about to start teaching art criticism.[38]

SM: Presumably it's right to say that one of the reasons artists were so prominent in *Artforum* is that the relation between criticism and self-criticism was right there in a way that no longer seems to be the case.

LC: And that included devising the critical frameworks for the interpretation of their work.

SM: Yes.

LC: Not only taking over the voices that criticism had occupied, but taking over the discourse itself.

SM: Yes, I think those are two slightly different sides of the same fact.

JE: I've never been entirely sure of the force of the observation that art criticism was pre-empted by minimalists and conceptual artists. It's been said many times, by Krauss, Buchloh, Foster, and others, but I don't see what kind of explanation it is, given the subsequent developments in the late 1970s, as Michael has mentioned. Could it be conceptualized as a particular understanding of the difference between criticism and self-criticism?

SM: It seems to me pretty clear that something happens to the idea of self-criticism in the late-1950s and in the 1960s, and that this change is pretty strongly registered in the now well-established use of "reference" as an active verb adequate to the relations one work of art might have to another work or to itself. It also seems to me that one's sense of what difference "theory" makes—for either art or criticism—depends on where one stands in relation to this kind of shift.

MN: During the second half of the 1960s the border between criticism and artists' writing became porous. Dan Graham, Robert Smithson and others started to use the magazine page as a medium. In *Fox* and *Art & Language*, artists pursued critique and a philosophy of art of sorts. And Victor Burgin and Mary Kelly functioned as theoreticians as well as art practitioners. This was both a challenge to the traditional role of the art critic, since practitioners would create the discursive context for their work, and an extension of what could count as criticism. Of course Donald Judd was publishing a lot of art criticism, in a very pragmatic style, but his writings remained recognizable as conventional art criticism. I don't think criticism was "pre-empted" by all this, but it was challenged to become something different.

DH: My perspective, having been there at the time, is that the rise of *October* marked the academic repudiation of French structuralism, or, more precisely, its radical Germanification. The day that Marcel Duchamp was transformed from a French dilletante into a Frankfurt schoolboy signaled the return of everything Structuralist theory had set out to repudiate. *October* reintroduced the so-called "human sciences," Foucault's bête noir, into beaux-arts discourse. Psychology, sociology, and anthropology returned along with their cruel stepsisters: the plague of intentionality, the myth of origins, the fiction of historical logic, the fantasy of auratic identity, and the whole imaginary superstructure of repression. Minimalism had washed that slate clean, I thought, and all of a sudden, all this stuff was back, and we were talking about Freud again. This was the mid-1970s, mind you, and people were talking about repression!

Not surprisingly, then, I regard that moment as end of visual rigor in the arts, a reactionary return to the woozy inheritance of German romanticism (with which American academia has never truly been out of love). Annette and Rosalind orchestrated a kind of putsch to take over the discourse from the people you're talking about, Lynne, and it worked. They won. Hardcore Frenchies like myself and Jeremy Gilbert-Rolfe, who was an original *Octoberite* himself, lost. And when you lose, it's always your fault. This doesn't make the distance between Rosalind and Sol LeWitt any narrower, however.

JP: There are plenty of contemporary artists who don't care a bit about *October*. But that is not the case with university departments of art history, where the *October* mafia has gained a stranglehold on the hiring process. It is now going to take the Rico Act to get *October* out of academia.

Ariella Budick: The *October* roundtable is hermetic, and they are not really writing to the public: they're writing to insiders, like-minded people. I think it is ironic that they call the subject of their roundtable art criticism, when that is a practice directed to a public. To the extent that they speak mainly to themselves, they are out of date.

JP: Is it an *October* surprise that we're here talking about criticism at an academic conference?

DH: Yes, it is.

SM: We're getting a little over the top here: *October* has published a lot of writing directly about art, and it has for the most part been good, strong, and properly influential criticism. There is, in its pages, plenty to argue about and with, but pretending it has contributed little or nothing to the practice of criticism is just silly. It also seems to me that the question of audience is a question art writing always faces; there is no "general public" for art or art writing, only the public artists and writers *make* for these things. *October* probably makes a smaller public than many other places, but that's not in itself much of an objection.

What Michael said about the dream of reconciling art theory and art criticism—and I'm speaking here not as a critic, but as an historian—is an important dream for art history. I don't think art history has actually gotten very far with this, but there is still the promise of seeing itself in a different relation to art criticism—in particular, a promise of seeing itself as a mode of criticism. This gets, I suppose, to James's remark about *October* in the university, where we can either go the well-worn route of the tenured radicals who have subverted or captured or whatever the institution, or explore the possibility that *October* might importantly figure in a properly disciplinary discussion about the practice of art history.

JE: It is interesting that so far in this conversation, those of us who are saying *October* is relevant are saying that it is so, in part at least, because it is a site for thinking about art criticism. But I think there are at least two other reasons why we might want to say we are connected to *October*. One of them is that a person aligned with the *October* project might want to claim that the most interesting historical discourse leads into and through *October*, so that contemporary thinking owes it serious consideration. That line of thinking leads into the theme of the histories of art criticism, so I will leave it until after the break. A third reason that *October* might be relevant is that it has completely captured the academic market, as James Panero said quickly a moment ago. As a question of institutions and market power, apart from content, that third reason may be the most compelling.

DH: Michael, you said a few minutes ago that the fact that there are so many people here signifies a new interest in criticism. I don't think it does, any more than proliferating "education schools" and "education majors" signifies a new interest in education. I would suggest that this roundtable is a death-knell for art criticism:

it marks a level of self-consciousness, creeping professionalism and narcissistic introspection that can't sustain the practice or be sustained by the practice.

MN: Perhaps I can slightly deflect those terms, and connect this theme with something Ariella and Steve just said, regarding the connection between art criticism and the public. I teach a class at the School of the Art Institute on the history of art criticism. In the years I've been teaching it, it's moved more and more toward a discussion of the relation between criticism and the public sphere. In a sense, if there isn't public space, then there is no criticism.

Now, what happens at the beginning of art criticism—say, the eighteenth century, and Diderot? You get an heterogeneous collection of people going to the Salon, which the critic addresses *as a public*. So in a sense the critic performatively constitutes the public, which will in turn support criticism. It so happened that a bourgeois public sphere was developing at the time, so the two things came together.

For various reasons, that configuration begins to close down; already in the mid-nineteenth century, public space becomes spectacularized. Richard Sennett writes about this in *The Fall of Public Man*.[39]

The question that arises for me is: Was the recent period of the crisis of art criticism—say, from the 1970s into the 1980s—to do with the closing down of a kind of unified public space? And if there is a new interest in criticism, does it have to do with an opening up of other kinds of public spaces? For example, the "blogosphere": is that a new kind of space for art criticism? And is there something enabling in the very fragmentation of public spaces and publics? So I don't agree with Dave: this isn't the death-knell of criticism. Some kind of fundamental public shift is happening, which is making criticism necessary again, but in a different way. Perhaps in relation to the current over-capitalization of the art world, various publics are demanding a more critical perspective.

DH: Uh, I don't think so. Occupations die all the time and this one is dead. We are sewing-machine repairmen, flat-boat operators, ferryboat polemen, night-time disc-jockeys.

MN: Anyone else? [*Laughter*.]

JE: I notice that Michael, that you and Dave are sitting at the far ends of the table!

MN: We're the two brackets.

DH: Well, okay, let me be specific: art history is not a linear progression, it moves forward according the logic of coup and contracoup, the radically fashionable is supplanted by the radically unfashionable and the art itself functions like a wild card. We find in it what we need, what mainstream technology takes away. Art goes where the mainstream culture is not. Pop and Minimalism repudiated the black-and-white graphic technology of the 1950s. Conceptulism repudiated the glossy incarnate technologies of the 1960s. Now digital, conceptual culture is dominant and the logic of dissent says that art, to give us back what technology gives away, might begin to concern itself with the physical word, with the haptic, the fractal and the tactile. In fact most art-types I know are happy as clams to be wallowing in mainstream culture, getting misty about the blogosphere and making themselves comfortable in a steady-state discourse. Criticism, at its most serious, tries to channel change, and when nothing is changing, when no one is dissenting, who needs criticism?

MN: I wasn't talking about art so much as public spaces for criticism.

AB: The *October* roundtable on criticism was only four years ago: we're not talking about a revolution in art or technology that has happened since then.

JE: Although yesterday, when we were talking in preparation for this roundtable, someone said they thought the *October* conversation took place in 1975.

JP: It's hard to believe that conversation took place in 2002.

AB: Right, so we're talking about the space of a few years. Did the audience expand from several hundred to several million in that time? I don't think it's a change in publics, but a move away from self-referentiality and hermeticism.

JE: We can perhaps leave this question of the current growth (or death-knell) of criticism, and the possible development of new public spaces, to the people who will write Assessments for the book. We should move on, so I'll just record what I consider to be the form of our disagreement about this issue. I started with a bad and a better reason why the *October* roundtable can be ignored, and we ended with three, possibly four, reasons why it cannot be ignored. I just want to note that those of us who *do* effectively ignore *October* do so for two possibly very different reasons: some, as in the first roundtable, feel that the conversation has simply changed. Others, and this pertains more to this roundtable, feel that they do something that is in some way an opposite of what *October* did. Those are profoundly different senses of historical sequence: from Jean Fisher's or Irit Rogoff's lack of interest in *October*, to Dave Hickey's conviction that he does something they do not. You can ignore something in the past because you think it's in a different language, from a different culture; or you can ignore it because you think you have figured out what counts as its opposite. Both, I think, are treacherous. But we should go on. History will re-emerge at the end of the afternoon.

II

JE: We have been circling around a subject that took most of the time in the first roundtable: the relation of judgment and art criticism. Especially the slow sea change from the openly judgmental and critical writing associated with Clement Greenberg, to the kind of writing in which judgments are not offered nakedly but interrogated, put into question, contextualized. What especially struck me in the *October* roundtable in that regard is their insouciance about *deciding* the issue of judgment: Hal Foster added up four models of criticism, and others appear briefly, but no one considered it a problem that the differences between the models were not directly addressed. It's the *lack* of concern about deeply contradictory pictures of judgment's place in criticism that puzzles me in the *October* conversation.

On this panel, we have a significantly wider range of practices in relation to this question of judgment. Some of us here—perhaps those to my right [*toward the end of the table with Dave Hickey, Lynne Cook, and James Panero*]—might be happy to say that judgment is more or less what they do; and others—perhaps those on my left [*toward Stephen Melville and Michael Newman*]—might rather want to say that the practice of art criticism involves other things, including "meta-critical" interests that work to prevent judgments from appearing, nakedly, on the page.

Let me open this subject by recalling Boris Groys's idea that the age of Kantian judgment (which he epitomized with a schema in which judgment is positive or negative, like electricity) is over, and we are effectively in the age of phenomenological judgment (the positive or negative noticing-of-something, and the neutral not-noticing-of-something). Boris calls those +/– and +/0 systems. (He was educated as a mathematician; he can't help it.)

DH: J.L. Austin observed, accurately I think, that all human utterance is dissent. The only reason you say anything is to dissent or to qualify. Governmental discourse and educational discourse, of course, are normative and coercive, but even so there is judgment in word said. This is axiomatic. I can't imagine that anyone now, in the twenty-first century, is pretending to transparency or disinterest. If that is in fact the case, they are welcome to it. So this is all mysterious to me: judgment is what we talk.

JP: As the one who represents the "conservative harangue" at this table, I would say that I do strive for a certain disinterestedness, and this is a subject on which Dave and I are fundamentally different. Dave, I think what you're interested in is interestedness.

DH: Yes, right.

JP: And the more you're interested, the better your writing becomes.

DH: I am interested in conflicts of interest.

JP: Exactly.

AB: When you write reviews, James, you have to show interest.

JP: The difference is that while I acknowledge interestedness, I try to avoid it. I think Dave looks for it.

DH: I probably should have noticed that.

JE: Is it just fortuitous, James, that what you just said about striving for disinterestedness and not achieving it echoes that famous statement of Greenberg's, that he may disagree with his own taste, but he has no choice in the matter?[40]

JP: I would say that I start with a dialogue between taste and judgment. I don't think criticism should be purely top down. And I think Greenberg was at his best when he operated that way too. But at the same time, by exercising judgment you to enter the higher powers of criticism. Taste is personal. It's tribal. It's charismatic. But with judgment you are appealing to higher laws. You can construct arguments through judgment. There may be a saying that there's no accounting for taste, but there is an accounting for judgment.

AB: I myself am very much committed to providing judgments, and I think it is necessary to set up a barrier between taste and judgment. Taste can play into judgment, but it should not be the determining factor.

I don't think of myself as giving advice to the buyer, like *Consumer Reports*, but I am making an argument based on my expertise as an art critic and historian; and the argument involves judgment: it involves saying, "This is good; this is bad." The judgment does not come from my taste, but from an historical sense of where the objects fits. Is the work derivative? Bad? Pretentious? Does it live up to its claims? Any of those things may play into my judgment, but in the context of my own experience and my understanding of art history. Ed Ruscha is an artist I don't particularly like, but I won't say his work stinks. That's also the difference between my visceral response and an intellectual argument.

DH: I may agree with James Panero here. Every critic writes best against his taste, when judgment overwhelms taste. Eventually, as a critic, you learn the kind of bullshit that you like and discover that you're reliable as a critic when you're writing about works that are totally outside of the area of "bullshit that you like." I'm better about Robert Gober than Ellsworth Kelly, I think, although I'm not uncomfortable with my reading of Kelly. Finally, I think that the privilege of judgment is one for which I pay by not working for the Man. I don't write for a publication, or a movement or a university, so when I speak it's just Dave Who Lives in a House on the Street. I'm not speaking through the instrumentality of an august institution. This is the price I pay to be foolishly candid. Should my interests coincide with a publication or institution, of course, we embark upon a short-term joint venture.

AB: There is no control or coercion from the editorial side in my experience at *Newsday*.

JP: Dave, in the interest of full disclosure, we probably all work for the Man. I certainly do. And for you, Si Newhouse is a man. He's a big man.

DH: What I am saying is that as a hired gun, I do not feel I bear the power of the institution, as Peter Schjeldahl does: he is the *New Yorker*, and he is the *New Yorker* talking. If I write for the *New Yorker*, it's just Dave. He is selling it for sure. He just doesn't have a pimp.

JP: But as an editor, I'd say that if the editor at the *New Yorker* doesn't like Dave, Dave doesn't get the assignment.

DH: That's true in fact. Last year I wrote a piece on Palladio for the *New Yorker*. It ended up in *Harper's*.

JE: May I ask the "other side" of the table to weigh in on this question?

SM: The things I most want to say are oblique. I will go back to your initial example, from Groys: I don't think a "Kantian judge" says "I like it" or "I don't like it." That's a Kantian taste for Chinese food, and it's a different matter.

JE: I agree: Boris uses Kant for his own purposes there.

SM: And I also want to avoid the interestedness/disinterestedness thing, because I think it *can* be avoided. What the form of a critical judgment actually is, seems to me a kind of question. In many cases, judgment happens as the critic registers that something is what it is, or fails to be what it is, in some way. It's something like that. It's not got the form, "Let me describe something and then I will arrive at a judgment about it."

JE: What I meant to point to in my initial framing of the so-called difference between the "two sides" of the table is that, given your description, it would be fair to say your interest is in that occurrence, in the form of judgment.

So, to take a counterfactual example, if you were a daily newspaper critic who had only two column-inches in which to report on an exhibition, your happiness would depend on your lack of interest in the forms and conditions of judgment, and in the pleasure in simply proffering judgments. It's an awkward example: I am trying to find a way to talk about the difference between art critics who judge, and those who consider judgments.

SM: But what I am suggesting is that at least for Kant, it is very hard to draw any line between judgment and description. A Kantian critic, if they exist (and sometimes Greenberg came close) matters because of their capacity to describe something. The whole picture of *a judgment*, of a sentence that has *I* as a subject and a judgmental verb, is a funny one in this context. I am trying to tilt the conversation a little bit.

JE: I don't think I would object to that, but I would still wonder if it is a way in which someone concerned about such things might talk to someone who isn't—someone who forms such sentences, and takes them as natural to, or even sufficient for, art criticism.

SM: I guess my thought is that someone like that has been persuaded into a bad picture and that the best way to address that is simply to drop back to more ordinary language and pay attention to the distinctions and phrasings we actually use in one situation or another.

MN: What Dave was raising was a question of the conditions of judgment. Boris Groys's distinction works on two levels. One concerns the conditions of judgment; the other concerns the object of judgment. The conditions of judgment include, now, the massive capitalization of the art market, and the fact that *any* attention given to a work is going to add to the value of the work. That may make "disinterestedness" all the more important, but the problem is that an apparently disinterested judgment from a supposed position of authority is all the more valuable to the market than one that has been bought. So in a sense the freedom and autonomy that "disinterestedness" was supposed to represent is systematically and not intentionally compromised.

"Disinterestedness" also involves a particular kind of object relation, since the object is not supposed to be an object of desire, or of use for some other purpose. I think that the transition from Boris's first model to the second has to do with a shift in the nature of the object of art since Duchamp, and certainly since the 1960s. It becomes interestingly unclear *what* it is that we're making a judgment of. It's not necessarily a painting or a sculpture. So part of the task of criticism comes to be to disclose, explain, create a discursive context for, this weird thing or activity that we're calling art. That has to take place *before* the plus or minus judgment is made, in any case.

I feel this very strongly in terms of the way my own practice as a critic has developed. The work that interests me is often work where it's not wholly clear what the work is, and the task is somehow to bring to light, so that one can begin to have a discussion, *what it is* that one is looking at or experiencing. In philosophical terms you could say the critical task regresses to another level, to the level of the constitution of the object—in a broad sense, since this can also involve a performance, a trace of an event, and so on—rather than the judgment of an already-constituted object.

LC: Our idea that things have changed so much from the 1960s until now seems somewhat naïve. Advocacy takes different forms; we don't have to like things as critics in order to talk about them. The two collapse into one.

I am reminded of a man called Willy Bongard, a German economist, who in 1970 began to rank artists, determining who were the most important and influential, the results of which were published under the title "Kunstkompass" in the magazine *Capital*. Bongard used an elaborate system to evaluate these hundred positions, based on the frequency of group and solo exhibitions, and I think also on the amounts of press coverage. I think you could make more or less the same model now, but perhaps the principal difference is the influence the market now has on an artist's perceived stature. Curiously, Bongard did not base his evaluations on financial data.

JE: There are contemporary parallels. Artprice.com gives artist rankings based on auction prices, lots sold, annual turnover, and bought-in lots rate.[41] Closer to your example is artfacts.net, which rates artists according to a very complex statistical model that includes reviews as well as market performance.[42]

DH: Michael, the issue of what we're looking at is trivial, I think. I hear people saying all the time, "You write about objects." That's not true. Physicists write about objects. Critics talk about how things look. Basically, all we're doing is addressing an excerpted fragment of the visual field and calling it art, trying to assess its standing and position in the category of other such excerpts that we call art. People write about Jackson Pollock as a performance artist. I write about John Baldesarri as a painter. Whether it's a nominal object or anything else is totally trivial.

MN: Can you judge a visual field? Surely it is just given. There is a passivity to that notion, an acceptance of the status quo. I'm widening the concept of the object—as object of a judgment—to suggest a reason why judgments have become problematic (as perhaps they always were).

AB: I want to address the first part of what Michael said, about Groys's ideas. There are two problems with not writing about something if you don't like it. First, there are too many things not to write about—that was said at the first roundtable. Second, there's a danger that the dialogue on art becomes only affirmative. That would be boring—it's boring to read, "This is great, this is great, this is great"—not just for the reader, but even for me as an art critic. I want debate, I want dialogue, fireworks, battles, energy. There's no energy in "I love this."

MN: That's a funny thing to say. Isn't love rather complicated and ambivalent? To go back to Boris's distinction: +/–, which involves thinking about how the work itself, transforms the framework according to which it is received; that is a lot more interesting than the banality of +/–, good/bad, which tends to leave fundamental assumptions unquestioned.

DH: I don't think it does. Professional evaluation demonstrates its axiological parameters, and bad art is important. As my friend Peter Plagens says, "Somebody's got to play defense." For instance, Damien Hirst is a bad artist, but he is a very important bad artist, because he's bad in a big way that reflects a lot of the bad things about the art world and cultural at large. There is a level of interest above interest. It is important that Jeff Koons is a major artist without having received one positive review, except for the puppy—and who hates a puppy?

AB: It's the critic's job at times to say that the emperor has no clothes. It is not enough to ignore Matthew Barney and pretend he doesn't exist, while his prices are rising, and the Guggenheim is putting up a huge retrospective. Somebody's got to get up there and say, "Matthew Barney stinks!"

JE: We are drifting a little off our subject of the difference between judgments of any sort, and contextualizations of judgment.

SM: Can I say one last word pertaining to Kant? I suspect that if for you the world divides up simply into subjects and the setting aside of subjectivity, that is called objectivity—it's a distinctively modern sense that the world does indeed divide up this way. I think you're not going to find very much of interest to say about criticism: it's not actually going to be a topic of its own. It'll be something you do, Jim, or Michael does, or Dave does, and that will be it.

What has made Kant recurrently interesting is that he has this idea that there are certain judgments that have to come out of an individual but are not subjective in that sense. One could say, as Kant does, that you are speaking in a "universal voice," but nobody believes that any more. Still, the idea that you could sometimes speak in a voice that is not merely your own is a very strong ground for an idea of criticism. In the absence of such an idea, criticism is a rhetorical activity some people are interested in, and others aren't, and there is not a great deal more to say about it.

JE: I need to call time on this. We haven't solved anything, but we have made some headway on the problem, which I think is unusual in these kinds of fora. To me there's a fascinating disconnect between (sorry to say it again!) the two "sides" of the table: it's a disjunction between the *ways* we choose to talk about the difference between proposing judgments, and talking about judgments. It's like the kind of problem Wittgenstein said he loved best: everyone who reads or writes art criticism knows that some people make judgments, and others don't. Among the others who don't are "descriptive critics," which the last roundtable considered, and academic critics who are interested in the conditions, forms, and histories of judgment, which we have here. Everyone knows that, but there still isn't quite a way to talk about the difference using a common language—that, for what it's worth, is my take on this part of our conversation.

Before we go on, I need to read into the record that we have a great parallel-universe phenomenon taking place as we talk. Gaylen Gerber, the artist on our panel, who is sitting here at my left, has actually made an artwork for this event, and it's been behind us all this time. We have literally turned our backs on it, since we're facing out, at all of you. So Gaylen the artist hasn't had a voice, and his work hasn't found its way into our conversation. It's a triple exclusion, of an artist, an artwork, and a critical context, while we've all be talking about criticism.

Gaylen Gerber: I'd like to say that the critical context of my backdrop exists whether we're distinguishing it from the field that surrounds it or not. It exists as the ground against which our conversation is being perceived. Listening to this conversation, I've kind of flip-flopped. I'm feeling more inclined towards *October* and towards its kind of critical writing in general; it's been very important to me. One of the things we've been talking about is the relation between representing an institutional position, being perceived as an institution, and taking a position that deviates from that institution towards something that is generally understood as more expressive. My interests are closer to representing the institutional position in this case because I am looking for common ground.

I am interested in trying to see the deviations, and I think the only way we can do it is by first trying to understand the norms that underlie any deviation. Trying to see the things that we all share—the things that visually, culturally, or critically we take as shared experience and then looking for deviation as a way to understand difference.

As the conversation went on, I was thinking that *October* has positioned itself, or is now perceived as an institution in its own right, as a ground against which we're interpreting new critical distinctions. And in that way I feel a real kinship with it. I like the sense of stoicism and stasis that it has come to represent, and I appreciate the way other cultural expressions become perceptible against the field of *October's* collected writings as if it were a unified field. We have been talking about *October* as if its position within the field of criticism hasn't changed: for me it's reminiscent of the Ramones, who in the beginning of their career felt so different. But over time, because they were so resolved in their expression, as listeners we found ourselves wondering, "What year is this?" Their interests just didn't seem to change—when they didn't change, it made it possible to readily perceive the changes in the things surrounding them. And in that way I think the conversation we're having is making sense to me in a way that it hadn't before. *October* has become an institution that may provide us with a ground against which we can see the criticism surrounding it—

JE: —You're also drawing an allegory of your painting, did you realize that?

GG: Yes. It's the relationship between norms and the expressions that I'm interested in making apparent in my work, and our conversation seems to have been framing a similar relationship between the canon of writing about art and the question of how to value more recent critical writings.

JE: Let's take a break now for questions.

Amir Fattal [*Question from the audience*]: Do you find that artists tend to take less interest than they once did in criticism or art theory?

DH: I find art students these days talk about criticism the way seminarians talk about the liturgy: they feel like they have to internalize it and make the proper noises. I don't think they have the faintest freaking idea what they are talking about.

JP: I think artists are more savvy than ever about *October*, but the difference is that artists today are fearful to be seen as operating in a tradition, and specifically in a tradition of modernism.

LC: In art schools, students are being taught to be professional artists, and much of their training is about how to present themselves in the art world, and be articulate in these terms. Many students spout Octoberese, or second- or third-generation versions of it, because it's thought to be a currency in which they will then enter into the next phase in their careers.

DH: Their professors think that, if they had done that, they would be famous artists instead of impoverished teachers. But honestly: you either write for the charts, or your write for the future. All that is solid melts into air.

All this crap is going to disappear. Go back and look at an *Artforum* from 1985. It's a haunted mansion: there's nobody there you've heard of. And I was there! Taking the conditions of the art world in the present as a donnée is crazy. You have got to make a change. You must deviate. There is simply no option. If you make art that looks perfectly like art, it will disappear like a song on a.m. radio. Everybody will say, "B+," and let you go out and get a job in Iowa.

GG: Everything I disagree with was just stated there in a nutshell. If it were possible to make art that was timeless and transparent, I'd be interested in seeing it. I'm interested in artists' intentions, and I am interested in the correlation between what the artist intends to express and our interpretation of their expression. I prefer the situation of the arts to be bigger and messier, in part because our assessments change as our interests and needs change, and this alters the criteria for evaluation. Some things that I thought were "crap" ten years ago (as Dave has characterized them), we now think are relevant and meaningful, and vice versa. I prefer to keep things open to reassessment and as a result it may be necessary for art to remain messy, and indulgent, and "crap." I can live with that. It's close to how I perceive the world we live in: it's not perfect but it is what we make of it that counts, and I'm comfortable with that. Producing art is not like a doctor operating on someone, or heating someone's home. Art is culturally privileged in that, for better or worse, it is charged with cultural expression and the culture affords it the necessity of running the gamut of expression from the profound to the frivolous. In my opinion the big asset that art has retained is that it can do so in the larger culture with some impunity. Unfortunately this also means that it often does so without much effect.

As I see it, whether it is art or criticism, our production helps the larger culture to perceive itself through re-presentation in a way that the culture has sanctioned. And so it's important or even necessary to deviate from those expectations in order to be perceived as meaningful, as Dave has suggested, because we equate deviation with significance. But deviation for deviation's sake is meaningless, and that's the crux of our dilemma.

III

JE: Our third topic is what we want to count as criticism. It was a large bone of contention in the first roundtable. It was said, for example, that daily newspaper art criticism shouldn't count, and my own notion that commercial gallery brochures are a kind of art criticism didn't exactly make any converts. I am guessing this panel may not have those qualms, but I wonder about the range of ideologies we have. There were—James, as you would say, "in the interests of full disclosure"—actually *complaints* about the constitution of this panel. Michael and I had originally planned to invite panelists using a strategy I called "ambush invitation": that is, don't tell the people you invite who else they will be sitting with. Now Dave is a huge draw, but I also got complaints that he was coming, and I have heard there were complaints that we had invited someone from the *New Criterion*. Maximizing and displaying those differences in what counts as art criticism were the main organizing principle for this panel.

James, at your lecture this morning, you bravely—given where he was, in the heart of the liberal art world—positioned yourself as an unrepentant modernist and member, as you said here, of the "conservative harangue." I thought you articulated that extremely well, and in an undogmatic style, but what puzzles me is this: why aren't you desperately unhappy?

JP: It's true; I'm not unhappy. Thanks for noticing that. I think I can function as a high modernist critic in the Greenbergian sense, and also deal with everything else that is going on, because in my mind I can separate what I view as art criticism from what I see as cultural criticism. When I go to the art fairs, I am mainly operating as a cultural critic in the journalistic sense. But I do still believe in the modernist project, and so as part of that cultural project I look for works that are part of that tradition, and engage them in a modernist critical fashion.

DH: I think that's an extremely viable position. I invited Robert Irwin to talk a while ago, and a student asked him about postmodernism. He said, "It would be fine with me if we had five hundred more years of modernism." Well, maybe not, but that doesn't change the fact that a number of the best artists I know are just straight-ahead, hard-core modernists who are spoken of in postmodern lingo: Bruce Nauman, Ellsworth Kelly, and Roy Lichtenstein, come to mind. As a general rule, most self-identified postmodern art is just modern art with a social agenda. It's that or journalism.

JP: I get the sense that you believe the modernist project is over, just as you think the *October* project is over. Do you think there is good modernist art around?

DH: Yes, absolutely.

JP: I too have have modernism on the mind, and I think this is particularly useful where cultural criticism and art criticism intersect. I think of the work in the Armory Show in New York, for example, as cultural, totemic objects. They are part of our quote unquote visual culture. But some products of visual culture claim to be works of art. They even claim a part of the modernist legacy. I have in mind, for example, John Currin. People think he works in a modernist vein, but when you actually go and look at his work, his style, his ability as a painter, stinks. There's nothing to it.

DH: You got it.

JP: There's nothing to it. He can't lay claim to being a modern artist.

AB: It sounds like you're equating what's modernist with what's good, and saying everything else stinks.

JP: Do you disagree?

AB: But in Greenbergian modernism, there is a teleology. Flatness and the other concepts have a purpose—art progresses toward some ultimate expression.

JP: Well, I'm not such a teleological person. But back to what I was saying before about good and bad art. You know, a great deal of contemporary art wants to be bad—bad in the modernist sense. Much of the stuff at the Armory Show sells itself on anti-quality. I think one of the reasons this work is so popular with high-stakes buyers is that it functions like a junk bond. These objects have little to no intrisic value. So for the speculative banker/art buyer, the price of this work could either go through the roof or it could tank. But from the start its value is purely speculative, because such art doesn't even have any value as a pleasant or impressive or beautiful thing.

DH: I remain a modernist in the sense that I have a serious commitment to articulated difficulty. Art that doesn't manifest some level of difficulty doesn't particularly interest me. Art that does not elicit a complex response is boring by definition. The presumption of difficulty is the crux of what I take from the modernist tradition. Art is not supposed to be easy. It's not for sissies, dummies, or education curators.

JE: I'd like to note, before we move on, the way that Gaylen's unremarked painting changes as our conversation changes: at the moment it's a difficult modernist piece, resisting easy reading.

But to pursue this question of the limits of what counts as art criticism. The conciliatory nature of this exchange between Dave and James is interesting. We are witnessing a collapse of several senses of modernism into a surprising agreement about what counts as art criticism (perhaps as opposed to "cultural criticism").

I would like to extend that collapse into another field, and that is contemporary curatorial practices that become mixed with critical practices. Curation seems an appropriate focus given that six of us have curated exhibitions. I participated, but not as a curator, in a small biennial in Rincón, Puerto Rico, called "PR 04."[43] Some if it comprised curatorial practices that seemed to be artworks, and art that seemed to consist only of curation. Artists and curators were trying on each other's identities, partly in the name of relational aesthetics, and I imagine many people there would have been happy to be called art critics. I wonder if that might be another way to talk about art criticism's increasingly wide and blurry boundaries.

DH: My position on curation is that the meaning of the show emerges from the show itself. The curator is a more or less inspired art-herder. I'm doing a show in Los Angeles now, big messy paintings by five artist with a wide generational span. When we put them all up, we'll decide what that's all about. The show is called "Step into Liquid," which is a surfer reference and kind of a control, I guess, but otherwise there is no pedagogical apparatus. As a curator, I am not being paid to think, I am being paid to do something that, when observed, will be thoughtful. Curators now, the ones who go to Bard or wish they had, think they have to generate a theme that subsumes all the art in their exhibition. They talk like parochial schoolmarms, act like whores, and—

JE: Including Lynne [*who was sitting next to Dave*]?

DH: Oh, would that she were! [*Big hug for Lynne from Dave.*] Anway, being a well-known whore myself, I was recruited to curate a little biennial in Santa Fe a few years ago. When I was putting the show together, I kept getting calls from the Dutch Consulate, the Danish Consulate, and German Consulate. They wanted me to put Danes, Germans, and so on, into the show, and I said, "I don't think I will." They said, "We will send you e-mails." I said, "I don't look at freaking JPEGs." They said, "We fly you. We put you in a very nice hotel. You will have camellias in brandy snifters on the terrace." It occurred to me at this point that this is what curators are doing: they are flying around to national capitals, taking government-paid tours to look at government-approved artists that are biennial-friendly. Curating is a very corrupt discourse.

AB: You have to make some distinctions: there are curators of contemporary art, and curators of more historical art in museums. I think the latter do act at the border of art history and art criticism. When they frame a show, they are proposing a theme, and that is what makes the art coherent.

LC: I'd like to go back to Jim Elkins's presumption that somehow curators are being swamped by artists who had curatorial agendas, and that they were coming in and either taking over the role of the curator, or in some stages pre-empting it. I suppose you may be thinking of people like Pierre Huyghe, or Philip Parreno, artists like that—

JE: Pablo Helguera, Pablo Léon de la Barra—

LC: But I think that curators have often asked artists to do their dirty work. I am thinking, for example, of Fred Wilson's work at the Maryland Institute in Baltimore, or other such invitations for artists to come in and recontextualize or rearrange the collection—to get the skeletons out of the cupboards. It is not a one-way activity: it goes in both directions, and you might ask why curators want artists to fulfill roles that they, the curators, feel unable to undertake.

JE: Yes, I agree; I think it's less a one-way street than a mutual confusion of roles, which could be understood as an expansion of art-critical activity.

LC: I don't think it's a confusion. It's an understanding of the differences permitted to each activity. Artists supposedly have license to do things that curators cannot do in collections. Consider, for example, the exhibitions at the National Gallery, London, in the 1970s, where senior artists such as Richard Hamilton or Bridget Riley were asked to come in and rearrange works into some set of precepts that they found interesting. In such shows you could see a Piero hung next to a Seurat; clearly there are relationships between those works, but no curator is going to ever feel they have the authority to rearrange a traditional chronological hang in the National Gallery in order to put those works side by side.

AB: But what about MoMA 2000?

JP: I think everyone agrees MoMA 2000 was a disaster. Those hangings were failures.

AB: I don't agree.

JP: The Tate Modern has already rehung its thematic hanging.

AB: The Tate is different.

DH: Well, thematic hanging is just philistinism. Jesus, you go into the Tate Britain and see paintings of beefsteak, or paintings about trout all nicely grouped together.

JP: I wish curators would have just a little more muscle. Can't we have an Alfred Barr today? Can't we permit that?

LC: What do you think gave Barr the stature he had?

JP: He had a powerful vision on what modern art was. He was a great educator. He was not afraid of making mistakes.

AB: If you look at the Whitney shows of the last few years; the reputation of someone like John Currin was the responsibility of Larry Rinder, who isn't there anymore. He was a cross between a critic, a curator, a dealer—he played all those roles, and he lost.

MN: Can we have a say down on this end of the table [*Michael Newman, Steve Melville, and Gaylen Gerber*]?

JE: Yes, and I'd like to ask a question *about* your end of the table, rather than *to* your end of the table. I wonder if your side of the table might be dissatisfied that there are still boundaries of this sort to be drawn between criticism and curatorial practices? Might that account for the silence of this half of the table?

SM: I think we might have different answers to that. My own silence was because I was trying to find a way to think about the distinction that was being drawn between curators and artists. That is certainly one area where things have been going on lately. The other is between curators and critics. I went to a symposium called "The State of American Art Now"; in it, curators and critics, including Arthur Danto, talked for six hours about the state of

American art in fairly predictable ways—but they managed to do so without using the word "criticism" once.[44] I thought that was kind of extraordinary, so I asked them if criticism was simply out of it. And they all, including Arthur Danto, agreed that criticism was simply out of it.

JE: —Even though he writes huge amounts of art criticism?

DH: At least by yardage.

SM: Yes, by yardage there is a lot of it. These were distinctly younger curators, and they were clear that critics were out of it because curators now did that job.

That has rankled at me. It's a funny kind of distinction I want to propose, but it seems to me criticism is crucially recognizable by the fact in it of a voice. Although curators have points of view, and often strong points of view, you might say the act of curating does not involve having a voice.

JE: But how would it be possible to walk through an arrangement of objects without finding a narrative in it?

SM: I am not saying there's not a narrative or an argument in curation, but there is not, or should not be, or traditionally has not been, something you would call a voice in it. I am not sure if I can make this stick, but it is a line I draw; and there is now a new generation of curators who are characterized by the fact that they want to have a voice. They don't simply want to have a point of view, and they don't simply want to make arguments.

JE: Could I say you are agreeing with distinctions between curating and criticism made by the other side of the table, but in completely different terms?

SM: I guess so.

JE: I mean, there are still lines there to be drawn.

SM: And I don't know if I am being retrograde or not. Times are changing, and I am telling you my sense of the distinction that matters to me.

JP: I think one thing that may be happening, and which we may agree on, is that everyone who operates around the creation of works of art—curators, collectors, critics—wants to be part of the art.

DH: Dear God.

JP: You disagree?

DH: No, go ahead.

AB: No one has mentioned the fact that curators now all have PhDs, and they're all basically academics. That never used to be true. You can kind of sneak your way in without a PhD, but—

JE: Does that make you more like an art critic? Or give you a propensity to act critically?

AB: I don't know: I'm just throwing it out there.

NM: Both Steve and I have curated shows, but I suspect we have done that as critics rather than as curators, in the sense that we were trying to get the exhibitions to elaborate a thought—although I did enormously enjoy putting the work up on the walls and deciding where it went. It's a pleasure I miss, and I haven't done it for a long time. (So: any offers?)

SM: I think we really were trying to act as curators, although I don't know with what success. I just mean that we did the show because we thought the only way forward with what had begun as an academic, and perhaps critical, argument was to see what showed (or failed to show).

MN: The point I'd like to make has to do with curating and criticism. Up to about ten years ago, criticism was one of the prime ways that works of art were mediated to the public. The critic was somebody who tried to interpret, explain, or judge the work for a public. Now that seems much less the case, and that curating has become much more the way the work is mediated. But, as has already been said, curators tend to see themselves as closer to the production of the work than the critics saw themselves. Criticism is more detached: it mainly uses a different medium—language—whereas curating functions according to a mode of presentation and contextualization, and that followed the moment in which art itself often involved activities of contextualization and recontextualization.

An example is Michael Asher's show that is currently here at the Art Institute.

So the boundary is more blurred between curating and art production than between criticism and art production. I wonder what, in the broader culture, explains this shift from a discursive mediation to a kind of near-immediacy of presentation? The appeal of curating sometimes seems not unrelated to the phenomenon of reality TV: curating seems closer to the reality of art than criticism, just as reality TV seems closer to unmediated reality than—

DH: I think that most curating is just jumped-up social climbing. Most shows I see are not curated: they involve a curator coming in and preempting the job of patron. They don't choose art for the show; they say, "Oh, we'll fly Inga in and she'll do some leaves." That is not curating: that is patronage. That's why the curators have such power: they can fly you to Santa Fe and let you fill a room full of leaves, and let you run up an enormous phone bill talking to your girlfriend in Puerto Rico, and then fly you home. The curator takes a step up, because the money that comes in, the dirty commercial money, is purified by flowing through a curator to an artist to do whatever he or she wants to do. This is such a stupid activity.

"Oh, and we'll get Ulf in, he'll do great, and he can get the tires he uses for his art right here in town." It sounds as silly as it is, but its driven by an economic model, by the budgetary constraints of running a contemporary museum. "Tires? Leaves?" Great. No shipping. No loans! No insurance! No climate control! No security. Just parties!

JP: I think I follow that. The problem I have with it, and I think we share this problem, is the sense that the curator adds a kind of modern cleanliness to shows of unmodern or anti-modern art. It's dishonest.

DH: Yes, right.

JP: Well, I think that's wrong, in that the museum is not operating in the modernist tradition, and when that's been exposed, we have had major crises in the museum world. For example, Thomas

Krens using the Guggenheim the way he does, paring Kandinsky with Matthew Barney. Or there was the "Sensation" show in Brooklyn.

DH: As D.H. Lawrence says, "trust the tale and not the teller." What we have today is curators who are not selecting art—they're selecting artists.

MN: I think this blanket condemnation is actually totally unhelpful. There are good and bad curators, just like there are good and bad artists and critics. One needs to come to some kind of decision as to what the criteria are for judging curators, just in the same way as artists. A sweeping condemnation doesn't help.

JP: I don't think we're condemning all curators.

DH: Neither am I. I am condemning a particular kind of practice.

AB: The closer you are to contemporary art practice, the better the chances that your hands will be sullied with the dirt of the market. There is a danger for any contemporary art curator of being bought by the market. Many curators are in the employ of collectors, or have unhealthy friendships—

MN: But a good curator can illuminate the work in new ways, make people think about it differently—

AB: I am just saying that they need to be careful. There was an Alice Neel show at the Whitney a while ago, and every single painting in it belonged to the Robert Miller gallery.[45] It's easy, if you're doing a show, to make a deal with a gallery and get all the work through them. But it's compromising.

LC: You speak as if there is some inside trading practice, but any curator worth their salt would not be interested in behaving like that.

JP: Not only do curators behave like that, they conceal it. Everyone knows what happened to Marcia Tucker after she gave the Whitney over to Richard Tuttle in 1975. She didn't keep her curatorial distance from the artist, and she was fired. Now, even if you agree with her curatorial practice, no one wants to be another Marcia Tucker.

LC: That happens very rarely, James, and when it does it is absolutely evident. I am much more interested in your question about why there aren't Alfred Barrs now. I think there is a move back toward behaving more like Alfred Barr; that wasn't the case when criticism was more powerful, persuasive, and visible, back in the 1960s and 1970s. You see that in Helen Molesworth's forthcoming show and in the show that Jean-François Chevrier did in the Museu d'Art Contemporani de Barcelona, which were attempts to re-read modernism in the twentieth century.[46]

Barr's contribution was to provide, through exhibitions and attendant publications, schemata for movements such as Cubism and its offshoots, Dada and Surrealism. Those were among the first publications in English that tried to write an art history of the twentieth century and did so through the museum rather than through an academic department. In the postwar years, academics tended to inhabit universities, rather than research positions in museums, and that's where such histories have been written. Today there are various efforts on the part of curators to regain this territory, and play out those debates *in* the museum.

JP: But is the curator writing the narrative, or just distilling the narrative?

JE: Especially when art historians contribute so much to the catalogues, for example, in the book announced for Helen Molesworth's show.

DH: I think you're putting up some art and seeing what narrative arises as a consequence. For this, "themes" are death since the attributes that any group of artists have in common is, by definition, the least freaking interesting thing about the work.

SM: I don't think that's true of the kind of show Lynne was just talking about, and I'm thinking particularly of Helen Molesworth's show. It's got a strong, complex argument, and the fit between the objects and the argument has an appropriate looseness to it—that is, there are objects that she knows belong in the show, but she doesn't know exactly why. I'm just afraid that shows like that don't get the criticism that it seems to me they demand. When shows like hers happen, more and more they don't travel, they go away . . . and there's a real failure there. Something has not happened that ought to happen.

JE: I need to exercise my prerogative as moderator to have the last word on this and then change the subject. I wanted to just remark that what we were supposed to be talking about was limits of what counts as art criticism. But I note instead the ease with which we find that we can criticize curatorial practices! I think the question of the limits of art criticism—its territory, its conceptual reach—will have to remain open for the people who write Assessments for the book.

IV

JE: So, on to our fourth and last topic, history. It is the most interesting of the four, I think, because throughout this roundtable and the first it has been the most deeply buried. The question would be something like this: what is the relation between current practice of art criticism and their potentially relevant histories?

There are at least two forms of this question. In the first, what is asked is the relation of what histories of art might be relevant to art criticism: when, or whether, contemporary art criticism should look to episodes in the history of art for its meaning or ground. In the second, the question is about what histories of art criticism are pertinent for the contemporary practices of art criticism. For example, Baudelaire is studied in most every class on the history of art criticism, but exactly how does his work impinge on contemporary practices?

Michael, your essay is a good place to begin, because you argue that certain understandings of current art criticism come from the generation of Kant or the generations just after him—and in that there's an implication that art criticism has particular relevant histories that it needs to take into account.[47] My generalized question would be: how are we to think of writers such as Baudelaire as being immediately pertinent to what we do?

MN: Let me frame my answer in three parts. First, is there a history of art criticism? And is it possible to place contemporary practices in relation to that history? I would say yes, and that contemporary ways of doing criticism, hopes for criticism, possibilities for criticism, do have relationships to crucial moments in the past. For example, the attempt within German Romanticism to create a kind of art community that would bring together art and life was directly related to a perceived failure of the French Revolution and the Terror, and the attempt to, as it were, displace politics into art. There is a long history of that displacement of the political into art, and I think one needs to understand that in order to understand things that happen in recent criticism. So yes, there is a relevant history of criticism.

What is very surprising to me, as somebody who teaches the history of criticism, is that to my knowledge not a single book has been written on the history of art criticism. That is absolutely astonishing to me, totally astonishing.

JE: Because Venturi's book is not about art criticism.[48]

MN: It's actually a history of art history. I tend to understand art criticism as beginning around the eighteenth century, in its modern form. Why is there no history of art criticism? This goes back to things Jim has said in his essay.[49] There are senses in which art history has a lot of difficulty with art criticism. Sometimes I think art historians would like a kind of benign inclusiveness, but it never seems to work. There is something involved in art criticism that is a problem for art history. It doesn't mean that the great art historians don't also have a critical dimension, but some aspect of criticism touches on something that art history has to repress or exclude within itself.

I think it has something to do with the different ways the object is determined in art criticism and art history. I would want to argue that in the classic period of art criticism, the object is fundamentally not an historical object. For art history, of course, the object is fundamentally historical: the problem is, they're the *same* object. So art history, in order to accept art criticism, has to accept that there is something about its object that is not historical. Now, what do I mean by that? Well, I don't mean that the object is not historical in virtue of some timeless essence, or that the values of art are eternal and therefore not historical. What I mean is that in a sense the object is transhistorical. Jeff Wall once said there is *only* contemporary art.

DH: Amazingly, he was right.

MN: That was in riposte to people who say to him, "You're an historical artist, you're an historicist, and you use art history in a bricolage way." But there is only contemporary art because now is when we experience it: even if it is Renaissance or medieval art, we are experiencing it now. I think a critical relationship with the object is fundamentally an existential relationship. The historian is going to be interested in the relation between the object and its historical contexts of meaning. The critic is going to be interested in whether that object survives, whether something about it—in a sense its immediacy—is carried over from one context to another. So I am not saying art criticism is above history or above context: I am saying overflowing context, or meaning that is carried through from one context to another.

This was a problem for Marx; he wondered why we appreciate works of art made for the Greek city state, when we no longer live in Greek city states. What is it about Greek sculpture that has crossed contexts? So it's fundamentally a matter of what art history has to repress.

JE: I think we can take the incorrigibility of art history as a given, and concentrate on art criticism. Let me ask a pragmatic version of my question: when you think of critical practices aside from your own, what is the deepest available history? Before modernism and modernist criticism, there is Romanticism, which I think is very much alive and well in current critical practices, perhaps especially in yours, Dave. But before Romanticism, is anything available as a history *for* criticism?

DH: Do you mean a pre-Romantic history of criticism? Probably not, although there are reams upon reams of classical and medieval commentaries of art and poetry, oceans of commentaries on these commentaries, even. Is there pre-Romantic art criticism? Probably not, because classical, Renaissance and Neoclassical discourse presume the unity of the arts. If we join in this presumptionn, Quintillian, Seneca, Vitruvius, Boccaccio, Vasari, Palladio, Sydney,

Scaliger, Dryden, Pope, and hundreds of others may be properly regarded as beaux-arts critics or theorists.

What a renaissance critic writes about *Orlando Furioso* is presumed to be applicable to cultural endeavors generally. That was sort of the idea of the Renaissance. Criticism begins with Aristotle, and then there's other stuff.

The diction of my own practice goes back to Baudelaire, Dickens, Wilde, Shaw, Lamb, Hazlitt, and DeQuincey, with a little bit of Alexander Hamilton thrown in, since my dream job would have been to contribute to the *Federalist Papers*. As an idiom, then, my practice is less high-Romantic than pre-Romantic, or low-Romantic if you wish. That's whence I come, and hopefully I've come a long way. In any case, I'm mostly about writing, about handling the non-fictional voice, and managing Shadyesque parataxis.

JE: But is it also about ideas about art and life, their interaction, immediacy, judgment, and so on?

DH: Probably, but it all begins with the word, with the idea of the word as an object. I am interested in the phonetics, in how it sounds when you read it, in the fluidity of the tempo, the graphic look on the page, and I'm interested in works of art with comparable attributes, so there is an element of circularity there. I'm interested in the text as it resolves itself in the world, and not in the footnote. I am interested in art as it resolves itself in the world and not in a footnote. A small thing, but mine own.

JE: You take formal inspiration, or writerly rhetorical inspiration, but not philosophic inspiration, from these sources that comprise your history.

DH: Right.

JE: There's a good book along those lines, Philip Lopate's *Art of the Personal Essay*[50]—

DH: I don't know it, but there is something in the modes of address devised by Wilde and Shaw that I find attractive. There is a kind of winsome, non-coercive arrogance in Shaw's music criticism, and in Wilde's "The Critic as Artist" that I have, on occasion, tried to emulate. It's a matter of how you handle your voice. Anyway, I can't imagine a history of art criticism, because it would be gigantic general history of beaux-arts commentary.

The Balkanization of art criticism has taken place during my lifetime. I started out writing about dance, rock and roll, art, movies, everything—I was a critic. Most of my colleagues did the same. The Balkanization of art criticism is just a sign of its escalating Philistinism. What is gone out of the culture now is the presumption of the unity of the arts, that poetry, theater, dance, art, and literature have some common language. And I know of no artist who does not believe this, so I should point out that we have been talking for a while here without mentioning Mozart, Balanchine, Shakespeare, or Donne. I mean, are we civilized or not?

JE: But isn't it important to distinguish between people in the past who you might include if you had to teach art criticism (that group might well include Vasari, or Boccaccio), and critics who represent some viable antecedent to your own practice as an art critic?

DH: Well, speaking for myself, I grew up with a practice that was called "new journalism." It was grounded in mid-nineteenth-century Victorian practices. It was Dickens, Ruskin, Hazlitt, and DeQuincey. All those people had a manner of address, and basically we just appropriated it. Tom Wolfe would tell you that; all of my old co-conspirators would tell you that. It's just Victorian prose. With Hunter S. Thompson it was more boring than with most, but—

JE: You're throwing a nice wrench into the works for academic critics who are compelled to teach the history of art criticism, as Michael is, because next time he is going to have to put Hazlitt in alongside Baudelaire—alongside genealogies that would be more normative.

MN: That's okay. Hazlitt is sitting on my shelves, along with Ruskin, Pater, and various others.

SM: Maybe we could put it this way. It seems to me that within the university, it is clear that criticism is always a secondary discourse. You can't have a department of it, and it can't be a discipline in the usual way. In the literature department, you have criticism because it is a continuation of the object you already have. (You're reading Shelley, so why not read the critical bits?) In the art history department, criticism gets in as a part of the contextualization of the work. It comes in as evidence.

Then, as Michael observed, some of the most genuinely compelling art historians understand their activity, at some deep level, *as* criticism. But then it is no longer a case of asking about the history of criticism; it is a matter of rethinking how you might do history.

DH: Here's a position I would propose. The tradition of writing history, criticism, and narrative is broad, deep, and intermingled. Even in these most general categories, it's hard to distinguish them and sort them out. As a consequence, when you sort history out and then sort art history out from the general writing of history—when you sort criticism out and then sort art criticism out from all other form of criticism, you don't have much. Also, you have introduced a second level of encryption that cannot be rendered clear. It is doubly encoded. You are missing vital information. To take an instance, I grew up around a generation of artist-writers (Don Barthelme, John Barth, and Thomas Pynchon) who wrote criticism. Barthelme has a little story called "The Balloon," which is a beautiful critique. *The Crying of Lot 49* is an act of criticism. Does that means it is not fiction or not criticism? I don't think we need to make boxes. What is not criticism? Even Raymond Carver is criticism; bad criticism, unfortunately.

JE: But I do think we can separate the problem of finding moments of criticism within, as, and for history (a subject Whitney Davis raised in the first roundtable), from the problem of the absence of art criticism in universities. (And here, as I've said, it is important to distinguish the many courses on Diderot, Baudelaire, Fénéon, and so forth, from courses that might lead to the *practice* of criticism.) For me, this latter question is practical, and that is why I was asking you [*James, Ariella, and Dave*] how far back you find viable, pertinent antecedents to your own practice: where, in history, do you draw relevant genealogies?

JP: Well, in *The New Criterion* we also talk about Hazlitt and other writers we've been mentioning, and we are also interested in the

British tradition of taste. And I agree with Dave that criticism is a nineteenth-century Romantic tradition, filtered through journalism. If you read Tom Wolfe's *Painted Word*,[51] it's very much in line with what you, Dave, have been describing as criticism. My problem with Wolfe, however, is his contempt for the history of aesthetics and for modernism. And look at what results. I can't stand those tacky artists he likes. I mean, Frederick Hart? That kind of taste gives Wolfe's species of conservative a bad name.

DH: You're right of course, although *The Painted Word* is a sorry book.

JP: But Jim, to your question: I agree with Dave that there has been no history of art criticism because until recently, criticism has had a unified history. There's that, and in addition art criticism was thought of as a debased enterprise, which wasn't worthy of thought or critique at an academic level.

JE: But still, people have had forty years since the academization of criticism in which to ponder possible histories—

JP: Yes, but academia moves very slowly.

JE: Perhaps—

JP: When I was an undergraduate—and that wasn't so long ago—I wanted to write about the summer 1967 issue of *Artforum*, I was told it was unheard of to do that.

JE: I would rather think there is a systemic reason for the absence of histories of art criticism, rather than just academic dilatoriness or caution. Criticism in general, even in literature departments, is exactly the site on which a great deal of work about "philosophy" and "literature" has been done, by people like Derrida, and now Hélène Cixous. (She is here for these events, but not, unfortunately, at our roundtable.) So I'd rather look to the history of critique after Kant, as Michael does, or to the deep-seated ambivalences about criticism and nonfiction in literature departments. (Art history, it seems to me, has its own limited and mainly inarticulate ideas about criticism.)

DH: I don't think a history of criticsm is of much value. Beyond its literary quality, it has the shelf life of milk. Why not just throw it out with the rest of periodical journalism.

JP: Without *October* there would be no academic history of art criticism. It would have been written within contemporary work, it would have been a continuation of practices, it would have been written in the present. There is a desire in this panel, I think, to put art criticism into an historical framework, and to remove its presentness.

JE: Well, that's not my question. I am concerned that art criticism seems to have no *worry* about its lineage. Can contemporary practice be content to have either no history (to be something grounded in experience) or else to have all of history (from Boccaccio, say, to the present)?

MN: To go back to what Steve said: I studied literature before I studied art history. When I studied literature, basically I thought I was doing literary criticism: I was learning to read texts in a critical way. Then I went into art history, and I discovered that it was supposed to be something very different; criticism was something you did outside the university. This has to do with the historical development of the disciplines, but also with the nature of the object. The object of literary criticism is a text, whereas traditionally the object of art criticism has been a thing, a physical object upon which you perform certain operations to do with its contextualization and interpretation.

Beginning around the 1960s, the object of art history came to be conceived of as a text, rather than as a thing, which opened the possibility of a new rapprochement between art history and criticism. That may also lie behind the *October* moment in relation to criticism.

JE: To me this conversation is completely bewildering, because we are supposedly wondering about criticism's relation to modernism, and antimodernism (or non-modernism, or postmodernism), and yet somehow by eliciting what happens under the name of criticism in literary studies, we have arrived at a place where the relevant history of art criticism includes William Hazlitt. We have leapt back before modernism and into Victorian literature—

DH: But doesn't modernism start in 1605?

JE: No, it doesn't.[52]

DH: Ah! Thank you.

MN: Well, maybe we're at another stage, after that textualizing moment. You could say the postmodern moment was the moment of the textualization. We're not quite clear what the moment is now, because—

JE: We are not unclear about it, because we are taking Victorian models as appropriate antecedents for our practice.

LC: But isn't the nineteenth century the very moment when the novel becomes a mass medium, and it is available to everyone?

DH: Right.

LC: And literary criticism went hand in hand with the novel, because everyone had access. Until very recently, even art history was done by people of a certain class who got to travel to see the objects. If you look back into early twentieth-century British art history, on the whole the art historians have a certain kind of background that enables them to go look at things—

DH: The Grand Tour.

LC: —and so on. Similarly, criticism must have some relation to access to the objects, and that must make it a totally different thing from literary criticism, after a certain point. If you can't see it, you can't write about it.

JE: I don't dispute any of that: I want to draw attention to the weirdness of a conversation on art criticism, held in 2005, which ends up with a list like Hazlitt, Pater, Wilde, Shaw, and Boccaccio! This list really is astonishing. It would never have come up after, say, Fry's generation: names like these were not proffered in *Artforum*, or *October*. They point to a new sense of possible histories.

DH: Might it not be possible that the much-heralded death of modernism opened its historical narrative at both ends—that things after modernism resonate with things before modernism?

AB: I was trained as an art historian, and then I made the leap to art criticism, so I have a foot in both camps. I think the goals are much the same. They are about understanding the object in its historical context, and in the context of other art. I take as my models people who are really good art historians and writers. For example, Leo Steinberg. A lot of art historians who wrote clearly, without a lot of jargon, and made arguments.

JE: But who are your favorite models among art critics?

AB: I like Adam Gopnik, who used to write art criticism for the *New Yorker*.

DH: He wrote a good piece on Watteau.

AB: He has the training . . . but I also like Meyer Schapiro. He has a love of the objects, and also a high level of expertise that transcended art history and moved into art criticism. Steinberg and Schapiro are good models, and they are within the field. And I like Ruskin. I do think there is something between Ruskin and now.

JE: Something!

DH: Let me interject something here. I think we have the question backwards. I don't think the problematic resides with criticism, which has always been contemporary commentary, which, as Foucault has pointed out, arises out of the enormous pre-modern (or pre-1605!) tradition of commentary. The problematic resides with art history, which, tenured or not, has hardly any history and no canonical masters. Art history is the new kid in town, not criticism, and in its very beginning, with Wölfflin and Riegl, it bit the poison fruit of "culture."

SM: It was okay with Wölfflin and Riegl; it was with Panofsky that things changed—

DH: Either way, art history is the parvenu deluded by romantic Kultural Kriticism (with capital K's). Criticism was infected at a later date.

JE: Ah, some more familiar names, but again not from art criticism . . . but we need to wrap this up, so we have time for questions.

Martin Patrick [*Question from the audience*]: I teach art history and criticism for Illinois State University, so I don't work for the Man, but for the State, which I guess is roughly equivalent. I teach the history of art criticism, with a number of texts. One of the people I would insinuate between, say, the panelists here and, say, John Ruskin, would be Lawrence Alloway. Nothing of his is in print—

JE: An anthology is being prepared.

MP: He was largely an autodidact, and he said he wrote "criticism with footnotes." And then, along with Donald Kuspit, he started one of the only art history programs created by art critics. There is a large gap in twentieth-century criticism, occupied by people like Alloway and Lucy Lippard, who have not been mentioned here. But it seems to me that when it comes to constructing histories of art criticism, you are on your own. There is a lot of art criticism in bookstores like Powell's [*a used book store*], because it goes out of print.

SM: So, imagine you put together an anthology of the history of art criticism. It has Baudelaire, Fry, Diderot . . . and then you say, "Okay, we're not going to do the bits that have been covered in the history of art course, and we're not going to do the parts that are covered in the history of theory, history of ideas, or history of philosophy. We are going to do the bits that belong to the history of criticism." Then I think what you're left with is the voice, and that's not a history. That's something else.

JE: Steve, this idea is not unrelated to the third most popular reason for writing art criticism in the Columbia survey—that is, to "write well." Our funny dramatis personae is as wide-ranging as theirs.[53] I won't go over the objections I had to that criterion of writing well, because they are different from the issues that arise with your concept of "voice." But I wonder if an account that turns on voice might work when it comes to questions of such things as books, courses, or institutional configurations. How—and I guess this is a version of the same question—might an account of voice be used to explain the absence of histories of art criticism?

SM: I was not trying to reduce criticism to voice. I was saying the reason you can't have a history of criticism is because the thing that would be an object of that history is not fundamentally historical.

DH: One reason I started writing criticism was that when I began, and I was writing fiction, I found I had this weird voice. It was too eccentric or ego-centric, if you will, for fiction. It was easier to render it transparent when I was writing about objects in the world.

JP: I think art criticism *is* more than voice, and it is something different from writing a novel, or writing stories. Maybe, too, we think criticism is a healthy enterprise, and not in crisis. The only way you can get a book published on it is for there to be in crisis, and that's why we read the *October* roundtable. It's not art criticism that's in trouble. It's *October* that's in crisis.

DH: *October* is like *Yellow Submarine?* I love it.

JP: But I think criticism is still vital, and doesn't want to reveal all its secrets.

AB: I would also mention Pauline Kael; she wasn't an art historian; she was just a good writer who was also a critic.

JP: Or Clement Greenberg, who is still startling in how closely he can read work.

JE: Our list is getting as long as the Columbia lists . . .

DH: Okay. The difference between writing art criticism and writing fiction is that, in criticism, the ethical imperative is absolute. You cannot cheat. You cannot betray the world as seen. You cannot engage in conflicts of interest. It is an absolute, straight-arrow, hard-core, down-the-line relationship with the reader. You are speaking on your own authority, and your authority is what you live by. If you screw up, you're screwed. We can all list art critics who have destroyed their reputations by collusion of one sort or another, Clem among them.

Michelle Sciumbato [*Question from the audience*]: How prevalent do you think it is for an art critic to invent or discover an artist for their own benefit?

DH: It's been done, but the accreditation process is much more complex.

GG: I heard you as asking something else, which is that there may be an agenda in place. You were wondering—tell me if I'm right—if critics look for examples to illustrate their ideas.

MS: Right.

GG: So that the text would come first, and the artwork would be the thing that would be its subtext, instead of the other way around.

DH: It doesn't work that way. Good art makes good criticism. Good criticism, invariably and without exception, makes bad art.

MN: Well, my own criticism is mostly longer essays, between say three thousand and eight thousand words. One of my motivations is to understand the work as well as it can possibly be understood, or explain it as well as it can possibly be explained. There's a dimension of that which is a project of mastery: I am going to understand that work better than anybody has ever understood it before, and better even than the artist is capable of understanding it. I am going to produce the best possible interpretation of that work. That's very dangerous, because it can result in a kind of closure. So there comes a point at which I feel I have to undermine my own investment in mastery, and so the question is: to what extent is that implicit in all criticism?

For example, I have written for many years about the work of James Coleman; he produces work that is about the most difficult to understand of any artist currently working. That attracts me a lot, because I want to penetrate the work and really understand it. But there is a moment when I find that the work is about my own failure to do that. The work, as it were, criticizes or undermines me as a critic. I think that's an important moment for criticism, when it is undermined or opened up, because that's when dialogue can happen, and when some kind of otherness is recognized.

DH: I think we must assume that all objects exceed our description of them. I like to write about art that's hard to write about, because it puts pressure on the language. I prefer writing about abstract art, because I don't like pictures of anything but Catherine Deneuve.

But, whatever I write, I am always excerpting an excerpt. My interpretation is a creature of the historical moment. The work of art, insofar as it survives, is trans-historical. Writing about art that doesn't survive is just war reporting or drama criticism.

JE: The open-endedness of criticism is a good note on which to conclude.

I think these two roundtables, spanning three thousand miles and six months, have made a good start on some fundamental issues in contemporary art criticism. I want to note three issues in particular, on which our indecision has been especially interesting.

First is the problem of judgment. In the *October* roundtable, Hal Foster seemed curious about forms of judgment, but overall they were content to let strongly contradictory versions of judgment circulate in their conversation. Our Irish roundtable was diffident about the prospect of defining forms of judgment. I think we have brought the conversation to an interesting place, where the issue seems to be resolving into a difference between writers "committed to providing judgments" (quoting Ariella there), and writers who intend either to describe without judging (a theme in the first roundtable), or to encounter works without judging (Irit Rogoff said judgment was "deeply alien" to her), or to find interest in the conditions, possibilities, and contexts of judgment (as happened on this roundtable). Whether the term of judgment is quality (Greenberg), art (de Duve), or "notice" (Groys), writing that offers judgments differs from writing that ponders the conditions, history, cogency, or sense of judgments. Talk about judgment in art criticism is stalled, I think. People who proffer judgments as their everyday business don't have a productive way of talking to people who don't. I think that in this roundtable we got close to the problem of trying to find a common language in which those two possibilities might talk.

Second, we broached the question of art criticism's histories, which had been a constant ghostly companion of both conversations. The strange lack of a history of criticism is a crucial fact for criticism. That missing history is a literal absence (as Michael noted, there is no textbook), but it is also a philosophic problem (as Steve noted), an institutional problem (as I suggested in the first roundtable), and even an historiographic problem (that became clear in our crazy lists of critical models, from Boccaccio to Pauline Kael). It would be good to have a way of talking about criticism's "historylessness" that could take all these into account.

Third and last, we made virtually no progress on deciding what counts as art criticism. The first roundtable focused on the difference between journalistic writing and "serious" criticism, and we wandered from questions of divisions within critical orientations (modernist, postmodernist) to problems of curation. Those portions of both roundtables dedicated to the subject of what counts as art criticism (it was the third topic in this roundtable, and the fourth topic in the earlier roundtable) are, I think, the least coherent. Could we conclude that art criticism has a crippling inability to talk about what it is?

And now I have a final question for Dave: what percentage of what we said this afternoon was crap?

DH: I have no idea. My own contributions were running at right about seventy-eight percent, maybe eighty-two.

Notes

1. *The Dictionary of Art*, edited by Jane Turner (New York: Grove's Dictionaries, 1996), with online updates.
2. It was advertised in that way: see the brochure "6,700 Scholars Have Joined Together to Change the World of Art History," edited by Jane Turner (New York: Grove's Dictionaries, 1994).
3. See my review of Newhouse, *Art and the Power of Placement* (New York: Monacelli, 2005), in *The New York Times Book Review*, Sunday, May 8, 2005, 22.
4. Boris Groys, *The Total Art of Stalinism: Avant-Garde, Aesthetic Dictatorship, and Beyond*, tr. by Charles Rougle (Princeton NJ: Princeton University Press, 1992).
5. *Force Fields: Phases of the Kinetic/Conception*, edited by Guy Brett (Barcelona: Museum d'Art Contemporani de Barcelona, 2000).
6. Julian Schnabel, *C.V.J.: Nicknames of Maitre D's And Other Excerpts from Life* (New York: Random House, 1987).
7. Yve-Alain Bois, Benjamin Buchloh, Hal Foster, and Rosalind Krauss, *Art Since 1900* (London: Thames and Hudson, 2004).
8. Michael Fried, "An Introduction to My Art Criticism," in *Art and Objecthood: Essays and Reviews* (Chicago IL: University of Chicago Press, 1998), 1–74.
9. The idea of "not caring how it comes out" is Richard Wollheim's opinion (personal communication, 1996). It can be seen in Fried, "An

Introduction," 73 n. 75. "Resolutely nonjudgmental" is in "An Introduction," 51.

10. Fried, "An Introduction," 51–52.
11. Kabakov, *Ilya Kabakov stellt vor: Leben und Werk von Charles Rosenthal (1898–1933): das Städel*, edited by Sabine Schulze (Frankfurt am Main: Stroemfeld, 2000).
12. Staatliche Hochschule für Bildende Künste, at www.staedelschule.de; School of the Art Institute of Chicago, at www.artic.edu.
13. State University of New York at Stony Brook, www.art.sunysb.edu/maphd.html.
14. For a discussion of art research, by which I mean art as a process of inquiry leading to new knowledge or understanding, see my "A Method of Search for Reality" in *The New PhD in Studio Art*, edited by James Elkins (*Printed Project No. 4*) (Dublin: Sculptor's Society of Ireland, 2005); the same essay also appears in *Thinking through Art*, edited by Lynne Holdridge and Katy Macleod (London: Routledge, 2005).
15. Parts emerge in *Thinking Through Art*, edited by Katy Macleod and Lin Holdridge (London: Routledge, 2005). My "Afterword" in that book is printed in expanded form in *The New PhD in Studio Art*, edited by James Elkins (Dublin: Sculptor's Society of Ireland, 2005). That book is no. 4 in the occasional series called *Printed Project*, published by the Sculptor's Society.
16. The survey yielded 169 responses, a seventy-three percent return rate. *The Visual Art Critic*, edited by András Szántó (New York: National Arts Journalism Program, Columbia University, 2002), quotations on p. 27. It did not include freelance writers, and did not poll art magazines on account of their lower circulations. The book is available as a free pdf at www.najp.org/publications/researchreports/visualarts.html.
17. Thierry de Duve, *Kant After Duchamp* (Cambridge MA: MIT Press, 1996), 304 and passim. See also vol. 1 of this series, *Art History versus Aesthetics* (New York: Routledge, 2006), in which de Duve elaborates on his sense of aesthetic judgment. [J.E.]
18. Reprinted as a Starting Points essay in this volume.
19. Documenta X and XI are currently archived under Documenta XII. For X see www.documenta12.de/archiv/dx/english/frm_home.htm. For XI, see www.documenta12.de/data/english/.
20. I am informed by Katy Deepwell that Documenta XI had the highest percentage of women artists—some forty-four percent. "What it failed to do, was include women from outside Europe" or even New York. The exact figures are in *Paradoxa* (July 2002). [J.E.]
21. Reprinted in this volume.
22. Rosalind Krauss, "Introduction," *The Originality of the Avant-Garde and Other Modernist Myths* (Cambridge MA: MIT Press, 1985), 1–2, repeated for example in "Poststructuralism and the Paraliterary," also in *The Originality of the Avant-Garde*, 292, 295.
23. *When Attitudes Become Form: Works, Concepts, Processes, Situations, Information*, exhibition catalog, edited by Harald Szeeman (London: Institute of Contemporary Arts, 1969); *Les Immatériaux*, exhibition catalog, edited by Jean-François Lyotard (Paris: Centre Pompidou, 1985).

24. Rosalind Krauss, *The Optical Unconscious* (Cambridge MA: MIT Press, 1993).
25. *After Criticism: New Responses to Art and Performance*, edited by Gavin Butt (Maiden MA: Blackwell, 2005). Texts like *ReMembering the Body*, edited by Gabrielle Brandstetter and Hortensia Völckers, with contributions by Bruce Mau and André Lepecki (Ostfildern-Ruit: Hatje Cantz, 2000) and the journal *Performance Research* are good examples of this new sense of critical writing; but as interesting as it is, I do not see how it can be justified as a response to temporal and ephemeral artwork in particular. I wonder why the same arguments could not be used to produce analogously experimental writing in response to, say, paintings. (And I think of writers such as Jean-Louis Schefer in this regard.)
26. See http://opensource.boxwith.com.
27. "Round Table: The Present Conditions of Art Criticism," *October* 100 (Spring 2002): 200–28.
28. "Round Table," 207.
29. "Round Table," 209.
30. "Round Table," 210.
31. "Round Table," 216–17.
32. Joselit: "So now you get the YBAs as a kind of popular cultural entity." Buchloh: "The YBAs?" Joselit: "Young British Artists. [*Laughter*.] That's probably a symptom." "Round Table," 203.
33. Perhaps especially because it continues to have measurable influence in North American and English departments of art history, and in some critical contexts such as the journnal *Texte zur Kunst*.
34. Since the roundtable in Ireland, the *October* roundtable, and my own *What Happened to Art Criticism?* were noted, obliquely, in Rhea Anastas, "A Response," *Art Journal*, 64, 3 (Fall 2005): 78–83, especially notes 1–3.
35. Buchloh says Hickey is a "rhapsodic substitute" for art criticism. He appears to resuscitate art criticism, in Buchloh's view, "by giving us something that has no social function, no discursive position, [and] that serves as a critical placebo." "Part of the appeal of Dave Hickey," Hal Foster observes, "is that he has developed a sort of pop-libertarian aesthetic, a neoliberal aesthetic." Robert Storr defends Hickey, and gets this from George Baker: "So Dave Hickey is the Robin Hood of Art Criticism." "The Present Conditions of Art Criticism," *October*, 100 (Spring 2002): 201–28, quotations on [J.E.]
36. The roundtable was part of a series sponsored by the School of the Art Institute. The roundtable itself was held in a packed auditorium, and turned away one hundred people. Talks given by Dave Hickey, Jim Elkins, and Hélène Cixous all had to be closed. [J.E.]
37. "American Sculpture," *Artforum*, 5 (Summer, 1967).
38. *Conference on Art Criticism and Art Education*, edited by David Ecker, Jerome Hausman, and Irving Sandler (New York: New York University Office of Field Research and School Services, 1970), 69.
39. Sennett, *The Fall of Public Man* (New York: Vintage, 1976).
40. The passage in "Complaints of an Art Critic" is discussed in my *What Happened to Art Criticism?*, excerpted in this book.
41. www.artprice.com.
42. www.artfacts.net/about_us/?Statistical_Resource.

43. www.mmproyectos.com/pr_04.htm, curated by Pablo Helguera.
44. "American Art Now: Aesthetics and Politics," Clark Art Institute, October 2003.
45. *Alice Neel*, exhibition catalog, edited by Ann Temkin (New York: Abrams, in association with the Philadelphia Museum of Art, 2000).
46. Helen Molesworth, *Part Object Part Sculpture*, exhibition catalog, with essays by Briony Fer, Rachel Haidu, David Joselit, Rosalind Krauss, and Molly Nesbit (University Park PA: Penn State Press/Wexner Center, 2005); Jean François Chevrier, *Art and Utopia: Limited Action*, exhibition catalog (Barcelona: Museu d'Art Contemporani de Barcelona, 2005).
47. Reprinted in this volume as one of the Starting Points.
48. Lionello Venturi, *History of Art Criticism*, translated by Charles Marriott (New York: E.P. Dutton, 1936). There is also *L'Invention de la Critique d'Art*, edited by Jean Marc-Poinsot and Henry Frangne (Rennes: University of Rennes, 2002). I thank Katy Deepweel and Michael Newman for drawing my attention to this.
49. *What Happened to Art Criticism?* reprinted in abridged form in this volume as a Starting Point.
50. *Art of the Personal Essay: An Anthology from the Classical Era to the Present* (New York: Anchor, 1993).
51. *The Painted Word* (New York: Farrar, Straus, and Giroux, 1975).
52. I would argue that as in *Master Narratives and Their Discontents* (New York: Routledge, 2005), saying modernism begins in 1605 is overly eccentric, because it cuts off too many of the principal theories of modernism's beginnings.
53. Excerpted in as one of the Starting Points in this vol.

4
Assessments

András Szántó

So Why Don't They Like to Judge?

Some years ago, I had the entertaining privilege of collaborating with the Russian artist duo, Komar and Melamid, on an installment of their survey project, in which they polled populations of various countries about what kind of art they like and dislike. Their tongue-in-cheek exercise had by then raised all sorts of surprisingly profound points about the status of art in society and who has the power to say what art is or ought to be. So, the artists decided, it was time to poll the experts.

Our survey of the membership of the North American Society of Aesthetics was undertaken in adherence to exacting sociological research guidelines. We presented our findings at the Association's annual conference in Montreal. A PhD student colleague of mine at Columbia University crunched the numbers. I did the analysis and wrote the final report.

By far the most rewarding part of my job was to suggest to the artists the key parameters that should govern the creation of an original artwork that would represent the statistical consensus of the polled individuals, who were academically credentialed professionals versed in the appreciation and analysis of art at the highest intellectual level. After carefully consulting the findings, I suggested to Alex and Vitaly that the theme of the work should be *prevarication.*

Why? Because the experts refused to give clear answers. Their favorite responses were "I don't know," "maybe," and "not applicable." Do they like paintings the size of TVs or refrigerators? It depends. Which color is their favorite? All over the map. What about preferring to see nudes or historical figures in a painting? Many experts on art history and aesthetics didn't even bother to answer such questions.

This refusal to commit to clear opinions stood in stark contrast to the surveys Komar and Melamid had conducted of average people in many countries around the world. Those plain folks were unequivocal about which color they like the best (blue, in most cases), where they stood on the matter of figuration vs. abstraction (figuration, all the way), and which season they preferred to see on a painting (spring). In other words, while laypeople have clear ideas about what sort of art they like, there appears to be something about expert knowledge that abhors categorical judgments. Hedging one's bets, it would appear, is a mark of erudition and sophistication, at least when it comes to art.

Komar and Melamid proceeded to paint a diptych consisting of two panels—one the size of a fridge, the other the size of a TV, and thus the work *in toto* being the size of neither. The picture had a lot of vagueness and murkiness about it it. It wasn't pretty. I wouldn't want to hang it on my wall. But it was brilliant in visualizing the statistical results.

Anyway, I'm relating this now in response to a section of the dialogue on art criticism that refers to another study of mine. That study appeared under the title *The Visual Art Critic: A Survey of Art Critics at General-Interest News Publications in America*, and its most frequently cited finding had to do with critics' relative disdain for what has traditionally counted as a fundamental aspect of art criticism—judging. In the survey, to the surprise of almost everyone connected to the project, judging came in last among the queried points of emphasis in art reviewing, behind describing, contextualizing historically, theorizing, and even writing well.

A panelist in the roundtable rightly noted that the survey included critics writing for mainstream media,[1] and voiced a concern that one shouldn't lump together "journalism" and "art criticism." Another speaker agreed that "reportage criticism" is cut from a different cloth entirely than criticism of the more high-minded variety. The writers of "reportage criticism," it was argued on the panel, are "not trained in looking at art," so we shouldn't take their responses as a benchmark of expert opinion on art criticism.

As it happens, the survey included only art critics, and not arts reporters. And the overwhelming majority of them were highly trained in looking at art. So could it be that the venue where they publish their criticism precludes them from placing a higher emphasis on judging?

That's true, to a point. In mainstream media, critics are supposed, above all, to inform the general audience about goings-on in art. They're not supposed to engage in inside-baseball debates. They're certainly not supposed to sound like they're resentful, or taking sides arbitrarily, or advancing personal convictions or agendas.

Obtuse writing is a no-no. Pious arrogance and surfeits of intellectualism are not appreciated. Most importantly, however, these critics are operating in an environment that, in every other respect (except on the editorial page), worships at the shrine of "objectivity." American mainstream journalism is a place where, as a matter of professional custom, opinions and personal judgments are erased out of the picture. All of which leaves critics in a somewhat odd position.

This certainly accounts for some of the wariness about judging, but hardly all. For the fact is that the critics in the survey were highly sensitized to recent changes in the art world that make passionate and categorical judging increasingly difficult, and to some, even suspicious. "The days of the chest-thumping oracle critic are over," said one, approvingly. Indeed, it may well be that "reportage critics" are the ones who are practicing the kind of enlightened, open-ended, accepting, and pluralistic art writing that rightly fits our increasingly globalized, multicultural, de-paradigmed, and omnidirectionally inclusive art world.

I, for one, haven't forgotten about the Komar and Melamid research. I have a feeling that judging may have fared equally badly in a survey administered to higher-end art critics. If you want to hear categorical judgments about art today, go to an art fair and listen to collectors talk about pictures. The vocabulary appears to consist of "I hate it" and "it's fabulous." You will search in vain for such clear expressions of taste in the groves of academe or in panel discussions of well-meaning accredited experts on art and culture. Academics may not want to hear this, but their predispositions toward the act of judging art may rank them closer to journalists than they think.

Katy Deepwell

A Feminist Response

I have described my own position as that of a feminist art critic and have tried in more than a few essays and books since 1987 to articulate what this position entails.[2] I not only practice my politics in and through the art criticism that I write, but also as an editor, a lecturer, an invited guest, an organizer, even, at times—I confess—a groupie, a fan, and an engaged reader. My practice involves making strategic choices—these are decisions in the sense of "exercising" judgments—

questioning my own enthusiasms, preferences and understandings while simultaneously researching and locating the spaces and possibilities where it might be purposeful to act, make an intervention, and articulate a different point of view. With reference to Marx these are all professional/personal judgments I make within circumstances which are not of my own choosing.

I want to begin by raising the question of "ethics," which was surprisingly not discussed. We orient ourselves within the world according to our ethics (or lack of them) and the situations in which we find ourselves confront us with ethical choices. Ethics, here, is the practice of a politics, even amongst those who declare the absence of politics as their politics and those who deny any conscious knowledge of everyday life as thoroughly infused with such choices. There are professional and personal ethics in how art critics respond and relate to the artists they write about which goes beyond the question of "identification," "embodiment," "or even friendship" with artists evidenced in a text. The issue is more complex than whether or not such interests are declared or known and whether procedures of "distance" or claims to "objectivity" are advanced. This is also more than reporting the "gossip" which makes up so much of the internal conversations of the art world. Who we choose to write about and where we put our energies defines us as much as the language with which we speak about our concerns. Boris Groys mentioned how "finite" he felt the possibilities for making changes to certain interpretations are—the weight of history, of canons and of pre-existing bodies of knowledge. I would concur, but this doesn't undermine the desire to seek to transform meanings, interpretations, evaluations even though it is done knowing that we are not "free" (or even uniquely privileged) nor possess infinite possibilities to play. The form of art criticism or critical writing was not discussed and there is a difference in what is possible in a one-hundred-word vs. eight-hundred-word exhibition review; a one-minute interview on TV vs. an hour-long documentary; a chat-show host's job vs. that of a five-thousand-word interview with an artist for publication; an endorsement of a commercial catalogue of five hundred words vs. an academic essay in a kunsthalle catalogue of four thousand–ten thousand words; a five-minute contribution to a panel discussion vs. a one-hour lecture. The art critic's role in the totality of dissemination and circulation of knowledge about contemporary art should not be overlooked: TV, print media, art press, academic journals, radio, Internet magazines, catalogues, books, lecture series, talks and conferences in galleries, universities and museums; all determine our "field" and they do mutually interrogate each other. Nor should the specific task of some critics—if they have a particular progressive agenda—be forgotten as this "work" generates attitudes, agendas and diverse forms of aesthetic, cultural, and political avant-gardism in our culture. Maybe this is where recognition of greater distinctions in the practices of art criticism, beyond academic and journalistic, was needed in the discussion. The "neutrality" pertaining to the text is illusory: as the context often produces a further "investment" in a form of critical discourse without any attention being given to its actual content.

Rolling like an undercurrent to these debates are some of the less ethical procedures fostered by certain cliques or circles of influence: a dealer's purchase of magazine space beyond advertisements, staking one's career in the active promotion of groups or tendencies as the next avant-garde, private collectors employing critics to promote their collection in publications, accepting hospitality from dealers or collectors or government agencies (and distinguishing this from outright bribery or pay-outs), exploiting contacts in networks between dealers, curators, and critics to raise artist's prices by producing and placing positive copy, a critic's acquisition of works by artists they have promoted, the impact of love affairs or the treatment of one's social, cultural, or political enemies in what gets published. For the reader, this is not just about distinguishing "promotion" and "hype" from a partial perspective, it is about how the text, the coverage, the media used itself announces these forms of "ethical" decision-making within communities of shared interests. Art critics do generally align themselves, even at different stages in their careers, with communities of artists—just as curators do. Sometimes these connections are only visible retrospectively. The discussion of the relationship between journalism and academic forms of art criticism (in the exhibition catalogue or the specialist art journal) did not address an important point: art critics are not all "jobbing" critics, sent on missions by editors, but they, and I, frequently choose to write about subjects which engage us in a self-elected and self-interested way. I chose my own strategy as an intervention in the status quo, namely, to write largely about women artists, to open up spaces where such work could be published, and to speak about discrimination as an issue. This was a choice, but one in which political allegiances, historical encounters, engagement with certain forms of knowledge as well as personal preferences all played a part. After more than thirty years of feminist art criticism and feminist critique as a recognizable discourse internationally, it also means investigating, questioning and considering what this legacy entails as a body of knowledge and as a resource for future work. Feminism may superficially appear to operate as repeatedly asking some basic questions about gender differences in representation and the unequal treatment of women in a liberal feminist vein, but the ramifications of such questions has led to the development of a large and diverse body of theory and knowledge touching on every subject in the canon and embracing a wide spectrum of political standpoints and perspectives from culturalist/socialist to radical separatist and queer.

Throughout the discussion about whether or not judgments are part of what critics do, or what kind of judgment was exercised in certain kinds of art critical writing, the alignment of judgments with forms of social/cultural/economic discrimination (on the grounds of sex, sexuality, race, ethnicity, religious belief, or nationalism) was not fully tackled. The exclusion of women on "quality" grounds was identified in the early 1970s as the alignment of a "prejudicial" aesthetic judgment with sex discrimination. Nothing has changed, the same trope repeats itself. Expressions of academic snobbery are also judgments. It is not the question of whether judgment is present or not, but whether the exercise of that judgment is the result of unfounded prejudice, bigotry, misogyny or hatred which is the issue (as Adrian Piper's work has so clearly identified). Feminist art history since the 1970s has found numerous examples of negative judgments against women—on every continent and in every language. Bigotry, hatred, and misogyny are the unpleasant "universals" which we should perhaps address when speaking about the discourses of art, art criticism and art history and their processes of selection. For example, what might the impact of an artist living and working in Madagascar be, who has a serious interview published in English for the first time: a passing interest in cultural exoticism, serious academic engagement, recognition of cultural innovation (for the critic), or will it lead to dilletantism and the promotion of a token? Will what she actually says ever challenge the canon, increase her market price or make her works more likely to be objects collected by world-class museums? Will her contribution be recognized as the subject of a "new" form of knowledge? Will it matter that she is regarded as "indigenous" or "in exile from a conflict," and what might be the differential impact of such assessments on any readings of her work if her family is regarded as American or that she trained in Europe?

The Art Seminars were very white, middle-class, and Anglo(Irish)-American, dominated by an internal debate between Dave Hickey, Michael Fried, *Artforum*, and *October*. If these represent the only hegemonic interests or reference points of concern, then this debate is redundant or very depressing. The arguments felt very dated: as if the 1980s and 1990s had never happened and as if distinguishing between critique and criticality was somehow important. This doesn't reflect the world in which I act or the developments in art criticism in which I am interested. Boris Groys's very important point about silence—about not writing—is probably the most effective strategy around today. What was silenced by this debate? With the exception of largely Jean Fisher's comments, it was the impact of feminist theory, cultural studies, post-colonial theory and post-structuralism in art theory and criticism today. *N.paradoxa* was founded to provide a space for critical discussion of the work of contemporary women artists and its relationship to the broader body of feminist theory. It was an intervention and is the only international art journal on this subject in the world. Perhaps when Documenta 12's publication project (2006–2007)—of which *n.paradoxa* is one of more than seventy journals of art criticism across the five continents in the world—will have developed, the global spread of different forms of art criticism (all neatly translated into English) will be more apparent.

While art theory had a brief mention in the conversation, and I would locate my interests there, cultural studies—and its academization—even as the background for the emergence of visual culture, did not get a mention. Cultural studies, feminist theory, and Marxism fuelled my own interest in the politics of knowledge production and, because of its attention to race, sex, and class, was taught not as a "systematic, hierarchized subject," a canon, a set of fixed subjects, but as an expanding framework—subject to revisions and transformations—an area where new concerns, innovative approaches, a politics of representation and a space for new subjects/objects of study would emerge against the grain of the "doxa." The notion within the first discussion of art history as not attached to the market, to curatorial and museum activities—to knowledge as power—seems laughable to someone coming from a training in the social history of art where insights of the sociology of art (H. Becker, P. Bourdieu, J. Wolff) were important. To study the mechanisms through which contemporary art is produced has been central to art school education—in spite of the decimation of art theory and criticism in the United Kingdom—in order to reveal how the field of contemporary art (variously defined post-1960s, because of art history's own sense of itself as a taught discipline) is continually being structured and restructured by its discourses (a process evident in/through curating and critical writing).

Ultimately, what structures my own desire to write is my curiosity to find out about art production in a global and dynamic sense beyond that which is dictated by fashion (even in academia). I think this spirit is in keeping with Lucy Lippard's approach of "changing" through encountering new phenomena, artists, and ideas during one's own lifetime and not just because they happen to be the "latest" thing. And like her, this is coupled with an acute sense of social injustice in which the problem of the continual marginalization of "others" is a constant concern, particularly those "Others" who form fifty-two percent of the world's population: women.

Daniel A. Siedell

Academic Art Criticism

Criticism is not only a cultural practice: it also circumscribes a social role. It is not only what a critic *does*, it is also what a *critic* does. This is important because a good deal of the *practice* of critics is in the cultivation of their *role* as critics. In arguing for the importance of the critic-intellectual to live in "metaphorical exile," Edward W. Said observed, "exile means that you are always going to be marginal, and that what you do as an intellectual has to be made up because you cannot follow a prescribed path."[3] An implication of not following a "prescribed path" is that critics spend a great deal of time talking and writing about what a critic is and what criticism should be. This is such a prominent feature in the history of criticism, and art criticism in particular, that it must be considered a primary aspect of what a critic is and what a critic does. This is in part why the Cork and Chicago panel discussions (as well as the infamous *October* roundtable that seems to lurk in the background) are so interesting: they are gatherings of critics and academics with a stake in what counts as criticism, re-enacting an important part of what criticism actually is. Consequently, these kinds of discussions are not, in the taxonomy of analytic philosophy, "second-order" analyses, but are in reality "first-order" practices. Or at least they *should* be.

Like all such discussions about criticism since the early-1960s, the Cork and Chicago panels function within the framework established by Clement Greenberg's critical practice in and around his publication of *Art and Culture* (1961) in which he retreated from the tentative projections and conjectures of his own "metaphorical exile" by revising his essays and reviews, many of them unacknowledged, in order retroactively to carve out a "prescribed path."[4] Greenberg's strategy proved a highly effective one for the reception of his criticism, which became inextricably bound to the development of the study of modern art and art criticism in the academy.[5] Therefore, much of art criticism's authority as a cultural practice is derived from academic entrenchment. An important means by which Greenberg accomplished his transformation in *Art and Culture* was to repress the journalistic aspect of critical practice, those aspects that reveal him to be feeling his way. He redefined himself through academia as a "theorist."

So it is not surprising that the Cork and Chicago conferences likewise pit academia against journalism. Elkins makes the revealing observation that there exists a massive chasm between academic art criticism, embodied in the *October* (and *Artforum*) circle and the "arts journalism" on display in the survey sponsored by the School of Journalism at Columbia, entitled "The Visual Arts Critic." He acknowledges his own difficulty in reading such arts journalism because it does not seem to sustain the kind of "close reading" he and his graduate students give it. This suggests that the seminar room is the intended audience for criticism and that art critical texts must be read in the same ways that academic texts are read.

Academic art criticism, that distinctive genre that coalesced as a result of the reception of *Art and Culture*, can be a provocative and powerful manifestation of criticism. But to assume that it alone is in the position to define what "counts" as art criticism is itself a failure to follow the virtues of metaphorical exile and a manifestation of an academic guild mentality that maintains a whiggish canon of art criticism that serves primarily to justify itself as *the* authentic form of art criticism. The academic aversion to arts journalism has become a repudiation of the critical spirit of modern criticism: the impressionistic, belles-lettristic, essayist, rhetorical, "journalistic" writing of non-academics, and non-professionals, that characterized the genre as a public discourse from the first quarter of the nineteenth century.

Because it attempts to reconfigure the relationship between criticism and art history, it is thus not surprising that Michael Fried's long introduction to his collected essays and reviews has not received the attention it deserves. In fact, it is dismissed by Elkins in the Cork panel discussion as "strange," and most of the panelists brush it off as too personal to be of much use.[6] But criticism is nothing if not personal (and "passionate, partisan, and political," to quote Baudelaire). Fried's essay is a remarkably frank, provocative, and problematic attempt to struggle with his role as a critic and its relationship to his work as an art historian. And what is more, it is *his* attempt to reconcile *his* role, *his* practice in a context in which there were no fixed rules or boundaries, and he was forced to make it up as he went along. This introductory essay is an attempt to reflect on this process. Like Greenberg, Fried is concerned about what criticism is and what his role as a critic is (and was). But his strategies and conclusions are quite different from Greenberg. In fact, Fried's publication of his essays and reviews function, in many ways, as an alternative *Art and Culture*.

From these and other panel discussions about the state of art criticism, it appears that what counts as art criticism is now defined exclusively by the academic guild. (And Fried's definitions are no exception.) Academics produce "authentic" art criticism, while non-academics produce arts journalism. If you have tenure, you can talk about what counts as art criticism. The problem with this is that it tends to absolve the critic of the responsibility and obligation to define and redefine her role as a critic and the function of her criticism as a constitutive part of the critical enterprise. Whether or not one has tenure and enjoys the fruits of an endowed chair, criticism remains the practice of an individual in metaphoric exile, one who, in Dave Hickey's words, "doesn't work for the Man." Authentic criticism is wrought from the realization that the authority to offer criticism must be continually achieved and re-achieved with each and every work, by each and every critic. Criticism that fails to recognize this is not criticism. It may get you tenure, but it isn't criticism.

Sheila Farr

Art Criticism: Who's Listening?

Audience is key to any discussion of art criticism, and got surprisingly little attention in the roundtables. Who are we writing for? Why should they care? The standard complaint about academic writing—whether it's categorized as history or criticism—is that much of it seems to be aimed at other academics. Journalists have a more diverse audience and the opportunity to entice those who know little about the subject while prodding the assumptions of those who do. Just because the opportunity is there, of course, doesn't mean we always take it.

I'm a daily newspaper critic, which some of the panelists consider an oxymoron. That's okay: I'm ambivalent about the title, too. Clearly much of the reporting (and even investigative reporting) I end up doing in my role as the visual art critic for the *Seattle Times* has nothing to do with critical writing. But those of us who write about art for newspapers are a diverse bunch. With a background in visual art, dance, literature, and poetry—not journalism—I never intended to write for a daily paper. But I love the opportunities and the audience it presents me, even if the drop-dead pace and hit-and-run style don't suit my temperament.

My first exposure to arts writing, growing up in the 1960s, was reading Tom Robbins. Before his debut novel *Another Roadside Attraction*, Tom was the art critic for the *Seattle Times*. Much like Dave Hickey, he wrote reviews with slam-dunk judgments and dazzling prose that were always fun to read and deeply intriguing, even if you couldn't figure out where those snappy judgments came from. (Tom once made headlines himself, arrested for indecent exposure at a Happening. It stuck in my mind then that a person must be fearless to be an art critic—and I've since learned from personal experience that it's true!)

I enjoyed working through transcripts of the roundtable discussions, dictionary at hand, even though at times it was a tough go. And naturally, being a critic, I'm glad to offer my assessment. First, Jim Elkins deserves applause for initiating the discussion and herding the cats. It's good to step back and take a hard look at what we do so fervently every day. The most focused part of the discussion dealt with the question of how history and criticism overlap. When it came to issues of contemporary criticism—should it describe or judge? What is its relationship to commerce? Should it be taught at universities?—the debate got more convoluted and tangential.

By the end, criticism was starting to look like a solipsistic endeavor, all wrapped up in itself. I couldn't help wondering, how are we serving art? (By that I don't mean gallery owners, publicists, artists, art collectors, and curators.) And how are we serving our readers?

If my early reading convinced me that art criticism can be engaging and even exhilarating, I've since developed my own ideas about its function. Here are some of them:

1. One of the greatest powers and responsibilities of a critic is choosing what to write about and what to exclude. In this respect, art historians are definitely critics when it comes to canon formation, no way around it.
2. Description isn't art criticism but it plays an important role, both in helping a reader picture the work in question and in helping the critic reveal the work's effectiveness. It's not a question of whether to describe or judge, rather how to present visual art in verbal terms.
3. Evaluation is essential to art criticism. Judgment is not. I agree with Michael Newman, who pointed out in the second roundtable that the act of weighing, comparing, contrasting, contextualizing needs to happen before a thumbs-up or -down. The most profound critical writing sometimes leaves

open questions. Our aesthetic should always be stretching. History has made lots of snap judgments look pretty silly.

4. Context matters—the framework of art history and contemporary culture, and the context in which the work is shown.

Readers come first in all this because writing is an act of communication. If art criticism isn't clear enough so that people understand it and compelling enough so they want to read it, we are writing to ourselves. It's our job to be interesting and relevant. That way, there's a chance of prying open people's minds.

Which is how we serve art. If a critic can inspire people to go look at art—be it a landscape painting, a multi-media video installation, an incendiary performance, or a sculpture made out of petroleum jelly—and consider it in a different, more expansive way than they would have done on their own, if we can change one person's set "I don't like that" or "my kid could have done it" attitude to a sense of curiosity and openness, we have done something right.

There is much more to it, of course, but that's where I like to start. Critical theory is a lot like theology. In order to debate it, you need to subscribe to a certain dogma and believe in something ineffable. All of us who write about art no doubt believe in it. But when it comes to defining what "it" is, we remain pretty much at sea.

Compartmentalizing visual art can be a futile enterprise, like dissecting a corpse to find the soul. For me, some of the most revealing writers about art have come from the ranks of poetry, philosophy, psychology, literature. As critics, we work in a strange zone where the validity of our judgments (those of us who make them!) can't be proven. The only real measure of our relevance is how readers—and the artists we write about—respond, and how well our ideas hold up over time.

Pier Dominguez

From Art Criticism to "Art" "Criticism"

After the appearance of a recent *New York Times* article which chronicled the results of a survey sent to certain critics and writers in an effort to select the greatest work of American fiction of the past 25 years, some of the writers who replied to the survey were allowed to discuss the results in an online forum. In the discussion, Michael

Cunningham noted that a request to name the " 'greatest' book of the last 25 years is different from a request to name one's favorite. I wonder if a second poll of the same people, one that asked only that we name the book that has meant the most to us, would produce different results."

I think it would have produced different results. In fact, many of the writers and critics who refused to participate in the survey for a variety of reasons, were still able to anticipate (correctly) that the winning novel would be Toni Morrison's *Beloved.*

This discrepancy: the refusal to name a "greatest" book juxtaposed with the ability to predict it, seems to me an interesting way of approaching the questions of art criticism vs. cultural criticism and of art criticism vs. art history, which were brought up in the panel.

First of all, I think that the problems raised by Elkins in these roundtables are very healthy questions, and I think that far from suggesting the "death of art criticism", as some panelists noted, they announce its vigor as a discipline. Disciplines constantly cleanse themselves, and questions like these force a discipline to confront the assumptions underlying its forms of knowledge.

The ability to predict which works of fiction would be judged "canonical" in the current cultural scene, by a specific constituency, suggests a hyper-awareness of the kind of issues that are taken into consideration in these judgments, and for many (some of whom wrote either whiningly or complaining) the issues are race and gender, and they *seem* extra-aesthetic.

I found the distinction, made in the roundtable, between criticism (judgment), critique (judgment and a focus on the values underlying it), and criticality (beyond critique) to be very helpful, and Michael Cunningham's comment suggests we are at a moment of criticality, almost hyper-conscious of critique, but there has been no understanding of what that means, practically, for popular arts criticism. If the *New York Times* article is any indication, it means an attempt at judgment that disavows—almost deconstructs—the very judgment at the same time.

My own conclusion, after thinking through the roundtables, is that ultimately there cannot be a "history of art" (partly because the very idea of "history" has been so provocatively taken apart); there can be archaeological writing, there can be histories of art criticism, there can be journalistic or academic accounts of art movements, but this idea of some objective, meta-narrative, history of art would ultimately be nothing more than, as Susan Sontag wrote in the preface of *Against Interpretation*, "case studies for an aesthetic, a theory of my own sensibility."[7] An individual critic's sensibility, however, can make history. After all, many interpreted *Against Interpretation* as an instantly canonical bit of 1960s art history: a *New York Times* review of the book immediately called it "a vivid bit of living history here and now, and at the end of the sixties it may well rank among the invaluable cultural chronicles of these years." (And reviewer Benjamin deMott was quite right in his prediction, at least with regards to Sontag's views about "high" and "low" culture as laid out in her "Notes on Camp.")

These issues were brought to the forefront more explicitly with the publication, twenty years later, of Rosalind Krauss' *The Originality of the Avant-Garde and Other Modernist Myths.*[8] Reviewer Yve-Alain Bois wrote in his rhapsodic review of Krauss in *Art Journal*: "one is struck in reading the book by its demonstrative stance, something that has as much to do with the polemical posture of a number of the texts as with the particular position of the author as both critic and historian—or rather, as historian because critic."

That is the key phrase: historian *because* critic, and despite the overwhelming differences of their critical styles (Sontag abhorred jargon and the only ostensible reference to structuralism in her book was her review of Levi-Strauss' *Tristes Tropiques*), I would argue that Sontag was also an historian because critic, but what is instructive is the explicit acknowledgment, outside of Krauss' and Sontag's texts, that they were so. The *Saturday Review* article on *Against Interpretation* described Sontag as "cultural historian, esthetician, tastemaker," which points to a perception of the collapsing of the criticism ("esthetician"/"tastemaker")/history ("cultural historian") binary. (And the description of her also as "literary critic, drama reviewer, film *aficionada*" points to Sontag's lack of specialization as compared to Krauss, who privileged static visual art—painting and sculpture—but was also, like Sontag, fascinated by photography.)

Bois goes on to note: "In her introduction Krauss presets herself as a critic and never uses the term 'history' to refer to her work. Yet it is my contention that it is precisely there, in the articulation or juncture between criticism and history, that the lesson of this book can be seen to lie: its theoretical and methodological thrust." Sontag similarly saw herself as a critic, and in explaining her role in the preface to *Against Interpretation* makes no explicit reference to history: she viewed herself as writing "meta-criticism" in which she "wanted to expose and clarify the theoretical assumptions underlying specific judgments and tastes." Krauss could not have explained her own project any better. Interestingly, like Krauss, Sontag also read Foucault and wrote about the influence that Roland Barthes and Walter Benjamin had on her own thought—before these figures were canonized in the academy.

These two thinkers suggest that a "history of art" would always still be one person's (or perhaps an institution's) interpretation of which art is important and why, but at the same time, as demonstrated by Krauss' influence in the academy and Sontag's in the media world (which produce two very different canons), these individual sensibilities do end up becoming more than that, making history (at least in part) by reshaping the conception of criticism and history.

I was surprised to see as the most e-mailed article of the *New York Times* one day, a headline announcing, "Revising Art History's Big Book: Who's In and Who Comes Out?" I had never heard of the *Janson History of Art*, but apparently it is very popular in introductory, survey art courses on college campuses (which probably explains how I found it as a coffee-table book in my brother's apartment), and the changes made in the book, removing certain "canonical" artists in favor of others, caused a stir in certain academic circles. The book was now being reorganized by Janson's son, which is partly what led to the changes, but this generational change (within the same family) made it clear that a history of art is ultimately a chronicle of one individual's sensibility—even if the academic community, for example, has a certain canon of its own that might coalesce around that individual's. (And why should that canon be more important than any other?)

When James Panero was asked why he wasn't desperately unhappy about the current critical/cultural scene given his own distinctly un-postmodern background, he explained calmly that he still believes in the high modernist tradition and that he look for works that are in that tradition and engages them in a critical fashion that is compatible with that work. That is exactly correct, and there is no reason why he should change his methods given that he's found a niche for his views in the *New Criterion*, and he probably feels that doing anything else would be a betrayal of his critical vision and the values he holds dear.

It was Ortega y Gassett (one of my favorite critics and by far the most fascinating Spanish critic) who wrote in the 1920s: "But the art of our time, from the end of impressionism in painting and symbolism in poetry lacks sanctioned codes of evaluation. The critic must operate at a threshold; at the same time that he judges the work, he must garner authority for the general rules he applies."

This is what one of the panelists meant when she said that a critic doesn't just report—he produces. (Joselit noted that she didn't just report on "a pre-existing phenomenon," but actually helped "produce a definition of postmodernism.") I would argue that only the "greatest" critics—and Sontag is one of them, as is Walter Pater—invent and impose influential sensibilities or theories.

Which means that unlike Sontag, James Panero probably won't be "making history," and neither will the art that he writes about—which suggests that the previous "history of art" might have been more accurately called "a history of the new in art"—whether in subject matter or content or occasionally, and most revolutionary, in both.

I don't believe, as Panero does, that he can really separate taste and judgment. This idea that floated around, that Clement Greenberg said he may disagree with his own taste, but has no choice in the matter, to which James replied, "There's no accounting for taste, but there is accounting for judgment," is incorrect insofar as "judgment" is simply the name given to an accounting for taste, and that needs to be recognized (and it could be argued that ultimately Krauss broke away from Greenberg in large part because of their incompatible *theoretical* views about this, even though interestingly, in *practice*, she was never, especially by contemporary standards and even when compared to Sontag, particularly interested in popular culture or arguing for its legitimacy).

Modernism believes in an objectivity of taste that everyone can agree on, and as the pop culture/high culture mishmash that is postmodernity clearly shows, that was not a correct assumption. (I think that by now, the idea of high/low cultural swinging is so entrenched everywhere, that to call Clement Greenberg or Dwight McDonald "elitist" is anti-intellectual, not to mention banal, and needs to be retired. The problem is that most academics today would rather be accused of vulgarity than elitism—because any potential accusation of "vulgarity" has been completely hollowed out.)

As James Elkins pointed out, the large quantity of writing on Michelangelo is itself some sort of criticism or curatorial work, which is connected to the idea that many panelists expressed about their reluctance to giving out negative notices because in today's publicity-driven art market, all publicity is good publicity. But aren't those "extra-aesthetic" concerns as well? Yet shouldn't these things be discussed within the criticism?

Obviously, the rise of cultural criticism is connected to the acknowledgment that the aesthetic/political is virtually inseparable. A cultural critic can read an "art critic" and pull out the underlying values of the critic's judgment, but an aesthetic reading of cultural criticism usually leads to banal complaints about the writing's complexity or lack of grace (like Roger Kimball in everything he writes, but most recently in *The Rape of the Masters*, or Camille Paglia in almost everything she writes, but most recently in *Break, Blown, Burn*, a poetry anthology that will be followed by a similar book on visual art, or Tom Wolfe in *The Painted Word*.)

I really enjoyed the moment when Boris Groys said he found *October* incredibly uninteresting ("an exercise in taxonomy") by quipping, "It's just not sexy." As someone who is uninterested in *October*, but who finds Rosalind Krauss' entire oeuvre incredibly sexy and full of intellectual excitement, I disagree with his comment, but I understand what he's trying to say (partly because I feel the same way about Arthur Danto), although comments on style are always ultimately about content as well, and I think this kind of comment might be directed at the "style" of writing that implements theory in general. (It was Krauss herself who described her writing as paraliterary).

Although Groys' seems a funny or harmless comment, it is in fact a recurring complaint throughout the history of art criticism. It reminded me of a comment Robert Rosenblum made about *Artforum*, which called the magazine's writing "intellectual and bone dry and never could correspond to the sensuous pleasure of looking at art." Sontag famously ended her *Against Interpretation* essay, which attacked Marxist/Freudian readings of art, with the line: "In place of a hermeneutics, we need an erotics of art." (I tend to think of Rosalind Krauss as the academic Susan Sontag—and in writing this I realized that I agree with the narrative that places Krauss and the rise of *October* as "one important symbol of the eclipse of serious non-academic critics like the New York intellectuals, and the rise of an academic intelligentsia in step with the post-GI Bill expansion of higher education.")

On the other end of the spectrum, Walter Pater's criticism was considered too sexy and caused a scandal upon publication, which led to his memorable complaint: "I wish they would not call me a hedonist, it gives such a wrong impression to those who do not know Greek."

What this talk of eroticism and sexiness brings into focus is the fact that art criticism, as a form of writing, is itself an art (or can be), and like any art it requires innate talent and cannot really be taught, it can only be nurtured. I think this is connected to why art criticism has not been institutionalized pedagogically. (As an undergraduate at NYU I took a course called "Literary Forms: The Craft of Criticism," believing I would learn how to write criticism in it. In fact, it wasn't even a survey of the most important critics, but simply a class in which we would read a canonical book like *The Scarlet Letter* and then study all the different kinds of criticism—new historicist, post-colonial, feminist—to which it had been subjected. However, unlike in (visual) art where James Elkins says there is no history of art criticism (although I think the work of David Carrier is an attempt at such a history), a number of people (I've only read Vincent Leitch) have set it upon themselves to write histories of literary criticism in the United States.)

I was disappointed that the roundtables focused exclusively on criticism of static visual art (painting) because that kind of art already has such a limited audience compared to literature, film, fashion, pop music (including music videos, which went, in such a short amount of time, from being conceived as advertising to being consecrated everywhere from MOMA to the Pompidou to the Academy (where videos were either analyzed for their transgressive sexual-political content or analyzed as a new aesthetic medium)), and even fashion, all of which is regularly and exuberantly reviewed.

One must be a very cloistered academic or writer to think that there could ever be some "death knell of criticism" or that it was dying until the "blogosphere" opened it up again.

After all, the most popular show in America, watched by tens of millions of people, is nothing more than a dramatized art criticism spectacle. In *American Idol*, a singer performs and then finds his work being analyzed by three different critics, with three different perspectives: Paula Abdul is a former pop singer, Randy Jackson is an American producer, and Simon Cowell is an English producer and considered the Clement Greenberg/Dwight McDonald (or the "elitist" critic) in the context of the show and is routinely booed when giving his forcefully negative notices. For the most part, these critics' criteria consists of comparing the singers' performances with their own previous showings, with their competitors' performances, with the original artists' renditions of their covers, and also by analyzing their command of the stage and even their wardrobe. (Most interestingly, in terms of the un-theorized criteria for being allowed into the show during auditions, is their idea of what constitutes a "good voice," which, as many television critics have noted, seems derived from a Mariah Carey-show-off-your-range model.)

People love engaging with art and seeing whether their assessments coincide with a given critic's. (My dad sometimes says, "See? I told you" when his own comments correspond with Cowell's.)

Ultimately, I think that most art gets the criticism it deserves, because art begets art. The most lively arts produce the most lively and interesting criticism. (Although there are interesting moments when the reverse is true, and a provocative history of art criticism could contrast those moments when art was catching up with criticism as opposed to the moments when criticism was catching up with art.) If there is a sense that "art criticism" might me moribund—and I think those "death of" claims, while intellectually provocative are usually too vague—one question to ask would be: What "art" are you talking about?

Lane Relyea

Impure Thoughts

Far and away the most striking thing about the two roundtable discussions, at least to my ear, is their constant insistence on pursuing the topic of criticism in terms of how it relates to the university and the humanities and to the discipline of art history in particular. It's not that this is the wrong approach, for reasons I'll get into. But why exactly the roundtables chose such a bias is never clearly stated, although it's easy to guess that it has to do with the two ambitious academic initiatives James Elkins mentions being involved in (one a PhD in Art and the other a graduate curriculum in art criticism). Then, as a kind of matching pendant to all the talk about whether it's possible to determine a teachable field of art criticism, one whose historical and epistemological parameters could nestle comfortably with those of the other humanities departments, reference to criticism as "applied," as a living daily practice, does get made albeit through the positivist method of the social sciences, the horribly quantifying statistical survey offered in *The Visual Art Critic*. Thus is consideration of criticism to be divided here between a theoretical discipline on the one hand and a batch of empirical data on the other.

It could be said that such a predisposition distracts from a consideration of criticism as a concrete political and rhetorical activity embedded in the back-and-forth of everyday cultural exchange and evaluation, the constant tussle over public meanings. Not just Dave Hickey but Craig Owens and Thomas Crow, among others, have expressed a preference for this sort of rhetorical framing of criticism's undertaking.[9] It certainly goes with a dominant definition of modern art criticism, one bound up in the Western history of the nation-state, its culture and citizenry, the rise of museums and coffee-house cosmopolitanism, the expansion of markets, of newspapers, and so on. But there are good reasons to view all that as belonging to some romantic picture of the past.

Tippy-toeing the ever-thinning line between advancing ideas and advancing careers has been art criticism's burden since its modern inception—never has it been either entirely free of the market nor totally absorbed by it. Today, however, these negotiations appear to have broken down. One can perhaps hear an echo of that breakdown in the first roundtable when, after the findings published in *The Visual Art Critic* are mentioned, Abigail Solomon-Godeau and others protest against equating journalism with art criticism. Yet the conversation quickly moves on. Where and how might one draw this distinction between "real" criticism and journalism (or should we say "pure" and "applied" criticism)? By severing its ties to journalism, doesn't art criticism risk losing its connection to "the public," one of its enabling conditions or fictions? Perhaps that connection is no longer a concern, since any credible semblance of a public sphere has all but vanished? Even though a majority of the roundtables' participants are academic art historians, some, like Solomon-Godeau and Jean Fisher, used to write mostly for art magazines, where their texts shouldered up against gallery ads (I had the honor of publishing their writings when I worked as an art magazine editor in the 1980s). At times they even wrote reviews, excellent ones—ones that rewarded "close reading." And that wasn't unusual, other smart people with principled theoretical positions wrote art reviews. It was called, in Solomon-Godeau's famous words, "living with contradictions."[10]

The university is indeed an issue, maybe a leading issue, when coming to terms with the conditions underlying the writing of art criticism today. But it has less to do with the obstacles blocking the critic's path into the university than with the ease by which academics have already streamed out, pervading the art world and its criticism, and, by the same token, the degree to which a corporate business mentality has taken over the university. It's pointless to train people to become critics since the critic has historically evaporated, the figure means nothing now, if only because the modern definition of the critic—as a citizen of culture, an enlightened amateur—has been universalized, at least according to current market ideology. Superseding the critic is today's ubiquitous figure of the "prosumer," the contemporary shopper as creatively signifying bricoleur who works a commodity landscape in which there is no more use value, everything is cultural, distinctive, and connotative. Once a particular concrete practice, a specific occupation that one might hold, criticism has now become disembodied, something like the floating ethereal mode Irit Rogoff calls "criticality."

In the eyes of an art world in desperate need of new resources of distinction, academics become all the more attractive because of the heavy educational apparatus that officially credentializes them as nonamateurs, as specialists. And so magazines like *Artforum* assign the few long, critical articles they still print to art historians, thereby erecting a new hierarchy in which the dual functions traditionally negotiated by criticism get separated out, with uncredentialed freelance critics relegated to the back of the magazine and the gallery-beat of reviewing, with its market complicity, while a loftier, more disinterested realm is preserved for historical and theoretical rumination. Perhaps the increase in such magazines of four-color glossy features promoting "young artists to watch in the coming year!" is compensated for by those few pages of elevated and supposedly noncommercial writings by academics who pride themselves on pursuing knowledge purely for its own sake. I hear this all the time: because I'm in a university studio department and considered a critic, I'll have trouble getting tenure because my writing for art magazines and exhibition catalogs is not lofty enough, it's too commercial. As the art historians down the hall like to tell me, "You only write about artists because you're paid to."

The field of art history might pretend otherwise, but it's as competitively cut-throat as any you can name. And to an art world increasingly reducible to the economic academics have flocked to take part in its hyperproduction of ever-new distinction and value, accepting writing assignments which in turn help inflate their own value on the academic job market. At the same time, the segregation of the pure and the applied helps keep the contradictions and complicities of this situation go unremarked. Unlike freelance critics, the work of academics is still organized around the unaccountability of their own position, which disappears into the presumed anonymity, neutrality, and objectivity of their profession and institution. The art historian looms transcendent, disembodied, purified, engaging in amorphous "criticality"—while for-hire critics, who'll write about nearly anything that comes down the art-world pike, appear by comparison overly visible, with too much bodily self-interest and no institution or discipline to hide it behind, speaking and acting individually and unendorsed. But is it really still critical for academics to wag a finger at galleries that sell art when the art world today is increasingly structured as a mixed economy of private, corporate and public monies, the kind of revenue structure that makes possible all those kunsthallen and avant-garde art festivals that deliver crucial assistance to municipalities conniving to insinuate themselves into the network of global commerce? In an information age that privileges programming and coding, in which no single TV show or pop song is as hot as the TiVO boxes and iPods that manage their organization, is it still critical to pit an inherently redemptive theoretical apparatus against an inherently commodifiable and corrupt art *objet*? In the shift from Greenberg's 1950s motto that "Feeling is All" to Hal Foster's 1980s dictum that "historical specificity, cultural positioning is all," there is perhaps charted the necessary modernization of the artistic sphere and its apparatus of reception so as to better align them with today's dominant protocols of information management.[11]

The terms that underwrote an older conception of criticism—notions of the public, of culture, of value—are in deep crisis, seemingly indistinguishable today from naming mere market functions in our transnational capitalist economy. These are the grounds for "criticality," the culmination of Rogoff's three phases, an era in which the figure of the critic doesn't survive. It's tempting to stretch Rogoff's tripartite scheme so as to cover the entire modern historical project of Western art criticism. Would what she calls "criticism" be responsible for canon formation, ideally a democratic process undertaken by critics as public citizens whose main object is the museum and salon, which in turn represents the national culture? Canon formation then gives rise to and is undermined by canon critique (the second of Rogoff's phases?), which parallels the rivaling of museums first by private galleries, then by alternative spaces, as well as the increasing social estrangement of the critic, who attacks as historically conditioned and temporary standing representations of cultural consensus from an ideological position that projects its own future inhabited by a more ideal constituency and consensus. While these first two modes work together dialectically, the third marks a radical break. Today there is no canon to form or reform, no grand historical project to advance, supposedly no more oppositional ideologies; global capitalism eclipses not only the nation-state but its whole attendant category of culture, and technological advances allow for more products to bypass any moment of public debut and debate and instead be delivered directly to isolated moments of private consumption. From my admittedly biased point of view, it's hard to see progress in the replacement of public argument between critics over cultural values by today's bureaucratic administration of values at the hands of multilateral corporatist elites who work the international circuit of mega-biennials. We shouldn't kid ourselves, these are difficult times for criticism, critique, criticality, what have you. How do they respond to the globalizing of "culture," the evaporation of the public sphere, and the shift in progressive aim away from the formations of canons and even consensus toward the construction of vigorous, inclusive dissensus?

Peter Plagens

Derriere Guard

Where you stand, some wise person once said, depends on where you sit. In the great wide, wonderful wacky world of art criticism, my derriere—by dint of that inevitable combination of circumstance, natural inclination, and experience—has been planted in the popular press. For about sixteen years, I've been the art critic at *Newsweek*, although during the last three as a nominally retired "contributing editor" (that is, freelance-with-a-conduit). These days, I write maybe half a dozen pieces a year. When I was a staff writer, I produced twenty to twenty-five (of all sorts, including reviews, profiles, news stories, and collaborations). While I do get to hold forth occasionally elsewhere (art magazines, the odd book review in *The Nation*, and so on), my main critical activity since about 1990 has been writing about almost any kind of art (usually in a museum exhibition)—from Old Kingdom Egyptian to the quilts of Gee's Bend to Paul McCarthy—for a general audience. So when I'm "doing criticism," I'm more concerned with making myself intelligible and somewhat entertaining to a lay reader than I am with producing something that'll be footnoted in a UC Irvine dissertation or get me invited to an international conference on cultural nomadism. (Heavy-duty "theory" is a matter of grudging intake for me—reading it, even in carefully calibrated doses, is enervating, but necessary; I can't, and don't, produce any.) Finally, I accept the fact that art criticism is reactive: it arrives after the fact of art, and responds to it. A simple truth: you can have art without art critics, but not art critics without art.

The two most significant-for-criticism developments over the last couple of decades in the part of the art world in which I operate (that is, the Euro-American gallery-and-museum sector) have been, in my opinion, (1) the emergence of "the market" and everything it entails (advertising, publicity, auction prices, cozening up to rich collectors, art fairs, strategic commissions, fashion tie-ins, and so forth) as the primary determinant of what ambitious young artists produce, and (2) the decreasing interest of the popular press in covering art, except when there's a money scandal or a censorship brouhaha. One would think that contemporary art's increased market orientation, its amplified desire to locate and amuse an audience (as opposed to its desiring to "address issues"), would *increase* the popular press's willingness to cover it. But the fact is that the number of staff art critics at metropolitan daily newspapers and general interest magazines is decreasing.

My preliminary guess is that the popular press's lack of interest has something to do with contemporary art not looking much like "art" anymore. A plurality of contemporary art vying seriously for critical attention these days looks a lot like movies, TV, music videos, theater and literature instead. (Accompanying me on a Saturday round of the Chelsea galleries, a book-reviewing colleague at *Newsweek* said about the installation artists we were seeing, "You know, they all really want to *direct*.") Contemporary art now appears to the popular press to be a "quick study" kind of thing, something any entertainment writer can, with a little bit of Googling as prep, handle just fine, thank you.

That said, I know there are dozens—perhaps hundreds—of writers about art out there who approach art as, in Aidan Dunne's memorable line in the *Irish Times*, "the continuation of sociology by other means." Compared to their socially reformative projects, I probably seem like either Nero or Marie Antoinette or both. But within my own critical first order of business ("Is this art any good or not?") lies a considerable quotient of "What's really going on with this art, anyway?" To sociological critics (mostly lodged in academe) more concerned with "socially constructed" and "performative" identities than with the *look* of contemporary art, I owe a lot in helping me with "What's really going on with this art, anyway?" But those critics, too, should be worried about the current, showbiz-like art scene and the popular press's paradoxical lack of interest in it. The same let-the-market-decide mentality that's driven MFA (Master of Fine Arts) candidates to obsess over what Jeffrey Deitch and Dean Valentine are going to want next has also dried up the NEA (National Endowment for the Arts), shrunk funding for grittier museum exhibitions, cut back the number of my-art-is-my-research college teaching jobs, and visited hardship upon state and municipal arts organizations. Sociologically-oriented critics depend more on these entities than writers for the popular press do. Of course, we critics in the popular press have to struggle more with our readers' market choices about which, if any, publications to read, than subsidized academic writers do.

Blogs? Fine. The more voices the merrier. But almost all bloggers give their criticism away for free and make their livings otherwise. As much as I admire economically selfless critical expression (however amateurish and ego-driven it sometimes is), I think that a good "state of art criticism" requires more opportunities than we have now for critics to make at least a good portion of their livelihoods being professional critics.

Blake Gopnik

Assessment of the Art Seminar

Two of the panels' central concerns are the demise of a genuinely critical art criticism, and the gap between art history and art criticism—especially in the mass media. I think there may be closely related institutional explanations for both.

As the number of full-time, salaried art critics shrinks—how many of us are there left in the US? a dozen? two score?—so does the number of truly independent, potentially critical voices. If you're trying to cobble together a freelance career as a critic—a hard enough task already—there's no up-side to writing pans. You're going to need the income from hired-gun gigs as a catalogue essayist and curator, or from other jobs where you end up in the role of advocate for the artists you're working on and with. There's no room for "negativity," or even usually for balanced evaluation, in that kind of work. (Though there ought to be, and Dave Hickey flirted with the negative in a recent essay he was paid to do for the National Portrait

Gallery.) Of course, negative positions taken elsewhere don't exactly endear you to that market for your work, either.

Another consequence of the impoverished market for freelance criticism is that the art magazines can't enforce much in the way of a code of ethics on writers to whom they can't pay a living wage. All of us know of countless magazine reviews where friends have written about friends, or where someone who has written a catalogue essay for a gallery or museum—for whom they would no doubt like to write more in the future—also writes reviews of shows in that same gallery or museum. And given the lack of financial incentives in freelance criticism, the social incentives of friendship and peer-group support often take over in getting a writer to pick up a pen. (The hallowed role of "artist-critic" involves potential conflicts of interest that weren't brought up in the panels, and almost never are, anywhere.) There's also more than a suspicion that many art magazines aren't keen to publish pans of their advertisers. (One of them makes this known more-or-less upfront to its writers—and often asks them to review negligible galleries just because they advertise.)

Full-time, salaried critics—especially for non-art publications, which is where almost all of us work—don't face those pressures. We could even be disciplined for writing about our friends, and (at the *Washington Post* at least) aren't allowed to accept work from the institutions and people we cover. As for pressure from advertisers . . . maybe if we reviewed department-store bras there would be an issue, but I've seen dealers storm into editors' and publishers' offices to demand the head of an "overly" negative critic, with the threat of pulling their ads, only to be told that the advertising space the newspaper sets aside for them actually *loses* money compared to other uses it could be put to.

If there's a problem in mass-media work, it's that editors—and readers—often enjoy the frisson that comes with a grand-slam pan, just for its own sake. The problem in the art press is exactly the opposite: the "front-of-the-book" articles are almost always feel-good features meant to validate and support their art-world readership; criticism, such as it is, is always buried at the back. It is strange that, at a few major newspapers at least—smaller newspapers and most popular magazines are a completely different story—criticism gets much better, bigger, front-of-the-section play than it does in the dedicated art magazines.

Of course, the independence of the salaried critic comes at a considerable cost. Because we earn our keep by covering the full range of exhibitions that could possibly come our way, we are often writing about material that we have limited expertise in. The best of us only have—*could* only have—true scholarly background in a subject or two. (In newspapers at least, many critics have no academic credentials, having been moved from beats as far afield as books or sports.) Which means that we don't only risk getting the answers wrong—we might not even know what the most pressing or even least hackneyed questions are to ask of, say, Egyptian funerary art or Mughal gold.

The popular critic's beat is, in important ways, constituted by art history—the objects we write about are almost always dependent on what art historians have decided is worth looking at—and yet time and workload issues make it impossible to keep up with what top scholars are thinking about in the range of fields we need to cover. And then, of course, there's the critic's fond (or foolish) hope of going beyond merely parroting what some expert thinks needs to be said about a work, and actually finding new insights that rival the scholar's. (Though that aspiration is admittedly almost as rare as any sign of success in achieving it, as James Elkins pointed out at the Irish roundtable.)

That's why I think it's a mistake to bemoan a lack of attention to the history of *criticism*. I don't trace my antecedents to critics such as Baudelaire or Zola as much as I trace them to art historians like Vasari, Wolfflin, Friedlander, and Gombrich and all of their most interesting descendants—all of whom are plenty studied in any decent academic program in art history. (The study of the historiography of art also helps a writer to critique the art historical premises behind museum curating—or the absence of such, as panelist Gemma Tipton pointed out as being more and more the case.)

The old cliché has newspaper journalism as "the first draft of history." I believe that good popular art criticism ought to aspire to being the first draft of *art* history.

Criticality is an important part of such art writing, especially when it comes to contemporary art. A good critic, like any and every art historian, plays an important role in the canon formation—and canon demolition and reformulation—that art history necessarily practices as it limits its field of study. By writing negative reviews, I hope to help shape (and pare down) the list of historically "significant" artists that scholars will be writing about in two hundred years.

Saul Ostrow

Criticism: Politics' Phantom Limb as an Exemplary Supplement (for JD)

Is criticism in a crisis? From the point of view of many the answer is yes, but no one is quite sure why. Most would agree that the influence of criticism has been lessened, given that everything today seems to be judged on its own merit, rather than in relation to a general set of expectations or in terms of its relevance to other practices. How did this come to be? No one is reasonably sure. There is a lot of speculation, and numerous causes are proposed. These range from the view that mass media and poplar culture have had a leveling effect on our cultural standards, to the notion that the collapse of modernism's master-narratives allow for the proliferation of practices, too numerous to account for.

All these estimations describe conditions that contribute to the crisis of criticism, but do not to really explain how it is that criticism's status actually came to be diminished. For instance, can one take seriously the idea that there is too much to account for, given that a consistent complaint concerning the critical enterprise is that it had the power to privilege one network of practices over another. Consequently, neither the dumbing-down of culture nor the return of the repressed actually offers up an explanation as to how criticism lost the power (if it ever had it) to determine what will, and will not be privileged.

Other explanations fair no better. For instance, the notion that art has appropriated criticism's role by addressing the issues of its own commodification, decay, and banality, as well as those of its social and institutional status, is a problematic idea. In the main, such self-critical approaches to cultural production rests upon positions formulated during forty years or more of critical debate. Rather than offering up alternative perspectives, models, or further insights concerning the value of this enterprise, those who produce these works seem instead intent on alleviating themselves and their audience's sense of alienation and hopelessness by means of proffering truism and platitudes. To blame art's adherence on the critical formulation that addressed its institutional existence for the fact that there is little or no contemporary critical discourse, seems circular thinking at best.

Another condition that seems to be a manifestation of this crisis is a general failure to differentiate between criticism and its specious competitor—art journalism, which being more accessible (less specialized) has come to colonize the terrain once occupied by criticism. While art journalism—reviews, news items, promotional articles (profiles) as well as editorial commentaries—share with criticism a nomenclature and genealogy, they do not share its intent. Criticism, unlike journalism, is more closely related to (and intimately engaged with) its object. Its task was to expose the terms by which a given act or practice (inclusive of itself) might come to be validated, substantiated, and in the end judged worthy of preservation. This process often included a self-reflective acknowledgment of how criticism itself conceals or obfuscates this process by decontextualizing or historicizing its object. The critic's role is not to speak for either the art or artists, but to locate them as a point of convergence within a complex network of ideological, cultural, and material elements capable of taking differing forms. The objective is to assess (analyze, evaluate, and judge) what of value is made aesthetically, socially, or culturally manifest by its object.

With the view that criticism is an act of validating and substantiating an act of evaluation, critical debates, such as those of modernism and its tradition-bound antecedents, can be viewed as concerning the values and standards by which culture as a noble and unifying mechanism might give rise to an autonomous and universal "Subject." This debate that marks the later nineteenth and early twentieth century, fed the debates of the 1930s that were preoccupied in specific with preserving modernism, and in general culture per se in the face of barbarism, while those of the 1950s to 1960s focused on safeguarding the modernist tradition and its ties to upward mobility and self-improvement. The debates of the 1970s to 1980s, though, were different in that they concerned a paradigmatic shift that was intent on doing away with the modernist subject altogether, because its mythology had become a fetter on our ability to realize our "self."

The eclectic body of thought identified with postmodernism promised to resolve the dichotomies arising from the contradictory and complex effects that were resulting from modernism's reified process of negation. The solution it offered was to discard modernism and allow free reign to our subjectivity by adopting a view of culture that was inclusive rather than discriminatory. It appeared that postmodernism (poststructuralist theory) could dissolve the problematic aspects of modernist which were stymieing artists' and critics' attempts to define art. The solution was to embrace a heterogeneity that would allow them to bypass modernist prohibitions.

Implicitly, postmodernism was self-reflexively preoccupied with fulfilling culturally and psychologically, if not politically, the goals of self-determination, emancipation, and self-awareness. These goals are an intrinsic aspect of the Western intellectual tradition of materialism, intent on dismantling metaphysic, as associated with both the enlightenment and modernism and their goals of self-realization and empowerment. The problem here was that the term "post" in this case came to mean in opposition to, in exclusion to, or as superseding modernism rather than merely "after." This resulted in the wishful pronouncements as the end of modernism, the end of art and all history, as well as a near-acritical embrace of novelty, be it in the form of eclecticism, art's appropriation of popular culture, digital technology, or middlebrow intellectualism.

So, while artists, critics and even art historians heatedly celebrated Western culture's liberation from the idealistic utopianism of modernism, they also ironically found themselves arguing against not only their own methodology but also the role they played as cultural mediators and interpreters. If this synopsis reflects the making of the contemporary cultural environment, then its genealogy begins in the pre-World War II era, when the heated debates concerning art's political and social functions versus its aesthetic ones began to undermined the liberals' belief in culture as an objective body of values and standards by which one could improve themselves. They came to believe criticism's main function had come to be the sustaining of a discriminatory hierarchy that served the marketplace while devaluing contending endeavors and tastes, creating an unnecessary sense of inferiority in individuals as well as society's middle and lower economic strata. Consequently, they viewed criticism as becoming too specialized, too jargon ridden, too pretentious, and that critics viewed what they did as more important than the cultural practices they were addressing. This lead liberals to become increasingly skeptical as to the value of criticism and intellectual debate as a means to achieve their political goals.

The liberal view bears significantly on the question at hand because the primary audience for criticism had been liberals who, uncertain of their social, economic, and cultural position, sought intellectual assurance that changes in their values, standards, and criteria would lead to economic and cultural reforms. Since the beginning of the twentieth century, the liberal solution was to put an end to culture's snobbish elitism by establishing the validity and intercourse of critical and common culture without concern for their alterity. Postmodernism appeared to advance both the liberal and generic left's project by supplying a philosophical and critical perspective in which all criteria are viewed as being derived from the ideological constructs that form our symbolic order and as such are subjective, arbitrary, or relative.

Yet the suspension of judgment and evaluation—the warp and woof of political liberalism—has been turned into a illness rather than a cure. The awareness of the artificiality of the symbolic order that we impose on events rather than producing the state of emancipation generated its antithesis; a cynical realization that the feared and fearsome notion that everything is arbitrary or at best subjective might just be real. This leads one to believe that all deliberate intentions—even one's own—cannot be taken seriously, and as such our actions lose a lot of their meaning in advance. This leads us to experience ourselves, and our social existence, as being in a constant state of trauma. Accordingly, we find ourselves individually and collectively salvaging and forming into assemblages; bits and pieces of history, political ideology, psychoanalytic theory, reason, semiotics, and desires from the belt of debris that surrounds our very existence. This ability to pick, choose, and rearrange is envisioned as operating as the symbolic representation of our ability to self-consciously realize our "selves." Given that this leaves us living in a recursive present premised on the aestheticization and standardization of all aspects of everyday life, seemingly cultural emancipation means little without its political co-efficient.

Given this scenario in which culture out runs its political base, if we are to evaluate or reconsider criticism's contemporary condition and the nature of its crisis, we are required to examine the role criticism plays in forming our conception of who we are and what is to become of us. In the context of contemporary culture, it is apparent that criticism cannot be conceived of as theory or history, though it may use both. For this reason it must be thought of as a node, a point of convergence within a dynamic system that cannot be codified, mapped, classified, or envisioned as a thing in itself. As a system of extrapolation and interpretation, no one model of criticism can circumscribe and address the totality of a given practice. Obviously, this requires criticism to be ideologically and methodologically diverse. Consequently, it is through the ensuing critical debates between the differing understandings, interpretations, and paradigms that criticism (and theory) comes to consciously, and unconsciously, order the point of view and expectations of both producer and consumer alike. It is in this effect that leads to the accusation that critics have too much power. Yet these models only remain viable if in practice their aesthetic and intellectual tradition can be sustained. If they do not achieve this, no amount of assertion will make them any more relevant. Critics do not determine the course of art, nor tell artists what to make or the audience what to like.

So while the shift in the form and content of culture can bring a critical paradigm to an end, a general crisis can only be attributed to the idea that postmodern art and culture has failed per se to generate a virtual collective Subject. In the context of how dominant models come to the fore and come to correspond to our understanding of our collective "self," it is worth looking at the model of subjectivity and agency that was encrypted within the now demonized formalism that was identified with the critic Clement Greenberg, which postmodernist have made to appear to be synonymous with late modernism.

For our purposes, rather than trace formalism from its art-for-art's-sake roots—it is more useful to set the stage with the years of mass media's emergent influence (1910s to 1930s.) Photography had already demonstrated that mechanical reproduction was not only a threat to the ideal of authentic experience, but because of its ability to change perception it also had the potential of reordering culture as a whole. In keeping with the post-World War II idealization of democracy and the relative prosperity of the time, culture was gaining a social status in direct proportion to the degree that painting, sculpture, architecture, and even nature was increasingly known only through book and magazine reproductions. Consequently, mass mediums, which had become the dominant means to externalize, objectify, synthesize, and communicate information and experiences, had, through reproduction, converted art into a class of images rather than a source of sensory data and self-reflection. Meanwhile, museums began to be reconceived of as educational institutions whose task was to make our cultural heritage and contemporary production more accessible to what was by then a thriving liberal middle class.

This mediation by technology and its alteration of the habits of daily life, expectations, and experience followed in the wake of the Depression, the shock of the horrors of World War, the Holocaust, and the threat of nuclear annihilation resulted in a conflicted sense of self that manifested itself as a desire for uniformity and security, as well as one for radical change. Faced with this ideal of progress without change, couched in absolutist terms, the formalists sought to defend culture from the penetration of capitalism's instrumental logic into every aspect of human existence by putting forth a vision of a transcendent subject embedded in a developmental concept of history. From their point of view, the only possible resistance to the encroachment of middle-class values and the banality of popular culture, which they viewed as a threat to the ideals of innovation, creativity, and self-expression, was an unwavering commitment to the ideal of an aesthetic experience which would constitute a moment of unalienated self-consciousness and self-reflection. The goal of the formalist project with its focus on the specificity of content was to secure art's identity (by establishing criteria that would allow us to differentiate between art and nonart) and maintain culture's highest standards, traditions, and ideals.

Formalism's insistence on self-referential specificity, though, contributed to the conditions under which artists seeking to make art more specific, increasingly revealed that art's self was an assemblage consisting of a multiplicity of practices circumscribed by a common history, which privileged at times a sub-category of objects with shared qualities adhering to common criteria. Art was not a conflicted self, but one that was segmented. The variety of material objects, situations and acts that came to be included in the category traditionally known as art, seemingly revealed modernism's critical discourses pro and con concerning those criteria by which art as a singularity might be sustained, might be interpreted as misdirected.

From the point of view of formalism, "art" has no worse enemy than the total availability of all forms, for this results in aesthetization and the regression of art into a world of arbitrary effects and objects which lead to a nostalgia for what had been (conservative reaction). In either case, "true" avant-garde culture would suffer, so the only way modernist culture could continue to exist would be by sustaining and protecting the Western tradition, its forms and practices, against the encroaching world of standardization, repetition, and middle-brow desire for an art that would represent their values and understanding. What this meant to them in practice was that quality and innovation was intrinsically tied to the development of the inherent historical and material imperatives of a given form that determined (its identity) membership within a certain class of objects (community).

In the face of the instrumental debasement of bourgeois idealism, formalism metaphorically articulates the necessity of change (recuperation) within a model, rooted in an ethical and historically valorized stance. This understanding resides in the recognition that the thing in itself (physically as well as conceptually) can be defined by irreconcilable conflicts and contradiction. Consequently, the formalist principles of working within the inherent qualities of a given form can be understood to reflect the view that in order to achieve self-representation and self-determination, we must restrict our choices in accord with nature of the conflict between traditional humanism and vulgar reductive materialism rather than being distracted by what appears to be a field of endless possibilities and opportunities. This view, which characterized the critical debates that demarcated the mid-1930s to the early 1970s, was itself circumscribed by an ongoing process of criticism seeking to identify for itself an ever-more elusive and fundamental, ontological "self."

Among the ranks of the formalist we find not only those drawn to metaphysics and idealism, but also those who are literal minded. It is such divergent understandings of essentialism that allowed for multi-perspectives in what is often represented as the monolithic vision of formalism. Harold Rosenberg, David Bourdon, Phil Lieder, Lawrence Alloway, and Max Kozlov are representative of critics, though critical of Greenberg's formalism, who did not dismiss formalism per se. From their point of view, formalism was a component of art, not the sum total of it. In accord with this view Lucy Lippard (even before turning to feminism and political activism), John Perreault, and Wiloughby Sharp viewed their own critical efforts as collaborative, or as a form of intervention. These activist critics focused their attention on evaluating the social and political terms and context in which works of art came to have meaning and institutional and market value.

About the same time, in order to secure for itself recognition as a discipline, criticism used philosophical discourse and art-historical methodologies to bolster its authority. It is at this time that art historians concerned with contemporary culture came to identify themselves as part of the project of criticism. These included young art historians such as Robert Rosenblum, Michael Fried, Robert Pincus Witten, Barbara Rose, Rosalind Krauss, Cindy Nemser, and Jack Burnham, who were to make criticism the central focus of their practices. While many of these identified with the formalist project of Greenberg, what they brought with them was a sense of professionalism as well as the methodology and perspective of their discipline.

Besides these critics, there was a growing tradition that seems to begin with Barnett Newman and Ad Reinhardt, Alan Kaprow, Fairfield Porter, of artists writing critically on their own work and that of their peers. By the 1960s and 1970s, a new generation of artist/critics was transforming the traditional relationship between artistic and critical practices. This reflected a significant change in these artists' orientation toward the object of art and the function of representation, criticism, and history. Committed to a philosophical analysis of art's existence, they respectively emphasized self-consciousness, concepts, and knowledge/experience rather than aesthetics as the basic tools of art making. In this the subject of criticism cannot be separated from the practice of its making. These practices acknowledge that criticism and its object (not its objective) had come to be joined to the cycle of production and distribution and replication/reproduction. So while their practice and understanding of art was informed by game and information theory, symbolic logic, developmental psychology, linguistics, and so on, their writings and discussions were peppered with references to the works of Ludwig Wittgenstein, Marshall McLuhan, Alfred North Whitehead, Herbert Marcuse, Thomas Kuhn, Karl Popper, George Kubler, Claude Lévi-Strauss, Maurice Merleau-Ponty, Susanna K. Langer, Robert Quinne, Morse Peckham, Noam Chomsky, Norman O. Brown, among others.

While tying criticism to art history or critical theory strengthened the critic's ability to substantiate judgments, it also contributed to the lost of identity in that criticism lost its concreteness. Theory is the hypothetical that informs the critical, the practical or applied criteria meant to advance the cause of its subject. Criticism is an evaluation of such hypothetical positions as they come to be realized in practice. Dumping criticism and theory together did harm to both. It was in recognition of this dynamic that the critical theory of Theodor Adorno and the Frankfurt school had, since the 1930s, attempted to create a methodological unity between the two practices. The problem, though, was that by the 1970s the fractured collage of mass-media and communications technologies offered a line of escape from formalism's dead-end by giving representation to a dematerialized world in which things (and events) appeared, as though on demand they could be re-mixed or assembled in accord with their appeal rather than their inherent qualities, made it increasingly difficult to repair the fracture that exists between the abstract and concrete. As such the materialist approach, and its ideological foundation, detached from the experience of the subject.

The result of this was that by the mid-1980s, theory rather than criticism had emerged as a guide to practice and formalism held little or no appeal, not having established an essential, irreducible commonness beyond institutional (conceptual) and material conventions for art (and our sense of "self"). The impact of this failure to secure identity on our social and cultural spheres effectively lead to an erosion of the boundaries between differing disciplines by exposing the symbiosis that existed between them. The result is a contemporary cultural sphere inscribed upon its surface the interlocking boundaries of mass, popular, sub, critical institutional, national, local and international, Western, non-Western, et al. culture rather than some simple oppositions or dualities. Consequently, the various positions concerning the identity and truth of art can be understood as constituting, by proxy, a debate concerning how we might come to understand the economy of fundamental propositions, compromise, and acculturation that circumscribed our being.

Today, in the wake of the abandonment of modernism, the issues of individualism, national identity, freedom, history, agency, and progress and authenticity as they were formulated by the dynamics of the political and cultural environment of the mid-1930s, are no longer capable of informing the individual and collective subject of society. The deterioration of critical culture, consequently, is not due solely to such environmental forces as mass media or pluralism, but has its roots in our changed conception of self that emerged out of the cultural conflicts that arose in the 1950s due to our existent paradigms having become fetters on our cultural development. This destabilized and undermined our trust in the existing systems of knowledge, labor, and morality, affecting our ability to construct a framework to assess, identify, index, and propose the standards and values by which the viability of these new structures might be judged. Paradoxically, these are the conditions under which we will have to attempt to construct/assemble a sense of self in the face of the subjectlessness induced by mass media's capacity to relegate every aspect of our sensory to its own individuated territory within a world of intangible representations.

The crisis of modernism and those critical practices that are associated with our sense of collective identity can also be linked with the initial successes and eventual failure of the last-ditch effort made in the 1960s to assert by means of political struggle the radical cultural reform that had been formulated in the late-nineteenth/early-twentieth centuries. The cultural revolution of the 1960s at first put into place a "subject" whose sense of "self"-actualization generated the potential for cultural as well as political change. This made the possibility of transforming or uprooting undemocratic and discriminatory cultural institutions a strategic goal of the struggle against racism (with its emphasis on racial pride), war and nuclear armaments (which challenged the culture of conformity and passivity), and sexism (women and gay liberation, whose main task was to undo the culture of omission). As these movements challenged the misrepresentation and suppression of its constituency, the accompanying youth and student movements promoted a vision of culture as the means to personally express one's freedom and imagination, devoid of value judgments and hierarchies. Just enjoying it was enough to make something good.

For an older generation of liberals and progressives the counterculture's anti-establishment and do-it-yourself ideology seemed like it would fulfill the long-held promise of using culture to regulate the contested ground of political power. The message of "finding yourself, and doing your own thing" represented a democratic approach to culture based not only on equal access but also on relative standards and values. In turn, the developing discourses of multiculturalism, feminism, and post-colonialism supplied the theoretical basis for the formation of new hybrid identities that might effectively challenge historically constructed ones. All thus while the cultural production of women, ethnic and national minorities, or the works of regional artists came to be acknowledged and promoted consciousness raising, and identity politics became a significant aspect of the struggle for political and economic power. As such the radical subjectivism that this gave rise to came to be understood as empowering individuals or groups by turning all social problems into psychological ones.

In turn this view gave rise to a confusion between the idea of subjectivity—the construction of one's identity or sense of self—and the idea of subjectivism, in which someone's belief or feelings are their own ultimate authority. In other words, representation is no longer the product of a hypothetical real, but a real that is reducible to its representation. As such, the form that this type of cultural politics takes does not concern the control of the means of the production but only that of representation. The type of self-empowerment that developed from such a situation results in an increased sense of isolation and powerlessness as one is moved further and further from the source of any type of power, even over one's own opinions, because one is now responsible for their own destiny otherwise they must think of themselves as a hapless victim. By creating this illusion that the contradictions that exist between the individual and society are personal, the bourgeois category of politics dissolves into the realm of cultural self-realization.

Capitalism's ability to adapt to this assault reciprocally could not be foreseen because the myths that sustained the ideals of individualism, self-determination, emancipation did not allow for it. Corporations, foundations, and cultural institutions promoted the notion of horizontal culture by exploiting the educative aspects of critical culture as well as its spectacular and fetishistic qualities. In this manner, art/culture's value becomes a social supplement rather than the space of a disruptive virtuality. This is done with the intent of bringing cultural production into line with the idea that the cultural sphere can become market/consumer driven. In this scenario the criticality of the cultural field turns in on itself and becomes little more than a harmless political critique of its own impotence or that of capital's encroachment into all areas of public and private life. The irony of this is that if art comes to be converted into nothing more than intellectual entertainment, capital would in turn lose one of its most valued and important areas of research and development.

The question that confronts us, therefore, is not how to differentiate cultural production hierarchically, but to search for the terms by which the diverse indeterminate and temporal values that now define our intellectual environment may serve the historical projects to which our society seems committed. To reinitiate our critical debates will require us to reorientate and rethink our identity. This will oblige us to abandon the fruits of hard-won victories, because the underlying assumptions they represent are no longer relevant or may be in need of significant reformation both methodologically as well as practically. The result would perhaps allow an agenda as to what is sociologically necessary to be proposed rather than assumed. Such a contingency plan would help us make better choices about what we do, and its implications would help us perceive more accurately the effects of our activities, which would allow us to construct a "subject" willing to make judgments and take actions. Within such a program, criticism as a tool for thought would again play a role in testing models in the ongoing process of self-emancipation.

Darby English

What Matters to Criticism?

I want to use the space of this Assessment to remark the curious and important difficulty that questions of history and subjectivity had coming to light in the conversations recorded here. To do this, I'll try to imagine a counter-figuration of the historyless, alocational, and unembodied critic assumed by many of the conversants, as it is by most of us when we tackle the topic of criticism.

The operational protagonist in the two roundtables printed here[12] presumes an obligation first and foremost to contemporaneity and immediacy. In this way, this figure retains a curiously modernistic cast and displays a comparably modernistic aversion to exigency and contingency. Both properties make this figure an obstacle to theorizing the act of the practice of criticism now. This is registered especially strongly in the atmospheric antagonism that diminishes the historical and dispatches with questions of subjectivity almost as quickly as they can arise. Despite counting among the talking points, in both forums history fights caricature and plain disavowal; thus the obvious fact of criticism's eccentric histories attracts some interest, but the more consequential question of how a virtually randomized historiography might redirect our conception of a practice still conceived in narrowly disciplinary ways was marginalized.[13] Because a number of the factors that arise when the subjectivity of critical acts—things to do with desire, sociality, ethics—receive similar treatment, it seems possible to address this antagonism by insinuating within these pages a notion of a *historical subjectivity* as central to any conception of critical practice, its precipitates being so central to discrete exercises of criticism.

Historical subjectivity is more than just a convenient compound encompassing the two principal terms of my complaint. It's also the determinant factor in critical acts that criticism more generally is at the greatest pains to camouflage. One experiences historical subjectivity in a kind of inertia: unless one is somehow the first or only subject of a given kind of experience, one's struggle to understand that experience necessarily will be caught up with countless others' struggles to do the same, albeit for themselves, as well as with the effects of those struggles as they're registered in the experience itself. That's to say, the form a given experience takes will to some degree reflect back to understanding the compromises struck during prior attempts to know it. This process entails series of interactions that violate the sanctified spaces of seer and seen, breaking up the field of knowledge they jointly constitute. Awareness of these interactions recommends a model of criticism in which a situated seer works out from a context of self-conscious relationship toward a reading that stands for a more or less agreeable compromise with the phenomenon seen. At work here is a quality of play that animates the judgment-making process by frustrating perception—and making knowledge richer in the process, oddly enough, by securing greater resemblance to that which it would clarify.

It will be clear that this view of criticism privileges the kind of intellectual work that the best art obligates us unexpectedly to do on our ideas and even our conceptions of self. If criticism can be said always to be a record of an artwork's provocations to thought, then perhaps it is at its best when it articulates such provocations in a way that *retains rather than assimilates* the elements of surprise and encounter that signify that a rearrangement of mind (or another provisional order) has occurred. When the surety of judgment and the subjective ground upon which it is enacted aren't in question, the play I just described is arrested and all the more easily disavowed. The question of criticism now concerns whether and how we're going to be accountable in our work for the place from which judgment is undertaken, for shifts in the shape of that place brought on by art events that exploit the libidinal, ethical, insistently, and irretrievably social aspects of "aesthetic" experience. (Let's not delude ourselves about the practical function of criticism in contemporary global art culture: more and more it's how many of us have learned to *see* the art at issue in a given debate context. Moreover, *art knows* that there are whole classes of people waiting to extract usable, representative knowledge from the experiences it offers. These facts alone should complicate business as usual for art criticism in massive ways, but hasn't seemed to, as yet.)

The few exceptions to this rule occurring during the roundtable discussions are worth underscoring for two reasons. First and most obviously, they attain a special force in a context so fiercely pitched against the rigorous and qualifying kind of self-awareness that could anchor a criticism more attentive to the sociality of representation (figurative, abstract, or otherwise) than those we've inherited. Second, the exceptions have as their authors participants who also felt it necessary to aver cultural difference in the course of their participation, speaking out against the trend as queer theorists, women, feminists, and/or general advocates for the un- or under-represented (I have in mind here Whitney Davis, Jean Fisher, Irit Rogoff, and Abigail Solomon-Godeau). While these participants sometimes linked their interventions to alternative positionalities, they did not do so to affirm or excuse corresponding critical positions. Instead these voices register a determined effort to append historical subjectivity and inexpugnable interest to a model of criticism which resisted them. I am less interested now in their "differentness" as such than in the way they qualify their own claims concerning criticism by locating their practices in relation to a norm both licensed not to locate itself and unable to see a model arising from "a kind of self-interrogation" that allows "an encounter with, and a reciprocal relation with, an artwork."[14] In this context, the dissenters stand for location not as an irrepressible, pluralizing tic but as an *elective inconvenience*, one that willfully suspends the possibility of unencumbered and indescribably fluent movement from perception to judgment, favors the thought to the claim, and in doing so shows an uncommon but entirely welcome measure of respect for the *rareness* of clarity in the experience of really effective art.

For me, the roundtable discussions generated a real thirst for a focused reconsideration of the place of desire in criticism, particularly in the critic's tendency to create the art she needs (as do we historians in perhaps a deeper and more widely implicated way). In the Chicago roundtable, Michael Newman speaks persuasively of criticism's work on the "level of the constitution of the object . . . rather than the discussion of an already-constituted object," but alas not about desire.[15] In differently interesting ways, Davis, Rogoff, and Fisher seem willing to risk far more in this enterprise, at least theoretically. Davis refers to a "theoretical threshold" faced by art historians who find themselves in relations of identification with artists (though one could just as well substitute artworks). Yet notably identification enters the present discussion as a position that has to be defended, and fails to reemerge in any form I can detect—as though there exists a type of relationship in the social realm that doesn't involve identification. It's not a question of how much identification occurs in our encounters with our subject matter, however. It's a question of how it informs or is absented from our *accounts* of these encounters. Paradigmatic here (again, for me) is a kind of criticism that has the courage to say of its object, "This is *so* important that it becomes a kind of tool for navigating, for differentiating between things in the world," without wielding that tool despotically.[16] Identification, the mechanism by way in which we determine where one stops and another begins, services us in just this way, making the work of identity (that is, being, saying, or knowing what one is, namely, what one is, not) both possible and terminally unfinished.[17]

It goes without saying that art is increasingly dependent upon social or parasocial relations as a precondition of its intelligibility. The still-dominant model of criticism is clearly at great pains to "correct" this development. As has been the case historically, a particularly effective corrective strategy involves the assimilation to the anesthetic, to the realm of nonart what more sincerely might be called a "relatively alien reality." Jean Fisher in this volume uses this term to speak of a criticism rooted in the spontaneity of relations (rather than always seeking the familiar in the new). In Fisher's words, this criticism privileges "choices about which pathways to follow when thinking about a certain art practice," choices "dictated by more by the nature of the practice and my horizon of knowledge than by any prescribed mode of aesthetic judgment." Fisher here describes an understanding that is reached mutually, on information gathered both prior to and during the encounter with "a certain art practice." What grounds it is a "relation between human and world."[18]

I find this critical position compelling because it is precarious, structured openly, and in tune with some particularly effective art's capacity to achieve itself by disallowing us simply to suppose our subjectivity and passively assert the primacy of perception. What would it mean for a critical practice to be "continuous" with aesthetic practices (this is how many of us describe patently good art criticism) that acutely undermine the ways that one establishes a comfortable viewing position in the first place? Such effects are commonly adduced in responses to works by Yayoi Kusama, Glenn Ligon, William Pope.L, Hanne Darboven, Rirkrit Tirvanija, The Atlas Group, Ilya Kabakov, Bruce Nauman, Vito Acconci, Dan Graham, and Mary Kelly. Surely *their* critical corollaries must be said to do a very different kind of work. Will this count as criticism?

Olu Oguibe

Between History and the Present

I

It is impossible not to derive exceptional pleasure from certain moments in the conversations that form the core of this book. One cannot ignore the ease with which they flow from one area of critical or visual art practice to another, from moments of shocking certainty to passages of complete cluelessness, and from manifestations of self-indulgent academicism that has little to do with the purpose and practice of criticism to occasional lucidity on the practical essence of critical engagement with cultural production. When Jean Fisher reminds us, for instance, that orthodox understanding of the purpose of criticism derives perhaps from asking the wrong questions, and that criticism might be better understood, or indeed might better understand its purpose, by looking at "what art does as engendering a process of thought" and approaching art "as the trace of thought linking experience to world" rather than dwelling on it "as object as such"; or Boris Groys notes that "art criticism is a kind of politics . . . part of the realm of injustice"; or Dave Hickey dramatizes the suspect preoccupations of contemporary art curators, the inchoate nature of these conversations begins to come across as a positive rather than negative condition, one instinctively lights up. When, for another example, the participants speak of a "paradigm shift"—*the paradigm shift the art world and art criticism are putatively experiencing now*—even when it is the case that no paradigm shifts have taken place yet, only the conditions have changed, there is nevertheless a transparent beauty that emanates from the nature of the exercise of conversation and underscores its enduring status as the most democratic mode of discourse. Elsewhere I have referred to this as *polynunciation*. As discourse emerges from the loosening grip of late-twentieth-century French philosophy and its masturbatory, Kantian centering on the supposedly illuminating reverie of the solitary intellect—the genius—conversation and dialogue are making a gradual return through the work of James Elkins, Maurice Berger, and to a slightly less reassuring degree, Doug Aitken, Hans Ulrich Obrist, and others. Culturally, the reach for voices remains largely restrained and monocular, almost entirely peroxide by inclination, one reason it is paradoxical to speak of paradigm shifts, but it is dawn still on creation day.

II

With regard to our present enterprise, the subject is now as tired as it is unpenetrated. In an article published in the January, 2006 issue of *Art in America* that almost seems intended to preempt the present book, Nancy Princenthal rehashes the recent history of the debate over *the crisis* in art criticism. Despite its grandiloquent and predictable conclusion that all art criticism is "bound to fail," Princenthal's article, read closely, is in fact a mere summation, albeit an elaborate one, of James Elkins's earlier treatise on the subject, *What Happened to Art Criticism*, with the singular difference that Elkins's essay concluded on a less emphatic note that seems to bear witness to its author's own doubts about the germaneness of the debate.

Art criticism may well be in crisis: criticism, after all, is about *crisis.* However, it does appear that the ongoing preoccupation with *the crisis* in art criticism, including the aforementioned efforts, is driven not so much by a sense of crisis or disaffection *within* art criticism itself as by a conviction or concern within art history and the academy that art criticism is in crisis.

Evidence of this may be seen quite clearly in the two conversations at the heart of this book. It is rather fascinating that these conversations about the state(s) of art criticism should not only begin with, but also focus so heavily on, *not* art criticism but art history.

III

Elkins sets the tone by asking: Might there already be criticism in art history? In what ways might it be said that there is criticism in art history? In other words, shouldn't we begin by acknowledging that criticism is in some way subordinate to art history, by confirming that the latches on this potential runaway coach are firm and secure, by *containing* criticism? We are left in little doubt of who is in charge of the discourse and how the two practices are hierarchically placed within it. Subsequently, a great deal of effort is spent in a circuitous search for what criticism might comprise, by looking at everything but criticism itself. And, failing to reach a definite consensus on this, art criticism is then cast as the indeterminate foster-child of all practices, the public goat that is in constant danger of starvation because everyone could claim it but no one takes responsibility for it. The idea of art criticism as an independent practice that may in fact be quite content with its perceived *crisis* is all but totally subsumed in the concerted effort to register it as impaired.

The discussions make a conditional concession, though, which is that the key difference between art history and art criticism is temporal; in other words, while one deals with history as its firm domain, the other merely contends with the present, the ephemeral and whimsical immediate without the gravitas of history. This, of course, is a traditional position carried over from the academy and the art history industry where trade organizations such as the American College Art Association reserve a separate trade publication (*The Art Bulletin*) for studies and narratives of art and culture from at least a century prior to the present, that is, for *art history*, while maintaining another, more laissez-faire organ (*Art Journal*) for discussions of contemporary art and culture, that is, for art criticism and whatever may fall within the no-man's land between *art history* and criticism.

The position is as conceited as the notion that art criticism may not be engaged without first acknowledging its subordination within art history. It is an erroneous position also, because it rests on the thin top soil of a fundamental misconception, namely, that history is, or is about, that which exists in the past. There are other ways in which history may be understood, and this is something that those who produce culture and history perhaps understand better than those who merely narrate them. History is much more than a narrative of remarkable occurrences in the distant past. History is transitive. History is presence, not precedence. History is not a mere recollection but a continual activity. It is not only the account of events but the events themselves. History is contemporaneous; history is now.

Such temporal delineations between *history* and the present where *history* metaphorically equates the past sifted and weighed, comprising nothing but pure, solid gold as opposed to the inchoate and gravelly slag of the present, no longer find favor even with social and political historians, apparently, and may now be found only in art history, which lends further credence to my contention elsewhere that art history may well be "the last bastion of backwardness" among discursive and scholarly practices in the modern world.

IV

Because these discussions issue from a *questionable* source, that is, an institutional practice or discipline that is set in its ways but nonetheless eager to be seen engaged in an act of gallantry—art history come to the rescue of criticism—they seldom deal with what many might consider the poignant questions. Instead, there is an effort, possibly unconscious but determined nonetheless, to import orthodox or institutional values and obsessions that belong to art history and impose them on art criticism so as to anchor it in the academy.

Among these is the obsession with *disciplinarity*, that is, the conviction that in order to be valid and command respect, a discursive practice must be *properly* institutionalized and legitimized by the academy. In practice this conviction explains why art historians often consider art criticism almost a fringe practice, a quackery of sorts, like sorcery or astrology, unregulated and unruly, even suspect and somewhat *illegitimate* because it cannot claim the recognition and approval of the academy as a valid, respectable and serious practice, that is, a discipline.

Although some of the participants in these conversations are critics whose relationships with the academy may only be described as circumspect at best, the first conversation nevertheless seems largely to affirm this conviction that a practice—art criticism included—is only valid or may only be taken seriously if it is *properly* "institutionalized or academicized." Boris Groys observes quite honestly that "academization makes every field less free" and notes that an argument could be made that dragging art criticism under the academy "involves creating privileged positions." Educating artists to the doctoral level would produce a dichotomy between artists "who are trained in criticism, and those who are not, and we would have created a new inequality." These observations are nonetheless prefaced by an affirmative declaration for academization. "*I am absolutely for the academization of art criticism in the university*," declares Groys, all arguments notwithstanding. The observations may be honest, if romantically so, but they are neither correct nor valid not only because there is no such dichotomy or hierarchy between artists who take PhDs and those who do not, thankfully, but also because they do not address the relevant question, which is that there is, in fact, no genuine reason that for the academization of criticism that is germane to the practice of criticism itself.

For one, art production, the practice that criticism preoccupies itself with, is not an academic discipline. Art instruction did become an academic discipline, and many would argue that art instruction met its death as soon as it was coerced into the academy. Those of us who were trained in the academy and remain in the academy as teachers but practice art beyond producing for the annual faculty exhibition or the college gallery solo exhibition aimed at attaining job tenure also know that the very best mode of instruction for the art practitioner is not in the academy but through the old system of studio apprenticeship. We know from direct experience that the academy seldom prepares artists for practice as professionals in the real world, and we know that in order to prepare aspiring artists for professional success we must train them the old way, by recreating the master studio in the academy and grooming them as apprentices.

Irit Rogoff states that at Goldsmiths College, London, where she teaches, a large number of students who come for PhDs in art "are people who have come back from the art world, after having been professionally active, because they need the space . . ." But it is not clear what space Prof. Rogoff is referring to. A space to work? A space to think? A space wherein to commune with other artists? A space to imbibe poorly masticated theoretical curd about the essence of contemporary cultural production? A space for a reencounter with Ardono and Kant? Because this writer did teach at Goldsmiths College—where graduate art students had no more than a pig pen for studios, by the way, and, at least at the time, a motley of "artists" without active practice for instructors—and found the studio program there so diabolically repressive to creativity that I resigned my position by facsimile.

But, then, there is certain verity to Irit's information; in the case of Goldsmiths and several other institutions, the academy is there not to train artists for professional practice but to receive those who, having already been partly crippled by the academy, return to its monastic safety in order to escape the demands of practice and engagement with the real world. The academy is there, also, to cater to those who have other needs to fulfill in their lives: egotistical desires, acquisition of status symbols, credentials for better placement in the job market, and the pursuit of natural curiosity. The academy is not there to help such individuals become better artists because that is not the purpose of the academy. Imagine Picasso returning to college for a PhD!

And if training for art practice does not require the academy, if indeed training for art practice suffers from the decrepit orthodoxy of the academy, why, precisely, does the practice of engaging with art and art making—which is what criticism attempts—require the academy? A retort to that might be: art history, after all, is the generation of knowledge and narratives about art and art production. If training for art practice does not require the academy, why does art history? And the answer to that would be: absolutely no reason other than the security and largesse that the academy provides for scholarship. Art history as a living practice—not as a unionized trade—does not require the regulations and equivocations that constitute academic *discipline*, but of course, in the absence of royal patronage, art history as a means of livelihood with a living wage, a mortgage, a pension, and justifications for statutory funding does benefit from *academization*. So does art history as pedagogy after the ascendance of the academy as the seat of pedagogy.

However, one does not require any number of credit hours or diplomas from the academy in order to produce—or possess the intellect and discipline to produce or relate—art history. Less so art criticism. And even much less so art. In effect a statement such as "*I am absolutely for the academization of art criticism*" has very little logical ground to rest on.

V

Guy Brett asks, rather meekly, "Why can't we have a discipline (read *practice*) that's not taught? A discipline (*practice*) that's self-taught?" To which James Elkins replies, teasingly yet quite seriously, "That is an incendiary opinion from a university standpoint!" Needless to observe that Guy's question does miss one very valid possibility, which is that a trade or practice needs not fall between *academized* and *self-taught* because the academy—the university—is not the only possible venue for learning. A trade could also be learnt through apprenticeship, and that includes a scholarly or intellectual trade.

Equally significant is the fact that literary criticism, as a discipline, has taught us over the past three decades, if not half century, that it is indeed possible to translate skills across disciplines by consistently challenging our claims to disciplinary authority as art historians and theoreticians. No matter what reservations we may harbor individually and as a discipline or trade regarding forays into art theory and criticism by literary critics—if we must hold them to their academic credentials and home departments—scholars from English, literature, cultural theory and even the social sciences have produced and continue to produce engaging studies of and speculations on art history, visual culture, and theory.

And not to be ignored is the similar example of curatorial practice. In the conversations here a great deal is made of the unruly nature of contemporary curatorial practice or, more precisely, curatorial adventures in contemporary art. In some instances the positive possibilities of contemporary art curating are acknowledged, and one occasion there is even mention of a paradigm shift having been instigated, if not accomplished, by recent curatorial interventions. However, the overall inclination is dismissive. What is relevant to our discussion here, though, is that several of the most influential contemporary art curators over the past four decades—that is, curators who have come close to instigating the paradigm shifts that are mentioned in these conversations—came from the social sciences, with little or no backgrounds in the disciplines of art history or the visual arts.

Alanna Heiss, who in 1971 founded the Institute for Art and Urban Resources in New York—later to become PS1 and eventually part of The Museum of Modern Art—came to curatorial practice and art administration from music, having received her bachelors degree in that discipline from Lawrence University in Wisconsin. Adelina von Fürstenberg, who founded the parallel Kunsthalle Genève, later the Centre d'Art Contemporain in Geneva in 1974, received her degree in political science, as did Okwui Enwezor, co-founding publisher (with this writer) of the first major journal for contemporary African art, director of both the Johannesburg Biennale and Documenta XI, and now Dean of Contemporary

Practice at San Francisco Art Institute. Carlos Basualdo, chief curator of the Philadelphia Art Museum and curator of numerous influential exhibitions over the last decade, received his degree in English. And the list goes on. These individuals are not guerilla curatorial adventurists but institution builders who have helped shape the public's engagement with contemporary art and its reception and narratives without having *disciplinary* backgrounds in art or art history. One might ask, is there any particular manner in which graduates of the Bard College program in curatorial studies, having gone through the *discipline* of art history and curatorial practice, might possibly contribute more to the promotion and understanding of contemporary art than these individuals? It is almost inconceivable.

Creative writing was *academized* in the late 1960s (at least one scholar dates it to the 1880s instead), resulting in an infestation of creative writing programs across North America in particular, and Europe. In what ways has the institutionalization of creative writing as a discipline or sub-discipline benefited the creative practice of writing beyond producing terrible, predictable formulaic fiction and hammering the ultimate nail on the coffin of American poetry? Creative writing may now be taught in all but the least endowed colleges, but the most significant creative writing be it fiction or poetry, continues to come from writers who have no diplomas in creative writing.

Which returns us to Guy Brett's question: why can't we have a practice that's not taught in the university, and intellectual endeavor that does not require the sanction of the academy? But what a precise and honest response from Elkins!

VI

Despite the fact that the conversations in this book touch on numerous subjects related, and sometimes unrelated, from the place and validity of judgment in criticism to the blurred demarcations between criticism, art history, and curatorial practice, one dwells on the question of *academization* for a reason. Even if lightly stated, the desire to see art criticism *academized*, to bring it under the regulatory aegis of the academy, to see it *disciplined*, accredited, and *legitimized*, nonetheless points directly to the root of our present enterprise.

The current concern over a supposed crisis in art criticism

belongs to a tradition of recurrent intellectual preoccupation with invented crises in the humanities and social sciences, and over the past two decades a great deal of energy has been spent on these *crises*: the crisis in art, the end of art history, the end of history, the demise of anthropology, the crisis in art criticism, the threat of the discourse of Others, feminism and its discontents, the plague of cultural studies, the mandate of inter-disciplinarity, and now the dreaded apocalypse of "visual culture", and so on and so forth.

That the academy has a need for these perennial *crises* is obvious: as fields of study become ever so narrow and disciplines turn myopic and anal, the academy needs its flashpoints and "crisis" moments almost the same way that the royal houses of Europe stumble from incestuous self-indulgence to scandal in order to regenerate sympathy for themselves and remain in the public eye. The real crisis, however, is a larger one: outside the well-funded sciences and the utilitarian disciplines of business studies, law, and the rest, the academy is caught in a permanent struggle of self-doubt and self-justification.

VII

Somewhere in the first of the two conversations here, Whitney Davis speaks of the "philosophic possibility" of judgment. One thing that emerges from these conversations, in addition to the absolute necessity of conversation as a democratic mode of discourse, is that they present all discourse and scholarship with an inescapable argument for a return to philosophy.

By philosophy one does not mean the exact same thing as does Professor Davis. Rather, one means a preoccupation with the discovery and generation of knowledge that is driven by genuine curiosity instead of the will to power and the desire to discipline. Understanding philosophy in this pristine sense allows one to speak not merely of philosophic possibility but of a philosophic imperative. It also allows one to separate the vocation of knowledge from the business of institutional regimen.

Regarding art criticism and its supposed crisis, James Elkins comes close to answering the major questions that he poses in these conversations in the conclusion to his earlier treatise on the subject. "All that is required," writes Elkins, "is that everyone read everything.

Each writer, no matter what their place and purpose, should have an endless bibliography, and know every pertinent issue and claim." Never mind the rather predictable headliners on Elkins's recommended reading list—Greenberg, or Ardono—but note his more significant admonition: "We should all read until our eyes are bleary, and we should read both ambitiously . . . and also indiscriminately—finding work that might ordinarily escape us." This is the philosophic imperative of discourse at the turn of the century; that it returns to an earlier age when to be enlightened meant to read—and explore—widely, ambitiously, indiscriminately; to venture into all areas of mystery in search of knowledge; to pay no mind to disciplines, delineations, or delimitations; and most importantly, to recognize that the desire for knowledge precedes all institutions.

Matthew Bowman

The New Critical Historians of Art?

That neither of the two roundtables managed to reach any consensus or decision with regard to the question "What is art criticism?" is perhaps not altogether surprising; not so much because art criticism is a highly diverse or pluralistic field that actively resists easy categorization, but because some of the most compelling art-critical and art-historical writings in the last two decades or so have, I think, effectively blurred—or insisted on this blurring—of art criticism and art history. How are art critics, or art historians for that matter, meant to understand Michael Baxandall's conviction that art history and art criticism are not distinguishable?[19] Should art critics perceive this as an unwarranted encroachment on their practice? Should art historians worry that Baxandall risks diluting the academic standards and rigor of their discipline? Following Baxandall, we should probably understand his books as deliberately interweaving art history and art criticism, and as providing models for rethinking both. In a similar fashion, it has been suggested that what is especially compelling in the art-historical works of T.J. Clark, Michael Fried, Joseph Leo Koerner, and others is a shared fundamental allegiance to art criticism as a dimension of those works.[20] If these examples have only referred to "art historians" so far (or critical historians of art), then it seems right to admit that there are several "art critics" who also possess this orientation. For example, a book like Rosalind Krauss's *The Optical Unconscious* is probably poorly read if it is merely read as a series of art-critical essays chronologically arranged and thematically linked, or if it is read as an art history text pure and simple. Much the same, I think, can be also said about Hal Foster's 1993 book on Surrealism, *Compulsive Beauty*.[21]

The last two examples, of course, are associated with the *October* journal, and I raise them because it was a disappointing feature of both roundtables that, despite the efforts of James Elkins, there was barely any credible acknowledgement of *October*; the participants at the first roundtable in Ireland declined to speak when the subject of *October* arose (which, oddly enough, was surely tantamount to a refusal to engage in criticism), while at the second roundtable the near-hyperbole of David Hickey and James Panero attempted to drown-out the more measured reflections of Stephen Melville and Michael Newman. What especially made it a shame that neither roundtable quite managed to engage with *October* is that, insofar as the journal has dominated the critical scene for nearly thirty years, it arguably provides a useful vantage point to meditate on and chart some of the transformations in art criticism. It is perhaps helpful, then, to consider the history and development of *October*. A comment made during *October*'s 2002 roundtable, "The Present Conditions of Art Criticism," seems a good place to start: about halfway through the conversation, David Joselit observes that Krauss' art criticism "helped to produce a definition of postmodernism, rather than merely reporting a preexisting phenomenon."[22] Joselit's comment here is on target. Krauss, and her fellow critics at *October*—Douglas Crimp, Craig Owens, Joel Fineman, and Annette Michelson, for example—indeed played a crucial role in defining a postmodern sensibility in a newly emerging generation of artists.[23] And today it is often forgotten that prior to *October*'s critical intervention toward the end of the 1970s, the theorization of postmodernism was mostly restricted to architectural discourse rather than any other cultural field, and the influential accounts of postmodernism expounded by Fredric Jameson and Jean-François Lyotard were not yet present on the Anglo-American stage. *October*'s achievement was to appropriate the *term*—although not the *concept*—"postmodernism" from architecture, combine it with inspirations taken from poststructuralism and Frankfurt school critical theory, among other sources, and render it applicable to a new artistic generation.[24]

My overriding sense of the art criticism at *October* during those early years, then, pertains to the powerfully generative effects it produced, and of its timeliness or its contemporaneity. *October*, Owens once said, did not so much write *about* young artists like Sherrie Levine or Cindy Sherman as *alongside* them, distinguishing between heroes and villains (that is, Neoexpressionism and its supporters) and conservative and progressive postmodernisms in the process;[25] polemics with other art critics (especially Hilton Kramer and Donald Kuspit) were common to *October*; and many of the poststructuralists it found inspiration in were still alive and writing. For Arthur Danto, the 1980s were "the *October* decade." But things are now rather different at *October*. To my mind, it is still very much the case that *October* is producing strong art criticism, but a shift in its immediate concerns is perceptible: it now appears that much of the journal's art criticism evinces a greater orientation toward art history, and is generally less interested in directly delineating, supporting, or contesting the present condition of art.[26] A cursory glance over the last twenty or so back issues of *October* brings up movements and names—many of which are often perceived as of mainly historical interest—like Dada, Surrealism, Constructivism, Carl Einstein, Barnett Newman. When living artists appear in the journal's pages, chances are it would be figures like Ed Ruscha, Robert Rauschenberg, James Coleman, Sherman, Levine—all artists whose careers have been long established. There are exceptions, of course, but these seem to derive from a younger generation of art historians and critics: Claire Bishop on relational aesthetics, for example, or Mark Godfrey on Tacita Dean, and there has been material on and interviews with Pierre Huyghe and Thomas Hirschhorn. Hal Foster, who out of the central quartet (with Bois, Buchloh, and Krauss) is arguably the most receptive to ongoing developments in art, wrote an essay arguing for an archival impulse in recent art, but somehow it lacked the conviction of his best writing. A very rough and unscientific census of the first twenty issues of *October* suggests that around two-thirds of the essays were dedicated to contemporary art and theory, while the most recent twenty issues (99–118) puts the percentage around one-third.[27] If it is really true that art students and younger critics are starting to feel there is something increasingly irrelevant about *October*, or that there was something hermetically sealed about the roundtable on art criticism, as Ariella Budick claimed, then it could be because *October* can appear to be less out of step with the times than running very fast in the opposite direction.

However, we gain very little if we just ignore *October*, or declare it "unsexy." The journal still provides a useful place for meditating on the part theory plays, or can play, in art criticism, and on the way theory and criticism might relate to the artwork. And indeed, in contemplating these questions, it can often become useful to see how specifically art-historical facts and matters might also play a significant role in our understanding of art. As such, art criticism generally doesn't figure in the more explicitly art-historical essays published in *October* as evidence to be marshalled (as Abigail Solomon-Godeau worried in the first roundtable); nor does it appear to be the case that art history functions as merely data for art criticism. This is not to claim that this is a new or recent orientation in *October*; it is only to claim that this orientation has become increasingly pronounced over the years. Nor would I wish to suggest that I always and consistently find *October* valuable for thinking through these questions and problems; *October* can be just as frustrating, disappointing, and infuriating as any other academic journal or popular newspaper, and the issues I am foregrounding are not always explicitly central to the journal's enterprise. Nevertheless, even if *October*, and some of the other names that I indicated in the opening paragraph, effect or insist upon a blurring of art history and art criticism, then it still remains to be answered why this should be. One answer might be that art history finds in art criticism analogies to literary criticism, and thereby techniques for close "reading" that register the materiality of the artwork; in art history, it is too easy to speak *of* the visual without speaking *to* it. Another possible answer might be, as Michael Newman suggested, that to a certain extent all art is contemporary art insofar as the art from the past continues to inform our present-day culture. Linked to that answer we might suggest another: that the value of past art needs to be critically re-established *in* and *for* the present, and the mere uncritical acceptance of that value as a transhistorical given risks just being thoughtlessness or convenience.

These reasons—and they are by no means exhaustive—all seem

plausible starting points for thinking why and how art history and art criticism interweave, but there is another that particularly interests me. During the course of the second roundtable, I was struck when Newman said that art criticism happens, or should happen, "where it's not wholly clear what the work is, and the task is somehow to bring to light, so that one can begin to have a discussion, *what it is* that one is looking at or experiencing." The remark struck me largely because it was reminiscent of Phil Leider's confession in Amy Newman's book *Challenging Art*. Thinking back on the development of art in the 1960s and the way that the art criticism in *Artforum* responded to those developments, Leider admits: "The verbal part, the theoretical part, sustained me through my doubts. Every time I began to doubt the way things looked, the value, the quality, the plain quality of the work as it looked to me, I was able to fall back on this structure of thought."[28] And Leider's confession reminds of yet another statement, this time from Adorno's *Aesthetic Theory*: "It is self-evident that nothing concerning art is self-evident anymore, not its inner life, not its relation to the world, not even its right to exist."[29]

All these comments, to my mind, tell us a great deal about art criticism's role within modernism, and perhaps within postmodernism as well. What they tell us, in one form or another, is that in modernism art was no longer a fully self-evident category, that it was no easy matter to identify artworks *as* artworks without some kind of critical-theoretical elaboration. Today, arguably, we have so grown used to—under certain conditions—identifying a signed urinal placed on a plinth as being an artwork, or a metal bin filled with rock taken from a quarry as an artwork, or a monochromatic canvas as being a painting, that it would perhaps be more controversial to declare them as non-art rather than as art. This is a shame, not because controversy or radicalism are to be valued in themselves, but because it obfuscates the very real battles waged in art criticism, and between art criticism and the artwork, that—at times only tentatively—conferred a status upon those works. Modernism, by violently unmooring itself from the conventions and materials that had defined art since the Renaissance, rendered it difficult to make objects that are art in any a priori sense. That is to say, it is seemingly characteristic of art under modernism that it is progressively less available to the immediacy of sensory perception and less amenable to historically earlier categories and conventions.

My sense of modernism, then, is somewhat less informed by the apparent certitude of Clement Greenberg's infamous account given in "Modernist Painting" than it is by the manifest uncertainty and conviction that is to be found in Stanley Cavell's philosophy (however, it must be noted that these two names do not represent polarities). His essay "Music Discomposed," for example, raises the issue of modernism's attachment to and detachment from history, and thus the difficulty art has in defining itself when all the conventions that have determined it are put radically into question.[30] In response to this situation, art has to more or less invented its own conventions, but there are no a priori rules or tests that will decide whether or not the invention of these conventions will be successful. Cavell's argumentation is complex, and it would be impossible here to chart it in any manner that would do it justice, but it is useful to underscore that this peculiarly modernist situation forces us to put our *trust* in artworks that look strange or unfamiliar or don't pertain to what we traditionally expect from art, and that this leaves us open to the risk of *fraudulence*; our trust can be betrayed.[31] For Cavell, these modernist circumstances place art criticism in a special but difficult position: art criticism is not simply positioned to judge the difference between good art and bad, but also to justify art as authentically modernist or condemn it as irredeemably fraudulent; what further makes the position of art criticism all the more difficult is that the artist does not deliberately make his work either fraudulent or authentic, and the critic can be fooled, made into an impostor. Art criticism (and the artwork), then, is less a solution to this conundrum than a symptom of it, but it is all we have.

All this is just to say that modernism makes art criticism all the more necessary and all the more difficult. And it seems to me that the growth of art criticism in the 1960s, the emergence of *Artforum* and similar publications, the greater role of theory and criticism in the writings of artists like Robert Smithson,[32] even the collapse of Greenberg's formalism and philosophy, all testify to modernism's problematic relationship to past conventions as described by Cavell. Along these lines, when Melville—correctly, I think—argues that *October* is "in part an attempt to inherit the very broad permissions that *Artforum* gave to criticism in the 1960s, so that it was born with a worry about art criticism as a part of what it is," I would add that this worry derives from modernist art criticism's openness to, and need to distinguish between, the authentic and the fraudulent, and that this worry does not disappear with the shift from modernism to postmodernism. One of the problems I have with the criticism and roundtable contribution of Hickey and Panero is that their art criticism and modernism is seemingly entirely protected from any self-doubt—safe from the risk of fraudulence and failure—despite Hickey's sounding the death-knell for art criticism.

I want to end by suggesting that if art criticism is now a vital component of art history, then art history inherits the worries and dangers that modernist art criticism partakes in, and it is doubtful that these worries and dangers can be avoided if one chooses only to refuse or deny art criticism's role in art history. And this does not just pertain to the modernist artworks examined in *October*, but also to much older works—works that we now presume ourselves to be thoroughly familiar with. I imagine, then, Dürer's epochal self-portrait of 1500, his eyes staring out at *us* in some fusion of horizons, making demands of *us*, still calling—always calling—to be judged authentic or fraudulent.[33] Dürer's painting calls to us, to Koerner, because no matter how historical and historically established it might be, it still remains a potent question that is yet to be answered with any degree of finality. And although it is now over five-hundred years old, and widely written on, and every nuance historicized, there is no guarantee that we have learnt to look at it yet, that is to say, no guarantee that we have met and acknowledged Dürer's stare.

Margaret Hawkins

Newspaper Criticism, Context and the Huh /Wow Factor

Newspaper art critics take a lot of flak. We're accused of wallowing in the shallow waters of bland irrelevance, pandering to an entertainment-oriented public, failing to make aesthetic judgments and abdicating serious discussion in favor of dumbed-down educational pap. Newspaper critics, we hear, have lost their place at the table, have become mere journalists who do nothing more than describe art to an uneducated and uninterested public.

I can only speak for myself but I suspect I'm not alone in saying that, however bad my writing or my judgment may sometimes be, my aim is always higher than that. In fact, it is embarrassingly lofty. I think of myself as a kind of stealth philosopher trying to conduct a public meditation on the nature of perception in the midst of bad news, gossip, and baseball scores.

This meditation includes judgment and criticism in the sense of sorting out the good from the bad, but mainly, as I practice it, it involves an exploration of how we see and come to know things and the related phenomenon of how the way an artist sees can reveal truth about the universe. In visual art this process is part optical, part psychological and part philosophical. Art criticism is as much or more about how the mind works as it is about how good or bad what we look at is.

In defense of my ilk I'd say newspaper critics have a unique and even an important place in the world of art writing. We are the first responders—we and only we rush to the scene of the crime, or the exhibit, and file the first report. We behold the thing, the object, the event, and attempt to divine its meaning before a public consensus has been reached. We write about experience, not theory. We are not historians and don't claim to be. Often we are self-taught in the sense that we did not study criticism; we studied painting or politics or biology. We are of the world, writers and viewers with opinions, unaffiliated though not unfamiliar with formal critical systems.

Most of us, I think, try to be both honest and clear. We avoid jargon, partly because our editors won't let us use it, but also because we want to find meaning and communicate it to a general audience and not obfuscate it in academic language. We hope what we write is thoughtful enough to hold up over time, but there's no question that newspaper reviews are about one person's aesthetic experience in the context of the moment and usually not about an exhibit's historical significance. To understand that, a writer needs time, and time is one thing the newspaper critic doesn't have. Closer to city hall reportage than art history, newspaper criticism is at best poetry on the run, at worst a useless mix of rehashed PR and glib opinioneering. Usually it's somewhere in the murky in-between.

One of the struggles for a newspaper critic is that her writing must remain serious yet be lively enough to compete with other kinds and tones of writing, often on the same page, not to mention with the pictures that accompany that writing which can create odd contextual juxtapositions over which she has no control. Some days my column runs as a solid block of text—no photo—next to an ad for a triple-X strip club. On other days it runs opposite one of Roger Ebert's movie reviews, illustrated with big color publicity shots. To read my nine hundred words about a painting show requires a significant shift in the mindset of the reader, who must stop planning his or her weekend and start musing on, say, the ephemeral nature of light reflected off aluminum. Though I suspect my column is often skipped over, it occurs to me (though my editors may not agree and have occasionally asked me to make my writing more "plebeian" and to stop using so many big words) that some readers may actually enjoy wandering in and out of states of mind as they riffle the morning papers. I do. I enjoy switching from the editorial page to the pet lovers' advice column, from the often-bloody headlines to the reassuring fluff of Wednesday's food section. Why not? Such is the texture of life. It's nether all grim nor all frivolous, and dailiness intrudes on even the most life-changing of events so why not add in philosophy in the form of a serious consideration of visual art, complete with challenging ideas and images. Maybe newspaper art criticism isn't irrelevant at all; maybe it provides a useful, even necessary, place for contemplation in the midst of the busy world, like a small park in the middle of a big city.

I had the opportunity to hear Peter Schjeldahl speak at the School of the Art Institute of Chicago in spring of 2005, and when he opened the floor to questions I asked him what criteria he used in judging art. He replied by quoting Ed Ruscha, who said that when you look at bad art you say "Wow! Huh?" and when you look at good art you say "Huh? Wow!"

It's as good an attempt as any I've heard at describing the process of aesthetic judgment and it captures for me, if not what art critics do, more importantly, how they do it. It's a story not about judgment but about perception, about listening to your gut or your right brain or what ever prelogical part of the human organism responds to visual experience, and then trying to understand what it's telling you before your intellect kicks in and starts bossing your brain around. Any newspaper critic who can do that and then write about it still has a rightful place somewhere between the front page and the used car ads.

Elaine O'Brien

An Assessment of State of Art Criticism

A significant feature of the roundtable conversations overall is the disparity between James Elkins's focused urgency of purpose and his discussants' seemingly willful lack of it. Some, for example Whitney Davis and Abigail Solomon-Godeau, question Elkins's efforts to define art criticism, asking for clarification about what is at stake.

When Elkins insists that the seminar must reconsider judgment, for him the key term of art criticism, Irit Rogoff and Jean Fisher assert that judgment is irrelevant to their practice. Such telling disjunctions and ellipses fascinate and position the speakers on the field. Elkins's commentary supplies sufficient centripetal force and offers the reader a bird's-eye view, as when he speculates that the inability to remain on topic might indicate the threshold of art criticism's self-consciousness.

There was little disagreement with Elkins's premise that art criticism is in crisis, or if not crisis, then decline. Some readers like me will reject this point of view since—even if the European tradition could be considered in isolation—it presupposes a linear theory of intellectual history that we don't hold. But more importantly, the strong differences of opinion among these eminent critics and critical historians of art, their wayward, often astute and sometimes brilliant intercourse do not tell a pessimistic story about the state of art criticism. They can be read against the grain as evidence that the defining independent, paradoxical, and intellectually promiscuous nature of critical culture is still vital.

What remains in doubt is art criticism's relevance to twenty-first-century art and life, whether or not the level of ethical prestige earned by modern and postmodern art criticism will be sustained. In view of the fact that for decades the education of critical thinkers has been the task of academe, I looked for signs of historical consciousness and responsibility in these seminars. Certainly they are present in Elkins's urgency.

As a response to his concern that art criticism doesn't worry enough about its history and his question to the Chicago seminar about looking to art criticism's relevant past for direction, I would like to suggest that certain disregarded aspects of the Baudelairean avant-garde tradition be reconsidered for academic practice. By including Dave Hickey's independent voice (however derisive in this context), Elkins brought living principles of Baudelaire's nineteenth-century vanguard criticism to the discussion. Except as history, these values have been ignored by academic art criticism, which achieved cultural dominance in the United States by the late 1960s. Thus the avant-garde values that Hickey tossed out in the seminar (as if not expecting them to be taken seriously)—intellectual autonomy, anti-academicism, broad literary erudition, and the significance of writing style—have been buried, turned over in the paradigm shift that divides the pre-academic era and our own.

Whether or not the ethical postures of Baudelairean modernism are relevant for today's globalized visual culture, or even possible for academic critics to adopt, is a topic for another occasion. Here I will point to one present-past intersection in this tradition: the affinities of theory and practice between Dave Hickey and Harold Rosenberg (1906–1978).[34] The production of each critic is unique, but both orbit around a core of shared principles. I will touch on two: anti-academicism and the significance of writing style.

"Art history is the death of art like the museum," Hickey asserted in 1999 with typical conviction.[35] Into the Chicago seminar he drops these discouraging words: "I would suggest that this round-table is a death-knell for art criticism: it marks a level of self-consciousness, creeping professionalism and narcissistic introspection that can't sustain the practice or be sustained by the practice." Such remarks, both in anti-institutional attitude and epigrammatic form, are pure Harold Rosenberg.

Rosenberg's art criticism can be read as a record of unrelenting combat against the academization of culture. "The Rape of Academe"[36] is the title Henri Peyre gave his review of Rosenberg's first collection, *The Tradition of the New*, in 1959. But Rosenberg had declared war much earlier, firing the first salvos in response to the fall of Paris in 1940. To him, that catastrophe represented a gross failure of critical nerve that he blamed on "the clerks": institutional intellectuals, "the herd of independent minds." For years he targeted former Marxist political and literary independents, but by the 1960s, with the stunning institutional success of Greenbergian formalism, it was the American academic art establishment that he pursued relentlessly.

As to the second point of comparison between Hickey and Rosenberg, the significance of writing style, it's clear that Hickey would, as Rosenberg did, identify himself as a "word artist." Rosenberg believed his first task as an art critic was to raise the conversation to the level of history and enrich the environment of words around artists, especially artist friends like Willem de Kooning whose lifestyle he shared and whose artwork was to Rosenberg a process of discovery like his writing. In much the same way, Hickey describes his own criticism as art talk that "provides the oxygen of art's social life."[37] Hickey explains in the Chicago seminar that he is "mostly about writing . . . interested in the phonetics, in how it sounds when you read it . . . and I'm interested in works of art with comparable attributes, so there is an element of circularity there."

The "circularity" Hickey notes, the creative relationship between art and art criticism, defined Rosenberg's art criticism as well. When James Fitzsimmons, editor of *Art International*, asked Rosenberg in a 1967 letter why art criticism is "so inferior to literary criticism,"[38] Rosenberg suggested that "one reason there is so much wretched writing about art is that the writers who produce it are simply not writers." He continued, "I would go further and say that since writing itself is an art, being able to write is the basis upon which a writer understands an artist."[39]

Much of Rosenberg's contempt for the young PhD art historian critics had to do with their failure in his eyes to develop individual creative writing styles, which he attributed to a doctrinaire attitude toward their subject and a lack of poetic sensibility. "Obviously," he wrote in a 1968 *New Yorker* piece on Baudelaire, "poetic criticism is not a program that can be attractive to ideologists, system builders, curators or art departments. By its nature it invites abuse, in that it seems to substitute colorful phrases for a serious analysis of paintings and sculptures. . . ."[40]

The literary sources of Rosenberg and Hickey, their impressive erudition in Western letters, can surprise university art historians and critics. "I want to draw attention to the weirdness of a conversation on art criticism, held in 2005," Elkins observes, "which ends up with a list like Hazlitt, Pater, Wilde, Shaw, and Boccaccio! This list is really astonishing. It would never have come up after, say, Fry's generation (his dates are 1866–1934): names like these were not proffered in *Artforum*, or *October*. They point to a new sense of possible histories."

I will let Elkins's remark on "a new sense of possible histories" conclude my assessment.

Maja Naef

The State of Art Criticism, Reviewed

I started to write art criticism while still at university, without curatorial experience or of having worked in the art business. Taking a critical stance on art from this starting point, with all the advantages and disadvantages of naïvety, made it necessary to reflect on the distinction of art critical and art historical *writing*. This dilemma is symptomatic for the question why art criticism is not an independent discipline, a question raised in the roundtable discussion. Equally, it highlights why no differentiated conception of art criticism existed, that I could have anticipated. This gave rise to two interrelated consequences: first, a dialectical and at times problematic relationship to art history underlies my conception of art criticism. That is, my art criticism does not aim at situating an object in its art historical context or at relating the work to generally observable trends in art, especially when engaging with events in a geographically limited environment. Second, I was of the opinion that I did not possess sufficient criteria to pursue what I naïvely took to be "true" art criticism, though all the while aware that no such thing existed clearly circumscribed: that is, that I needed an objective originary ground to which the expressed judgments of the artwork refer: What, then, are the preconditions *for* and the specific knowledge *of* art criticism? This raised the question of an art criticism that didn't continuously falsify its own writing with greater urgency.

One of the central insights, exclusive to the praxis of art criticism, was the impossibility of recouping the experience of the artwork in writing; and that it is precisely this irretrievable residuum that motivates this form of writing. My art-critical curiosity sought out an impetus inherent to writing that communicates the object or the exhibition space and enables an experience of art inimitable to language, both for the writer and the reader though distinct and separate. Because it is not only the negotiations of art, especially the author's production and the reader's response, that depend fundamentally on language and on texts; that is, on a form of knowledge available to language.

Thus I consider language and experience as the referential ground for the praxis of art criticism, replacing the parameter of the merely descriptive or primarily evaluative writing. The act of writing in art criticism enables the emergence of the verbally irretrievable experience inimitable to the artwork. As such art criticism can be understood as a performative act, what Gemma Tipton aptly called "criticality" in the first roundtable discussion. Writing stands-in for a process of negotiations, allowing the discontinuity between the experience of the individual object in its particular constellation and its appropriation to be paraphrased.

In this sense my conception of art criticism is sedimented in writing itself, in that it records a searching motion accompanied by the verification of *how* one experiences, that is, *how* experience is translated into writing. And in this I understand art criticism as a form in the present, articulated in the choice of its object. Art criticism occurs not solely in the expression of an opinion, the opening of a discourse, or the articulation of judgment. Art-critical writing enables the experience that art gives rise to something that makes language itself a productive problem, and not the mere means of judging.

–Translated by Timothy Grundy

Victoria Musvik

On the Virtue of Cultural Flux

I have mixed feelings about what was going on during the two roundtables on criticism. Or rather—keeping in mind the main subject of this book—"mixed press" would perhaps be a much better term. I started reading it in hope that certain questions that I have about my own critical activities would be if not answered, then at least raised by influential critics and art theorists that Jim managed to get together in Ballyvaughan (I have even looked the place up on the map) and Chicago. I finished reading it in a completely blurred state of mind, thinking that, however exciting this discussion might be (and I have found this "parade of voices" very thought-stimulating), much of what has been said has little or no use to me in either my own everyday critical practice or university teaching.

What makes it difficult for me to stomach this discussion is the absence of dialogue; or rather, the absence of a conscious effort of dialogue. In fact, I find the way that its participants do not hear each other and sometimes arrogance or even hostility that can be read between the lines—and this in a roundtable that was supposed not only to show the array of possibilites that exist in contemporary criticism but also to come to more general conclusions about its nature—quite sad. I must say that for me—for an academic with a critical "voice," for an outsider who was not there when the roundtables were taking place, and for a cultural outsider who, though white, is not Western European or Northern American—these things were quite obvious. And much to my surprise (though perhaps I was not as surprised as I should be), I think it was the academics that were not "really" listening the "other side of the table." Their vis-à-vis, it seemed to me, were just trying to defend something about art criticism that somehow was not quite clearly articulated.

Now, mistrust of the outsiders (and after all, art critics are mostly outsiders for the university) is quite understandable: academia is a corporation with its own set of rules and practices. The problem is that it was not questioned, apart from some irony about it, or put into light in any serious way that could provoke reflection not only on the nature of art criticism, but on the nature of academia as well. Unfortunately, this happens quite often: as academics we "do research" on other spheres of culture without asking ourselves why we are doing it. What worries me most of all in this context is the absence of self-reflection on the part of the university side of the discussion on why exactly we want to connect criticism in any way with academia—and (especially!) invite these so-called newspaper critics to such roundtables. Ironically, I do not see the opposite movement, that of "less serious" critics trying to find out what academia thinks about them; in fact, I have a feeling that they do not really bother, may be because, as university graduates, they know it well. So the most important question arises: why do we as academics want to talk to non-academic critics, mire them into our own ways of talking, and then tell them that they are doing the wrong sort of things with art? Or, to put it in a more simple way, if we do not value some of these fellows and the stuff they are writing about art, if we consider them not up to the snuff, why do we want them to talk? Is it just because we find criticism an interesting subject of research? Is it because we want to teach it and so create new university positions? Is it a form of self-assertion? Is it something comparable to Orientalism—the simultaneous fetishization and annihilation of the Other that has been brilliantly described by Edward Said and his followers? Or is it, maybe, because we secretely think that art theory (and theory on the whole) is at the moment at a kind of dead-end and need to find something in the practice of criticism that is radically or dramatically different—a different approach to art, to culture, to the outside life or maybe even methodology of writing and connecting things? However, given the dislike that the "serious" academics show to more volatile genres of criticism, I cannot see the later question even being formulated, let alone answered.

My personal position is rather flexible. I am used to constantly playing with these two faces—that of a newspaper critic (and even—yuk—of a writer about art for glamour magazines or, come to think of it, my blog) and that of an academic—in my own professional life. In fact, I do not see why I have to renounce any genre of criticism in favor of another. I write mostly about photography but sometimes also about contemporary art and historical exhibitions for Russian newspapers (I was a staff writer of a major Russian publishing house Kommersant for four and a half years, and left it last year choosing to be a freelancer), websites, professional photographic magazines, and "serious" cultural analysis for political magazines; I also teach visual studies at the university and do research on early modern subjects. There is no opposition between university and journalism in my life, and I cannot say that I am a "writing academic" or a "teaching journalist": university and criticism are two separate practices that co-exist and, depending on circumstances, aims, and my interests, it is either one face or another that I represent to the world. In fact, in certain situations I prefer to act as a newspaper critic, because of the possibility of immediate reaction, the influence that I can exercise on the things emerging, shortness and coherence of utterance and quick feedback from the audience (though sometimes it comes from very strange people). On the other hand, my university background helps me to pose new questions in newspaper criticism, to keep proper critical distance, and to constantly (re)define my intellectual position.

It might be of course that, as a critic operating in a culture that faces problems quite different in many ways from the ones that those Great White Westerners have been discussing, I have my own kettle of fish to boil. I, a 31-year-old Russian critic and a university lecturer, live in a society where so many things are just emerging after so many years of being absent or simply repressed (including newspaper or academic criticism of contemporary art). In the situation when the society is messed up, one is going to get lost without shrewd understanding and questioning of one's roots, prejudices, and masks. There are too many lacunae to fill in, such a long way to walk in such a short time, and so few critics, university researchers, or just intelligent people able of sober, unbiased, and realistic reflection on the contemporary state of the art field in Russia (or culture on the whole, for that matter) that one finds oneself constantly being torn apart by opportunities and emerging fields. The burden of responsibility is sometimes enormous: whatever you write, you may be the first one ever to write about it.

It might also be that the society of critics I know is quite different from that which the participants in the roundtables were talking about. First, it is definitely smaller. Second, for the past ten or fifteen years the Russian market has been (and still is) full of opportunities of quick intellectual development and even fame for creative specialists, but not, I regret to say, in the sphere of academia. In fact, the almost total collapse of university values and the current financial situation has led to the flight of young specialists from the university. Young people of outstanding intellectual and creative qualities are forced either to move from Russia or, if they want to stay, to earn money in more "down-to-earth" professions, including cultural journalism (which pays much better than work at a state university). Third, almost all art critics I know are quite young and there is a generation gap: the thirty-year-olds are the first "free" generation that had an early opportunity to travel as well as having a whole new range of possibilites for development. Many people of that generation have returned to Russia with the desire to make changes. When I compare people of my age in this country with those of the same age in Britain or the United States, I have a feeling that we had to grow up faster and had more cultural flux and uncertainty to deal with, but there were also more possibilites for development. The result is that by thirty, many have already established their own reputations. And fourth, in the early-1990s when both contemporary art and photography markets were undeveloped in Moscow, a conscious effort was made by several cultural editors to raise a generation of "educated critics" in the newspapers. The result is that almost all art, photography, literary, and so forth critics I know in major Russian newspapers and art magazines are young (under forty, and sometimes even under thirty); many of them have PhDs in relevant fields of the humanities, some of them continue to do university research or teaching, but on a part-time basis, and none of them sees any part of their experience as "not relevant," be it academic writing or newspaper criticism.

It might also be that I, as a person whose first degree was in literary theory and history, see that the tradition of art theory reflection on itself is too young (compared, in fact, to criticism itself) and just does not have the necessary tools to deal with criticism—yet. I do not think, however, that my "different" experience and the position of an outsider (in many ways) has much to do with the main argument of my assessment. The main issue, as I see it—and this may or may not be the case—lies somewhere far beyond the clash of wills of the people in these two roundtables. I think the problem with criticism for the university is that it is organized on a compleatly different set of principles to those of academia. These are exactly the things that one has to cut down in oneself if one wants to be a "good academic" and have a proper distance from the subject of research. This is why I value criticism: I can be a critic where I cannot be an academic, and there are parts of me and my experience that I just do not want to repress. To name but few, good criticism, in my opinion, means having a voice that is instantly, from the very first lines, recognizable in one's writing (I think it is this that is meant by "writing well" and not just any sort of general observation), a strong connection with the "world outside" (art in this country at this particular moment) and the audience, including the so-called general public. I value the instantaneity of reaction, emotional response, and connection to one's own feelings to the point of vulnerability; however, these three points do not mean the lack of intellectual background or education in a particular field, or a carte blanche to make factual mistakes.

But the main principle of criticism as I see it is the ability of this field to encompass different practices, including minor voices, without trying to "structure" them in any way. To the outer world, criticism might seem a disarray of very different practices, but this might be just because the outer world has no tools to deal with this kind of thing. I would compare this to a medieval manuscript with its overlapping marginal notes or the early modern ideas of the world as a book full of signs, similarities, and resemblances. For me, this is a quality of culture that is definitely pre-Enlightenment, and to understand it we have, in a way, to jump over the head of our own tradition, but I would stop here because I do not want to go too far in a small assessment like this. Suffice it to say, in my opinion this is why criticism (as some other practices of the same kind and with the same organization) works well in the world of cultural flux, changes, and "instabile creativity" and the university does not. I find it funny how no one asked in the discussion one important question: if we want art criticism to become part of the university, why should art criticism become part of academia on academia's terms? Should we not better interest ourselves in the questions that might be crucial to the art-critical society as a whole structure, not as a subject of analysis or dissection? The same questions come over and over (what practices are criticism? what is judgment? how is criticism included in the art market?), but no one asks critics themselves to formulate questions that they would think the most important problems in criticism as a professional experience.

Having said that, I do not want my assessment to be seen as an attack on academia—either Russian or Western. It is indeed the university, in Moscow, London, and Washington, that has taught me irony, detachment, and proper critical distance from the subjects I am writing about—both as a critic and as a researcher—and it is at the university that I teach people all these things. But it is with a growing feeling of something that can be only called sadness that I get more and more experience of other cultural spheres that work as well as academia, and in some senses (for example, in the mechanism of their interaction with the society or contemporary culture) better than academia, such as criticism, cultural journalism, exhibition organization, and the art market. I cannot bring those knowledges and practices back into academia, except in some very marginal ways. I am worried that the inability to deal with systems that are organized (epistemologically, historically, methodologically) on different, indeed opposite principles than those of the university structure of the humanities leads to a constant leak of "minor" ideas (as compared to those currently shared by the majority) and creative specialists into other spheres of culture. In spite of all current changes and fashions, in spite of all national differences, academia is a corporation whose main, indeed basic structure of interaction with the world is still very positivist. This means that we frequently want to impose the structure of our own field or discipline on other phenomena without reflecting on the way our own field is organized in the first place. I see this is a rather serious deficiency, to notice cultural structures that are compleatly different not just as the subjects of research or heavy irony, but as a living force which we should not only tear apart, but from which we can also learn something useful.

I have a feeling that recently this has been realized; witness various attempts in the universities all over the world to "deal with" such things as, to name but a few, everyday experience, emotion, creativity, or indeed criticism. Unfortunately academia is trying to draw these "unruly" things inside and dissect them, rather than walking quietly into someone else's house to observe, as a guest or a witness. I think that we have to find ways of letting art criticism as a system teach art theory and visual studies something that it knows and we do not—and yet to keep a proper distance from it. This is a difficult task—a much more difficult one, in fact, than inviting leading critics and then assigning them roles that we have thought of in advance, but it seems to me that academia would greatly benefit from such a way of looking.

Mark Bauerlein

A Commentary on the First Roundtable

Early in the first conversation on the principles and practices of art history, Whitney Davis identifies a central need in the discipline: "in art historical contexts it is often unclear what the object of critical or historical analysis itself *is*. There needs to be a kind of critical clarification of that problem." Davis goes on to judge it "the essential critical activity in art history."

If that is the case, then the discipline of art history is in bad shape. If an inquiry isn't sure of its subject matter, it can't pose focused questions or formulate clear hypotheses about it. It can do other things, for instance, theorize about objecthood, or produce long-winded reiterations of the epistemological dilemmas that, far from advancing an inquiry, paralyze it. And it can highlight artworks whose boundaries are fuzzy, and make that fuzziness into a virtuous trait. But as for compiling the kind of knowledge that may assist future generations in their engagement with the artwork, which is the sign of a healthy discipline, inquirers uncertain of their object don't even know where to start.

There is another aspect to Davis's statement that reflects poorly upon the state of the field: we've heard it before, many times and for many years. The questioning of terms and assumptions and operative premises has been a staple of humanities scholarship and criticism ever since the advent of High Theory four decades ago. In literary studies, theorists coming out of graduate school in the late-1960s and early-1970s made careers as "metacritics," people who put the conceptual tools of criticism (text, evidence, objectivity, interpretation, and so on) under the scrutiny of Derridean, de Manian, and other ruminations. For a time, the approach seemed invigorating and acute, a needed injection of new ideas from philosophy and the social sciences into literary study. It was a form of epistemological skepticism, to be sure, disabling for traditional scholars, but it was remarkably productive for others, and it proved highly adaptable to the expansion of criticism into political and institutional issues—for instance, the conversion of linguistic difference as theorized by Saussure, Levi-Strauss, and Derrida into racial difference and sexual difference as theorized in quarterlies such as *Critical Inquiry* and *Signs* in the 1980s.

Art history picked up this reflective turn in the mid-1970s, according to the participants here, and they single out Rosalind Krauss as a leader. Late in the conversation the turn is identified as "critique," the critic's "interrogation of her own assumptions regarding judgment." In fact, the self-examination ritual pops up in different versions several times, as in Davis's assertion that "the activity of hermeneutic interpretation and judgment in art history as a critical possibility needs to be actively and self-reflectively recognized and theorized." Gemma Tipton, too, exclaims, "I can't understand how one can believe themselves [sic] to be writing about something without judgment being implicated. It's there fundamentally in your choices of words, of emphases, of going to a particular exhibition, and then of electing to write about it at all. And if you don't acknowledge that, and pretend you're neutral, you are in a sense cheating the reader."

James Elkins notes how common and, indeed, normative the reflective turn has become in the discipline: "as art historians, we're all taught this first thing: we're instructed, as students, that we're not writing objective texts, and that neutrality is an incoherent proposition. But it seems no one knows what to *do* with that information. How might it influence what you say, or how you say it?"

Reading these statements in 2006, thirty years after *Knowledge and Human Interests*, forty years after *Les mots et les choses*, 100 years after *Pragmatism: A New Name for Some Old Ways of Thinking*, and 120 years after *The Will to Power*, one wonders what the discussants are up to. Why are we still making this tiresome point about neutrality and self-awareness? Davis and Boris Groys cite numerous figures in the Continental tradition, but the participants nonetheless treat it as a live insight, as if it needed to be rehearsed because (presumably) of all those people out there operating in, as Husserl called it, the "natural attitude." But who in the orbit of art history needs to hear it? In truth, this phenomenological backstep is familiar to every graduate student, indeed, to every college sophomore who's taken a couple of humanities courses. Warnings against bias, partisanship, ethnocentrism, and so on are routine, and every time the words "theory," "critical thinking," "diversity," and "multiculturalism" are spoken, a pedagogy of critical self-reflection is at work.

Nevertheless, here and elsewhere, the professors rehearse the caveat, and the gesture has worn thin. This may be seen in how, in order to assert the importance of critique, the participants must pose its opposite in such extreme and caricatured ways. Abigail Solomon-Godeau says, "I would begin by saying that the existence of a *canon* in art history attests to the fact that criticism has made its way into what is ostensibly an objective, scientific discourse. Insofar as one accepts the idea that the canon is a kind of natural, organic element of art production, one obscures the fact that criticism, in the sense of making determinations of value, has already been at work." And Irit Rogoff refers to "the Olympian notion of judgment," that is, the adjudication of art works from an incontrovertible height. But nobody in the humanities today thinks that the canon is an "objective, scientific discourse." Nobody affirms an "Olympian judgment." Nobody "pretend[s] to be neutral." The absence of real antagonists in the academic world shows just how empty the assertion has become.

Added to its deadening familiarity is the fact that the phenomenological backstep isn't as binding as the participants assume it is. If we tie it to the concrete problem it purports to address—the possibility that bias might skew a conclusion or finding—and not to the resentment or anxiety that seems to fuel it, the backstep has an important but limited function. It helps guard against mistaken or unwarranted inferences, but it does nothing to show inquirers how practically to avoid them. Once it has made inquirers aware of potential bias, it has done all the work it can. At that point, we need methods to handle the problem, not reiterations of the problem.

Humanities professors appear to believe that there are no solutions. Hence Professor Elkins's statement "no one knows what to *do* with that information," which is all-too-true in humanistic settings. But in the sciences, inquirers and theorists have been working on the bias problem for a couple of centuries. One of the greatest philosophers of science, Charles Sanders Peirce, devoted much of his career to explaining how science can work given the situation that, as he acknowledged, an individual viewpoint is necessarily partial. As Peirce said once, "Individualism and falsity are one and the same," and he criticized Cartesian philosophy precisely because it claimed that "the ultimate test of certainty is to be found in the individual mind."

For scientists, on the other hand, knowledge was to be found in a community, not an individual. Only when individuals submit their notions to a community of inquirers who observe common scientific standards but who, individually, have different interests and biases do we arrive at reliable knowledge. It's a messy process of peer review and duplication of efforts, but in the long run knowledge is established. Peirce compares the scientific community to a cable made up of hundreds of filaments. Each filament bends and snaps easily, but together they form a super-strong connection, just as each scientist is a biased individual but the community is able to come up with extraordinary and reliable discoveries and improvements. We don't need to warn the scientists again and again that various interests and ambitions threaten their work. We just need is to ensure that the method of peer review remains fair and transparent.

Art history isn't physics, of course, and while physical experiments aren't valid until they've been repeated by others with the same results, scholars don't rewrite each others' interpretations. But the general difficulty of reaching sound conclusions despite individual bias is the same in both fields. Scientists have found ways of dealing with it, and humanists should respect their achievement. Let's waste no more time dithering over our partial perspectives and buried assumptions. They are always present in humanistic work, more or less so, and when they are egregious they shall be struck down. They should be taken on a case-by-case basis, as a practical matter. To treat them as a theoretical matter in this day and age is no longer a sign of critical acuity. It's a symptom of decadence.

Robert Enright

Criticism: The Zoo of Many-backed Beasts

I must confess my delight in reading (and re-reading) the two roundtables over the last few months. The experience falls partially into the category of guilty pleasure, since there is much in them that is quixotic and ambulatory, not to mention simply outrageous. This is exactly what you would expect if you gathered together in the same room such a varied and "contestable" cluster of theorists and critics. It occurs to me that I may have the wrong collective noun for this particular congregation. A pride of critics may be closer to the mark, perhaps a murder.

Two things are immediately apparent. We are in the early stages of theorizing art criticism, and while we're not exactly grunting and grimacing at one another before we pull out the clubs, there is something inchoate about the way the conversations proceed. It is a deficiency which James Elkins frequently brings to the attention of his unruly colleagues. In his double-barrelled role as convenor/

moderator, he is obliged to keep the participants on topic, and you sense there are numerous occasions where he would prefer to drop the *politesse* and become an enforcer.

In truth, you have to go much further back in time to locate the figure who best explains the sense of drift traced by these conversations. In the *Euthyphro*, an early Socratic dialogue, Plato's eponymous companion laments that nothing seems fixed in their conversation: "Somehow or other, our arguments, on whatever ground we rest them, seem to turn around and walk away from us." Euthyphro insists that Plato is "the Daedalus who sets ideas in motion," and while the philosopher acknowledges a familial relationship with the maze-maker, he would clearly prefer an opposite role. "I would give the wisdom of Daedalus, and the wealth of Tantalus, to be able to detain them and keep them fixed." Because the ideas in the roundtables, like the notions raised in the dialogue, "show an inclination to move," Elkins would most assuredly say both amen and ibid. to Plato's wishful conjecturing.

In the Chicago session, Elkins is concerned about the cavalier manner in which the Cork participants dismissed the *October* roundtable, and in making a case for Rosalind Krauss, Benjamin Buchloh, et al., he emphasizes their critical engagement with "a whole zoology of options." To characterize the choices open to readers of the roundtable discussion and practitioners of the mercurial act of writing criticism, he might have been more economical and said "zoo." He could have gone further still, by referring to art criticism as a zoo of many-backed beasts. The designation, an alteration of Catullus, makes the intercourse among them more suggestive.

I feel a sense of permission in responding through the prism of a Roman poet, since the list of antecedents cited by the roundtable participants includes a diverse array of writers, many of whom are not art critics in any usual sense of the term, and who come from the traditions of fiction, the essay, theatre, music, and poetry. Initially Elkins responds to this inventory of influences—Hazlitt, Pater, Wilde, Shaw are bookended by Boccaccio and Pauline Kael—with combined frustration and bewilderment. He emphasizes the "weirdness of the conversation" and the "astonishing" list that has arisen from it, but his conclusion is that these forerunners "point to a new sense of possible histories." Elkins's acquiescence to this new configuration of critical influences is an example of how the roundtables frequently operate. "The exciting thing about criticism is the plethora of forms and modes it takes," Gemma Tipton says, and in the saying, declares that art criticism draws its strength, Antaeus-like, from its diversity.

There is something apposite in turning towards language to discuss contemporary art criticism. Certain of the participants, most notably Dave Hickey, argue persuasively for the primacy of language in any critical formulation. "I'm mostly about writing," he says. "It all begins with the word, with the idea of the word as an object." In one sense, he carries the *belle lettrist* baton handed him by Peter Schjeldahl from the *October* roundtable in 2002, the ghostly presence of which haunts the proceedings in Cork and Chicago. For art critics, October is clearly the cruellest month.

Hickey is an apologist for writing, not just for style, but for a way of using language that proceeds through looking, seeing, comprehending, and composing. All of these acts demand unwavering concentration, beginning most critically with close observation. When Michael Newman declares his interest in art, "where it's not wholly clear what the work is, and the task is somehow to bring to light, so that one can begin to have a discussion, *what it is* that one is looking at or experiencing," he is underlining this necessary attentiveness. We must be all eyes before we can become all words. There is no criticism without objects looked at. Criticism is not an abstract process, and for it to work well, I am persuaded that it can never be disinterested.

What calls this articulated but impossible objectivity into question is the degree of personality revealed by the roundtables. Elkins needn't have bothered pointing out the spatial arrangement in Chicago; if we weren't told that Michael Newman was on one end of the table and Dave Hickey at the other, we would have guessed it on our own. There is a disruptive "range of ideologies" apparent in the discussions, and there are unquestionably occasions when the differences among the participants are maximized and displayed. This is often a function of personality, and in that steeplechase, Hickey outdistances the field. His conversation is performative and unpredictable; over the course of the Chicago proceedings he elegantly explains his attraction to modernism as "a serious commitment to articulated difficulty"; and then he unfairly drops a reference to the "yardage" of Arthur Danto's criticism. To use a portion of his own self-description, sometimes he's just the whore of babble on. There are many ways that criticism involves what Boris Groys calls "the realm of injustice." (While Hickey's tendency to be "foolishly candid" can be tedious, it's preferable to the over-exercised caution that Irit Rogoff displays in admitting that she finds the consideration of collaborating with Raphael "an interesting possibility, but it's not something I've thought out—and I don't want to just start speaking nonsense for the sake of speaking." But why not? The roundtables are works-in-progress, which makes having thought through them an impossibility and an element of speculation a necessity. Few of us have, either by will or divine intervention, what Joyce's *Stephen Hero* calls "the gift of certitude.")

But it's Hickey's "I" that plays a major role in his roundtable participation and in his criticism generally. "I am a non-conforming critic," "I am a creature of the marketplace," and "I'm always happy to dine my enemies." These self-descriptions are consistent with the overall sense of personal declaration that informs the roundtables in both cities. I mention this only because one of the undeclared but obvious traits of criticism is how much the personality of the critic informs the criticism they write. The roundtables aren't only the beginning of formulating the history of art criticism, but also an early articulation of the autobiographies of the very critics involved in shaping that history.

Finally, there are two other absences from the roundtables worth remarking. While I can't say with any certainty that they would have added anything conclusive to the proceedings, I can say why I think their perspectives would have been useful. With the exception of Ariella Budick from *Newsday*, there are no representatives of newspapers or magazines. The Columbia University survey adds to the mix a good deal of information about the popular press, but it doesn't afford an articulated response to any of the issues raised (and overlooked) in the roundtables. I sense Solomon-Godeau's question—"is arts journalism the same as art criticism"—to be a rhetorical one, but so what? How are they different, and how should we regard their differences? Popular criticism plays an important role in the discourse around contemporary art and it is part of a larger continuum of writing about art that has to be better understood if the theoretical framework of the practice is to be advanced. (As I write this assessment, two international art magazines—*Frieze* and *Art Monthly*—came in the mail and both issues focus on art criticism.) If these practitioners are disembodied and voiceless, their role will continue to be underestimated and misunderstood. The various kinds of art criticism occupy the center of a fundamental issue in art, what Stephen Melville calls "the question of audience," a question "art writing always faces." Art audiences and art writing constantly intersect, and one of the prerequisites of good criticism is figuring out who you're writing for and in what way. Criticism is a three-way negotiation that concerns the writer, the thing written about, and the audience, and each one has to be honoured equally. There are different audiences, and I am convinced that there is no reason to dumb down to write to any of them. It is a question of bringing together our skills with language, and the acuity of our powers of observation. Hickey says "art is not supposed to be easy," and neither is writing about it.

The second, and more telling, absence is the number of participating artists. This was a problem in the *October* roundtable, where Andrea Fraser's burden was to keep up the art-making side, and in these more recent gatherings, Gaylen Gerber supplied a backdrop painting for the symposium and the occasional observation. But there are numerous artists who, in addition to making significant art, have written and are able to speak about what they do with sophistication and a conceptual awareness of where they are situated. I'm thinking of artists as different as Jeff Wall and Mike Kelley, David Bachelor and Michael Craig-Martin. I have spent the last thirty years focusing my critical practice on interviewing artists for broadcast and publication, and am utterly convinced that intelligent conversation is a way of understanding and contextualizing the production and reception of art. Any sense of the special insights artists have is conspicuously missing from the roundtables. I would reverse Shakespeare's directive and ask for "more art, less matter." When artists are missing from a conversation, so is the art they make, and the effect on these roundtables, so rich in ideas and energy, is to reduce them to artistic impoverishment. How is it that talking to artists about art objects has become a taboo subject in our embryonic attempts to theorize art criticism?

Felipe Chaimovich

Greenberg After Oiticia: Teaching Art Criticism Today

I would like to address the issue of teaching art criticism. I think James Elkins misses the point when he says, during the first roundtable, that art criticism doesn't exist in art schools as a structured field. If we consider art criticism as a philosophical practice, it is possible to create a systematic experience of it for undergraduate students in an art faculty, independently of deciding how their future professional practice will be determined by the media where they would publish.

I also disagree with Boris Groys when he states that we don't have a canon of contemporary art criticism. Contemporary art criticism is defined by the central position of Clement Greenberg's work.[41] It is a coherent set of writings, and it can be considered as the basis for a theoretical model of art criticism. In his text "Modernist Painting" (1960), for example, a threefold model for painting criticism is proposed: "The limitations that constitute the medium of painting—the flat surface, the shape of the support, the properties of the pigment."[42] First of all, students of art criticism could be taught to analyze Greenberg's writings, and to apply his theoretical model to judge paintings from an exhibition chosen for the exercise.

However, art criticism in the last decades was also about the debate *against* Greenberg. Many other theoretical models were proposed. So students of art criticism should also experience an opposite point of view, a theoretical model that would constitute an antithesis to Greenberg's.

In Brazil, Helio Oiticica proposed a model for art judgment that can be considered as opposed to Greenberg's. In "Esquema geral da Nova Objetividade" (1967), Oiticica lists the points that would define the new object of art, created by Brazilian avant-garde against dictatorship, underdeveloped culture, and dependency from Europe and the United States. This sixfold list, explained along the text, can be considered as a theoretical model: "1. General constructive will; 2. tendency to the object, while denying and overcoming the easel painting; 3. participation of the spectator (with the body, the tact, the vision, and semantics); 4. addressing and taking sides on political, ethical, and social problems; 5. tendency to collective proposals, and therefore abolition of the 'isms', characteristics of the first half of the century in today's art (a tendency which can be understood as part of Mario Pedrosa's concept of post-modern art); 6. reappearance and new formulations of the concept of anti-art."[43]

Students could then analyze this second model. The inclusion of political, ethical and social problems in Oiticica's text implies the discussion of the local versus the global, opposing Greenberg's view of eternal values for art. The issue of collective proposals denies primary importance to individual style, opposing Greenberg's definition of modernism as an autonomous state of art.

At this point, students would apply Oiticica's model to judge works from other art students in the same faculty. The problems of participation of the spectators and collective proposals could lead to a reflection about actual conditions of art making in their own environment. The sense of community and the responsibility to address their peers would raise problems within the group, pointing to real ethical issues in art criticism.

I agree with Boris Groy that there is a need to take responsibility on the inequality generated by art faculties between those artists that are trained in art criticism by academies and those who are not. Opposing theoretical models and creating real ethical problems are means to confront such a task.

As a result, art criticism would be experienced as dialectic. Students will get the responsibility for any synthesis, and they should be encouraged to find as many problems as possible for this synthetic point of view, in order to picture the contemporary debate as an open forum.

Sue Spaid

Getting Over the Hoopla and Under the Art

Getting over It

One of the many topics that these panelists ruminated upon was the rumor that "rock star" curators wield all the power and critical voices have gone mute. If curators are so powerful, why do exhibitions and collections the world around resemble one another? Couldn't the truly powerful cast their nets wider than some predictable A-list?

When did critics ever call the shots? In distinguishing criticism as "what happens matters,"[44] art historian Michael Fried spotted the critic's lot, yet who could spare a lifetime waiting around for one's wagers to win? Having new bets to place, we return to the race. Few artworld roles carry greater expectations, though none is more misunderstood. A "What do critics do?" panel stacked with peripatetic snoops and sneaks keen to inspect criticism's status is long overdue. (Of these panels' seventeen participants, two are artists, yet only a few are self-employed critics, working double-duty to recognize interesting art and to lure editors to publish their views. Most participants are practicing art historians, though some are critics and one is a curator.)

Only critics for a weekly, such as the *Village Voice, LA Weekly*, or a cultural-capital daily (such as those in Boston, Chicago, DC, Houston, Los Angeles, Miami, NYC or Philadelphia, St. Louis) can expect art lovers to follow their work. If you write art criticism for a magazine, chances are, few will value your efforts for years to come.

You're probably wondering who would spend hours writing articles for such a small audience. Why do art magazines even exist? Who reads articles later than sooner? In addressing these questions, I hope to shed light on criticism's significance: why it can't be taught; why its voice is far-reaching, despite its impotence; and why it's unfair to expect the nation's 169 newspaper reporters covering art to do more than describe it clearly and accurately, while providing enough background to make exhibitions more inviting for their public.

Let's start with this last point. Being prepared to make judgments about art requires experiencing hundreds of museum and gallery exhibitions annually in dozens of cities, a feat that requires good reasons for spending all of one's time and discretionary income researching art. Unless one experiences a lot of art, it's hard to imagine that one would have a broad-enough picture to discern the best from all the rest, so why expect judgments from newspaper critics whose beat butts up against city limits? When I moved to Cincinnati in 1999, the full-time *Cincinnati Enquirer* art critic bragged that he hadn't visited NYC in twenty years, so he was ill-prepared to judge whether Contemporary Art Center exhibitions surpassed those at PS1.

Those critics who see tons of shows, yet overestimate an artist or artwork's importance—"the year's best painting show," the "most important emerging artist," let alone "I know of no other postwar American male artist whose work more completely approaches the condition of poetry, that reads as richly as it looks"[45]—sound just plain supercilious, if not malicious (an obvious swipe at Cy Twombly, the poster boy for painterly poetry)! Make arguments for the work's significance, inspire readers to learn more about the artist's oeuvre, but let us draw our own conclusions, thank you. And curmudgeonly critics like Adam Gopnik, who bizarrely bemoan the abundance of bad art, yet overlook the good stuff, should just stay away! It's obviously not their forte.

There are several reasons why art criticism need not be academized. Perhaps a ten-week certificate that introduces burgeoning critics to practicing art writers, willing to critique attendees' writing samples (submitted before the program), would prove an invaluable experience. Similarly, one-week refreshers could update journalists working in the hinterlands regarding recent artists on the scene. The best way to teach students how to write about art is to assign them to review their peers' exhibitions (fellow art students) or to write essays for student shows. Whenever I request "art writing" classes to review gallery or museum exhibitions, students submit rather stale papers that tend to parrot press material. Not only does challenging the official story require access to behind-the-scenes information, but young writers' peers warrant their energy more than famous artists. In addition to caring more about their peers, their peers' projects typically dovetail with their own generational interests, a point eluding most academics.

School can enrich and encourage criticism's crucial tools—values, interests, and a sense of place—but young critics need to read a massive number of catalog essays, research unfamiliar artists, and experience every show possible. If this needs to be assigned, they're already behind! Even active critics typically devote their energy to artists who stand most to benefit from their efforts or whose works they're so eager to figure out that they're willing to spend time getting under another's work. No matter how you slice it, criticism eats up heaps of time.

Getting Under It

Since saying "thumbs up!" or "thumb's down!" seems so Siskel and Ebert, what should critics do instead? Rejecting this +/– dualism, panelist Boris Groys proposed the analog 0/1, as in ignore/cover. I have in mind something else. Art critics bear witness to what Wittgenstein termed the " 'dawning' of an aspect."[46] After experiencing as much art as possible, critics select particular exhibitions or oeuvres to analyze in depth. To this end, they study everything about an artist that they can get their hands on, so that they can put forth something fresh that justifies (implicit in the article's existence) the work's significance. (Even if few critics work this way, readers expect this. Given the limits of time and money, critics rarely see as much work as they'd like. I can't tell you how often ticket sellers stare at my AICA press pass as though it's a parking ticket, which leads me to believe that AICA members don't get out much. Judging from the rather mundane outcome of the 2007 AICA awards, I worry that its members cast their ballot more on hearsay than eyesight. In addition to their prestigious exhibition awards, AICA should recognize those who see and review most!) While Elkins notes that art historians never reference criticism, a loathsome thought I must accept, reviews written early on in an artist's career or articles offering groundbreaking analysis remain historical markers of who knew what when. Art lovers relish articles penned by critics who spent time getting under the work, articulating what made particular works remarkable for their era.

The view that critics, curators, or anybody "discovers" artists is absurd. At most, they recognize attributes or features in works that others have overlooked or underestimated. By the time particular artists attract an art historian's radar, aspects that critics once identified as rare no longer loom disputable. Already absorbed into the prevailing discourse, such critical frames appear so obvious that footnoting seems redundant, yet some critic's perspective, triggered by his or her particular art experience, first focused this lens. How does this story's popularity jive with my view that reviews go unread? Perhaps key readers doggedly spread ideas by word of mouth.

What do I mean by perspective? In the course of explaining, justifying, or interpreting works, critics choose, select, frame, emphasize, connect, specify, analyze, and identify those aspects that are relevant for their arguments. Hardly communication tools, as some panelists claim, works of art exemplify acts of discovery, whose outcomes elicit physical experiences. Catalysts for novel concepts, works of art unwittingly inspire otherwise unavailable ideas. Criticism thus provides a public record of those related thoughts befalling dalliances with art. Critics must also contend with the motive and context underlying each artist's discovery. To this end, I found the Irish roundtable's juxtaposing art history as neutral and art criticism as judgmental, leaving art history's criticality a debatable point, quite odd. While I appreciate art history's goal to record stories as accurately as possible, thereby solidifying a work's "static immanence," as Irit Rogoff termed it, I was surprised to learn that criticism carried such negative connotations.

Jean Fisher even asked, "What kind of knowledge does art criticism actually involve and produce?" No doubt, singular critics do not produce "knowledge." The art world rather circulates perspectives that either find adherents or disappear. Unlike critics who favor works that require sweat equity, good curators don't limit their selections to personal preferences . . . they display veritable wild cards to goad audience reactions! The art-historical practice itself is already premised on questions that are nothing short of judgmental: Why record an artist's history? Why is his or her oeuvre significant? Why store this work? When would be the best moment to premiere it? Which artists did this work influence? Why is this work more "memorable" now than before? It's difficult to imagine questions that critics and curators routinely address as remaining beyond an art historian's purview, especially when he or she is getting ready to publish a monograph.

Even if the responses to such questions appear "subjective," critics and curators always offer argument and evidence for their positions, so their conclusions are no less subjective than those of an art historian who suddenly challenges some prior history. Yes, such judgments are exclusionary, and too often reflect personal interests or institutional biases, yet our tacitly accepting an author's assessments effectively legitimizes his or her claim's objectivity. Critics, curators, and historians alike must either challenge their peers' premises as flawed, outdated, incomplete, simplistic, and so forth or uphold their propositions. Revisionist art historians like Ann Gibson, Anna Chave, or Linda Dalrymple Henderson, who have demonstrated prior historians' erroneous assumptions, cannot be said to be practicing criticism, even when they introduce alternative values or frames instead of art-historical evidence. The very visibility of works of art, whether this painting or that pot will ever see the light of day, wholly depends on art historians' capacity to judge the merit of particular objects or eras. While the critic might bemoan what's hidden from sight, he or she is typically stuck with what's currently on deck.[47] That these art historian panelists consistently undermined their judgmental prowess seemed strange indeed.

Let's say that critics' and curators' arguments for works are temporarily subjective, but gain objectivity as they withstand the test of time. If art historians don't appear on the scene until the oeuvre has withstood "the test of time," it's no wonder they fail to footnote earlier efforts. Museums are the worst offenders. Even though everybody knows that a cadre of dealers, critics, and collectors endorsed a particular artist for decades before the museum ever took notice, museums behave as though they alone discovered/made the artist, ignoring everyone who came before. And everybody goes along with this, leaving the museum to select which earlier exhibitions and reviews qualify as "important" enough to be "recorded" in the artist's "official" biography. Art historians who credit earlier critics, curators, and dealers are better prepared to navigate museums falsely framing artists' careers. It's horrifying how far museums/historians/dealers go to snuff the efforts of earlier risk-takers, whose labor laid the table for later feasts.

Polyandry

How many lovers can you take? And how many can you service simultaneously? Art criticism tests such skills. What impresses me most is not what I loved at first sight, but what I first detested but later grew to love wholeheartedly. That is where subjective taste becomes conviction, a surprisingly unshakeable conviction, I might add. Given the abundance of art that I love and admire, it's often quite difficult to decide where to focus my energies. While I can easily blog two thousand words in a day (this is description, not criticism), criticism, like essay writing, persists for days on end, just to produce five hundred *fine* words. Rather than pull punches, I typically take aim at thematic museum exhibitions, while reserving constructive and fresh analysis for solo exhibitions.

Art criticism entails genuine love affairs. Some last only a few weeks (during the writing process), others manifest long-term commitments, verging on addictions. I would be embarrassed to say how much time and money I've spent traveling to experience some exhibition . . . Why??? I can't reply. Certainly not for the fee, which is so puny it's not worth discussing. Hoping to enhance an ongoing relationship (no longer on assignment), I'm pushed to rendez-vous with friends or ignite an old flame. Like most flings, I always learn ten times more about a show or an oeuvre after I've spent time analyzing it. Freshly released from some intense romance, readers end up on dates with me, absorbing my stories, imagining why I was so enthralled with that lover. Even when romances are short-lived, I rarely fall out of love. Keen to greet tomorrow, I daren't dwell on past lovers. Only true love occasions groundless judgments.

I have been pleasantly surprised to watch old flames develop and change over time, enabling them to lure new lovers. Viewers' interests in, analyses of, or reactions to works depend heavily on prior personal experiences (with other works of art and in life), their knowledge base (art history as well as every other field), their imagination's capacity to navigate unchartered territories, their ability to thrive or not during unfamiliar events, and so much more. Love interests border on the ridiculous! I would be shocked to read a review whose writer reacted to, pointed out, or even mentioned what I have. My efforts to write a totally unique review or essay for each artist, let criticism sketch my future (that's the opposite of the way a memoir works). Such responses are volatile, because they're spontaneously triggered, guided, driven, maneuvered, and inspired by the lover at hand. Perhaps those art historians who consider critics so lecherous (although that sounds downright Barthean) are bound by serial monogamy. Art criticism anticipates the ride of a lifetime.

Kim Levin

Separate Conversations

There is a certain undeniable luxury in being the invisible guest, commenting on a conversation that already has taken place, a conversation about the state of art criticism. Criticism having long been spurned by academe—supposedly seldom theorized and hardly investigated—that, I recall, was the attitude at the Institute of Fine Arts when I was a student decades ago. Functioning as a critic was a definite liability to one's career in academe. How can you do it? demanded my horrified archeology professor when he learned I was writing criticism for an art magazine, as well as working toward a doctorate in Egyptian archeology. How can I do what? I replied. His eyes narrowed ominously. How do you know you're right? There are no primary source materials, no experts, no authorities, how can you be certain that you're right? I grandly proclaimed that I would never claim to be right: I would be the primary source material for the archeologists of the future.

I thought we had come a long way from those days. But apparently not. Among critics around the world, there has been ongoing discussion of the critical issues as they develop—from modernism to postmodernism to multiculturalism. We've dissected the components of the self and the other, gender and ethnic identity, as well as paramodernism, hypermodernism, and antimodernist backlashes, as well as modes of art criticism—formalist, poststructuralist, whatever. We've pondered the way these facets reflect variously from different geopolitical positions, different latitudes, longitudes, and histories.

But none of that counts. Apparently we're still back in the days of Michael Fried and the reign of *October*. Baudrillard footnotes may be out of style, but what about Barthes, Foucault, or Paul Virilio? What about Slavos Zhijek or numerous others who certainly have more to say about the world we have inherited? And as for history, it wasn't until perhaps page seventy-two of the transcript that I came across Clement Greenberg's name. In the midst of this bizarre imaginary intellectual feast, I imagine myself seated between Boris Groys and Dave Hickey, fellow critics out of their element. Dense versus lucid? I'd rather express complex ideas in a lucid manner than obfuscate simple ideas in impenetrable prose.

I am horrified at the notion of criticism becoming a branch of art history. The profession, or vocation, is precisely the opposite: in terms of the so-called canon, in terms of scientific methodology, in terms of the whole academic conversation. It's not just that the conversation has changed, utterly and completely. It's that there were always two utterly separate conversations going on. Art criticism has little to do with canons and much to do with contexts and reassessments—political, geographic, philosophical. It absorbs and digests—unscientifically, semi-subjectivally, almost poetically—all sorts of information.

Criticism subsumed into art history? No thank you. I say this as someone trained in art history, someone who has worked as art historian, curator, and educator, as well as critic. That would be the demise of art criticism. We don't require tenure. What we seem to require is total freedom, including perhaps the freedom of not being paid nearly well enough to silence our judgments, stifle our independence, or buy our opinions.

Art criticism is not art history. It is not curating. It is not an academic scientific endeavor. I would never dare propose the quasi-imperialistic notion of subsuming art history into criticism. But, as James Elkins remarks, "we're still all White, and we're all from North America or Western Europe." And, I can't help but note, nearly all male. It's not as if there were a dearth of serious thinkers, theorists, curators, and critics from eastern Europe, Asia, Latin America, the Mideast, or Africa. So what can I say? Let's just chalk it up to the same anachronistic institutional lack of imagination, or else to a curious form of academic timewarp.

Róisín Kennedy

A Dysfunctional Relationship: Art History and Art Criticism

A number of problems in defining criticism are evident in the roundtable, as highlighted by James Elkins in his concluding comments. My response is written from the perspective of the art historian rather than the critic, thereby acknowledging that in my opinion the two activities—art history and art criticism—are discrete. While there was much talk of the (American) academic debate on criticism, it is by its nature a populist pursuit—the rise of criticism coincided directly with that of public exhibitions of visual art. This public context resulted in some of the clearest voices in art criticism, as mentioned by several participants in the roundtable—Hazlitt, Ruskin, and Baudelaire. Their writings continue to be models of how criticism can provide a framework for evaluating the art object and its role in the wider culture. But such writings ultimately relate to the particular circumstances in which they were conceived and published. Their primary value to the art historian is in explicating the processes by which certain artworks were understood and perceived at specific moments in the past. Furthermore the comments of these famous critics have to be taken within the wider critical contexts in which they were generated.

Art history's parasitic relationship to art criticism can all too often see the latter as a source of easily available and useful commentary which can be grafted onto art historical accounts of specific works, artists, or movements. These dislocated comments are used to illustrate or validate an already established art historical viewpoint. A dismissal of the value and meaning of art criticism reflects the hierarchical nature of the academic discipline of art history and its pejorative view of colloquial art criticism. Compared to art historians, critics are marginal figures without established institutional roles.[48] Rarely is any serious attention given to the critic, the publication or the context in which the comments appear. With regard to contemporary art this is no longer the case, but as evidenced in the roundtable, academics continue to take the academic- or institution-based critic seriously while largely ignoring the role of the non-academic. Indeed, at certain points in the roundtable there seemed to be a concerted effort to categorize art criticism, whereas its overriding significance lies in its ability to transcend institutional control and to operate independently of the academy and the institution.

The uses of art criticism as an object of study lie not in identifying or promoting it as a kind of objective autonomous activity or even as a critically engaged one, but in understanding it as a function of the artistic field. It is an unwieldy and complex function and one that does not necessarily concern itself with ideological issues, but it is likely to continue in spite of the (alleged) current crisis.

Matthew Jesse Jackson

Conversations with God

To remain true to the experimental character of the seminars, my "assessment" will explore only my most offbeat observations. So here goes.

The real issue at stake in these conversations seems to be not so much the state of art criticism, or criticism's status as an academic or popular undertaking, but rather the articulation of contrary conceptions of art's social function. In the seminars, we encounter two divergent approaches to art criticism: one is rooted in what might be called *urban uncertainty*—a zone of doubt and difficulty defined by the valorization of innovation, criticality and hybridity; the other, its opposite term could be described as something like *suburban legibility*, an orientation characterized by frank judgment, pungent description and the narration of convictions. (Roughly speaking, Whitney Davis, Jean Fisher, Gaylen Gerber, Boris Groys, Michael Newman, Stephen Melville, Irit Rogoff, and Abigail Solomon-Godeau occupy the former camp; the latter includes Ariella Budick, Lynne Cooke, Dave Hickey, James Panero, and Gemma Tipton.)

Around the globe, urban zones require superior skills of translation and the ability to assimilate torrents of new information rapidly. In such environments, the interdependence of opacity and opportunity defines the social sphere. For the upwardly-mobile urban dweller, what she does not know—such as tomorrow's final stock quote—constitutes the crucial field of possibility that may lead to future rewards. Over time, every productive denizen of urban space becomes an unconscious connoisseur of the uncertain. The situation is exactly the opposite in the suburban office park. The worldwide suburbia of mushrooming mallscapes and prefab neighborhoods presents the challenge not of high-stakes multicultural multitasking, so much as the necessity of overcoming an all-enveloping social and professional anomie. The inhabitant of the suburbs inevitably finds herself searching for stable, hard and fast foundations on which to establish communities of judgment (epitomized by the sociability of Oprah's Book Club and its progeny). Of course, these demographic terms should not be taken too literally. I am speaking of the "urban" and "suburban" as frames of mind, not as windows onto the seminar participants' lifestyles, though it is appropriate that Hickey extols the virtues of the most suburban of cities, Las Vegas, while Groys lectures in three languages as "Global Professor" at NYU.

In simple terms, the urban critic wants the art object to emit a powerful, almost overwhelming charge of psychic indeterminacy (to reach a state of "maximal aconceptuality" in Elkins' words), while the suburban critic treats the artwork primarily as an "excerpted fragment of the visual field" to be evaluated with gusto and descriptive precision. Moreover, the suburban critic does not think that the project of art criticism is all that complicated. For her, above all else, the critic renders professional verdicts as persuasively as possible. She informs the public when "the emperor has no clothes." She expresses dismissive opinions of, say, John Currin or Matthew Barney, or contributes unexpected insights into the pictoriality of John Baldessari's work. The ideal medium for the suburban critic is painting, more specifically abstract canvases, since they read most readily as High Art for a suburban audience, as the polling data from Komar and Melamid's "People's Choice" project demonstrated.

In essence, the critical model grounded in suburban legibility is not that different from the mechanisms at work on *American Idol*, *America's Next Top Model*, or *The Apprentice* (or numerous other examples of "judgment television" in contemporary America). In fact, it's not that hard to imagine *America's Next Modernist Masterpiece* featuring Hickey as the show's jovially acerbic host and Panero as the Conservative Harangue sidekick. The charismatic charm of confident pronouncements drives the suburban critical enterprise, and I will not deny that it can be fun to watch. It also goes without saying that anytime these two "sides of the table" clash, suburbans will always beat the stuffing out of urbans. It's an unfair fight. Reading the Michael Newman/Dave Hickey colloquy calls to mind the Muscle Beach Bully manhandling the Bookworm Geek (I identify with Newman, by the way). Newman offers self-deprecating analyses of his critical paralysis before certain artworks, while Hickey kicks the sand of Strong Judgment in his face time and time again.

My take on urban uncertainty goes something like this: for the urban critic, art criticism is utterly unlike restaurant criticism, theater criticism, or music criticism, whereas for the suburbanite, all critical operations are interchangeable (that's why Hickey decries the

"Balkanization of art criticism," and why Pauline Kael is cited as an art critical resource by Budick). For the urban critic, art criticism is different from other forms of criticism, because art is different in kind from other forms of cultural production, though it might look very much like many other things (Gerber's painted Backdrop makes this ambiguity explicit). The urban critic understands the forms of art to be supremely contingent. As Davis notes, there is no sure ontological foundation underneath it all. (Or, in Panero's disparaging assessment, much art "functions like a junk bond.") This is not the case with other medium-based forms of criticism, because their objects of discussion are bound by much more stable categorical distinctions. We more or less know what theater is. We more or less know what music is. Bottom line: in some terribly important way, we never know what art is. (An urban critic would probably agree with this statement, whereas a suburban critic might not.) That is, if the urban critic were to write restaurant criticism, she'd be the kind of person who would analyze an establishment's forks and knives. In food criticism, of course, there is a tacit agreement that cutlery is functionally indispensable, yet critically irrelevant. In art, the urban critic might argue, nothing exists outside the critic's responsibility, because important artworks always work on the category *of what counts as art*. From this perspective, art functions as the default category for all uncertain cultural products: whether a "drilled-through dissertation" or a book framed in iron, all unstable creations as if automatically become potential artworks.

The underlying message of the seminars seems to be that art criticism is too academic to be genuinely experimental, yet too impressionistic to be sufficiently rigorous. To renovate art criticism, one must come to terms with the limitations of art history's conception of art criticism—or, in Elkins' words, "a limit of how art history conceptualizes itself." We must encourage art criticism that performs labor on the very possibility of the critical act. This transformation would not entail a further round of "damping pluralism," but rather a heightened degree of self-reflexivity that goes beyond mere "meta-criticality." We need a new range of critical identities and authorial voices, or, to paraphrase Hickey, we need art criticism that does not look like art criticism. We need a situation in which criticism becomes, in Gerber's phrase, "bigger and messier." We need spoken criticism, performed criticism, silent criticism, criticism of criticism, criticism of the criticism of criticism, sung criticism, anti-criticism, painted criticism, CRITICISM, "criticism," filmed criticism, environmental criticism, geological criticism, afterlife criticism (that is, criticism from beyond the grave), criticism that destroys the objects of its criticism, and so on and so forth. Without such a collective effort of productive rediscovery, art criticism will continue to inhabit an obsolete social universe. In the end, one must conclude that Dave Hickey is a quick-witted cultural critic and a first-rate performance artist, but he is not an art critic in any particularly meaningful way. Of course, it's not his fault: no one is an art critic in a particularly meaningful way today. Claiming that you are an art critic is now akin to announcing that you converse with God.

Alexander Alberro

The Elephants in the Room

There are a number of rather large elephants sitting at the Art Criticism panels. One beast is the critical journal *October*, for decades now at the forefront of writing on art. When near the end of the first meeting James Elkins tries to steer the conversation toward an assessment of the roundtable on criticism organized by the editors of *October* in 2002—"The Current State of Art Criticism," *October* 100—the participants balk. Their replies range from Boris Groys' witty dismissal of the journal ("It's just not sexy"), to Jean Fisher's confession that it has been a long time since she's found *October* inspirational, to Abigail Solomon-Godeau's terse characterization of the editorial board: "As a group they seem extremely judgmental, and yet they appear reluctant to acknowledge that judgment is any significant part of their critical tradition." Perhaps so as not to be thwarted again, Elkins raises this topic at the very beginning of the second roundtable in Chicago. Here, the response is more vigorous, and produces a lengthy dialogue. But for the most part, the panelists' engagement is marked by *ad hominem* attacks, *penni ante* accusations, and loquacious nonsense. Dave Hickey, one of the most vocal at the Chicago roundtable, pontificates that "the rise of *October* [in the 1970s and 1980s] marked the academic repudiation of French structuralism, or, more precisely, its radical Germanification." Ariella

Budick of *Newsweek* whines that from a mainstream perspective "The *October* roundtable is hermetic, and they are not really writing to the public; they are writing to insiders, like-minded people . . . they speak mainly to themselves, they are out of date." James Panero of the rightwing journal *The New Criterion* is even more scathing in his attack, which is duly tinged with a call for law and order: "There are plenty of contemporary artists who don't care a bit about *October*. But that is not the case with university departments of art history, where the *October* mafia has gained a stranglehold on the hiring process. It is now going to take the Rico Act to get *October* out of academia." In short, at both events the discussion of the *October* roundtable on criticism goes nowhere—spinning in circles, as it were, and producing little, if any, insight.

The trashing of *October* by the panelists is symptomatic of another, related anxiety prevalent in the contemporary art world: the academicization of art criticism. This elephant also looms large over both roundtables. Skepticism and objections to the idea of doctoral degrees in art criticism comes from different quarters, and ranges from Irit Rogoff's fear that private art galleries might manipulate established graduate programs in art criticism to Hickey's warning that if left to academics the arts would be divided into singularized mediums and genres and the common languages they share would be overlooked. Indeed, although Rogoff's and Hickey's views here seem overly hyperbolic, the majority of the panelists are apprehensive about the prospect of art criticism's formal integration within academia. The institutionalization of the critic, the rarification of the terminology and concepts of criticism, and the increased elitism of the profession, are among the concerns (spoken and unspoken) about this prospect raised at the two roundtables. I imagine that Whitney Davis's astute observation that the traditional functions of art criticism have been intellectually absorbed by critical theory stunned most of the panelists (and utterly terrified those at the second roundtable).

But there is a third mammoth in the room at the States of Art Criticism meetings—a pink elephant whose massive and vulgar presence is forcefully pushed into a corner. Davis comes closest to recognizing this beast when he cunningly notes "the dominance of well-entrenched economic structures of display, distribution, publication, dissemination, remuneration, in which a whole tier of artists, academicians, gallerists, and public relations people are all co-participants, co-exploiters, co-exploiteds." Ironically, while Hickey is quick to attack curators for functioning like "whores" and taking in "dirty commercial money," he stops short of reflecting on the connections between art criticism (let alone his own writing) and the ever-growing art market. In fact the taboo of the market is so strong that even when Stephen Melville describes *October* as "inheriting the very broad permissions that *Artforum* gave to criticism," no one mentions the crucial and blatantly obvious difference between the two journals: namely, the ratio of advertisements to text (or "grey matter" as it is caustically referred to in the business). The art magazine was traditionally the site where critics could explore the complexities of art. Magazines also functioned as venues for critique, places where some of the problematic aspects of the works in question could be taken apart, analyzed, and assessed. But the degree to which this can be maintained today is dependent on the view one has of the impact of commercial sponsors on art magazines that are largely comprised of—and dependent on—advertisements. In 1973, Richard Serra and Carlotta Schoolman produced a six-and-a-half minute videotape, *Television Delivers People*, that strung together textual excerpts on a rolling screen to highlight the manner in which the horizon of subject matter on television is tacitly determined by the economic sponsors of the medium: "It is the consumer who is consumed. . . . You are delivered to the advertiser, who is the customer. He consumes you. The viewer is not responsible for programming—you are the end product." That no one at the roundtables took up the crucial question of what the relationship between the advertisers, the art scribblers, and the readers of art magazines might be today was, in my view, a lost opportunity. Rather than perpetually returning to discourses of connoisseurship and judgment, or pathetically trashing the agenda of an art journal such as *October* (one of the few remaining that keeps advertisers at bay), the economics of art criticism—who and what is written about, by whom and why—are issues that need to be more openly addressed.

Julian Stallabrass

The Ideal of Art Criticism

The term "criticism" is fairly reputable, but with the prefix "art" ceases to be. This might be thought to be connected to art criticism's close connection to the mechanisms of an increasingly large and vulgar market, being tied to the manufacture of hype, but its lack of reputability is old (think of Empson's steady iron-hard jet of nonesense), and the term seems more sullied than comparable practices in other areas where there is certainly the same association with a market—"film criticism" or "literary criticism," for example.

Perhaps that lack of reputation is due to what some critics would see as the area's greatest virtue: the fundamental lack of clarity, or "undecidability" of its objects, statements and judgments, and of any empirical knowledge of the way art objects act on viewers. For Whitney Davis, such undecidable matters require "our speculative, theoretical and critical reconstruction," and surely the allure of such work is connected with that of the act of creation itself, being the promise of unbounded and unalienated labor. Michael Newman makes a connected point, asserting that aesthetic judgment is on principle groundless, and that part of its purpose is to highlight its own groundlessness.

Frequently, though, art criticism's overt lack of grounding is seen as the sanction for the spinning of partisan writing in the service of an industry in which what counts as "art" is decided by institutional fiat, in which the worst forms of mystification are applied at all levels (from the idiocies that are frequently found in newspaper and art magazine writing to the higher-level intellectual bullying and invocation of theoretical authorities in academia). At its best, this partisanship is at least overt: Boris Groys and Irit Rogoff in different ways see themselves as developing critique in partnership with suitable artists. Both Davis and Newman make remarks that demonstrate their understanding of the force of such critiques, talking respectively of the way in which a pliant "criticality" may end up serving the principles of neoliberalism, and of how an apparently high-minded, disinterested criticism is of more use to the market than lower forms of publicity.

The circularity of the discussions, which always seem to be returning to first principles, demonstrates the equally ungrounded character of knowledge about art criticism. At first sight, this may seem to be because two incommensurate discourses have been jammed together: the publicity-driven journalism of the newspapers and art magazines, and the products of academia. Yet more unites them than may be imagined: in each there is a decline of overt judgment (as Davis notes); or one might say that what judgment does appear is performed through various types of celebrity persona—that it is not the judgment itself that readers are meant to take seriously and act on, but rather that the performance itself is enjoyed, whether it be the light irony of Hickey and Collings or the baleful pessimism of Buchloh or the postmodern affirmation of Danto. In both, too, the ideal of the indescribably complex viewer facing and realizing itself in the similarly complex work is faithfully held to. Thus the various attractions to art criticism of psychoanalysis and theories of vitalism (which Groys rightly mocks in his discussion of Deleuze).

Two dark clouds, rapidly approaching, threaten the clear skies of this idealism. That such mystification can be held to is in part governed by art's exclusivity, its narrow band of elite ownership, its display and conservation in hallowed institutions. Such conditions were brought about by art's rarity and exclusivity, but as artists increasingly move into reproducible media, the ground of such restrictions comes to appear more visible and arbitrary. The many fans of the Barney's *Cremaster* series cannot buy DVDs of the five films on the open market, but copies circulate on peer-to-peer networks. If art becomes more widely owned, more regularly seen, and seen in uncontrolled circumstances, the liberties currently allowed critics may come to seem absurd when tested against the detailed and practical knowledge of that public.

The other cloud is the precipitate development in knowledge about the human brain, opened to detailed scrutiny from the 1990s onwards by new scanning techniques. The highly modular character of many brain functions undercuts faith in the bases of what passes for thinking about the mind in art criticism. As empirical knowledge is acquired about the way humans respond to works of art, there will be two effects: first, a falling away of the idealist faith in the ungrounded and ungoverned response; and second, a greater awareness on the part of viewers in how they are worked upon by works of art, and with it at least limited means for assent or dissent.

An exchange between Jeffrey Skoller and Jim Elkins

The Place of October

This exchange began with a comment, inter alia, by Jeffrey, who attended the second roundtable and felt it was a "kind of ideological polemic against politically engaged or cultural studies oriented art criticism."

Dear Jeffrey,

I beg your pardon? Where was that polemic? In whose statements? And do you mean you thought that was part of the book project?

Jim

Dear Jim,

You indicated that the discussion and people's remarks would be transcribed and put in the book. Is that not true?

The roundtable certainly seemed to be constructed like a polemic to me. The first part of the discussion was a round robin *ad hominem* trashing (with the exception of Michael) of *October* for hijacking art criticism and scholarship. Their focus on the social and political nature of art, for example, the Frankfurt school (and other "Aryan theories of the aura," !?!, as Hickey put it), as well as its integration of other cultural theory as a tool for criticism was blamed for moving art criticism away from judgment to description leading to the currently soft dispassionate forms of criticism and art.

1. That current art history and criticism is now dominated by meta-criticism rather than the taking of bold stands and opinions about quality. (Stephen Melville)
2. The discussion of the necessity of separating art criticism from cultural criticism, which liberal art critics no longer do. (Panero)
3. The criticism of the hermetic nature of dominating art criticism that no one outside of academia can understand and no one reads. (Ariella Budick)
4. The problem of curators with PhDs turning museum exhibitions into academic and political statements rather than foregrounding the art works. (Budick again, I think)

There was so much generalizing going on, that it seemed simply ideological and polemical. Again, with the exception of Michael (who was really great), the tenor of the discussion was one of resentment about the current domination of left-liberal artists and scholars who insist on politicizing art world discourses using critical theory and institutional critique that has moved academic art criticism away from the discourses of connoisseurship and enlightened judgment to the appropriation of art merely for social and political critique. There seemed an overriding melancholia about the loss of an earlier art world that focused on art practice as object making, buying and selling, and the role that the critic played in creating value and so on. This led to more *ad hominems* (of course dominated by Hickey) against, art professors insisting on the use of critical theory and shallow art students who make soft meaningless art while spouting empty theory, and curator whores (Hickey) with social and political agendas looking for hand outs and so forth.

There was very little discussion of the historical reasons why such changes have occurred other than a kind of cynical will to power. Who gets inside, who gets left outside and so on. Little was said in positive terms about the changing concerns of artists and critics who are thinking differently about their roles in contemporary culture in light of mass and corporate culture and the emergence of new technologies. Or the ways artists and critics with different cultural backgrounds and references or others who are working in new art forms have become part of art world discourses and have enlarged, enriched and changed the terms of art criticism. For me and my generation, for example, the importance of *October* was that it was the first place that really insisted on the idea that avant-garde cinema, video, and photography had a serious place in art history. That one needed to know about the history of cinema and the ways artists were influenced by it and used it, to understand twentieth-century art. As an experimental film-maker who wanted to make art, those discussions helped me find a place in art history, rather than as some sideshadow in the history of Hollywood cinema.

Other things that might have widened the important discussion about the ascension of curators over critics as taste makers: a discussion of the effects of the attack on arts funding in the 1980s and 1990s which led to the dismantling of not-for-profit alternative, artist-run spaces. This included spaces in which to make work, exhibit unconventional work, and money to make work the wasn't created to be bought and sold. The loss of publications to do criticism outside of the big art magazines. This loss of such a counter-art world has led to the centralization of art exhibition in those "contemporary art museums" that have been popping up in every city as the alternative spaces closed down in the face of urban gentrification, and defunding as local and state money was redirected to such emporia, for example, MCA, Yerba Buena, and so on. This has made curators more important and powerful to the success of artists who more than ever have to rely on them to have a place to show their work. In the face of the loss of arts funding, curators have become producers and benefactors who actually decide which works get made. This is particularly true for media art, where galleries and museums are becoming film producers.

Anyway, I think it was wonderful that you put together this discussion about the current state of art criticism and that there was so much interest. But it seemed that the vision of its impoverished state was so consistent that I could only interpret it as a polemic and assumed that this would be basis of the book.

Best, Jeffrey

Jeffrey,

The main purpose of this roundtable, and the other one in Ireland, was to have as wide-ranging a talk about art criticism as possible. Previous fora have been limited: hence the invitation to Hickey. He does not represent anything I agree with—and I'd say the same is probably true of most of the other panelists. I can see from the quotations you chose that Panero and Budick might seem similar: but of course they aren't!

Then, the reason I brought up *October* is that in the first roundtable, I talked at some length about the *October* roundtable on criticism, quite sympathetically. I have attached the transcript so you can see. And yet no one wanted to talk about it. And (note!) the people who did not want to talk included Irit Rogoff and Jean Fisher, two people absolutely committed to social action and visual culture. So I was puzzled by that refusal, and I brought it up again in this roundtable to see if people might want to be more sympathetic.

Part of what you're registering here is widely typical of journalistic art criticism, which Hickey represents (much as he would deny it). I'm actually glad to have gotten a panel that could voice such positions because of their uniquity. However, your assessment is mainly of James, Ariella, and Dave, who are very different politically and as writers. Note, too, that of the panelists, Steve is closely aligned with *October* contributors and interests.

In regard to the lack of interest in responding to *October*: it seems to me it might be symptomatic of an interesting moment in current criticism, in which some people who are committed to politics find their genealogies in *October* and others don't. I was skeptical of the disengagement of the first roundtable, because I doubt that interesting models of political commitment and cultural intervention can be as free of the influence of *October* as Irit and Jean suggest.

You write, "There was very little discussion of the historical reasons why such changes have occurred other than a kind of cynical will to power. Who gets inside, who gets left outside and so on." Here I completely agree. The reasons for the changes are the subject of my booklet, *What Happened to Art Criticism?*, which is something all the panelists had read, and that might be another reason the subject did not come up.

My interest in this book is twofold: (1) I would like to represent the entire field of art criticism, and I think the two roundtables together do a fair job of that; the forty-odd assessments will make this one of the most representative books on the subject; and (2) I want to understand everyone's positions. The things that went unsaid here are therefore of interest to me for that fact alone.

You observe that "little was said in positive terms about the changing concerns of artists and critics who are thinking differently about their roles in contemporary culture in light of mass and corporate culture and the emergence of new technologies. The ways artists and critics with different cultural backgrounds and references or others who are working in new art forms have become part of art world discourses and have enlarged, enriched and changed the terms of art criticism." Much was said about that in the first roundtable, by Irit and others. I won't add anything else; these are all open issues, which I hope the book as a whole will develop.

I am sending the transcript of the first roundtable, together with some of the texts that were precirculated.
Best, Jim

Jim,

Thanks for your responses to my screed. I read the transcript to the Ireland roundtable with great interest. It was the kind of discussion I was hoping for at the SAIC roundtable and most upsettingly, I didn't find. It would be interesting to try to figure out what made the one in Ireland so ranging and forward thinking and the one here so polemical and filled with resentment and nostalgia?

As to the question of it all being a polemic: I would ask, why with all the talk in Ireland about new paradigms in art criticism and art as research as well as the need for a more politicized activist criticism, in the ways Whitney or Abigail spoke about; or the reasons for the emergence of Third Text as a way to deal with emerging post-colonial art that Jean spoke about, why weren't there those kinds of critics or scholars included in your discussions? It would have been an extraordinary experience to have had the voices of the likes of Lucy Lippard, Moira Roth, Kobena Mercer, George Baker (you mentioned in the first roundtable you had planned to invite him and Helen Molesworth. Why didn't they make it?), Hilton Als, Greg Tate, Michelle Wallace, Douglas Crimp, David Deitcher, Coco Fusco, just to name a dozen or so critics and scholars who immediately come to mind. All have tried to

expand the terms of art criticism to include new models for criticism and have engaged artists from other communities with different cultural approaches to art practice. Given the discussion of the emergence of the artist as critic in the first roundtable, it would have also been valuable to have had an artist/critic speaking about their practice and those issues. The exclusion of these kinds of voices is what gives the roundtable such an ideological cast. I for one, and I'm sure others, would like to know why such voices were not included.
Best, Jeffrey

Jeffrey,

There's a reason why the roundtable was like that, and it's a reason that I hope to explore in the book: I wanted this book to be truly inclusive. The James Paneros, Dave Hickeys, and Ariella Budicks of the world outnumber the Steve Melvilles and Michael Newmans. I am interested in the sum total of criticism, and how it might cohere (or not). So, even though George Baker and Helen M. were invited (they couldn't make it), I still had hoped the conversation would be—as you say—nostalgic, because that reflects the tenor of the critical world.

Most interesting to me, so far, is the emergence of the fact that some politically active critical thinking disavows *October* . . .
Best, Jim

Jim—

Yes, I think the centrality of *October* in contemporary progressive art criticism has been over for a long while. As far back as the late-1980s when Douglas Crimp broke with *October* over the issue of the AIDS crisis and the ways he felt it needed to be responded to actively and critically, signaled for many of us the end of *October*'s importance as a politically engaged forum for art criticism and theory. But that moment opened onto an extraordinary period of art practice and criticism that attempted to engage the cultural and political crises of the 1980s and 1990s. Importantly there were many attempts to integrate art practice with cultural critique and art criticism.

The counter-history of art in the 1980s was an unprecedented joining of artists and critics, theory and practice to engage the public sphere. This was a movement away from the academicization of art criticism as embodied by *October*. As Irit alluded to, there were extraordinary experiments in collective critical practice—PADD, Gran Fury, Group Material, Repo-history, Paper Tiger TV (and this was just in NYC where I lived). A different approach to art criticism emerged. A journal like *Afterimage* was very important in the ways it combined aesthetic, theoretical, and activist concerns across a broad range of art forms. For examples of this kind of criticism that has little to do with *October*, see anthologies such as *Art, Activism, and Oppositionality: Essays from Afterimage* and *Art Matters: How the Culture Wars Changed America* for the range of artists and art critics doing activist, non-academic art criticism.[49] But this kind of melding of artist/critic, criticism as activism, theory and art making was too promiscuous for the mainstream art critics like Hickey et al., who can't stand the idea that artists and activists are also engaged in art criticism. Connoisseurship was now being displaced by politics and collective work between artists and critics. No longer was it one man in front of one painting deciding on its importance. Of course this was an intolerable situation for most professional art critics. What is an art critic to do? Well, in the case of Hickey, Panero, Budick, and so on, you trash everything going on around you while pining for the good old days of yore, when one man's judgment could still sell a painting. . . .
Best, Jeffrey

Jan Verwoert

Talk to the Thing

On the whole, I enjoyed reading the discussion and find the questions that were raised concerning the history of criticism and the politics of making judgments very relevant. I do, however, think that the debate is marked by the absence of a particular topos, namely the question of how criticism originates in the *experience of art*. What is it about the experience of art that makes you want to speak as a critic?

What does it mean for criticism as a practice that it is elicited by this experience? How can we account for the *indebtedness* of criticism to the experience of art when we try to describe the function and relevance of criticism? It seems to be the irony (as much as the joy) of our work as critics that we remain indebted to an experience that we can neither produce nor contain at will. Our discourse is engendered by an experience which lies on the limit of this discourse and thus also constantly interrupts it. Art does not belong to us. It is not ours. Because of this inability to fully contain the foundational instance of our discourse—art—within this discourse, we find ourselves unable to treat criticism as the self-contained enterprise we would have to pretend it was to pass it off as a proper profession, consistent historical tradition, or independent academic discipline.

Michael Newman, in fact, points towards this indebtedness of criticism to an experience that both engenders and prevents it from ever founding its own "proper" discourse when he argues, in the second roundtable, that "a critical relationship with the object is fundamentally an existential relationship (not a historical one)." I completely agree with his conclusion that to acknowledge this existential tie between criticism and art, however, would not mean to search for affinities but to be attentive to moments, as he puts it, "when some kind of otherness is recognized." In the daily practice of criticism, I believe, these moments occur whenever you struggle to find words and develop ideas in response to a work. No doubt, these words and ideas will have been yours. The recognition of "otherness," however, is implied in the very urge or urgency to respond and say something that would do justice to the work. It lies in the feeling that you *owe* something to the work—as well as to your potential reader. The work and reader is the other that founds your discourse, because it is this other you address when you start speaking. Consequently, an appreciation of the indebtedness to this other may simply manifest itself in the commitment to avoid dumb judgments. You owe it to the other, the work and reader, to say something worth saying. Whether what you said will indeed have been worth saying, however, is the right of the other, the reader, to decide. The denial of the obligation to the work and the right of the reader is the key feature of self-righteous judgments that seek to overwrite the experience of the work and preempt possible dissent from the reader through the assertion of authority. To grant the other the right to judge your judgments would, on the contrary, mean to find ways of writing that put your arguments and ideas at the disposal of the reader.

An ethics of criticism based on the recognition of its constitutive indebtedness to the work and reader would therefore imply an approach to writing which is both committed and relaxed, that is *fully committed* to the development of ideas which does justice to the work and is worth reading and at the same time *sufficiently relaxed* about the prospect that this commitment guarantees nothing. You cannot force criticism to be right and apt. Naturally, any halfway self-critical critic will have an intuition about whether or not a piece of criticism has a point and will try to check and make sure that it does. Still, the aptness of criticism in the end remains contingent on the experience of the work and perception of the reader. In the face of the work and in the eyes of the reader, criticism may always turn out to be inapt. Again, it is the experience of the other in which criticism originates and to which it is directed (as it addresses the work and the reader) but which it can neither fully contain nor control. But this also means that there is no way to certify that the debt which criticism owes to the other by virtue of being indebted to the work and reader can ever be fully settled. There is no way to square things up with the reader and work once and for all. The deal always remains open. The potential of criticism to be or become proven inapt puts it in a constant state of debt.

The good news is, however, that precisely because criticism is in this constant state of debt, it can never become obsolete. Someone who still owes something will not be allowed to dodge his debts and sneak off. As long as there is art, the debt persists, and so there must be criticism. In this sense I do not share Dave Hickey's view that the critic is out of business today. To declare criticism outmoded to me seems like filing for bankruptcy in order to evade standing debts. At the same time I do think that there is something significant about this melancholy pose of the obsolete juror. In a sense it is a vivid manifestation of the moment of misrecognition that Heidegger targeted in his critique of aesthetics: by construing our relationship to an artwork as the static positioning of a distanced subject of perception vis-à-vis an object of judgment, aesthetics obscures the intimate tie between viewer and work that, in the experience of the work, precedes and first of all engenders the positioning of the subject and object of aesthetical reflection—this tie being the "existential relation" Michael Newman talks about and which I, riffing on Derrida's notion of the debt, have now tried to describe as a primary relation of indebtedness to the work and reader. If we disregard this intimate indebtedness, we must indeed come to misrecognize ourselves as an outdated trade of lonesome jurors stuck in the job of assessing aesthetic objects. But we are not alone. There is always also art. I was surprised to see that, of all critics, it should be Hickey assuming the position of the alienated aesthete when his writing otherwise speaks so clearly of the joy of taking on that debt and trying to give back to the work and reader what you owe them.

It should be said that there is, in fact, a joy in giving what you owe, because this debt is neither a burden nor does the ethical commitment it implies have any moral connotations. This debt is without guilt, and there are no standards or taboos here that would make you a better person if you obeyed them. There is, on the contrary, something about this debt that enables the agency of criticism. As the open debt cannot be settled and the deal is never closed, it in fact could be said to create the "horizon of openness" of criticality that Irit Rogoff speaks about. This openness, as I see it, is defined by a particular mix of urgency and contingency: the debt urges you to act but there are no fixed rules or protocols for dealing with it. As there are no objective standards that would make a criticism right or apt per se, there is no fixed currency in which the transaction between criticism, art, and the reader should be carried out. Any currency from, figuratively speaking, hard cash to sea shells will do as long as it makes an exchange possible. This critical exchange is free in the sense that it can have any form or outcome as long as it faces up to the debt in whatever way. But you can only give what you can give. And for a critic this is words and thoughts. Therefore I agree with Jean Fisher when she argues that an adequate way to respond to the experience of a work through criticism would lie in "engendering a process of thought." To recognize the debt in Fisher's terms would then mean to unfold the existential relation to the world that a work opens up through a form of writing that likewise opens up a "new configuration of reality."

To speak of the potential of criticism to create the "new" here seems crucial. It needs to be emphasized that criticism, in being reactive, is always proactive. The agency of criticism could be seen to lie in the practice of making a reaction become a creation. Paradoxically, then, criticism is empowered by its indebtedness to the work and reader to develop its very own modes of articulation. So, beyond the moment of commitment, the ethical use of the term *debt* should not suggest the need for a false humbleness or modesty. It's a debt that sets you free to say whatever has to be said. Now, in relation to our understanding of this agency of criticism, Irit Rogoff raises an vital question by asking whether the horizon of criticality should really be seen as unfolding from one particular point, the attention to a work, or whether we should not rather understand this horizon of criticiality as originating in the overall condition of "contemporaneity," of being in the world together with others today? This shift of focus would imply the recognition of a "common set of concerns" rather than the commitment to a singular work as the point from where criticism begins. The argument is that by putting the work of art in the privileged position of the chosen subject of criticism we submit to and affirm the aura and authority of art and its institutions. The conclusion would be, in a sense, to shift the debt, and understand that we speak as critics because we owe it to those we live with and not to art. The primary reason to speak would be the feeling of, as Rogoff puts it, being "implicated in the lived conditions of which we're a part" and not a sense of being primarily indebted to art.

If the critic is to speak with the voice of the intellectual and not just that of an art expert, I agree, the horizon of criticality has to be understood in these broad terms. And I also admit that an unreconstructed use of Heideggerian terminology may indeed inadvertently serve to reinstate the aura of art and invoke an attitude of mythical devotion to the work through the sanctimonious character of its ethical and existential terms. So there is, no doubt, a need to dust off the phenomological vocabulary for speaking from the position of immanence and being in the world. In this sense "implicatedness" is actually a much better and less morally charged term than "indebtedness". There is definitely also no inherent reason why art should assume a privileged position in relation to the agency of criticism and intellectual discourse—other than that it is a very rewarding medium to engage with when you are curious to see, feel, and find out more about what it means to be implicated in the lived conditions of today. As such a medium, art certainly has a particular history. Still, I would hesitate to fully identify the history of a medium with the power of the institutions which claim the right to represent this history and subsequently build their authority on that right of representation. I would instead advocate the pleasures of making a medium work for you through a close engagement with it that is maybe *too close* to it to ever figure properly—and that is largely—in the broad picture of institutional representation. This perspective would bring us back to Michael Newman's observation that criticism may be too implicated or entangled in its subject to ever construe this subject as a unified scientific object of study. In the close encounter with the medium that criticism arises from, I would argue, art ceases to be a monolithic institution and instead falls apart into an infinite series of works.

To seek this close encounter with a particular medium through criticism—be it art, literature, philosophy, music and so on—as a means to recognize and practically intensify your implicatedness in the lived conditions of today in this sense would mean to go against the grain of the institutional administration of the history of these media and, as Irit Rogoff says, to "actualize" them. The close critical engagement with a work and medium would then be less a privileged form of access (or access to a privilege) but rather a practical and pragmatic approach to immersing oneself in implications. Beyond institutions and authorities, criticism could simply be a form of living with the things that *talk to you*, be it works, books, people, as well as social, political, and emotional events. For me the primal scene of criticism, therefore, is a moment I remember from an *Alice in Wonderland* cartoon when the coffee cup on the table suddenly starts talking to her and she feels obliged to talk back. I see this as a paradigm case of finding yourself implicated in a situation and indebted to a person or thing through the implications of an experience. When the cup talks to you, you owe it a response. What chance do you have? For the duration of the coffee party, this is the conversation you will have to make. So you might as well talk to the thing and get to know its take on life. The challenge but also the joy of this obligation to talk back is that you have to invent a new language to speak to the thing. And how often to you get the chance to converse with strange things that talk? All the time actually when you do art criticism.

Joseph Masheck

Don't Trust Anybody Dressed in Black

It's nice to be asked to contribute "staircase wit" after not having been at the party; though to be honest, this wasn't my idea of a party. I have never been much concerned with talking or writing about criticism as such, that is, instead of writing or talking critically about actual works of art of any period. However, as one devoted to art per se, I find that in every generation art criticism must be rescued from belles-lettrists armed with newly fashionable ways of taking the most accomplished works as just so much conveniently pre-processed roughage for their presumptuously higher-echelon text production. Now forms of "theory" oblivious, when not contemptuous, of art as art now often make matters worse by exercising a harmless show of radicality without the slightest threat to the way things are in the world, in which toughies always dressed in black effectively police a cynical game increasingly reserved to the well-off young.

In reviewing the transcripts of the two roundtables organized by James Elkins, I was pleased to find that I have colleagues who do care about the state of art criticism today, and I think the best I can do is to respond to certain points, in both sessions successively, in the form of a gloss of discontinuous remarks, like interruptive comments blaring from a face on a satellite screen. I must first confess, as I tend to be downright skeptical of skepticism, that the cause for which I most always find it impossible to summon any hope is the next ad hoc committee concerned to diagnose whatever latest dis-ease seems prevalent in art criticism. One reason must be Nietzschean: I just don't know what to do with the sometimes declared wish that criticism were more popularly accessible. Most people often do, I believe, entertain aesthetic judgments, most freely in regard to athletic or musical performance; as far as plastic form is concerned, the human body is usually the only abiding concern, with the exception, or better, extrapolation, of an automobile as thinly sublimated next best thing. As far as I can tell, this accounts for why, though, so few most people read criticism, so many like making fun of it—as affected folly, quite regardless of the critical outlook.

The question of art history and art criticism at odds always reminds me of a moment of contradiction precipitated in me as a young art historian just setting out for criticism by a typically casual diktat of Henry Geldzahler as curator at the Metropolitan, many years ago. Speaking in the museum auditorium, Geldzahler said that art history was finished, and had nothing to offer contemporary art. I was boggled because I was working in Renaissance and Baroque, mainly architecture, under Rudolf Wittkower and Dorothea Nyberg, both of whom, it happens, were encouraging studies in garden design that set me up for an interest in Smithson; indeed, I would spend a long night telling him all I knew about the subject, thanks to them. But though I was frustrated by Henry's cavalier dismissal of art history, any number of times since I have encountered similar clashes of hip and square, or reformed and unreformed, understanding. Shouldn't generalizations about the theatre and theatricality, for instance, by modernists of art, by rights have to take into account the likes of Brecht and Beckett as exemplary and definitive fellow moderns? Isn't it dissembling not to? I believe that the relation of art history and criticism is ever unsettled because there is always hip and square on both sides of the border.

Two other points of distinction. I know that it's politically correct to go for immanence, so as to show that one shuns whatever might be considered, perish the thought, transcendence; but I suspect that Whitney Davis was momentarily confusing immanence (the inherent) with imminence (the impending) where he says "as opposed to acknowledging fully emerged . . . qualities." And, to risk infraction against the American rule of one idea per person: quite besides Eastern immanentist mysticism, there is even in the West an ontological and even theological immanence as well as transcendence. Another "ideo"-problem: Boris Groys's is a refreshing voice, but I wonder about his thinking that showing "totalitarian" art alongside modernist art has never actually been done owing to vague "political and moral reasons," where the obvious problem is that most ordinary viewers, who pretty much think that art criticism is something somewhere between "dowsing" for water and an upper-class parlor game, would surely prefer the totalitarian art, and the kitschier the better, as Lenin, even when relatively culturally liberal, already understood.

A tangential point of conventional vs. unconventional critical modality as well as of "critical lag." Because it does not seem to imply any want of research, Abigail Solomon-Godeau's remark, as much as seconded by Jim Elkins, that there's never been any "serious criticism" of Julian Schnabel, is problematic in its effective assumption that critical time counts off not from when the critic or his or her own generation first encountered something—"people like us"—so that the qualification "serious" is effectively defensive and as such problematic. I don't think the Schnabel remark is supposed to allow of a certain line-by-line parody of an *Artforum* article by that painter which I published as "Snake Oil for Sprained Hearts: Julio Schnitzel Speaks to Joe Masheck"[50] (*New Observations*, 24, 1984), and reprinted in my *Modernities: Art-Matters in the Present* (1993); but why, after all, not such a thing? I certainly think that an extended parody ought to count as part of any critic's critical intervention, so I have to wonder how open critical theory really is to an unconventional intervention in practice. Interested in appropriation, I also published an accurate but pseudonymous article on paintings that I myself had ordered painted by mail order in Hong Kong, one of which—after Picasso—I showed in the same year over my own name in "The New Portrait," curated by Jeffrey Deitch, at PS1.[51] It may matter that during this time I was teaching as a critic in the studio program, not the art history department, at Harvard.

Jim Elkins's sense of the problem of art criticism in the university art history context, rather than as more practice-oriented in the art school, reminds me that it was a very twentieth-century, revisionist-modern thing (of which Stephen Melville seems aware in Chicago) to convert English departments from purveying "literary history" to "literary criticism," and in part this entailed a shift to the analytics of the "New Criticism" of literature, which was really the most important "formalism" in the English-speaking world between the Fry and Bell generation of World War I and "Greenbergian" formalism after World War II. Groys is no doubt right that there can be no proper academic treatment of art criticism without a canon. Warning, however: at present it is not in the interest of the sovereign economic powers to permit such a manifestation of criticism's identity and rightful function, which could only impede the sham "play" of market forces on one side and the "millionaire Marxists" on the other. Stimulated by Jim Elkins's rethinking of the academic-curricular problem, we might also demand that our art historians show some active and inevitably critical interest in arts of all times, in all formats and modalities—which should hardly have to be any more "utopic" than with the longstanding modal and stylistic catholicity of most musicologists as compared with art historians. For whatever their "periods," most musicians understand most music—what is great in Ella Fitzgerald side by side, as it were, with Buxtehude. Indeed, I suspect that the biggest educational-institutional problem in our field is that there are now far too many art historians who have no sophistication at all in any pre-modern art, which must be all the worse for those who, besides, have lost all faith in modernity. Hardly the way to evangelize for better than reactionary art!

Speaking of an art-historically informed critical office and practice, notwithstanding its underestimation by litterateurs and, somewhat differently, by theoreticians, Davis's quip "If you've read Adorno, you're ready to be an art critic" is to me quite problematic. As much as I approve ideologically of our dutiful reading of Adorno, let's face it, even he serves often enough as just another kind of literary software. If one is sufficiently visually perspicuous, and provided he or she understands enough about music to analogize what Adorno says about music to art, only then should one be considered Adorno-capable of art criticism.

Sorry, but a PhD in studio art is a horrendous idea! (A point of cultural history: Irit Rogoff thinks that the postgraduate model of education is a North American thing, but it was imported from Germany to the United States in the nineteenth century, at Johns Hopkins and Columbia, as a research-based alternative to essentially British-style undergraduate education.) I also disagree with Groys on the desirability of academicizing art criticism. Good critics thrive on wide artistic experience and wide reading; as it is, too much art study has become "theory" in the bad sense of just the same books taking in each others' laundry.

In no doubt, every symposium such as this in the past thirty or thirty-five years, one could expect to find a ritual denunciation of formalist aesthetics as not the only standard of value in art. But because I'm not sure that Gemma Tipton realizes all that is at stake, I think she went wrong in saying that most contemporary architectural criticism is bad because "It's still grounded in description and formalism . . ." A modicum of formal description is so necessary to "ground" what specifically architectural or otherwise artistic features and properties are at stake that slighting it should be cause for suspicion. Analogously, if you would be just as happy considering any painting of an available barmaid other than Manet's, you just aren't critically engaging the visual aspect as such; nobody is equipped to be a critic who cannot see how much better *The Bar at the Folies Bergères* is than any other painting offering the same social content. However ironically, this is more obvious with respect to painting, where for a hundred years an "objective" has been altogether optional. But in architecture, I would insist that it is glaring insensitivity to formal value, compounded by the affectations of philistine speculators, that in recent decades has loaded Dublin with the worst new architecture in Europe.

From a position further beyond formalism, Solomon-Godeau calls critical attention to a matter that is important in our ever-more ignorant, vulgar, and repressively totalized money culture: how a sense of "anything goes," under the ensign of pluralism, effectively terminates dialectic and makes efficacious criticism impossible. In neoliberal free-fall, even negative criticism must count as just that much more advantageously controversial publicity. The opposite of that sort of publicity used to be forthright individual advocacy of new art, which it used to be possible for the in-house or independent critic to discover and present ahead of commercial consensus. I was surprised to read Jim's relay of Rosalind Krauss at *October* to the effect that one of the critic's jobs is to scout things out, because I never thought of that as one of *October*'s capabilities. My own experience in initial or early advocacy has been both rewarding and frustrating. One of the strangest things in life is that if you were ahead of others before and they are stupid, they will only recall that they couldn't understand what you meant then, and they will think they must always be right because now you seem out of it too, or rather still! But you do tire of waiting twenty years until the party-hip writers of the glossies, including too many poets moonlighting as sensibility technicians, decide to pick up on what you were already literally writing for their parents about—something of an answer, surely, to Guy Brett's wondering about "a popularization of art" comparative to science writing.

Here, for examples, are some of the dates at cases in which I first published essays on the named artists, confining myself to the more distant past: Robert Smithson (1971; museum essay, 1974); Chris Wilmarth (1972; museum essay, 1974); Bernd and Hilla Becher (1973); Richard Serra (small exhibition curated, 1974); Robert Grosvenor (1974); David Diao (1977); Sean Scully (1979; museum essay, 1981); Tom Nozkowski (1981; small exhibition curated, 1985), Mike Bidlo (1986); Maureen Connor (1986); Jonathan Lasker (1987). As editor of *Artforum* from 1977 to 1980, my mission was to seek out significant new art—especially painting, to which there was outright pseudo-revolutionary hostility as well as simple lack of interest in favor of newer conceptual modalities of art. When I put a Sean Scully drawing on the front of the November 1979 issue, in connection with one of my own omnibus articles inside, the publisher, Charlie Cowles, who did produce *Artforum* as an act of noblesse oblige and secured my editorial freedom, still said "I see you are putting your friends on the cover."

The later case of Mike and Doug Starn is curious. I discovered the photographers when they had barely finished at the School of the Museum of Fine Arts, Boston, while I was at Harvard. A British editor offered me a thousand dollars to write an article on a still-unknown artist I considered important, so I wrote on "The Starn Twins"—a name suggested by me for their New York debut in a 1985 exhibition that I curated for 55 Mercer Street, and first used on its poster by David Wojnarowicz. But the article was rejected because the same editor had never heard of the artists! Then, after I published it in *Arts Magazine* for March 1986, a New York belles-lettristic critic published a piece which he claimed was the first on the Starns—despite the better part of a year elapsed between the writing of my article and its New York appearance, which was still, even so, earlier than his. Moral: critical acumen in scouting unknown art will likely be punished, while all advocacy of already-hyped art will be rewarded.

Turning to the Chicago discussion: I can't tell from the transcript just how amusingly outrageous Dave Hickey meant to be in saying that what he does as a critic is practically the same as what *October* people do. In any case, I could hardly feel that way myself: despite sharing "revolutionary" hopes, as a Christian socialist I have always found their undialectical materialism part of the problem (almost just like bourgeois materialism!) and not part of the solution. It seems to me that keeping any real possibility of social democracy at bay might as well be the realpolitik behind the art world's high-class pseudo-revolutionary discourse. Why else all the posturing as impossibly More Rad Than Thou when we can't even get a real Democratic mayor for New York?

I was pleased to see Stephen Melville's picking up on a problem that lingers on from the last generation or two in art criticism: that by Kantian rights, judging art by application of any principle will disqualify the judgment as aesthetic—a good centre of gravity for the problem of admitting worthwhile social analysis or commentary together with definitively art-critical criticism. Otherwise, Jim makes a very promising point about minimal and conceptual art as presumably preempting criticism. The problem would be a good topic for another roundtable. Judd's rather slam-bang judgments as an art critic, early on, could be entertained, but also the bigger questions of minimal and conceptual work as frustrating the commercial concentration on the sub-critical consensuses of whether "it's a good one" of whatever it is (so mercantile!), and of how we art folk do in fact judgmentally tackle minimal and conceptual works. After all, Kant himself might have been interested in what criticism could still do if and when art, possibly for good reason, went poker-facedly *an*-aesthetic.

But then Melville, it seems to me, got backed into conceding *October* the role of radical *directoire* that it had always presumed: I would rather venture to imagine that in the next generation, by c.2025, more about how we got where we are now will be accessible art-historically by studying the now defunct *Arts Magazine*, thanks to the sheer permissiveness of Richard Martin, and despite an advertising policy about which we had the luxury of having scruples, than by limiting consideration to what was properly registered with *October*. *Arts* had a lot of junk in it, but it has also had its Smithsons and Dan Grahams decades before *October* deigned to recognize such frightfully un-Ivy-League misfits or nerds. I admit, however, that even I prefer the Octobrists to the way-too-many charmingly vapid art texts of New York literary folk, when it gets like Laura Ashley on painting.

Thank God that Michael Newman tells it like it is in regard to "the massive capitalization of the art market"; but speaking of Kanty, we should make clear that the uninterest or lack of aesthetic interest of the investor is by no means a form of aesthetic disinterestedness. Then Melville's reminding all of us of the proper Kantian sense of "speak[ing] in a voice that is not merely your own" strikes me as a forthright challenge to do something critical that might be neither solipsism nor quasi-political wheeling and dealing.

I see something like the contradiction between unreformed and reformed understandings of "theatre" in the overestimation of "curation" as a veritable art-making process in its own right. Obviously nobody wants to be a spoilsport by denying what somebody else does who wants to think of himself or herself as a creative artist. James Panero says that nowadays "everyone who operates around the creation of art—curators, collectors, critics—wants to be part of the art." Well, there's the logical modern problem that if we allow curator-artists and collector-artists and critic-artists, even if for the sake of convenience we abolished the tiresome old artist-artists, wouldn't there soon be collector-artist curators and collector-artist critics, and so on? No doubt the trouble started well before the insider-traders, money-launderers and such, with the collectors of the pop generation and after who discovered how easily they could gain quasi-intellectual standing as highbrow patrons of culture just by buying two of whatever they are, giving one to an institution and covering themselves with the secured value of the other. Needless to say, that could only work as long as being deemed an intellectual commanded respect; but as long as it did, new money got to bask in the glow of culture when that was by definition "high."

I would certainly rather hear Michael Newman go on about the German Romantic critical response to the Reign of Terror (and the Schlegels, to whom I assume he alludes) than Dave Hickey toying with Hazlitt, which strikes me as like the way at a certain moment Jasper Johns played archly with the name of Tennyson for its sheer cultural piquancy. Newman is right about the problem of the transhistorical dimension, but first we should recall that not so long ago it was fashionable to delete the whole "diachronic" aspect of art history. Also, it didn't require Jeff Wall (admittedly a not uninteresting artist) to say "that there is only contemporary art," as Newman reports. The more complete form of Matthew Arnold's famous but ever-truncated utterance being that "in literature *we have with us in the present* all the best that has been thought and said" (emphasis mine). This is quite relevant to a conception that has long interested me: that what art history really offers art criticism is a tremendous random-access-memory data bank, just asking for lively interaction. Newman is quite right about what happened when the art object began to be called a "text," but it would be better to say *texte*, because what was hopelessly French about it was the pigheaded refusal to concede that a good century of non-objective art had any consequence for theory of "representation." Even Derrida with his goddamned Adami: *puleeze!*

Lynne Cooke on travel and access to objects rightly implies a way of recovering a sense of something more than—okay, *better than*—a text—better because incarnate. It would be interesting to hear her consider how the newly "global" circuitry of exhibitions and biennials already keeps a canon, however elastic it be, circulating to a point of absurdity where there should as a rule be no good reason to ship "another one" of such-and-such artist anywhere that already "has one" of its own, since only an art critic could even care much whether, or how, one was better than the other anyway. Well, I suppose it's probably better than keeping everything in crates in Zurich airport.

I have to say, before signing off, that notwithstanding his other insights, Melville does, in my view, make a typical litterateur's mistake of putting far too many chips on Panofsky as his representative art historian. After all, his 1927 essay on "Perspective as Symbolic Form" has no more importance for modern thinking about art than he had interest in modernity. It is possible to take his little book on *Gothic Architecture and Scholasticism*[52] in an Umberto Eco kind of way, but that's that. The whole thrust of his greatest work, precisely as iconographic, was not only anti-modern in interest but anti-modernist in its workings. During his later life in New York his only cultural importance to culture was as a dead weight for those who cared about the spiritual import in modernity to push against, such as Barnett Newman and, on his behalf, Meyer Schapiro. Too bad there is still such a business in blab about Panofsky, much like all the merely literary blab about Wittgenstein as mere "culture star."

I hadn't intended to end these rambling comments with a lesson, but having touched several times on the threat to our subject and our work as critics of those litterateurs who now affect a voluntary post-Maoist, can't-be-too-rigorous, ultra-literary black—the latterday cassocks of the rad elect—I can end with the thought that such conformist asceticism has not been seen in such monotonous profusion in America since the age of the Man in the Gray-Flannel Suit, in the 1950s. This is no way to promote any sort of aesthesis. The only excuse for all the architectural students is that for the sake of their very art they have to practice crawling for money. Of course, I can only speak so freely about this mostly ever-so-literary affectation because I didn't see what anybody was wearing in Ballyvaughan or Chicago. But it's not what they wear that makes our too-literary friends such a danger to art criticism; it is how crudely they tend to process art, whether politically or poetically. Even the poets are often the equivalent of tone-deaf without seeming to realize, not to mention superficially aware of art history. It will do to report that I once heard Susan Sontag say, when somebody called her attention after a lecture to that basic principle, since Wölfflin, of Northern art as categorically interesting vs. Italian art as categorically beautiful, that she thought that sounded like a good idea!

Notes

1. The survey did include freelancers, since most art critics in newspapers, alternative weeklies, and magazines do not have a full-time jobs.
2. These include: Katy Deepwell, "Issues in Feminist Curation: Strategies and Practices" in *An Introduction to New Museum Theory* edited by Janet Marstine (Williston VT: Blackwell, 2005); "Models and Questions: issues in feminist art criticism" Art Gamadas (2003–2004), Vol. 3. (Kumamoto: CAMK, 2005); "Défier l'indifférence a la différence: les paradoxes de la critique d'art féministe" in *L'Invention de Critique D'Art* edited by Pierre-Henry Frangne and Jean-Marc Poinsot (Rennes: Presses Universitaries de Rennes, 2002, text in French), 191–205; "Torture, Gender and Representation: Against the Torture of Women" in *Art of Tortures and Execution—Art Against Tortures and Execution* (Kaliningrad: Open Social Network Art Project, National Centre of Contemporary Art, 2002), 20–35; *New Feminist Art Criticism: Critical Strategies*, edited by Katy Deepwell (Manchester: Manchester University Press, 1995).
3. Edward W. Said, "Intellectual Exile: Expatriates and Marginals," in *The Edward Said Reader*, edited by M. Bayoumi and A. Rubin (New York: Vintage Books, 2000), 379–80.
4. For an analysis of some of the differences between Greenberg's initial essays and their form in *Art and Culture*, see Daniel A. Siedell, "Art Criticism as Narrative Strategy: Clement Greenberg's Critical Encounter with Franz Kline," *Journal of Modern Literature* 26/3–4 (Summer 2004): 47–61.
5. For a more in-depth analysis of this process, see Daniel A. Siedell,

"Contemporary Art Criticism and the Legacy of Clement Greenberg, or How Artwriting Earned its Good Name," *Journal of Aesthetic Education*, 36/4 (Winter 2002): 15–31.

6. Michael Fried, "An Introduction to My Art Criticism," *Art and Objecthood: Essays and Reviews* (Chicago IL: University of Chicago Press, 1998), 1–79.
7. *Against Interpretation, and Other Essays* (New York: Picader, 2001 [1966]).
8. The Originality of the Avant-Garde and Other Modernist Myths (Cambridge MA: MIT Press, 1985).
9. Craig Owens, "Analysis Logical and Ideological," *Art in America*, 73, 5 (May 1985): 25–31; Thomas Crow, "Critical Reflections," *Artforum*, 30, 9 (May 1992): 104–5.
10. Abigail Solomon-Godeau, "Living with Contradictions: Critical Practices in the Age of Supply-Side Aesthetics," *Screen*, 28, 3 (Summer 1987): 2–23, reprinted in Soloman-Godeau, *Photography at the Dock: Essays on Photographic History, Institutions, and Practices* (Minneapolis MN: University of Minnesota Press, 1991).
11. Clement Greenberg, "Feeling Is All" (1952), in *Clement Greenberg: The Collected Essays and Criticism. Vol. 3: Affirmations and Refusals, 1950–1956*, edited by John O'Brian (Chicago IL: University of Chicago Press, 1993), 99–106; Hal Foster, "For a Concept of the Political in Art," *Art in America*, 72, 4 (April 1984): 19, reprinted in Faster, *Recordings: Art, Spectacle, Cultural Politics* (Port Townsend: Bay Press, 1985).
12. I am not speaking here to the discursive context created by the addition of the "Starting Points" texts to the transcripts of roundtable discussions in Cork and Chicago.
13. For example, in the volley between Whitney Davis and James Elkins that closes a session of the first roundtable.
14. James Elkins, First Roundtable in this volume.
15. Michael Newman, Second Roundtable in this volume.
16. Irit Rogoff, First Roundtable in this volume.
17. On this subject, a key text is Diana Fuss's *Identification Papers* (London: Routledge, 1995).
18. Jean Fisher, First Roundtable in this volume.
19. Michael Baxandall, "The Language of Art History" in *New Literary History*, 10, 3 (Spring 1979), 453–65; reprinted as "The Language of Art Criticism" in *The Language of Art History* edited by Salim Kemal and Ivan Gaskell (Cambridge: Cambridge University Press, 1991), 67–75.
20. My list of "critical historians of art" is borrowed from Stephen Melville's assessment in *Art History versus Aesthetics*, edited by James Elkins (London: Routledge, 2006), 224. The term "critical historian of art" is, of course, appropriated from Michael Podro, *The Critical Historians of Art* (New Haven CT: Yale University Press, 1982).
21. Rosalind Krauss, *The Optical Unconscious* (Cambridge MA: MIT Press, 1993); and Hal Foster, *Compulsive Beauty* (Cambridge MA: MIT Press, 1993).
22. "The Present Conditions of Art Criticism" in *October* 100, (Spring 2002), 217.
23. See, for example, Rosalind Krauss, "Notes on the Index" parts 1 and 2, in *October*, 3 (Spring 1977), 68–81, and in October 4 (Fall 1977), 58–67;

Krauss, "Sculpture in the Expanded Field" in *October*, 8 (Spring 1979), 30–44; Douglas Crimp, "Pictures" in *October*, 9 (Spring 1979), 75–88; Crimp, "On the Museum's Ruins" in *October*, 13 (Summer 1980), 41–57; Crimp, "The Photographic Activity of Postmodernism" in *October*, 15 (Winter 1980), 91–101; Craig Owens, "Earthwords" in *October*, 10 (Fall 1979), 120–30; Owens, "The Allegorical Impulse: Toward a Theory of Postmodernism" in *October*, 12 (Spring 1980), 67–86, and in *October*, 13 (Summer 1980), 61–80; Joel Fineman, "The Structure of Allegorical Desire" in *October* 12 (Spring 1980), 47–66.

24. The characterization of *October* appropriating the term, rather than the concept, of postmodernism from architectural discourse is taken from Anders Stephanson, "Interview with Craig Owens" in *Beyond Recognition*, edited by Scott Bryson et al. (Berkeley CA and London: University of California Press, 1992), 299.
25. Owens's contention that *October* wrote *alongside* artists is from Stephanson, "Interview with Craig Owens", 307.
26. A comment made by Hal Foster admits the shift I am describing: "As a young critic in the 1980s . . . Now, as a not-so-young art historian in the 2000s . . ." See Foster, "Dialectics of Seeing", *Art History, Aesthetics, Visual Studies*, edited by Michael Ann Holly and Keith Moxey (Williamstown MA: Sterling and Francine Clark Art Institute, 2002), 215.
27. At a guess, roughly 95 out of 158 essays in *October* 1 to 20 were dedicated to contemporary art, while in *October* 99 to 118 it is something like 60 out of 164 (what counts as contemporary is, of course, very open to debate). The chronological structure of *Art Since 1900* is perhaps also quite revealing in this respect. For the most part, the *October* quartet manages to provide an entry for close to every single year until 1977, then gaps begin to appear in the 1980s and 1990s and Foster's contributions to the book become more frequent. See Foster, Krauss, Bois, and Buchloh, *Art Since 1900: Modernism, Antimodernism, Postmodernism* (London: Thames and Hudson, 2004). Statistics, however, tell only part of the story: it also seems evident that the term "postmodernism" no longer features with the same regularity or necessity in *October* today than it used in the early years of the journal.
28. Phil Leider quoted in Amy Newman, *Challenging Art: Artforum 1962–1974* (New York: Soho Press, 2000), 295.
29. Theodor W. Adorno, *Aesthetic Theory*, translated by Robert Hullot-Kentor, edited by Gretel Adorno and Rolf Tiedemann (London: Continuum, 1997), 1.
30. Stanley Cavell, "Music Discomposed" in *Must We Mean What We Say: A Book of Essays* (Cambridge: Cambridge University Press, 2002), 180–212.
31. For a useful guide to this essay, see Jonathan Vickery, "Art and the Ethical: Modernism and the Problem of Minimalism" in *Art and Thought*, edited by Dana Arnold and Margaret Iversen (Oxford: Blackwell, 2003), 111–28
32. Insofar as the question of artists using criticism and theory as a dimension of their work was briefly raised during the second roundtable, I agree with Elkins and admit feeling skeptical about the claim that those activities somehow *preempt* art criticism, especially as those writings often require critical interpretation themselves,. For a strong account of Smithson's writings, see Craig Owens, "Earthwords."

33. For an exemplary art critical-historical response, see Joseph Leo Koerner, *The Moment of Self-Portraiture in German Renaissance Art* (Chicago: University of Chicago Press, 1993). I wish to thank Margaret Iversen and Katherine Whitebread for the useful advice that helped bring this assessment to completion.
34. Rosenberg's art criticism is the subject of my 1997 doctoral dissertation.
35. Dave Hickey, "Simple Hearts: Still Writing Talk," *Art Issues*, 57 (March/April 1999), 11–13.
36. Rosenberg, "Aesthetic Assault," a review of *The Boys in the Back Room*, by Jules Romains, *New Masses* (30 March 1937), 25.
37. Hickey, "Simple Hearts."
38. James Fitzsimmons, Letter to Harold Rosenberg, (20 February 1967), Harold Rosenberg Papers (Santa Monica CA: Getty Research Library).
39. Harold Rosenberg, Letter to James Fitzsimmons (15 March 1967), Harold Rosenberg Papers (Santa Monica CA: Getty Research Library).
40. "Discovering the Present," *The New Yorker* 43 (10 February 1968).
41. See Charles Harrison, "Introduction: The Judgment of Art", in Greenberg, *Homemade Esthetics: Observations on Art and Taste*, edited by Clement Greenberg (New York: Oxford University Press, 1999).
42. Clement Greenberg, *The Collected Essays and Criticism*, 1957–1969 (Chicago IL: University of Chicago Press, 1995), 86.
43. Oticica, "Esquema geral da Nova Objetividade", in *Objeto—Brasil anos 60*, edited by Peccinini (São Paulo: FAAP, 1980), 77.
44. James Elkins makes this point early on in the Irish panel.
45. Holland Cotter, "Bull's-Eyes and Body Parts: It's Theater, From Jasper Johns," *New York Times*, February 2, 2007, E31 and E37.
46. Ludwig Wittgenstein, *Philosophical Investigations* (New York: Macmillan, 1968), 194e.
47. The artworld foodchain proceeds from artist to independent curator to dealer to critic to museum curator to art historian, leaving successive players more dependent, yet exclusive.
48. David Carrier, *Artwriting* (Amherst MA: University of Massachusetts Press, 1987), 163.
49. Art, Activism and Oppositionality: Essays from Afterimage, edited by Grant Kester (Durham NC: Duke University Press, 1998); Art Matters: How the Culture Wars Changed America, edited by Philip Yenawine, Marianne Weems and Brian Wallis (New York: New York University Press, 1999).
50. In *New Observations*, 24, 1984 and reprinted in Masheck, *Modernities: Art-Matters in the Present* (University Park PA: Pennsylvanian State University Press, 1993).
51. "China Trade: Discourse with W.D. Barnes," *Arts Magazine*, September 1986.
52. *Gothic Architecture and Scholasticism* (Latrobe PA: Archabbey Press, 1951).

5
Afterwords

THE STATES OF ART CRITICISM

James Elkins and Michael Newman

September 8, 2006

Dear Michael,

I thought it might be appropriate to break with the series format and exchange some letters as a way of thinking about what's happened here. The series is half done now, so I have a fair idea of the range and feel of the volumes. This book, I think, is the most disorganized, the one that's closest to being incoherent.

Volume 1, *Art History versus Aesthetics*, has a particularly wild roundtable conversation. Afterward, Arthur Danto said it was like herding cats. Yet the sources of that wildness, and the kinds of misunderstandings between art history and aesthetics, were clearly articulated. In that respect the book is very arguable: it's easy and inviting to argue with the different positions its contributors take. Danto, Jay Bernstein, Thierry De Duve, and many others in that book argue very sharply and it isn't hard to discover productive points of disagreement.

Volume 2, *Photography Theory*, has deep disagreements about what a theory of photography might be, and some pitched arguments between Joel Snyder and Rosalind Krauss about Peirce's concept of the indexical sign. Some people who wrote Assessments for that book seemed completely to miss the point of trying to articulate a theory of photography at all. They talk about other things instead, and there's the argument—which Walter Benn Michaels dismisses in a footnote—that you shouldn't try for a theory of something like photography that isn't a single subject. (Walter says of course you should.) But like the disputes in volume 1, the claim that it is misguided to try to conceptualize photography is itself not much of a moving target. It's possible to start from it, and go somewhere. It's the same with Joel's and Rosalind's argument about the index: you can see the sides, and compare the arguments.

The abstract problem here, aside from indexicality or photography, is how much logic one should demand. Joel and I think of art discourse somewhat differently. He is interested in clarity: he would like people to give reasons, support their claims, justify themselves. Now there are ways to be against logic (I think, for example, of Deleuze's writing on Lewis Carroll, or Jean-Jacques Lecercle's philosophy of nonsense), but even without subscribing to such theories it's possible to accommodate what Joel might call poor reasoning. For me, the art world is, among other things, the sum of many incoherent, incompletely articulated, badly reasoned, impressionistic, ex-cathedra, ad hoc, a priori arguments. So I'm content and engaged when, in *Photography Theory*, the conversation wanders from theory to anti-theory and back again. The idea that a given subject ought not to have a theory is itself a conventional move, an articulable kind of incoherence. So are arguments about whether or not Peirce's index is relevant to photography. These arguments can't be resolved, but it is possible to take them *as differences*, and go on from there.

Volume 3, *Is Art History Global?* raises some very serious questions, to do with whether art history is Western, and how one might think outside the boundaries of Western critique. It is my favorite in the series so far, because it is absolutely full of new information and unusual perspectives. And yet the species of disagreements in it are themselves well defined. For instance there is David Summers's position, that Western concepts can be made capacious enough to address experiences of art across many cultures. Against that there are doubts about how universal art experiences are, how limiting Western languages and metaphysics might be, and how blinding Western institutions might be. So again the problematic is not about to be resolved, but the species of disagreement are themselves agreed upon.

By comparison this book is incoherent in a different way. For example—just one example—there is an enormous range of ideas here about whether art criticism has a history. For some people, like Dave Hickey, art criticism's history is just whatever creative writers the critic likes. For others, like Steve Melville, by its very nature art criticism doesn't have a history, because it depends on the individual act of judging. And there are many other alternatives that turn on differing senses of history, relevance, reading, judgment, criticism . . .

I am interested in the subject of whether art criticism has a history, and if so what kind of history—but I'm mentioning it as an abstract problem. What I want to say is: the range of ideas about whether art criticism has a history is itself much broader than the range of opinion about, say, the index in photography, or aesthetic terms in art history. It is a deeper incoherence.

My sense of art criticism is that it is a different creature than the subjects of the other books in the series. What do you think—are we dealing with something conceptually distinct?

Saturday, September 16

Jim,

The answer is probably yes and no. It's striking that no adequate history of art criticism has yet been written. This can't entirely be because art criticism isn't taken seriously, because it has had quite a profound historical effect in creating the various contexts for the reception of art. Also, historians like Michael Fried and T.J. Clark have given a central place to art criticism in their books. Fried, in particular, uses Diderot to chart a decisive shift in the eighteenth century in the relation of the picture to the beholder. And who can discuss modernism without referring to Clement Greenberg's criticism? So the reason for the lack of a history cannot be that art criticism is unimportant.

A reason might be that art criticism tends to be in itself a practice without much historical consciousness. I don't have the sense that art critics spend a lot of time reading their forebears. Art historians tend to be more aware of their predecessors. And, at least in the Continental tradition, it wouldn't make much sense to do philosophy without reading, absorbing and arguing with philosophers from Plato onwards. By contrast, critics, especially the journalistic ones, tend to write as if no one had ever done it before them. But it's not only a problem of journalism: the turn to theory from the late 1960s into the 1970s also tended to void writing about art of its history. For example, at that time theory and practice were part of a common project to decenter the subject, so the point was not the historicity of art, and of writing about it, but rather that both would finally reveal the truth about subjectivity, a truth that would itself be quite unhistorical. So a history of preceding criticism could really only be a history of error.

But I think that there may also be a more profound reason why it seems to be so difficult to write a history of art criticism, which necessarily would also involve historicizing art criticism, relativizing its insights. There may well be a fundamental incompatibility between art history and art criticism, in relation to their respective takes on the status of the artwork. This is related, I think, to the role of judgment in criticism, but it is not simply because criticism involves judgment that it can't be historicized. Rather, it may be that criticism, partly though not exclusively through judgment, responds to a non-historical dimension of the artwork. For that reason, criticism may actually have a closer affinity with philosophy than with art history—although as a discipline (if it can even be called that) it certainly has much less self-consciousness than either. A history of criticism would have to account for the fact that in some fundamental sense criticism is not historical. And perhaps for art history criticism, if it is not simply instrumentalized as a period document, is something of an embarrassment, since it hints at the necessary failure of art history to saturate its object, the artwork—to account for why artworks exceed their historical contexts.

Obviously this claim is a rather general one, and we'll have to get more specific. But I wonder how it strikes you, as an art historian.

September 20, 2006

Michael,

Ha! ("As an art historian"!) Seriously, the absence of a history of criticism is a difficult issue. There is a lot of truth, I think, to your "rather general" observation: I like that line of explanation better than the one that was proposed in the second roundtable, namely that the absence of a history of criticism follows from the nature of judgment: that seems difficult to elaborate on the level of individual texts. It works as a ground of explanation, but I don't see how it can be elaborated as a practice of reading—at least the Assessments in this book don't try. But we could elaborate on art history's "embarrassment." I think it isn't often felt as an embarrassment, or even a lack, but it does leave traces.

Through this whole project, I have been very curious to see what reception your Starting Points essay would have. As it turns out, it was scarcely mentioned in the roundtables, even though one person—Whitney Davis—knew the text in its French version. The Assessors hardly mention it. I think it's a spectacular essay, and it is marked by its strong difference from the conversations that followed it. If there is a *rejection* of criticism's possible history, as opposed perhaps to an oblivion, or an insouciance about that history, then your essay would be a good place to begin. I'd very much like to know what you think about the place of your essay in our project. I'll ask two things:

First, what kinds of parallels would you draw between the historical moments described in your essay and things we've heard contemporary art critics say? As I read your essay, it is full implications for contemporary practice. Echoes of the Romantic and late-Romantic moves away from theory, from philosophy, and from history, are all embodied in our roundtables. And yet the "prehistory" you explore wasn't brought in. Why, I wonder? Would it be possible to imagine a version of your essay that included thoughts about the echoes of Romantic ideas in contemporary critical practices?

Or would you prefer to let the essay stand as is, without links to the present? And since I assume you're at least reasonably content to let it stand as is, in what ways do you see it functioning? (Perhaps as historiography? As a philosophic inquiry that is without immediate pertinence to questions of art criticism's history? Fulfilling what function in relation to contemporary criticism?)

Sunday, October 1

Jim,

You are generous towards my essay. At the time it was published in 1992 in the proceedings of a conference on art criticism held in Brittany, I thought I had made a transition from working as an art critic to philosophy. In fact, I started working as an art critic during the winter of 1976–77, before I studied art history. After I finished my undergraduate studies in English at Oxford, I had a place to do graduate studies at the Warburg Institute, where I proposed to work on the idea of the encyclopedia from the Renaissance to the Enlightenment. In the interim, I got a job working on a yearbook for an art magazine in London, and began to do reviews. I became fascinated by contemporary art, and decided to switch to the Courtauld Institute. So for me art criticism came before art history, and I think in some way it still does. Jeff Wall, who is often accused of cannibalizing art history, once said to me that for him all art is contemporary art. That is another way of explaining what I mean by the priority of art criticism, or, specifically, a critical moment in the relation to the work of art. It has something to do with judgment, but I think that there is also a pre-judgmental element to this: an absolutely unmediated, visceral response to the work of art. If judgment sustains the subject in his or her autonomy, this pre-judgmental moment of response puts the subject at risk. This is also another way of elaborating what I mean by the non-historical dimension of the artwork, to which I think it is the responsibility of criticism to attend.

By 1992 I was trying to sort out the relation between my different roles, as art critic, art historian, and apprentice philosopher. I began the serious study of philosophy—in the "Continental" tradition—in mid-career. After a period at the University of Essex in England, and at the Sorbonne in Paris, I was about to take up a fellowship at the Catholic University of Leuven in Belgium, which has the Husserl Archive and is the major center for the study of phenomenology. Michael Podro once said to me that I wrote about artists as if they were philosophers, and philosophers as if they were artists. I don't think he meant it as a complement. Nonetheless, I learned a great deal about philosophy through artists: for example, Richard Deacon led me to understand the importance of Heidegger, and John Stezaker introduced me to the writings of Maurice Blanchot. I found these kinds of encounters much more fruitful than the rather mechanical application of so-called theory that was taking place in the art world, and about which I was very skeptical. The essay for *the Archives of Art Criticism* in Rennes provided me with an opportunity to excavate the history of the relations between philosophy, criticism, and theory, and it seemed to me that German early Romanticism was where they were first articulated in a way that, for me, had a direct contemporary relevance. At the time I was also very much in discussion with Jay Bernstein, who was teaching both Hegel and the Frankfurt school at Essex (he is now Chair of Philosophy at the New School), and he encouraged me to make the connection between contemporary critical issues and German Idealism. In Paris I had moved more in the direction of phenomenology, and my advisor, Françoise Dastur, helped me to see the connection between phenomenology—Husserl, Heidegger, Merleau-Ponty—and the poetry and prose writings of Hölderlin, as a radical alternative to the line that runs from Hegel to Adorno. So, once again, a crux at the intersection of German Idealism and early Romanticism. When I talk of the unmediated dimension of the work of art, this is ultimately a phenomenological claim.

So, underlying the explicit question of my essay—what is the relation between art criticism, philosophy, and theory and where does their entwinement come from?—is an implicit question of critical practice concerning the relation between Frankfurt school critical theory and phenomenology. Do we need to preserve a phenomenological, and therefore descriptive, moment within criticism itself? Since the period of high expectations for theory has passed, I think that it is probably this that is the "live" question for criticism today. And perhaps, given the current context of the hypertrophy of the art market combined with the evisceration of the old critical discourses, the problem is to find a critical basis to prevent the phenomenological-descriptive moment from collapsing into collusion with the powers-that-be.

To begin the task, what is needed, I think, is a historical investigation of the relation of criticism to the development and disappearance of the "public sphere." Here it would be useful to look once again at Arendt, Habermas, Negt and Kluge, and Richard Sennett, as well as some other more recent studies, such as Michael McKeon's *The Secret History of Domesticity*. I honestly believe that if there is a crisis of criticism today, it is not because critics are writing badly, nor because of journalistic pressures, nor because of the academicization of criticism, but because this crisis is linked to the problem of constituting a new public sphere. This is a performative condition for criticism; by which I mean that critical writing in its rhetorical performance constitutes its "ideal" reader—as it has done since Diderot and Baudelaire—but cannot succeed alone in *actually* constituting the sphere in which it will have been read. This for me is the political dimension of criticism, which is not to say that criticism—or art, for that matter—should be instrumentalized in the service of a political project, but rather that its relation to the constitution of "the political" needs to be considered. This is also, of course, a question of philosophy: the German Idealists and Romantics called it *Stiftung*.

Monday, October 16

Dear Michael,

I was going to reply—I was going to write something asking how the phenomenological moment isn't recognized as a problem even by people who are committed to performative criticism, or even explicitly phenomenological criticism. But no.

I think we've reached a wonderful moment. I'm imagining this book is about four hundred pages long. It's got opinions from across the spectrum and then some—people who are somewhere off in the infrared, or the radio frequencies. There is virtually no agreement even on the basic issues: the Assessments are, well, all over the place. In the Art Seminars, I was trying to frame things by talking about judgment and its absence. I was interested and a little bewildered to find that many people writing Assessments didn't see that *as* a problem, never mind that they might of course disagree with what was said about it. That disparity is what made me write that opening letter, and it's why I asked about the use-value of your Starting Points essay. But now I see we are about to go in an entirely different direction, and so I want to stop. It's not because I'm not interested in pursuing this! It's because I do not want to cover the wildness of this book with a blanket of theory. The *Art Seminar* series is intended to capture forms of disagreement and misunderstanding. If we turned this into an occasion for meditating on ways the phenomenological moment is occluded in current criticism, we'd risk imposing a false (well, really, and ineffectual) coherence.

So let's continue this discussion out of print. I am happy to end just by noting that despite some very extended efforts, over several years—including two roundtables on two continents, e-mails to all four thousand AICA members, and hundreds more to individual critics in over fifty countries—our project has been burst by the disarray of the field. I think it's accurate to say art criticism is the single least well theorized subject in the humanities.

Tuesday, October 17

Jim,

Maybe that is also its strength. "Least well theorized" doesn't necessarily mean badly theorized. It could mean that theory has a peculiar difficulty in getting a grip on art criticism.

Given the commitment of criticism to the artwork, theory has to reach it through its object. But is the object the same? Or, more precisely, is the relation to it the same? Theory must be concerned with the "constitution" of the object, that is to say, its conditions of possibility. Criticism must be concerned with the response to the object. At some level, this response needs to be absolutely honest and unguarded. Theory depends for its effectiveness on a logical coherence that can easily appear over-defended in relation to the object. Criticism, on the other hand, can often seem extremely vulnerable—indeed, this is, I think, an index of its quality. This is because criticism has to do with exposing oneself to the artwork, a radical passivity. If I discussed in my previous letter the relation of criticism to the public sphere as a political task, there is a hint in what I am writing here of an ethics of criticism.

Tuesday, October 17

Michael,

You're definitely right about the risk to theory. Our exchange here reminds me of Fredric Jameson's idea of theory as a risk taken outside philosophy, or Philippe Lacoue-Labarthe's essay "Oblivion," on how mute writing is within philosophy. Except that in this project, "theory" is what is safe, potentially systematic, immune from the open dialectic. Criticism stands for the wildness just outside the safety of theory. We're in the wilderness outside the wilderness.

So much is necessarily unclear. "Response needs to be absolutely honest and unguarded"—I can imagine an entire essay, a book, on that sentence. "Absolutely"? For the writer? Under what conditions and for how long? And at what "level"? Are there levels? And what does it mean, "exposing" oneself to art? And an ethics?

Personally, I'm glad to close on a note like this: there is nothing like real, obdurate confusion to make me want to start again.

The State of Art Criticism, Reviewed

Maja Naef

For my first exhibition review I drove across the country. I arrived in the Swiss city of Saint Gallen and entered the gallery space expectantly. Adrian Schiess, busy with installing the industrially lacquered panels typical of his art, acted as if he didn't notice me, although he knew why I was there. My insecurity, which had been connected with this assignment from the beginning, grew. That I had read in preparation every text published on Schiess's work suddenly seemed to provide only questionable knowledge. The spacious gallery seemed constricted—in any case it was too small for me to go unnoticed and remain anonymous. The situation only eased when Schiess and his assistants took a break and a lively discussion ensued. I was again able to draw on the knowledge I had acquired through my research on the artist and his work. I won back my terrain, even if it would remain somewhat insecure. And above all: I was ready to engage with the artwork.

I mention this experience because I believe it illustrates important characteristics of what I call the "art critical situation": first, there is the (all too) dutiful preparation of the art historian; then there is the blunder of entering the gallery at the wrong moment, so that one feels like an intruder or at least a superfluous person; these frustrations are resolved in the conversation with the artist; and finally there is the sense that, freed from the social stress of the situation, the task of art criticism can begin, that is, the challenge of considering the installation *as* artwork.

Does not all this belong to the art critical situation? As an art critic one is also always an art historian. One quickly feels excluded, in the wrong place; one seeks the society of artists and even their gallerists. These three different moments—the intellectual preparation, the marginal (often also touchy) position, as well as the contrary longing for a sense of community—play into the experience of the art critic in his or her engagement with an artwork. Precisely when the art critical activity turns to its most important task—the spontaneous formation of judgment—these three moments are covered over and forgotten. And this forgetting perhaps stands for an even larger one, namely that of the prerequisite assumptions and the historicity of art criticism.

If it is possible to further supplement the extensive roundtable discussions, the animated debates about Assessments and Starting Points, with something that has not explicitly been said but that is nonetheless connected, such a phenomenology as the one briefly sketched here could be of use. It could then be seen that much of what has been formulated as an historical or culture-critical diagnosis can be illuminated through phenomenological analysis of the art critical situation. Likewise, the lament that art criticism is more plentiful and yet more irrelevant than ever before (Elkins[1]) can be related to the structural position of the art critic: he or she is a marginal figure in the triadic relationship consisting of artist, art dealer, and audience. If anything, it is not so bad that this position remains unchanged, despite the increased quantity of art critical publications, because the meaning of art critical judgments does not lie in their influence. Also, the problematic relationship to art history and even the question of a discipline of art criticism cannot only be discussed on an institutional level, but must also be decided in concrete practice (Melville[2]/Elkins/Groys/Oguibe/Rogoff). The art critic who has prepared herself so well—just as she learned to do as an art historian—encounters the limited value of this knowledge as soon as she enters the uncertain terrain that emerges in a new work of art. Here, one can speak of an "embarrassment of history," as Michael Newman aptly put it, because criticism implies "the necessary failure of art history to saturate its object, the artwork." It is then worth examining "why artworks exceed their historical contexts." To put it pointedly, this "embarrassment" of history vis-à-vis criticism brings with it another question: who owes whom which history? Does art criticism need art history in order to compensate for its own lack of historical safeguard? Or is it not art history that needs art criticism as a productive exemplification of history? As both are the case, the relationship of art criticism to the history of art could be defined as both deficient and excessive. In any case, in the phenomenological analysis of the art critical situation it can be seen that the historical understanding of art criticism, because of its very nature—that is, the spontaneity of the formation of judgments and the urgency of concrete experience—must be precarious.

What is gained through such a phenomenological reformulation? For one thing, the discussion about art criticism might be less dependent on culture-critical diagnoses, to which the suspicion of false generalities is always attached. For another, greater accommodation might be made for the fact that art criticism is a specific, in many ways paradigmatic, space of subjective experience.

Taking this as my point of departure, I would like to present my reading of this volume from two different viewpoints, which are grouped around the main problem of the multiply diagnosed "crisis of art criticism": should, may, must art criticism judge?

As art critics we all judge, explicitly or without acknowledgement (and the clearest manifestation of this is in the choice of what a critic writes about). The notion that judgment is no longer possible because there are no more binding criteria ("after quality"[3]) is a mistaken one: it is precisely *because* there are no criteria that judgment is necessary, since judgment does not refer directly to criteria. The activity of judgment is distinct in that it does not presuppose any objective decidability, but nevertheless offers itself to public discussion. The subjective experience of an art critical situation and its reflection takes this as given.[4]

Judgment and writing

A striking commonality between the roundtables published in this book and those organized by the journal *October* in 2002 is that various participants in these otherwise different roundtables seem convinced of a profound opposition between academic and literary writing in art criticism (the "belletristic model,"[5] see also Elaine O'Brien, who refers to "anti-academicism" and the "significance of writing style," of which Dave Hickey is an iconic example). If there is in fact a crisis in art criticism, then it can be found precisely in this distinction: that art criticism must choose either the one or the other possibility of writing about art, and that art criticism must thereby be conceived of as an academic discipline or even as indistinguishable from a history of contemporary art. But successful art criticism is always a third entity between academic writing and literary ekphrasis; although it often overlaps these other forms, it is nonetheless distinct. To come back to the *October* roundtable, one suggestion for taking this situation into account and formulating it in a new way would be to refer to George Baker's model of the "explorer."[6] Two interesting aspects of this comparison are that narratives of discovery represent a hybrid form between science and literature, theory and adventure story, and that explorers as well as art critics become different subjects through their respective experiences. This subjectivizing is expressed in the public sphere in different ways: for the explorer, in knowledge and maybe also wealth, for the art critic, in judgment. Melville plays on a similar model, when he says that it is characteristic for a critic to be walking around, in order to participate in a "certain urban situation and history." But Melville also problematizes the fact that today critics fly to the same locations, and thus circulate through the same channels, as curators ("a sort of airport-and-kunsthalle community"), since this development might have an effect on the language of contemporary art criticism, resulting in a "reduced version of languages once central to criticism's way of embedding judgment in description—of saying what's what: it now seems enough to note that a given work 'references' another or refers to itself or to art to imagine that one has somehow made contact with the whole complex issues that were once carried by the term 'self-criticism.'" It is certain that a purely descriptive approach can be of service to the maintenance or re-installation and cultivation of stable premises. Indeed, precisely because description happens from a particular perspective, it holds an important communicative possibility: it allows the reader to take part in the art critical situation (Schreyach) and also to mediate the "visceral" reaction, or else the (however biased) judgment, of the author (Newman).

Hence, art critical writing, which shares in the academic and the literary but which is never either one or the other, is mobilized through the act of judging. In itself, judgment already has a linguistic structure that requires a textual unfolding: "X is good" is not an art critical text, but the *movens* that unfolds a text and that a text unfolds. What is at issue, then, is a motivation that is urgent and that cannot be so easily regulated as if it were a matter of choice; in this motivation, the Here and Now of the art critical situation (see Elkins's comments on choice, position, and "stance") is condensed.

The act of judgment as the motivation of art critical writing is, in the process of this writing, not merely explicated but also put to the test and complicated in fruitful ways. The fact, in itself trivial, that the work of art cannot be attained through writing provides a second *movens*, that unattainable excess which brings the art critic to further his engagement with the work and with the act of judging in order to further his engagement with writing. The art critical activity addresses a moment inherent in writing itself, through which an object or situation can be mediated and through which—for both the critic and the reader, albeit in entirely different ways—a language-specific experience of art becomes possible. Thus, the art critical judgment is contained in writing, because it records a process that associates a certain revisability with *how* we perceive: art critical judging denotes the threshold that registers and reviews how perception is carried over into language.

Judgment and community

To return once again to the comparison between the roundtable discussions published here and the *October* discussion, a certain hesitancy to engage with theses published in *October* is apparent. Instead, the suspicion was voiced that the journal constitutes a power monopoly (for example, Alberro/Bowman). From a distanced perspective, I would therefore like to allow myself one further note: the problem of the formation of coalitions, whether *October* is one or not, should not be dismissed, because the question of alliances belongs essentially to art criticism, and as I see it, not only to the social reality of art criticism but also to its utopia. I would like to assert that the formation of cartels is in effect the flip-side of one of the utopian dimensions of art critical practice, that is, the formation of community. The community dimension needs to be considered in terms of inclusion and exclusion: the consortium of which one feels oneself a member needs to be examined from without and from the perspective of what tends to be its corruptible aspects. The public character of art criticism is such that it not only remains obligated to its utopian dimension of community formation, but also that it conceives of this community as political, in the sense that a community is designated through cross-purposes and antagonism (Jackson[7]). Judgment—which can be shared or not—is also in this perspective the most important basis and condition for the formation of a community, which—precisely because it occurs performatively in the Here and Now—cannot in any way be historicized, nor can that which coalesces out of uncertain and unsighted terrain demand a common ground.

Art critical judgment begins with an exposure of the self before the artwork, and it necessarily and deliberately gives the reader the potential to bring the subjective position of the author into discussion and to reflect upon its public character. Darby English refers to this art critical process as an "identification"; the mechanism "by way of which we determine where we stop and another begins, services us in just this way making the work of identity (that is, being, saying, or knowing what one is, namely, what one is not) both possible and terminally unfinished." (see Assessments p. 279). Not the content of judgment, but rather the activity of judging produces the political dimension that can transform the experience of subjectivity into one of community.

—Translated by Elizabeth Tucker and Timothy Grundy

Notes

1. "Art criticism is massively produced, and massively ignored", James Elkins, *What happened to Art Criticism?* (Chicago IL: Prickly Paradigm Press, 2003), 3.
2. Stephen Melville, "Critics often came from the university, in the sense that they were educated there, although not often in the field—art or art history—central to their activity as critics" Stephen Melville, "Is This Anything? or, Criticism in the University". The others are represented in the Starting Points essays in this volume.

3. George Baker, "Round Table: The Present Conditions of Art Criticism", *October* 100, Spring 2002, 200–228: 210.
4. Hannah Arendt writes in "Judging," the third and incomplete part of her work *The Life of the Mind*, that only when all criteria of judging have been disposed of can the ability of judging find its actual task. For Arendt, judging is the opening up of a cul de sac, the resolution of a hopeless situation. Because only when we are constantly judging are we able to give the world a meaning for ourselves. Judging makes possible the prospect of regaining human freedom. Hannah Arendt, *Lectures on Kant's Political Philosophy*, edited and with an Interpretative Essay by Ronald Beiner (Chicago, IL: The University of Chicago Press, 1982), 124.
5. James Mayer, *October*, "Round Table", op. cit., 216.
6. For the art critical work, George Baker avails himself of the "model as explorer": "locating silences, articulating repressions, providing a space for certain types of work and certain artistic aspirations to continue and to evolve." With this, Baker also implies that judging cannot be something in principle, but can only be an unveiling of something hidden. *October*, 210.
7. Assessments in this volume. For Jackson, it is not the status of art criticism itself that is at risk; instead, he localizes the crisis in two diametrally opposed conceptions of the social function of art conveyed through art criticism: on the one hand there is the "urban uncertainty" and a fundamental opening to possible spheres of community, and on the other hand, there is the "suburban legibility," that operates with a precise description and sees itself commited to coherent narration and conviction.

Notes on Contributors

Alexander Alberro, Associate Professor of Art History at the University of Florida, is the author of *Conceptual Art and the Politics of Publicity* (Cambridge MA, 2003). His essays have appeared in a wide array of journals and exhibition catalogues. He has also edited and co-edited a number of volumes, including *Art After Conceptual Art* (Cambridge MA, 2006), *Museum Highlights* (Cambridge MA, 2005), and *Recording Conceptual Art* (San Francisco CA, 2001).

Mark Bauerlein is Professor of English at Emory University, and has recently served as Director of Research at the National Endowment for the Arts. His books include *Literary Criticism: An Autopsy* (Philadelphia PA, 1997) and *Negrophobia: A Race Riot in Atlanta, 1906* (New York, 2001). His scholarly essays have appeared in *PMLA, Yale Review, Partisan Review*, and *Philosophy and Literature*, and his occasional pieces have appeared in *The Wall Street Journal, Washington Post, TLS, The Weekly Standard, Reason Magazine, Education Week, Times Higher Education Supplement*, and *The Chronicle of Higher Education.*

Matthew Bowman is presently a PhD candidate at the University of Essex in the Department of Art History and Theory, and is completing a dissertation, titled *October and the Expanded Field of Art and Criticism*, which examines the early formative years of the *October* journal in relation to the radical transformation of the idea of what constitutes an art medium in the post-Greenbergian art world. He is also the author of "Automatism: Proving Reality Undone," a catalogue essay written to accompany the "Reality Undone" exhibition held at the University Gallery at the University of Essex. (mattbowman100@hotmail.com)

Guy Brett is a London-based art critic and curator; he is the author of *Force-fields: Phases of the Kinetic; Camargo: Esculturas;* and *Exploding Galaxies: The Art of David Medalla*, amony many others.

Ariella Budick is a writer for *Newsday*.

Felipe Chaimovich works at the Faculty of Fine Arts at the Fundação Armando Álvares Penteado in São Paulo, and is the curator of the Museum of Modern Art of São Paulo. His publications include *Iran do Espírito Santo* (São Paulo, 2000); *29th Panorama da Arte Brasileira* (São Paulo, 2005); "Space and Democracy: Places for art in Brazil since the 80's" in *Espaço Aberto/ Espaço Fechado*, edited by Stephen Feeke (Leeds, 2006), 92–102; and "Objects or Reflection: Brazilian cultural situation" in *On Cultural Influence*, edited by Steven Rand and Heather Kouris (New York, 2006), 20–26. (Apinagés, 731/ 32 São Paulo, Brazil; fchaimovich@hotmail.com)

Lynne Cooke has been Curator at Dia Art Foundation since 1991, where she curated shows of works by Richard Serra, Jorge Pardo, Roni Horn, and others. She was co-curator of the 1991 Carnegie International, Artistic Director of the 1996 Sydney Biennale, and has curated exhibitions in numerous venues in North America, Europe, and elsewhere. She has taught and lectured widely at schools and universities throughout the United States and Europe. From 1979 to 1989 she was a Lecturer in the History of Art Department at University College, London. In addition to teaching at Columbia University in the Graduate Fine Arts Department, she is on the faculty for Curatorial Studies at Bard College. Among her numerous publications are recent essays on the works of Rodney Graham, Jorge Pardo, Diana Thater, and Agnes Martin. She was the recipient of the 2006 Award for Curatorial Excellence from the Center for Curatorial Studies at Bard College, the Independent Curators International Agnes Gund Curatorial Award in 2000, and four awards from the International Association of Art Critics, for exhibitions of Hanne Darboven (1996), Jessica Stockholder (1996), Juan Muñoz (1997) and Robert Irwin (1998). Born in Geelong, Australia, Ms Cooke received a BA from Melbourne University and an MA and PhD from the Courtauld Institute, London University.

Whitney Davis is Professor of History and Theory of Ancient and Modern Art at the University of California, Berkeley, where he also directs the Arts Research Center. His publications include *Replications: Archaeology, Art History, Psychoanalysis* (University Park PA, 1996), *Pacing the World: Construction in the Sculpture of David Rabinowitch* (Cambridge MA, 1996), articles on prehistoric, ancient, and modern archaeology, art history, and art theory, and three forthcoming books: *Forms of Likeness and the General Theory of Visual Culture; Sexuality and Aesthetics from Winckelmann to Freud and Beyond;* and *Visuality and Its Discontents: Essays on Art Theory in World Art History.* (Department of History of Art, University of California at Berkeley, Doe University Library 416, Berkeley, CA 94720–6020; wmdavis@berkeley.edu)

Katy Deepwell is editor of *n.paradoxa: international feminist art journal*, which she founded in 1996. She is Reader in Contemporary Art, Theory and Criticism and Head of Research Training, University of the Arts, London. Her publications include (as editor): *New Feminist Art Criticism: Critical Strategies* (Manchester, 1995: Valencia, 1998), *Dialogues: Women Artists from Ireland* (London, 2005), and *Art Criticism and Africa* (London, 1997); and (as author) "Défier l'indifférence a la différence: les paradoxes de la critique d'art féministe," in *L'Invention de Critique D'Art*, edited by Pierre-Henry Frangne and Jean-Marc Poinsot (Rennes, 2002, text in French) 191–205.

Pier Dominguez is a graduate student in American Studies at Columbia University. He has written for *New York Newsday* and his article "The Sexualized Male: Why Feminist Criticism is Only Half-Right" was published in the *Columbia Journal of American Studies* (May 2007). A summa cum laude graduate of NYU, his last book was *Christina Aguilera: A Star is Made—The Unauthorized Biography* (2002). (pd2220@columbia.edu, pierdominguez@hotmail.com)

James Elkins teaches at the School of the Art Institute of Chicago.

His most recent books include *Visual Studies: A Skeptical Introduction* (New York, 2003), *On The Strange Place of Religion in Contemporary Art* (New York, 2004), *What Happened to Art Criticism?* (Chicago, 2003), and *Visual Practices Across the University* (an edited volume; Munich, 2007). (jelkins@artic.edu)

Darby English teaches at the University of Chicago; he specializes in postwar American art and visual and cultural studies. He is the author of *How to See A Work of Art in Total Darkness* (2007) and a co-editor of *Kara Walker: Narratives of A Negress* (2003).

Robert Enright is the University Research Chair in Art Criticism in the School of Fine Arts and Music at the University of Guelph, and the Senior Contributing Editor to *Border Crossings* magazine. He is the author of a monograph on Eric Fischl, along with Arthur Danto and Steve Martin, (New York, 2000), and a collection of interviews called *Peregrinations: Conversations with Contemporary Artists* (Winnipeg, 1997). He has written over thirty introductions and catalogue essays on contemporary artists, including Leon Golub, June Leaf, April Gornik, Terry Winters, Alex Katz, A.A. Bronson and Diana Thorneycroft. He writes regularly for the *Globe & Mail*, Canada's national newspaper. In 2005 he was awarded the Order of Canada.

Sheila Farr is arts critic for the *Seattle Times.*

Jean Fisher has written extensively on native issues for numerous art periodicals including *Artforum International.* She is an editor of *Third Text: Third World Perspectives on Contemporary Art and Culture.*

Gaylen Gerber's work as an artist often incorporates other artwork and activities in its realization. Gerber asks others to cooperate with him and let their work be installed against the ground he provides. In doing so he focuses our attention on a central aspect of perception, which is that to perceive something at all you must first be able to perceive it as distinct from its context or background. By positioning his work as the contextual ground against which we see other artwork and activities, Gerber draws attention to the permeability of the distinctions between object and context and fundamentally questions the stability of perception itself. Gaylen Gerber has exhibited widely, including recent exhibitions and cooperative projects at the Musee d'Art Moderne Grand-Duc Jean in Luxembourg; FRAC-Bourgogne and Musée des Beaux-Arts, Dijon, France; Kunsthalle Bern, Switzerland; and The Art Institute of Chicago, Illinois.

Blake Gopnik is the chief art critic of the *Washington Post*, where he publishes regular reviews and features on all aspects of fine art. He has also published scholarly articles on notions of pictorial mimesis in Renaissance art and culture. He holds a doctorate in art history from Oxford University.

Boris Groys is Professor for Philosophy and Media Theory at the Academy for Design (Hochschule für Gestaltung) in Karlsruhe, Germany. His publications include *Gesamtkunstwerk Stalin* (Munich 1988); *Die Kunst des Fliehens*, with Ilja Kabakov (Munich 1991); *Die Kunst der Installation*, also with Ilja Kabakov (Munich 1996); Kierkegaard: Schrifte (as editor) (Munich 1996); *Logik der Sammlung* (Munich 1997); *Kunst-Kommentare* (Vienna 1997); *Unter Verdacht: Eine Phänomenologie der Medien* (Munich 2000); and, in English, *The Total Art of Stalinism: Avant-garde, Aesthetic Dictatorship, and Beyond*, translated by Charles Rougle (Princeton, NJ: Princeton University Press, 1992).

Margaret Hawkins writes a weekly column of art criticism for the *Chicago Sun-Times* and is Chicago correspondent for *ARTnews*. She has written for *American Craft, Art and Antiques, Camerawork, Photograph, New Art Examiner, Dialog, Chicago Artists' News* and Chicago Public Radio. Her essay "Art Crimes, Context and the Problem of Graffiti" appears in *[de]construction*, edited by Christopher Hauck (Atlanta, GA 2006), 46–50. She teaches writing at the School of the Art Institute of Chicago and at Lake Forest College.

Dave Hickey is Shaeffer Professor of Modern Letters at the University of Nevada, Las Vegas. His publication include: *Prior Convictions: Stories from the Sixties* (Dallas, 1989); *The Invisible Dragon: Four Essays on Beauty* (Los Angeles, 1993); *Air Guitar: Essays on Art and Democracy* (Los Angeles, 1997); *Stardumb* (San Francisco, 1999).

Matthew Jesse Jackson teaches in the Departments of Art History and Visual Arts at the University of Chicago. His publications include "Para-Performative Practices and Late Modernism: On Contemporary Art and the Museum," *Museum International*, September 2007; "Managing the Avant-Garde," *New Left Review*, March/April 2005; a revised version of this text appears in *The Uncertain States of America Reader*, edited by Brian Shollis and Noah Horowitz (New York, 2006); "Alternative Artists AT 'Alternative' Institutions," *Ilya and Emilia Kabakov: An Alternative History of Art*, edited by Jill Snyder (Cleveland, 2005). (262 Cochrane-Woods Art Center, 5540 South Greenwood Avenue, Chicago, IL 60637; mjjacksn@uchicago.edu)

Timothy Emlyn Jones is the Dean of the Burren College of Art, Ireland. He is an artist who has exhibited internationally and is represented in public collections in a number of countries, his most recent exhibitions having been in Beijing, Galway, Sydney and Venice. His publications include: "A Method of Search For Reality: Research and Research Degrees in Art and Design" in Printed Project No 4: *The New PhD in Studio Art.* edited by James Elkins (Dublin, 2005); and in *Thinking Through Art*, edited by Lin Holdridge and Tracy Mcleod. (London, 2005); "The Studio Art Doctorate in America" in *Art Journal* Vol 65.2 (New York, 2006); and "Performance and Protest," an interview with Heike Roms in *New Welsh Review* No 76 (Aberystwyth, 2007). (Burren College of Art, Newtown Castle, Ballyvaughan, Co Clare, Ireland, TEJones@burrencollege.ie)

Róisín Kennedy is Yeats Curator at the National Gallery of Ireland. Her publications include *Dublin Castle Art: The Historic and Contemporary Collection*, (Dublin, 1999); "Made in England. Louis le Brocquy's A Family," *Third Text* 76 no. 19 (September 2005), 475–87; and "Critical Writing on Irish Art," in *Irish Modern and Contemporary Art: History and Perspectives*, edited by C. Marshall and Y. Scott (New Haven CT, forthcoming).

Kim Levin is an independent art critic and curator. Her essays have appeared in magazines, journals, anthologies, and museum catalogues in the US, Europe, and Asia. From 1996 to 2002 she was international President of AICA (Association Internationale des Critiques d'Art). Her publications include *Beyond Modernism: Essays on Art from the '70s and '80s* (Harper Collins NY 1989; Tokyo Shoseki

1991). She edited *Beyond Walls and Wars: Art, Politics, and Multiculturalism* (Midmarch Press, NY 1992); co-authored *Transplant: Living Vegetation in Contemporary Art*, edited by Barbara Nemitz (Hatje Cantz, Germany, 2000); and was Guest Curator/Editor of *Unconditional Love*, Printed Project #07, (Visual Artists Ireland 2007). She has been Guest Curator of major museum exhibitions in Europe and Asia, including the Nordic Biennial Borealis 8, titled *The Scream*, at Arken Museum of Modern Art, Copenhagen, 1996–97. (52 West 71 Street, New York, NY, 10023; kimlevin@earthlink.net)

Joseph Masheck is Centenary Fellow and Visiting Professor of History of Art at Edinburgh College of Art (affiliated with the University of Edinburgh). His most recent book concerns Cézanne: *C's Aesthetics: Philosophy in the Painting* (Philadelphia PA, 2004). In production are a translation, in *Luna Park* (Paris), of "The Carpet Paradigm," his 1976 text on the roots of the modernist notion of pictorial flatness in nineteenth-century design theory, with a book version in production at Edgewise Press, New York. Underway are a book of essays on Adolf Loos and a book on Malevich's legacy in painting. (Department of Fine Arts, Calkins Hall, Hofstra University, Hempstead, NY 11549; AdolfLoos@earthlink.net)

Stephen Melville works at the Department of History of Art at Ohio State University. His publications include *Philosophy beside Itself: On Deconstruction and Modernism* (Minneapolis, 1986); *Seams: Art as a Philosophical Context* (New York, 1996); and, with Philip Armstrong and Laura Lisbon, *As Painting : Division and Displacement* (Cambridge, MA, 2001). He is editor of *The Lure of the Object* (Williamstown, 2005); co-editor, with Bill Readings, of *Vision and Textuality* (London, 1995); and co-editor, with Philip Armstrong and Erika Naginski, of *Res* 46, *Polemical Objects*, (Autumn, 2004). (Melville.3@osu.edu)

Musvik, Victoria works as a freelance photography and cultural critic and teaches Theory of photography and Aspects of creativity at the European Humanities University (Vilnius) and Visual studies at Moscow State University. Her academic publications include "Word and Image: Andrea Alciato's 'Emblemata' at Georg Dietrich Von Brandt's *album amicorum*," Emblematica (2002); "And the King of

Barbary's Envoys Had to Stand in the Yard': Perception of Elizabethan Court Festivals in Russia," in *European Court Festival: Art, Politics and Performance*, edited by J. R. Mulryne and Elizabeth Goldring (2002). She has also published numerous articles on photography and reviews of photographic exhibitions and is currently working (together with a colleage) on Alexander Grinberg's biography. (Moscow, 117452, ulitsa Yaltinskaya, d.4, k.3, kv.257; bookcase74@mail.ru)

Maja Naef is an art historian based in Basel and Chicago. Her publications include various essays for art magazines and exhibition catalogues as well as "Zeichnen als Leseverfahren: Überlegungen zu Raymond Pettibon" in *Randgänge der Zeichnung*, edited by W. Busch, O. Jehle, and C. Meister (Munich, 2007), 343–62; "Dieter Roth, Schreibszenen" (together with Jörg Wiesel) in *Über Dieter Roth, Beiträge und Aufsätze*, edited by B. Soentgen and Th. Vischer (Basle, 2004), 36–86; "Schneiden und Verschleifen. Eva Hesse's 'Mechanical Drawings'" in *Figur und Figuration: Studien zu Wahrnehmung und Wissen*, edited by G. Boehm, G. Brandstetter, and A. von Müller (Munich, 2007, 91–118); "Location Plan. Überlegungen zur Archäologie der modernen Abstraktion bei Terry Winters" in *Struktur, Figur, Kontur: Abstraktion in Kunst und Lebenswissenschaften*, edited by C. Blümle and A. Schäfer (Berlin/Zurich, 2007, forthcoming).

Michael Newman teaches in the Department of Art History, Theory, and Criticism at the School of the Art Institute of Chicago. His publications include *Jeff Wall: Works and* Writings (Barcelona, 2007); *Richard Prince: Untitled (Couple)* (London, 2006); "Salvage" in *Tacita Dean*, exh. cat., Musée d'Art Moderne de la Ville de Paris (2003); and numerous essays on modern and contemporary art, art theory, and continental philosophy (mnewman1@artic.edu)

Elaine O'Brien is a professor of modern and contemporary art and criticism at Sacramento State University, California. Her MA and PhD theses were on the art criticism of New York intellectual Harold Rosenberg.

Olu Oguibe is Professor of Painting and African American Studies at the University of Connecticut and author of *The Culture Game*

(Minnesota, 2004). From the late 1980s till the mid-1990s he wrote art, literary, theatre and cinema reviews for several weekly and monthly news publications in Britain, and currently contributes to art magazines such as *Frieze*. As an artist his work has been exhibited in museums and galleries worldwide, as well as major international biennials and triennials, including the Venice Biennale. His permanent site-specific work may be found in different sites in Africa, Europe, and Asia. Oguibe has also curated exhibitions for institutions and venues such as Tate Modern, the Venice Biennale, and the Municipal Museum in Mexico City, among others, and made significant contributions to New Information Technology Studies.

Saul Ostrow is Chair of Visual Arts and technologies at The Cleveland Institute of Art. He is the editor of the *Critical Voices in Art, Theory and Culture* series (Routledge, London) and the Art Editor of *Bomb Magazine* (NYC). His publications include *The Persistent Mythology of Modernism: Interpreting Post-Modernism/Postmodernism/post-Modernism. . . ., Philosophy, Art, History, Future*, edited by Vladimir Marchenkov (Athens OH, 2007); "Photography and the Visual Arts 1900–2000," *Encyclopedia of 20th Century Photography*, edited by Nancy Stuart (2007); "Consuming Emancipation: Ethics, Culture, and Politics," in *Ethics and Art*, edited by Elaine King and Gail Levin (New York, 2006). (2568 Overlook Road, Cleveland, Ohio 44106, or 162 West 21 Street, NYC 10011; sostrow @gate.cia.edu)

James Panero is the Managing Editor and an art critic of *The New Criterion*, for which he writes the monthly "Gallery chronicle" column. He is a regular contributor to a number of publications, including *The Wall Street Journal, The New York Sun, National Review*, and *The Weekly Standard*. He is co-editor of *The Dartmouth Review Pleads Innocent* (Wilmington DE, 2006). (900 Broadway, Suite 602, New York, New York, 10003; www.jamespanero.com)

Peter Plagens is Contributing Editor at *Newsweek* magazine, where he was art critic and Senior Writer, 1989–2003. His publications include *Sunshine Muse: Contemporary Art on the West Coast* (New York, 1974), reissued as *Sunshine Muse: Modern Art on the West Coast, 1945–1970* (Berkeley CA, 2000), *Moonlight Blues: An Artist's Art*

Criticism (Ann Arbor MI, 1986), and *Time for Robo* (a novel; Seattle WA, 1999). In addition, he has written essays and reviews since 1965 for, among others, *Artforum, Art in America, Art News, The Nation, New England Review, The New York Times*, and *Los Angeles Times*. He is also a painter, whose retrospective exhibition appeared at the University of Southern California, Columbia College of Art in Chicago, and The Butler Institute of American Art in 2004–2005. Plagens has received both Guggenheim and National Endowment for the Arts fellowships in painting. (imedajinsokt@aol.com)

Lane Relyea is Assistant Professor of Art Theory and Practice at Northwestern University. His essays and reviews have appeared in numerous magazines including *Artforum, Parkett, Frieze, Art in America*, and *Flash Art*. He has written recent monographs on Polly Apfelbaum (Boston MA, 2004); Richard Artschwager (New York, 2002); Jeremy Blake (Houston, 2002); Vija Celmins (London, 2004); Toba Khedoori (Basel, 2001); Monique Prieto (Los Angeles and London, 2002); and Wolfgang Tillmans (Chicago and Los Angeles, 2006). Among the exhibition catalogs he has contributed to are *Public Offerings* (Los Angeles, 2001) and *Helter Skelter* (Los Angeles, 1992). His most recent publications include "Clem Everlasting," *X-tra* 9, no. 4 (Summer 2007), 13–19; "Your Art World: Or, the Limits of Connectivity," *Afterall* 14 (Autumn/Winter 2006), 3–8; "Allover and At Once," in *Critical Mess: Art Critics on the State of their Practice*, edited by Raphael Rubinstein (Lenox MA, 2006), 49–59; "Paul McCarthy: A Few Words for *Dead H*," *Parkett* 73 (2005), 102–11; and "House Monument," in *Kate Ericson and Mel Ziegler: America Starts Here*, edited by Bill Arning and Ian Berry (Boston and Sarasota Springs, NY, 2005), 62–9. (3–400 Kresge Hall, 1880 South Campus Drive, Evanston, Illinois, 60208–2208; lrelyea@northwestern.edu)

Irit Rogoff is Professor of Visual Cultures at Goldsmiths, London. She writes extensively on the conjunctions of contemporary art with critical theory with particular reference to issues of colonialism, cultural difference and performativity. She is author of *Terra Infirma—Geography's Visual Culture* (2000), editor of *The Divided Heritage: Themes and Problems in German Modernism* (1991) and co-editor, with Daniel Sherman, of *Museum Culture: Histories, Theories, Spectacles* (1994).

Michael Schreyach is a Lecturer in the Department of Art History at the University of Southern California in Los Angeles. He is currently revising his dissertation, on pragmatism and abstract expressionism, for publication. (Department of Art History, Von KleinSmid Center 351, University of Southern California, Los Angeles, CA 90089; mschreyach@sbcglobal.net)

Daniel A. Siedell teaches modern and contemporary art at the University of Nebraska-Omaha. He is the author of "Contemporary Art Criticism and the Legacy of Clement Greenberg, or How Artwriting Earned its Good Name," *Journal of Aesthetic Education* 36/4 (Winter 2002): 15–31; "Art Criticism as Narrative Strategy: Clement Greenberg's Critical Encounter with Franz Kline," *Journal of Modern Literature* 26/3–4 (Summer 2004): 47–61; "Rosalind Krauss, David Carrier, and Philosophical Art Criticism," *Journal of Aesthetic Education* 38/2 (Spring, 2004): 95–105; and "The Art Criticism of Weldon Kees," in *Weldon Kees and the Arts at Mid-Century* edited by Siedell (Lincoln NE, 2004): 75–104. Siedell has an MA from SUNY-Stony Brook and a PhD from The University of Iowa. He writes art criticism for *artUs*. (dsiedell@mail.unomaha.edu)

Jeffrey Skoller teaches at the San Francisco Art Institute. He is a filmmaker and writer; in addition to numerous articles he is author of *Shadows, Specters, Shards: Making History in Avant-Garde Film* (2005).

Abigail Solomon-Godeau teaches in the Department of the History of Art and Architecture, University of California Santa Barbara. Her books are *Photography at the Dock: Essays on Photographic History, Institutions and Practices* (Minnesota, 1992); *Male Trouble: A Crisis in Representation* (London and New York, 1997); and *The Face of Difference: Race, Gender and the Politics of Self-Representation* (Durham, 2007). Her numerous articles have appeared in journals such as *Afterimage, Art in America, Artforum, October*, and she is the author of numerous exhibition catalogue essays.

Sue Spaid, an independent curator/critic/lecturer, is a regular contributor to *artUS*. Her publications include "Loser Paradise: The Drifting Spectacle of the SI," *artUS*, (Los Angeles, 2007), "The

Work of Art in the Age of Femmage" in *The Handmaking* (Abington PA, 2007); "Shrinking Cities: Expanding Opportunities" in *Shrinking Cities* (Cleveland OH, 2007); "Where Older Critics Greet Younger Artists" in *SWAP/meet* (Philadelphia PA, 2007); "The Treasure Map," *Domus* (Milan, 2007); "Going Places: Jackson to Nachez and Back Again" in *Mississippi Invitational*, (Jackson MS, 2006); "Set Theory: A Set is a Set is a Set" in *Sabina Ott* (San Antonio TX, 2006); "Being Here: Wrestling with Resemblance in an Antirepresentational Era" in *Presence* (Louisville KT, 2006); "Thomas Hirschhorn: Camotopia," *artUS* (Los Angeles CA, 2006); "The Gist of Isness," *X-tra* (Los Angeles CA, 2006); "Flirting with Femininity, Freedom and Femmage" in *Ruby Osorio*, (St. Louis MO, 2005); "The Experiential Paradigm: The Power to Cause Things to Happen," *artUS* (Los Angeles CA, 2004); and *Ecovention: Current Art to Transform Ecologies* (Cincinnati OH, 2002). (Wyncote, Pennsylvania; suespaid@hotmail.com)

Julian Stallabrass is a writer, photographer and lecturer. He is Reader in art history at the Courtauld Institute of Art, and is the author of *Art Incorporated* (Oxford, 2004), *Internet Art: The Online Clash Between Culture and Commerce* (London, 2003); *Paris Pictured* (London, 2002); *High Art Lite: British Art in the 1990s* (London, 1999); and *Gargantua: Manufactured Mass Culture* (London, 1996). He has written art criticism regularly for publications including *Tate, Art Monthly* and the *New Statesman.* He is an editorial board member of *New Left Review* and *Third Text.*

András Szántó is a Senior Lecturer at the Sotheby's Institute of Art in New York City. A writer, researcher, and consultant whose work spans the worlds of art, media, and philanthropy, he was formerly the director of the National Arts Journalism Program at Columbia University, where he continues to direct the NEA Arts Journalism Institute. He was recently the Marian and Andrew Heiskell Visiting Critic at the American Academy in Rome. He has published numerous studies on arts, media, and criticism, including the widely cited report, *The Visual Art Critic: A Survey of Art Critics at General-Interest News Publications in America* (2002). His journalism has appeared in *The New York Times, Los Angeles Times, Architecture, Print, I.D., The Art Newspaper, International Herald Tribune*, and other publications.

Recent articles include "Editing as Metaphor" in *Cautionary Takes: Critical Curating*. (New York, 2007).

Gemma Tipton is an independent writer and critic of contemporary art and architecture. Based in Dublin, she contributes regularly to art and architectural publications, panel discussions, lectures, radio and television programmes in Ireland and internationally. Reviews, features, and interviews are published in *The Irish Times Magazine, Art and Architecture Journal, Artists Newsletter, Irish Arts Review, Circa, Fuse, Irish Museums Journal, Apollo, VAN*. She has been manager of *Circa* magazine and editor of *Contexts*. Gemma has also been a judge for the Museum of the Year Awards, and for the AIB Prize. Gemma is the editor of *Space: Architecture for Art*, an investigation of the architecture of contemporary art galleries; and author of *Home*, a study of contemporary memorials. In 2001 she was awarded the Arts Council's Critic's Bursary in Contemporary Architecture Writing. She also writes catalog essays, has had a series of exhibitions of her own work, and has worked as an independent curator.

Jan Verwoert is a contributing editor of *Frieze*. He is editor of *Die Ich-Ressource: Zur Kultur der Selfst-Verwertung* (2003), and author of Wolfgang Tilmans (2002) and *Bas Jan Ader: In Search of the Miraculous* (2006).

INDEX

Printed in Great Britain
by Amazon

82654030R00242